PENGUIN CLASSICS

# WOMEN'S INDIAN CAPTIVITY NARRATIVES

Kathryn Zabelle Derounian-Stodola is a professor of English at the University of Arkansas at Little Rock. She is co-author of *The Indian Captivity Narrative, 1550–1900* and editor of *Early American Literature and Culture: Essays Honoring Harrison T. Meserole* and *The Journal and Occasional Writings of Sarah Wister*. She has also published numerous articles on the Indian captivity narrative and on early American women's writings.

# WOMEN'S INDIAN CAPTIVITY NARRATIVES

---

EDITED WITH AN
INTRODUCTION AND NOTES BY
KATHRYN ZABELLE DEROUNIAN-STODOLA

PENGUIN BOOKS

PENGUIN BOOKS
Published by the Penguin Group
Penguin Putnam Inc., 375 Hudson Street,
New York, New York 10014, U.S.A.
Penguin Books Ltd, 27 Wrights Lane,
London W8 5TZ, England
Penguin Books Australia Ltd, Ringwood,
Victoria, Australia
Penguin Books Canada Ltd, 10 Alcorn Avenue,
Toronto, Ontario, Canada M4V 3B2
Penguin Books (N.Z.) Ltd, 182–190 Wairau Road,
Auckland 10, New Zealand

Penguin Books Ltd, Registered Offices:
Harmondsworth, Middlesex, England

First published in Penguin Books 1998

3  5  7  9  10  8  6  4  2

LIBRARY OF CONGRESS CATALOGING IN PUBLICATION DATA
Women's Indian captivity narratives /
edited with an introduction and notes by
Kathryn Zabelle Derounian-Stodola.
p.  cm.—(Penguin classics)
Includes bibliographical references.
ISBN 0 14 04.3671 5
1. Indian captivities—United States.
2. Women prisoners in literature.
I. Derounian-Stodola, Kathryn Zabelle, 1949–
II. Series.
E85.W85   1998
305.48'969—dc21      98-21291

Printed in the United States of America
Set in Sabon

*For their courage and kindness,*
*I lovingly dedicate this book to my mother,*
*Kitty Derounian,*
*my godmothers, Catherine Brown and Anahid Gorgodian,*
*my mother-in-law, Betty Stodola,*
*my aunt, Armine Hartman,*
*and my English teacher,*
*Doris Cox*

# ACKNOWLEDGMENTS

I gratefully acknowledge support from a National Endowment for the Humanities Summer Stipend, held in 1997, which allowed me to complete the bulk of this project. Three research trips in 1992, 1995, and 1997 to the Newberry Library (Chicago) allowed me to use its outstanding holdings of Indian captivity narrative materials. For help at the beginning phase of this project, I thank the Newberry for a Short-term Fellowship and the Office of Research and Sponsored Programs at the University of Arkansas at Little Rock for travel funds.

# CONTENTS

# INTRODUCTION

THE term "Indian captivity narrative" refers to stories of non-Indians captured by Native Americans. Cowboys-and-Indians stories are the most popular manifestation of this literary form, but they are a relatively late adaptation of the genre, which has been part of the American psyche since the earliest European–Native American contact. Of the thousands of Indian captivity narratives in existence, a large number are by or about women, including some of the most famous. Indeed, the Indian captivity narrative is arguably the first American literary form dominated by women's experiences as captives, storytellers, writers, and readers.

In the larger sense, "the captivity narrative" encompasses any story with a captor (usually from a minority group) and a captive (usually from a majority group). This taxonomy accommodates such distinct, but sometimes overlapping, forms as the slave narrative, the spiritual autobiography, the providence tale, the UFO abduction story, the convent captivity narrative, and the sentimental novel of seduction, as well as the Indian captivity narrative.

Within that larger classification, "the Indian captivity narrative" is a discrete American literary form that involves accounts of non-Indians captured by Indians in North America (generally in what is now the United States of America and, to a lesser extent, in Canada). Almost invariably the Indian captivity narrative concerns the capture of an individual or several family members rather than larger groupings, and its plot is most commonly resolved with the captive's escape, ransom, transculturation, or death. While some texts were published in languages other than English and a few featured African-American or Mexican hostages, the vast majority of Indian captivity narratives, and certainly the most famous, were written in English and featured Europeans. Some critics believe that the Indian captivity narrative functions as *the* archetype of American culture, or its foundation text, in which initial contact between Europeans and Native Americans inevitably evolved into conflict and finally colonial conquest. But whether a reader prefers to see the Indian captivity narrative as part of the wider captivity narrative tradition or as a separate literary form, when pared down to its essence, the genre is all about power and powerlessness.

From the beginning of their publication history, Indian captivity narratives have appeared both as separate books and as stories embedded in longer works. In the former category are such texts in this collection as Mary Rowlandson's *A True History*, James E. Seaver's *A Narrative of the Life of Mrs. Mary Jemison*, and Sarah F. Wakefield's *Six Weeks in the Sioux Tepees*, and pamphlet-length ones such as Jemima Howe's *A Genuine and Correct Account* and Shepard Kollock's *A True Narrative of the Sufferings of Mary Kinnan*. The latter category would include the very famous tales of Pocahontas (not reprinted here) and Hannah Dustan, for example. Other captivities appeared not as separate publications or within someone else's longer work, but as short pieces in a magazine or almanac, including many versions of the "Panther Captivity." In fact, narratives arise in such disparate sources as interviews, newspaper stories, folklore, tall tales, poems, sermons, plays, dime novels, histories, broadsides, ballads, military correspondence, and biographies. Seaver's edition of the book-length Jemison text incorporates oral testimony from Jemison herself, biographical and historical information from others, as well as the editor's own observations. Including such varied texts dramatically increases the corpus but further contributes to the form's protean quality.

A traditional view of the Indian captivity narrative's development holds that there were three distinct phases: authentic religious accounts in the seventeenth century, propagandist and stylistically embellished texts in the eighteenth century, and outright works of fiction in the late eighteenth and into the nineteenth centuries. Yet although these divisions may indicate a trend, they do not adequately account for the presence of both fact and fiction throughout the form's history and they do not go back far enough to incorporate the sixteenth-century accounts or forward enough to anticipate the twentieth-century ones. At each end of the definitional pole lie fact and fiction, but it would seem more apt to designate the texts in between as "factive," meaning tending toward fact, and "fictive," meaning tending toward fiction, and to recognize that both factive and fictive texts use appropriate narrative strategies. Thus Mary Rowlandson's, Cotton Mather's, Elizabeth Hanson's, Mary Godfrey's, and Emeline Fuller's texts are essentially factive and seemingly "authentic" in their discursive details, James E. Seaver's and Sarah Wakefield's are in the mixed factive/fictive category of (auto)biography, Mary Kinnan's and

Jemima Howe's are fictive because they convert history into story, and the "Panther Captivity" is entirely fictional.

It is useful to correlate the development of the Indian captivity narrative with other literary forms. For instance, in the sixteenth and seventeenth centuries, accounts of captivity were influenced by, and sometimes incorporated into, histories, as with John Smith's most extended account of the Pocahontas story in his *Generall History* (1624). Many nineteenth-century histories by such well-known authors and antiquarians as Washington Irving, Samuel Gardner Drake, and Francis Parkman included captivity accounts, too.

Captivity narratives were also heavily influenced by religious writings such as sermons, providence tales, and spiritual autobiographies. For example, Cotton Mather's first telling of Hannah Dustan's story was indeed oral since he used it to conclude a sermon he later published in *Humiliations Follow'd with Deliverances* in 1697. The Puritan narratives especially used strategies of seventeenth-century English providence tales, which showed God's intervention and omnipotence in everyday events (Hartman). As its name suggests, a spiritual autobiography charts the spiritual, rather than secular, life of its subject. Filtered through different denominations, including Catholicism, Puritanism, and Quakerism, the Indian captivity narrative became a parable of the soul's thralldom to evil and showed the role of the captivity experience in bringing the erring soul closer to God.

Many of the factive captivities can be classified as autobiography, biography, or even both. For example, Mary Rowlandson's *A True History* and Sarah Wakefield's *Six Weeks in the Sioux Tepees* are autobiographical, but include historical and ethnographic information. But Seaver's story of Jemison incorporates the competing voices of Jemison herself and Seaver, blending the autobiographical and biographical. Autobiography preserves the subject-author's biases and blind spots, but biography, although it often claims greater objectivity, also includes the biographer's prejudices.

From the beginning, the Indian captivity narrative's strong story elements of plot, character, and conflict encouraged writers to fictionalize. But of course there is a difference between a fictive or fictionalized text and one in which the elements of captivity have no factual basis at all but are transformed into fiction. The development of an entirely fictional plot parallels the rise of fiction and the increasing secularization of American society. Thus, in the familiar formula, early texts were written for edification; whereas later ones were written and read for entertainment as well. The brief "Panther Captivity" is the only wholly fictional example in this collection, but its publication in 1787 anticipated a series of full-length novels on Indian captivity by Susanna Haswell Rowson, Charles Brockden Brown, James Fenimore Cooper, Lydia Maria Child, and Catharine Maria Sedgwick, as well as countless others throughout the nineteenth century. The early novels used the strategies of sentimental and gothic fiction and historical romances, including epistolary technique. According to Christopher Castiglia, it was not men but women such as Rowson, Child, and Sedgwick who first popularized frontier romances by adapting the Indian captivity narrative.

Indian captivity continues to fascinate twentieth-century fiction writers including Thomas Berger, whose epic parody of the subject, *Little Big Man*, was a best-seller in print in the sixties and later a popular film. Perhaps most interesting of all, Angela Carter's short story "Our Lady of the Massacre" (1986) criticizes white society's sense of moral superiority and gives voice to a seventeenth-century working-class white woman captive whose own culture gagged her. If we use the wider definition of captivity narrative, thousands of contemporary fictions continue to develop and modify the form.

Propaganda has been yet another strong influence on the Indian captivity narrative throughout its literary life. Indeed, the captivity narrative has often served as a convenient vehicle for propaganda and as a catalytic text in reinforcing other institutionalized beliefs. In the Dustan account and on the surface of the Rowlandson story, the blatantly anti-Indian propaganda manifests itself in the many racial slurs against Native Americans. Yet while much of the propaganda is anti-Indian, other accounts tie together anti-Indian with anti-British or anti-French biases, capitalizing on the politics of the times for maximum "spin." Witness the impassioned anti-British commentary in Mary Kinnan's text.

But propaganda can be for as well as against certain groups. Naturally, the anti-Indian, anti-British, and anti-French narratives also include ethnocentric commentary praising whites or Americans. However, two of the narratives in this collection promote a positive view of Native Americans: James E. Seaver's *Narrative* of Jemison and Sarah Wakefield's *Six Weeks in the Sioux Tepees*. Jemison, who chose to remain with her captors, praises her adoptive Seneca mother and sisters; she describes her two husbands—Sheninjee, who died after three years of marriage, and then Hiokatoo, to whom she was married for fifty years—as noble, just, and kind; and she describes the Indians in peacetime as morally "uncontaminated," faithful, honest, chaste, temperate, and moderate.

Unlike the transculturated Jemison, Wakefield was captured for only six weeks in the Dakota War of 1862 and had far more to lose by defending the Sioux on her return. Before the attack on the Upper Agency in Minnesota, Wakefield describes how she had arrived there with many negative stereotypes of the Dakotas; however, through open-mindedness, Christian charity, and everyday contact with them, she soon overcame her prejudices. Wakefield uses her narrative as apology, confession, and vindication to accuse the real culprits: the U.S. government and the U.S. military.

Why did Native Americans take captives at all? Although captivity of Indians by Indians predated colonialism, continued war practices and resistance to European-American encroachment made captivity a historical reality as well as an intensely feared possibility for whites. From earliest times, the European colonial enterprise involved exploration, trade, missionary work, settlement, and expansionism on the ever-shifting American frontier. Each activity brought the newcomers into contact with the indigenous peoples in different ways. Even though Columbus's *Journal of the First Voyage to America, 1492–1493* documents *his* captivity of friendly Indians, Indian captivity in the colonial record generally referred to Native American captors and European captives. Since the first colonial arrivals were men, early captivities usually concern males captured by males. The stories of Indians captured and enslaved by whites until the African slave trade proved more profitable were rarely recorded. However, it is important to understand that different tribes had different attitudes toward captive-taking. Some tribes did not take prisoners at all, while others were keen to convert captives into adopted tribal members.

Statistics on the number of captives taken from the fifteenth through the nineteenth centuries are imprecise and unreliable since record-keeping was not consistent and the fate of hostages who disappeared or died was often not known. Yet conservative estimates run into the tens of thousands, and a more realistic figure may well be higher. For some statistical perspective, however incomplete, consider these figures: between 1675 and 1763, approximately 1,641 New Englanders were taken hostage (Vaughan and Richter, p. 53); and during the decades-long struggle between whites and Plains Indians in the mid-nineteenth century, hundreds of women and children were captured (White, p. 327).

Indians took prisoners for various reasons. The urge to demonize Native Americans in the captivity literature made revenge a dominant motive, yet the historical record shows that this claim was greatly exaggerated. Gender played a role, and revenge and torture among certain Indian groups were a more likely fate for male, rather than female, prisoners of war. For example, when Father Isaac Jogues and his companions were ambushed in 1642, he describes how their Mohawk captors inflicted such tortures as amputation of fingers, near-death beatings, and ritual burning.

One gendered aspect of the revenge motive concerns whether or not Indians raped captured women. The narrative record shows two dominant and differing responses: overt or covert appeals to white women's vulnerability and Indian men's alleged sexual prowess (often made by male writers or editors) and decisive claims that rape was virtually nonexistent in Native American culture (often made by women writers or captives). Both discursive strategies play into the "sexualization of the captive's vulnerability" in which loud protests for white women's safety mask "a prurient white fantasy" (Castiglia, p. 211). While it is true, then as now, that women may be loath to admit they were raped, the historical record indicates that rape was rare, especially among Northeastern Indian peoples, because of different cultural aesthetics, incest taboos (in the case of adopted captives), and beliefs in warrior abstinence (Axtell, *Invasion Within*, p. 310). Among Plains and Midwestern Indians, however, the historical record tells a different story, although some historians believe that by the nineteenth century, these Indians had merely assimilated what was originally a white cultural practice. Still, rape was not widespread, but there were some documented instances. For example, in *Six Weeks in the Sioux Tepees*, Sarah Wakefield states that while her Dakota captors did not violate the vast majority of captive women, she did know of two cases.

Native Americans also took captives to trade either with other Indians or with non-Indians for goods, cash, or prisoners and to force them into servitude or actual enslavement. However, the line between trade and slavery was not always clear since captives destined for trade might have the status of chattel slaves. But from the late seventeenth to the nineteenth centuries, a major reason Native Americans systematically seized captives was for bounty or ransom. Guilty and distraught relatives, as well as self-righteous and Indian-hating communities for whom captivity signified civilization threatened by barbarity, willingly paid for captives to be returned. Native Americans exploited this phenomenon, and ransom amounts in the nine-teenth century could run to hundreds, occasionally thousands, of dollars. The incentive of a reward presumably helps to explain why some hostages were targeted for capture and why they were well treated: they were worth much more alive than dead.

A final important reason that Indian groups took captives and cared for them is that many were destined for adoption. Even hos-tages initially intended for trade or enslavement might find their status changed and become adopted as tribal members. Many Native Americans did not possess the same constructs of racial purity as Europeans and found it perfectly acceptable to replace tribal mem-bers lost to war and disease with people of other races. Since adopted captives essentially disappeared from white view, complete numbers cannot be known. A study of Indians and New Englanders in the colonial period found that white captives came from both genders and all ages as long as they were hardy (Vaughan and Richter). Any-one sick, old, needy, or particularly resistant would probably be killed in the initial attack or abandoned en route.

In early America the "prime candidate for transculturation was a girl aged seven through fifteen" since Puritan culture would have encouraged her, even more than a boy, to accept authority (Vaughan and Richter, p. 64). Because a woman's role in white culture tradi-tionally has been passive, later female captives from the eighteenth and nineteenth centuries were also probably better candidates for transculturation than males. Mary Jemison (Dehgewanus) illustrates this premise well. In 1758, when Shawnees carried her into captivity, she was about fifteen years old. As with almost all captives, her initial experience was traumatic and her transculturation was not immedi-ate. But gradually she embraced the life of the Senecas who adopted her, married, had children, and refused to return to white society when given the opportunity to do so.

The writers of Indian captivity narratives—whether actual ex-captives or editors—often kept an eye on the market, though their personal reasons for composition and publication varied. One un-stated motive in the fact-based texts was to counter captivity's dis-unifying and disordering effects by unifying and ordering the experience in print. Since the captive woman was often presented as more traumatized than the captive man, this urge probably can be discerned more in her texts, as seen, for instance, in Mary Rowland-son's, Elizabeth Hanson's, and Emeline Fuller's accounts.

But other reasons were more obvious. Ex-captives sometimes

needed to write for economic support when their previous livelihood had disappeared, and there was certainly money to be made in publishing captivities (although the captives themselves did not always reap the profits since editors and printers also stood to gain). Indeed, Rowlandson's *A True Narrative* and Seaver's *A Narrative of the Life of Mrs. Mary Jemison* were contemporary best-sellers (Mott). In addition, friends and relatives often encouraged the captive to publish his or her story. In the women's narratives, this claim was especially made in the seventeenth and eighteenth centuries when it was considered improper for a female to initiate such public recognition. "The Preface to the Reader" before Rowlandson's narrative states this very objection, but counters it by saying that not only had Rowlandson been prevailed on to publish, but she had yet another reason for so doing, namely, to praise God. Other narratives assert a providential rationale, too.

Publication also allowed the captive or narrator to set the record straight by furnishing insider information. *Six Weeks in the Sioux Tepees* attempts to exonerate Sarah Wakefield and most of her Dakota captors and to castigate the American government; however, more often the eyewitness reinforced prevailing propaganda demonizing Native Americans. Some narratives claimed to provide ethnographic information about Indians, though obviously it was not necessarily objective. The urge to furnish details about Native American culture was strongest in the seventeenth century, when promotional information (often wildly exaggerated) for prospective colonists was needed, and in the nineteenth century, when Indian peoples had been scattered and subdued and white society could afford the luxury of antiquarianism and genocidal guilt. Of course there were other, more idiosyncratic, rationalizations for publication too, including (to cite two examples not reprinted here) the wish to warn naive young women against missionary fervor in Mary Barber's *The True Narrative of the Five Years' Suffering* (1872) and the attempt to peddle an Indian blood tonic in Edwin Eastman's *Seven and Nine Years among the Comanches and Apaches* (1873)!

The ten representative narratives in this anthology span the seventeenth through the nineteenth centuries, the period when the most Indian captivity narratives were produced, and include both familiar and unfamiliar texts. Mary Rowlandson's *A True History* (1682), the earliest full-length Indian captivity narrative published as a separate book, has long been canonized as an early American classic, as have Cotton Mather's versions of Hannah Dustan's infamous captivity and escape, which he included within three books published from 1697 to 1702. Rowlandson, Dustan, and Mather were Puritans, but another famous early captivity, Elizabeth Hanson's *God's Mercy Surmounting Man's Cruelty* (1728), concerned a Quaker woman. These first three texts are based in fact, but the next one in chronological order is the entirely fictional "A Surprising Account of a Lady" by the pseudonymous Abraham Panther. Commonly referred to as the "Panther Captivity," it too has been very popular since its publication in 1787.

Less well known is Jemima Howe's *A Genuine and Correct Account* (1792), important because despite its factual foundation, it exploits the growing popularity of sentimental fiction to boost sales and enhance readability. The much better known *A True Narrative of the Sufferings of Mary Kinnan*, first published in 1795, is also fact-based but fiction-oriented, and its editor/writer uses the strategies of melodrama and literary stylization to heighten its anti-British and anti-Indian propaganda. James E. Seaver's *A Narrative of the Life of Mrs. Mary Jemison* (1824) forms one of the most famous accounts of a transculturated captive, namely, someone who although initially abducted, crossed cultures to become a "white Indian," as Mary Jemison (renamed Dehgewanus) did.

The *Authentic Narrative* of Mary Godfrey, which first appeared in 1836, has received relatively little attention, but its significance lies in the fact that it is set in Florida during the Second Seminole War—not, as many of the early narratives, in the Northeast—and its hero is a black Seminole (an escaped slave or free black who joined the Seminole Indians). African-American characters, let alone heroes, rarely feature in captivity narratives. Sarah F. Wakefield's *Six Weeks in the Sioux Tepees* first appeared in 1863 as the captive-author's attempt to vindicate herself against charges of being an Indian lover. It is attracting renewed interest for its radical critique of white society's hypocrisy and political exploitation of Native Americans and women.

The last text concerns Emeline Fuller, one of the few survivors of the Utter-Myers party bound for Oregon in 1860. Technically, her narrative, *Left by the Indians* (1892)—which is much better known as a historical document than as a literary one—does not deal with her capture but with short- and long-term survival after an Indian attack, though she does mention others who were taken captive. Unlike the earlier Puritan and Quaker captivities, Fuller's text does not claim a religious basis, but exposes bogus piety. Like them, however, Fuller's story derives its power from stark details and a spare style.

The ten texts thus represent chronological range, spiritual and secular diversity, and geographical variety as the American frontier pushed farther south and west. They chronicle different hostage experiences and durations of captivity among various Indian peoples including Seminoles, Dakotas, Narragansetts, Shawnees, and Senecas. Some "captives" were not captured at all, just scattered after hostilities; others stayed for days, months, or years with their captors; and some never returned to their original culture. In the case of Fuller, although Indians attacked her party, she was never actually taken, yet the Indian captivity narrative as a genre can incorporate even this discursive pattern of non-capture. After a Seminole raid, Godfrey hid in a swamp for several days accompanied by her four young daughters, but was captured for only a few minutes until her would-be captor had a change of heart. Dustan was taken hostage for about six weeks until she scalped her captors and escaped, while an alliance of Nipmuck, Narragansett, and Wampanoag Indians held Rowlandson captive for almost three months.

Kinnan's and Howe's hostage experiences lasted several years: Kinnan among the Shawnees and Delawares, and Howe initially among the Abenakis and then the French Canadians. During a confinement of that length—and sometimes during a much shorter period—a captive might well become acculturated, that is, she might temporarily accept and adapt to cultural differences. Howe's narrative shows signs that she attempted to do so. But Mary Jemison permanently transculturated to Seneca life. Although initially a captive, Jemison no longer held captive status once Senecas adopted her and she in turn adopted a new culture.

While the historical record shows that Native Americans took captives of both sexes, the narrative record usually differs in style and story according to the captives' gender. The following distinction oversimplifies the situation but nevertheless recognizes certain archetypes. The social construction of men saw them as active subjects, with public as well as private roles and the ability to make choices; the accounts with male subjects therefore emphasized their physical and mental qualities as individuals, particularly their strength, endurance, and intelligence. However, women were socially constructed as passive objects, with a predominantly domestic and private role, and the inability, often, to choose for themselves; the narratives with female subjects therefore targeted women's physical frailty and emotional nature.

Almost all the women's accounts emphasize that captivity inevitably sundered families. The narrative pattern—but not necessarily the historical reality—records a husband, father, or teenage sons either absent or killed early on; a pregnant or recently delivered woman; a baby who died in the initial attack or soon thereafter; and surviving children who were separated from the rest of the family, teenage girls being seen as particularly vulnerable. Not used to fending for herself, the narrative claims, the captive woman suddenly found herself witnessing her family's dispersal. Predictably, the women's texts focus on the roles of mother, daughter, wife, and sister and often recognize these designators in an extended title. For example, the 1728 edition of Elizabeth Hanson's captivity is titled *God's Mercy Surmounting Man's Cruelty, Exemplified in the Captivity and Redemption of Elizabeth Hanson, Wife of John Hanson*.

Throughout the captivity literature, women are generally depicted as either helpless victims or provoked avengers. Traditionally, Rowlandson is the prototype of woman as victim and Dustan of woman as avenger, yet deeper analysis reveals aspects of victimization and survival—of being removed and removing herself—in both women. Therefore, rather than being a static set of women's images, each individual text reveals variations on, and even reversals of, gender and cultural archetypes concerning identity. Sometimes in the same text, the narratives incorporate complex and competing images of women.

Rowlandson's *A True History* provides a good starting point because it presents a multifaceted main character in a richly textured narrative. The first few pages detailing the Indian attack establish Rowlandson within a torn web of family relationships: mother to a badly wounded child who dies and two others from whom she is parted, sister to a woman who is slain, and wife to an absent husband. Additionally, one of the hallmarks of Rowlandson's narrative is that she tests her own behavior under duress against that of three women—her elder sister, Elizabeth Kerley; her companion captive, Goodwife Joslin; and her captor mistress, the Indian squaw sachem Weetamoo—perhaps as a way of revalidating herself within Puritan culture.

Symbolically, Rowlandson stands between her elder sister, Kerley, who asked to die and was gunned down, and her surrogate younger

sister, Joslin, who despaired and was also killed, in accepting the
trials of captivity. These trials involved the physical dangers of starvation and abuse; the spiritual dangers of pride and despair; and the
psychological dangers of permanent emotional damage, depression,
and guilt. To survive, Rowlandson adapted to her wilderness condition, turned to her Bible, and shrewdly traded her sewing skills and
other commodities for food. But Rowlandson, as well as some other
women captives, can be seen in the role of author/writer, as Nancy
Armstrong and Leonard Tennenhouse recognize. Through the act of
writing, they claim, Rowlandson legitimates herself as a valid subject
of her text and passes on this sense of authority to her readers on
both sides of the Atlantic. Victim, survivor, Puritan model, author—
Rowlandson reveals all these roles and more in her narrative.

Hannah Dustan displays some of the same roles but in different proportions to Rowlandson. Dustan's much briefer story, told
through a succession of male authors, focuses on the captive as communal scourge and providential instrument and recalls Old Testament values. Male commentators like Cotton Mather had increasing
difficulty in melding Dustan's maternity with her vigilantism. Hers
was one of the earliest captivities to use what became a standard
narrative icon and propagandist ploy to stress victimization and to
rationalize the woman captive's ensuing vengefulness, namely, a recently delivered woman whose baby was killed by having its head
banged against a tree. Propaganda often demonizes outsiders by accusing them of such barbaric behavior as terrorizing mothers and
babies (Ramsey) because brutalizing men does not generate the same
degree of reader outrage. While Rowlandson also uses this device in
discussing Goodwife Joslin, in a forty-page text she devotes only a
couple of paragraphs to it; it dominates Dustan's three-page story.

God's Mercy shows Elizabeth Hanson in the roles of wife, mother,
victim, and spiritual guide, but not avenging angel. In fact, the most
significant way in which this narrative differs from the Puritan accounts is in the detachment, passivity, and stoicism that Hanson exhibits. In some ways this is surprising since Quakerism saw gender
roles as fluid, not fixed, and early Quaker women preachers were
known for their activism. But Hanson's story appeared at a time
when the Society of Friends was reevaluating the "aggressive public
presence" of the earlier Quaker women missionaries and requiring
that they accept patriarchal authority (Carroll, " 'Taken,' " pp. 114–
18). Passivity also enhances another dominant narrative role of hers,

that of the captive as ethnographer, in which the narrator includes objective-sounding details. The most memorable concern the constant attempt to stave off hunger, as in Hanson's description of eating pieces of beaver-skin clothing, nuts, berries, and roots. As ethnographer too Hanson details and attempts to rationalize the Indians' behavior, both good and bad.

Set in 1786 with a significant Revolutionary flashback to 1777, the "Panther Captivity" presents a female character who at the beginning and end of the narrative—in white culture—recalls the sentimental novel's weepy heroine and the captivity narrative's victim. In the central portion, however, she is the independent frontier woman who, after escaping an Indian attack and brief capture, then killing what seems to be a mythic giant with Indian characteristics who had threatened to rape her, lives alone for nine years until the frame narrator, Abraham Panther, finds her. The unnamed woman displaces and survives all the male characters in the story who failed or tried to harm her: her father, her fiancé, the Indians, and the giant.

Pre-twentieth-century readers would have been titillated by the sexual vulnerability of a single woman in the wilderness who eloped, symbolically castrated the giant, and dealt genteelly with Panther and his companion, Camber, even though they too could have taken advantage of her. However, many (male) readers would also have felt uncomfortable that a white woman like the lady of the story could independently kill a giant and live alone, in other words, that a white woman could become defeminized. Because this brief fiction is a composite of several genres including the adventure story, the captivity narrative, the sentimental novel, and the fertility myth, it has many different interpretations (Kolodny, *Land*, p. 60), but all of them recognize the power and threat of women in the new republic.

In the late eighteenth century, Jemima Howe's story was appropriated by three male editors: the Rev. Bunker Gay, David Humphreys, and Jeremy Belknap. Although parts are told in the first person as if by Howe, the editors "traffic" in her text by making her body a focal point of the narrative (Castiglia, p. 80). In this way, they convert the Indian captivity narrative into another eighteenth-century fiction: the novel of seduction. Although Howe is not molested while among the Indians, when she is sold to the French both her new master and his son pursue her. Like many an eighteenth-century heroine, Howe discusses her attempts to remain virtuous in this predicament. Indeed, when Gay takes over the narrative again

for the last two pages, he refers to Howe as "the captive heroine."
Howe also acts as a mother figure in trying to rescue her two teenage
daughters, Mary and Submit, from their own captivities.

A True Narrative of the Sufferings of Mary Kinnan—again told
in the first person, but heavily mediated by its printer/author, Shepard Kollock—casts the title character as the victimized heroine of
sentimental fiction. Her role is heightened by the text's melodrama,
sentimentality, sensationalism, and excessive stylization, which counteract the opening paragraph's claim that this is an "unaffected and
unvarnished tale." The narrative also displays the eighteenth-century
view that women should have a civilizing effect, which makes the
Shawnee women's supposed cruelty a crime against her sex.

In Seaver's Narrative, we find a white, male, establishment author
who is loath to allow Mary Jemison, a fully transculturated woman,
to prevail. Yet along with Seaver's voice, readers can discern Jemison's own voice penetrating and, according to one scholar, even ma-
nipulating the text (Walsh). Thus, despite the biographer's selectivity
and subjectivity, the dominant image of Jemison is that of a transculturated woman with far more freedoms in her adopted culture
than in her culture of origin. Certainly Seaver and Jemison provide ethnographic information, but Jemison's main agenda was to
show how transculturation gave women like her "physical, matri-
monial, and economic space" that was unavailable in white culture
(Castiglia, p. 36).

Much of the twenty-four-page Authentic Narrative of the Seminole War is a white interpretation of the first years of the Second
Seminole War (1835–1842). But the opening eight pages of background build up to two versions of Mary Godfrey's story: one in the
third person by the anonymous author of the entire document, and
another written in the first person because it was "received from [her]
lips." This double echo reinforces Godfrey's propagandist role as victimized wife and mother and authenticates the first-person account.
The introduction to the third-person version explicitly recognizes
Godfrey's roles as wife and mother and the vulnerability of her and
her four daughters in saying that the most providential aspect of the
entire attack on many households was "the miraculous preservation
and deliverance of Mrs. Mary Godfrey, the wife of Mr. Thomas
Godfrey, and her four female children, one an infant at the breast."
Like Kinnan's narrative, Godfrey's claims that only divine providence
turns the escaped slave, initially bent on destruction, into what the
first-person account calls "the humane African (our deliverer)." But

like Kinnan's narrative too, the religious interpretation takes second place to the text's main interest, which lies in the multiplied vulnerability of the five females.

In the seventeenth and eighteenth centuries, those women captives portrayed as victims were exploited by Native Americans or enemies such as the British or French; while some nineteenth-century texts continued this theme, others complicated the assumption of victimization by another culture. Both Wakefield and Fuller tell stories of victimization, but in both cases the worst exploitation is by whites, not Indians, and perhaps for that very reason these narratives sound particularly bitter. It is only through the acts of writing and publication that the two women can voice and publicize their altered sense of civilization and barbarity.

Wakefield functions as a corrective to white stereotypes of American Indian cruelty and European justice. She bolsters her defense of Native Americans and her condemnation of European-American culture on a Works-based, rather than a Faith-based, Christianity, using the same arguments that abolitionists turned against slaveholders. In this narrative published during the Civil War, she even says at one point, in defending Chaska (her Lakota protector) and herself against accusations of having become lovers, "I know that . . . my feelings were only those of gratitude toward my preserver. I should have done the same for the blackest negro that Africa ever produced; I loved not the man, but his kindly acts." She declares that her court testimony exonerating Chaska was virtually ignored by patriarchal white culture and that the mix-up by which Chaska was murdered (her word) instead of another Indian named Chaskadon who really did commit atrocities was at best careless, at worst intentional.

Emeline Fuller's *Left by the Indians* tells of the dispersal of the Utter, Myers, Van Ornum, and Chase families following an Indian attack. After both her parents died, thirteen-year-old Fuller shepherded five of her siblings across the plains with survivors of the other families. While Fuller does discuss the Indians' captivity and torture of others, she reserves the most scorn for the Myers family. Mr. and Mrs. Myers, as parent substitutes, did not protect Emeline and her siblings but acted in an authoritarian way, exploiting the children's vulnerability and insisting that they gather and share food while the Myers family prayed.

Gender also affects two other related areas in the captivity literature: authorship and mediation in the texts. For although male editors could and did intervene in the accounts of both male and female captives, they were more likely to mediate the women's texts. The title of this collection, *Women's Indian Captivity Narratives*, is deliberately ambiguous in order to signify narratives "of," "by," and "about" women. Each text features a main character who is female, but readers should be skeptical of the authenticity and authorship of all the narratives here. Even texts claiming veracity in their title may simply be using a standard publishing ploy to boost sales. Thus, Rowlandson's *A True History*, Howe's *A Genuine and Correct Account*, and Godfrey's *An Authentic Narrative* are certainly not completely true, genuine, correct, or authentic. No more valid is the assumption that narratives written in the first person and given a named female author should be taken at face value.

For example, at least five of the narratives were edited, written, published, or circulated with ecclesiastical oversight. Rowlandson's *A True History* and the retellings of Dustan's captivity were influenced by Puritanism, specifically by the Puritan ministers Joseph Rowlandson (Mary's husband), Increase Mather, and his son Cotton Mather. Hanson's *God's Mercy Surmounting Man's Cruelty* was molded by important (male) members of the Society of Friends. The convoluted publication history of Howe's *A Genuine and Correct Account* involves the Rev. Bunker Gay, from an unidentified Christian denomination, as well as other male editors. Finally, James Hughes of the Methodist Episcopal Church pieced together Fuller's story from her own words and other sources and published it under Fuller's name as *Left by the Indians*. Three other accounts—the "Panther Captivity," Godfrey's so-called *Authentic Narrative*, and *A Narrative of the Life of Mrs. Mary Jemison*—appeared under the names of, or within texts by, male writers who wrote with propagandist or pseudo-literary agendas. Only Wakefield's *Six Weeks in the Sioux Tepees* seems to have been composed by Wakefield herself without editorial intervention.

The process by which a verbal relation becomes a printed narrative may involve a transcriber, editor, ghostwriter, publisher, or other intermediary, each with his own agenda. The following statement of editorial method is by Shepard K. Kollock, a Presbyterian minister and son of the Shepard Kollock who printed and composed *A True Narrative of the Sufferings of Mary Kinnan*, and comes from the preface to his *Pastoral Reminiscences* (1849), a series of case studies illustrating the Christian life recounted by individual parishioners but recast by Kollock.

The following narratives, *substantially* authentic, are partly the effect
of recollection, and partly of notes taken at the time of recurrence,
when the impressions, new and vivid, were committed to writing.—
No truths have so much power as those which we have acquired by
*experience;* there is in them a mingling of sensation and emotion with
fact and reasoning, which seems to throw us completely under the
control of the lessons which are inculcated by our feelings as well as
our understandings. Hence may arise the superior influence of those
instructions which are presented in the style of narratives; they intro-
duce the reader into the midst of the events that are related, make him
a participator in the living scene, and produce a stronger and more
lasting impression on his mind and memory than abstract rules, or
mere lectures upon morals. (Kollock, p. xii)

First, like Kollock, the editors of many women's captivity accounts
were male ministers with interpretive status and authority. The Puritan divine Cotton Mather, the group of Quaker men, and the Methodist cleric James Hughes serve this function in the Dustan, Hanson,
and Fuller texts respectively. Second, Kollock's paradoxical claim
that his narratives are "*substantially* authentic" is echoed in the prefaces of many captivities where an author or editor capitalizes on the
factual but simultaneously acknowledges its gaps. For example, in
the prefatory remarks before Hanson's narrative proper, the unknown author says that Hanson's "Relation, as it was taken from
her own Mouth, by a Friend, differs very little from the Original
Copy, but is even almost in her own Words." The paradoxical claim
"almost in her own Words" actually means that the text is not in
her own words.

Third, Kollock acknowledges that report (the written document,
in this case the editor's notes) and recollection (the mental process,
in this case the individuals' memories) interact to produce a powerful
text in which "sensation and emotion" mingle with "fact and reasoning." The resulting narrative is what we now term "multivocal"
or "heteroglossic," that is, composed of layered voices that a reader
cannot necessarily separate or identify within the composite text.
Such is the case in many captivity narratives where, to use Tara Fitzpatrick's term, the voice of the captive "duels" with the voice of the
editor, though it is not always clear whose voice represents emotion
and whose represents reason, as the dueling voices of Seaver and
Jemison exemplify.

Fourth, Kollock establishes the didactic potential of narrative because it both recounts an individual's experiences and makes each

reader participate in the drama. Since narrative makes the act of reading experiential, the reader's involvement leaves a more permanent impression than "abstract rules, or mere lectures upon morals." In other words, Kollock uses his case studies as instructional vehicles. Similarly, many captivity narratives existed to further political, moral, religious, or propagandistic ends, and the figure of a captive woman made those lessons particularly memorable, as seen especially in the Dustan, Kinnan, and Godfrey accounts. More details on authors, editors, and other mediators appear in the introductions to individual narratives in this collection.

The background information contextualizing these ten captivity narratives should not obscure the major reason for their enduring appeal: they are a good read. But being aware of the complexities involved in the historical record versus the narrative record, the definition and development of the form, gender issues, and authorship and mediation allows readers today to understand the cultural work these seemingly straightforward narratives performed.

# SUGGESTIONS FOR FURTHER READING

## BIBLIOGRAPHIES

Vail, R.W.G. *The Voice of the Old Frontier*. 1949. New York: Octagon, 1970.

Vaughan, Alden T. *Narratives of North American Indian Captivity: A Selected Bibliography*. New York: Garland, 1983.

## PRIMARY WORKS

"The Bloody Escape of Hannah Dustan: A Cultural Reader." *American Voices, American Lives*. Ed. Wayne Franklin. New York: Norton, 1997. 109–130.

Calloway, Colin G., ed. *North Country Captives: Selected Narratives of Indian Captivity from Vermont and New Hampshire*. Hanover, N.H.: University Press of New England, 1992.

———, ed. *Our Hearts Fell to the Ground: Plains Indian Views of How the West Was Lost*. Boston: Bedford, 1996.

———, ed. *The World Turned Upside Down: Indian Voices from Early America*. Boston: Bedford, 1994.

Diebold, Robert K. "A Critical Edition of Mrs. Mary Rowlandson's Captivity Narrative." Diss. Yale, 1972.

"Female Fortitude." Poster advertising the *Authentic Narrative* of Mary Godfrey, 1836. The British Library, London.

Fuller, Emeline, *Left by the Indians*, and Carl Schlicke, *Massacre on the Oregon Trail in the Year 1860: A Tale of Horror, Cannibalism and Three Remarkable Children*. Fairfield, Wash.: Ye Galleon, 1992.

Hughes, Geraldine. Letter to Edward Eberstadt, New York. 22 May 1936. The Newberry Library, Chicago.

Kollock, Shepard K. *Pastoral Reminiscences*. New York: M. W. Dodd, 1849.

Levernier, James A., and Hennig Cohen, eds. *The Indians and Their Captives*. Westport, Conn.: Greenwood Press, 1977.

Rowlandson, Mary. *The Sovereignty and Goodness of God*. Ed. Neal Salisbury. Boston: Bedford, 1997.

Seaver, James E. *A Narrative of the Life of Mrs. Mary Jemison*. Ed. June Namias. Norman: University of Oklahoma Press, 1992.

———. *A Narrative of the Life of Mary Jemison*. Rev. Charles D. Vail.

New York: American Scenic and Historic Preservation Society, 1925.

Slotkin, Richard, and James K. Folsom, eds. *So Dreadfull a Judgment: Puritan Responses to King Philip's War, 1676–1677*. Middletown, Conn.: Wesleyan University Press, 1978.

VanDerBeets, Richard, ed. *Held Captive by Indians*. 1973. Knoxville: University of Tennessee Press, 1994.

Vaughan, Alden T., and Edward W. Clark, eds. *Puritans among the Indians: Accounts of Captivity and Redemption, 1676–1724*. Cambridge: Harvard University Press, 1981.

Wakefield, Sarah F. *Six Weeks in the Sioux Tepees: A Narrative of Indian Captivity*. Ed. June Namias. Norman: University of Oklahoma Press, 1997.

Washburn, Wilcomb E., ed. *Narratives of North American Indian Captivities*. Vols. I–III. New York: Garland, 1977.

## SECONDARY WORKS

Anderson, Gary C. *Kinsmen of Another Kind: Dakota-White Relations in the Upper Mississippi Valley, 1650–1862*. Lincoln: University of Nebraska Press, 1984.

Anderson, John R. *Editor for Freedom: The Story of the New-Jersey Journal in Chatham, 1779–1783*. Chatham, N.J.: Chatham Historical Society, 1975.

Armstrong, Nancy, and Leonard Tennenhouse. *The Imaginary Puritan: Literature, Intellectual Labor, and the Origins of Personal Life*. Berkeley: University of California Press, 1992.

Arner, Robert D. "The Story of Hannah Dustan: Cotton Mather to Thoreau." *American Transcendental Quarterly* 18 (1973): 19–23.

Austen, Barbara E. "Captured . . . Never Came Back: Social Networks among New England Female Captives in Canada, 1689–1763." *New England/New France, 1600–1850*. Boston: Boston University Scholarly Publications, 1992 (Annual Proceedings of the Dublin Seminar for New England Folklife, 14 [1989]). 28–38.

Axtell, James. *After Columbus: Essays in the Ethnohistory of Colonial North America*. New York: Oxford University Press, 1988.

———. *The Invasion Within: The Contest of Cultures in Colonial New England*. New York: Oxford University Press, 1985.

Baker, Charlotte Alice. *True Stories of New England Captives Carried to Canada during the Old French and Indian Wars*. Cambridge, Mass.: By the Author, 1897.

Barnett, Louise K. *The Ignoble Savage: American Literary Racism, 1790–1890*. Westport, Conn.: Greenwood Press, 1975.

Berkhofer, Robert F., Jr. *The White Man's Indian*. New York: Knopf, 1978.

Breitwieser, Mitchell R. *American Puritanism and the Defense of Mourning: Religion, Grief, and Ethnology in Mary White Rowlandson's Captivity Narrative*. Madison: University of Wisconsin Press, 1990.

Burnham, Michelle. *Captivity and Sentiment: Cultural Exchange in American Literature, 1682–1861*. Hanover, N.H.: University Press of New England, 1997.

———. "The Journey Between: Liminality and Dialogism in Mary White Rowlandson's Captivity Narrative." *Early American Literature* 28 (1993): 60–75.

Calloway, Colin G. "An Uncertain Destiny: Indian Captivities on the Upper Connecticut River." *Journal of American Studies* 17 (1983): 189–210.

Carroll, Lorrayne. " 'My *Outward Man*': The Curious Case of Hannah Swarton." *Early American Literature* 31 (1996): 45–73.

———. " 'Taken from her own mouth': Women's Captivity Narratives and the Uses of Female Authorship." Diss. Johns Hopkins, 1997.

Castiglia, Christopher. *Bound and Determined: Captivity, Culture-Crossing, and White Womanhood from Mary Rowlandson to Patty Hearst*. Chicago: University of Chicago Press, 1996.

Coleman, Emma L. *New England Captives Carried to Canada between 1677 and 1760*. Portland, Maine: Southworth Press, 1925.

Davis, Margaret H. "Mary White Rowlandson's Self-Fashioning as Puritan Goodwife." *Early American Literature* 27 (1992): 49–60.

Demos, John. *The Unredeemed Captive: A Family Story from Early America*. New York: Knopf, 1994.

Derounian, Kathryn Zabelle. "The Publication, Promotion, and Distribution of Mary Rowlandson's Indian Captivity Narrative in the Seventeenth Century." *Early American Literature* 23 (1988): 239–61.

———. "Puritan Orthodoxy and the 'Survivor Syndrome' in Mary Rowlandson's Indian Captivity Narrative." *Early American Literature* 22 (1987): 82–93.

Derounian-Stodola, Kathryn Zabelle. "The Gendering of American Fiction: Susanna Rowson to Catharine Sedgwick." *Making America/ Making American Literature*. Ed. A. Robert Lee and Wil Verhoeven. Amsterdam: Rodopi, 1996. 165–81.

———. "The Indian Captivity Narratives of Mary Rowlandson and Olive Oatman: Case Studies in the Continuity, Evolution, and Exploitation of Literary Discourse." *Studies in the Literary Imagination* 27 (1994): 33–46.

———. "Indian Captivity Narratives." *Teaching the Literatures of Early America*. Ed. Carla Mulford. New York: MLA. Forthcoming.

————, and James A. Levernier. *The Indian Captivity Narrative, 1550–1900.* New York: Twayne, 1993.

Dietrich, Deborah J. "Mary Rowlandson's Great Declension." *Women's Studies* 24 (1995): 427–39.

Downing, David. " 'Streams of Scripture Comfort': Mary Rowlandson's Typological Use of the Bible." *Early American Literature* 15 (1981): 252–59.

Drinnon, Richard. *Facing West: The Metaphysics of Indian-Hating and Empire-Building.* Minneapolis: University of Minnesota Press, 1980.

Ebersole, Gary L. *Captured by Texts: Puritan to Postmodern Images of Indian Captivity.* Charlottesville: University of Virginia Press, 1995.

Ellison, Julie. "Race and Sensibility in the Early Republic: Ann Eliza Bleecker and Sarah Wentworth Morton." *American Literature* 65 (1993): 445–74.

Fiedler, Leslie. *The Return of the Vanishing American.* New York: Stein and Day, 1968.

Fitzpatrick, Tara. "The Figure of Captivity: The Cultural Work of the Puritan Captivity Narrative." *American Literary History* 3 (1991): 1–26.

Gherman, Dawn L. "From Parlour to Tepee: The White Squaw on the American Frontier." Diss. University of Massachusetts, 1975.

Gould, Philip. "Catharine Sedgwick's 'Recital' of the Pequot War." *American Literature* 66 (1994): 641–62.

Green, Rayna P. "The Pocahontas Complex: The Image of Indian Women in Popular Culture." *Massachusetts Review* 16 (1975): 698–714.

Greene, David L. "New Light on Mary Rowlandson." *Early American Literature* 20 (1985): 24–38.

Griffin, Edward M. "Patricia Hearst and Her Foremothers: The Captivity Fable in America." *The Centennial Review* 36 (1992): 311–26.

Haberly, David T. "Women and Indians: *The Last of the Mohicans* and the Captivity Tradition." *American Quarterly* 28 (1976): 431–41.

Hacker, Margaret Schmidt, and Cheryl J. Foote. *Cynthia Ann Parker: The Life and the Legend.* El Paso: Texas Western Press, 1990.

Hartman, James D. "Providence Tales and the Indian Captivity Narrative: Some Transatlantic Influences on Colonial Puritan Discourse." *Early American Literature* 32 (1997): 66–81.

Heard, J. Norman. *Handbook of the American Frontier: Four Centuries of Indian-White Relationships.* 3 vols. Metuchen, N.J.: Scarecrow, 1987–93.

————. *White into Red: A Study of the Assimilation of White Persons Captured by Indians.* Metuchen, N.J.: Scarecrow, 1973.

Henwood, Dawn. "Mary Rowlandson and the Psalms: The Textuality of Survival." *Early American Literature* 32 (1997): 169–86.

Holte, James Craig. *The Conversion Experience in America: A Sourcebook on Religious Conversion Autobiography.* Westport, Conn.: Greenwood Press, 1992.

Howe, Susan. *The Birth-mark: Unsettling the Wilderness in American Literary History.* Hanover, N.H.: University Press of New England for Wesleyan University Press, 1991.

Hoxie, Frederick E., ed. *Encyclopedia of North American Indians.* Boston: Houghton Mifflin, 1996.

Jennings, Francis. *The Invasion of America: Indians, Colonialism, and the Cant of Conquest.* Chapel Hill: University of North Carolina Press, 1975.

Kilgore, H. D. *The Story of Hannah Duston.* Haverhill, Mass.: Duston-Dustin Family Association, 1984.

Kolodny, Annette. "Among the Indians: The Uses of Captivity." *New York Times Book Review,* 31 Jan. 1993, 26–29.

———. *The Land before Her: Fantasy and Experience of the American Frontiers, 1630–1860.* Chapel Hill: University of North Carolina Press, 1984.

———. *The Lay of the Land: Metaphor as Experience and History in American Life and Letters.* Chapel Hill: University of North Carolina Press, 1975.

———. "Review Essay." *Early American Literature* 14 (1979): 228–35.

———. "Turning the Lens on 'The Panther Captivity': A Feminist Exercise in Practical Criticism." *Critical Inquiry* 8 (1981): 329–45.

Leach, Douglas Edward. "The 'When's' of Mary Rowlandson's Captivity." *New England Quarterly* 34 (1961): 353–63.

Levernier, James A. "The Captivity Narrative as Children's Literature." *Markham Review* 8 (1979): 54–59.

———. "The Captivity Narrative as Regional, Military, and Ethnic History." *Research Studies* 45 (1977): 30–37.

Lewis, James R. "Assessing the Impact of Indian Captivity on the Euro-American Mind: Some Critical Issues." *Connecticut Review* 11 (1989): 14–26.

Littlefield, Daniel F. *Africans and Seminoles: From Removal to Emancipation.* Westport, Conn.: Greenwood, 1977.

Logan, Lisa. "Mary Rowlandson's Captivity and the 'Place' of the Woman Subject." *Early American Literature* 28 (1993): 255–77.

Mahon, John K. *History of the Second Seminole War 1835–1842.* Gainesville: University of Florida Press, 1967.

Minter, David L. "By Dens of Lions: Notes on Stylization in Early

Puritan Captivity Narratives." *American Literature* 45 (1973): 335–47.

Mott, Frank Luther. *Golden Multitudes: The Story of Best Sellers in the United States*. New York: Bowker, 1947.

Namias, June. *White Captives: Gender and Ethnicity on the American Frontier*. Chapel Hill: University of North Carolina Press, 1993.

Nash, Alice N. "Two Stories of New England Captives: Grizel and Christine Otis of Dover, New Hampshire." *New England/New France, 1600–1850*. Boston: Boston University Scholarly Publications, 1992 (Annual Proceedings of the Dublin Seminar for New England Folklife, 14 [1989]). 39–48.

Pearce, Roy Harvey. "The Significances of the Captivity Narrative." *American Literature* 19 (1947): 1–20.

Ramsey, Colin. "Cannibalism and Infant Killing: A System of 'Demonizing' Motifs in Indian Captivity Narratives." *CLIO: A Journal of History*Literature*Philosophy of History* 23 (1994): 55–68.

Riley, Glenda. *Women and Indians on the Frontier 1825–1915*. Albuquerque: University of New Mexico Press, 1984.

Rister, Carl Coke. *Border Captives: The Traffic in Prisoners by Southern Plains Indians, 1835–1875*. Norman: University of Oklahoma Press, 1940.

Robe, Stanley L. "Wild Men and Spain's Brave New World." *The Wild Man Within: An Image in Western Thought from the Renaissance to Romanticism*. Ed. Edward Dudley and Maximillian E. Novak. Pittsburgh: University of Pittsburgh Press, 1973. 39–54.

Saillant, John. " 'Remarkably Emancipated from Bondage, Slavery, and Death': An African American Retelling of the Puritan Captivity Narrative, 1820." *Early American Literature* 29 (1994): 122–40.

Salisbury, Neal. *Manitou and Providence: Indians, Europeans, and the Making of New England, 1500–1643*. New York: Oxford University Press, 1982.

Scheick, William J. "Logonomic Conflict in Hanson's Captivity Narrative and Ashbridge's Autobiography." *The Eighteenth Century: Theory and Interpretation* 37 (1996): 3–21.

Schultz, Duane. *Over the Earth I Come: The Great Sioux Uprising of 1862*. New York: St. Martin's Press, 1992.

Seelye, John. *Prophetic Waters: The River in American Life and Literature*. New York: Oxford University Press, 1977.

Sewell, David R. " 'So Unstable and Like Mad Men They Were': Language and Interpretation in American Captivity Narratives." *A Mixed Race: Ethnicity in Early America*. Ed. Frank Shuffelton. New York: Oxford, 1993. 39–55.

Shannon, Donald H. *The Utter Disaster on the Oregon Trail: A History of the Utter and Van Ornum Massacres of 1860.* Caldwell, Idaho: Snake Country Publishing, 1993.

Sieminski, Greg. "The Puritan Captivity Narrative and the Politics of the American Revolution." *American Quarterly* 42 (1990): 35–56.

Slotkin, Richard. *Regeneration through Violence: The Mythology of the American Frontier, 1600–1860.* Middletown, Conn.: Wesleyan University Press, 1973.

Smith-Rosenberg, Carroll. "Subject Female: Authorizing American Identity." *American Literary History* 5 (1993): 481–511.

Stanford, Ann. "Mary Rowlandson's Journey to Redemption." *Ariel* 7 (1976): 27–37.

Stutler, Boyd B. "The Kinnan Massacre." *West Virginia History* 1 (1939): 30–48.

Tate, Michael L. "Comanche Captives: People Between Two Worlds." *The Chronicles of Oklahoma* 72 (1994): 228–63.

Tilton, Robert. *Pocahontas: The Evolution of an American Narrative.* New York: Cambridge University Press, 1994.

Toulouse, Teresa A. "Mary Rowlandson and the 'Rhetoric of Ambiguity.' " *Studies in Puritan American Spirituality* 3 (1992): 21–52.

———. " 'My Own Credit': Strategies of (E)valuation in Mary Rowlandson's Captivity Narrative." *American Literature* 64 (1992): 655–76.

Trigger, Bruce G., and Wilcomb E. Washburn, eds. *The Cambridge History of the Native Peoples of the Americas.* Vol. 1. New York: Cambridge, 1996.

Ulrich, Laurel Thatcher. *Good Wives: Image and Reality in the Lives of Women in Northern New England, 1650–1750.* New York: Random House, 1982.

Vaughan, Alden T. *New England Frontier: Puritans and Indians, 1620–1675.* 1965. Rev. ed. Boston: Little, Brown, 1979.

———, and Daniel K. Richter. "Crossing the Cultural Divide: Indians and New Englanders, 1605–1763." *Proceedings of the American Antiquarian Society* 90 (1980): 23–99.

Voorhees, Oscar M. "A New Jersey Woman's Captivity among the Indians." *New Jersey Historical Society Proceedings* 13 (1928): 152–65.

Walsh, Susan. " 'With Them Was My Home': Native American Autobiography and *A Narrative of the Life of Mrs. Mary Jemison.*" *American Literature* 64 (1992): 49–70.

White, Lonnie J. "White Women Captives of Southern Plains Indians, 1866–1875." *Journal of the West* 8 (1969): 327–54.

Whitford, Kathryn. "Hannah Dustin: The Judgement of History." *Essex Institute Historical Collections* 108 (1972): 304–25.

# A NOTE ON THE TEXTS

Often written, edited, printed, and reprinted hurriedly to capitalize on their currency, Indian captivity narratives are at best textually unreliable. Even when editors today can establish which text might be desirable or definitive, it is not necessarily available. For example, most scholars presumably would prefer to use the first edition (Boston, 1682) of Mary Rowlandson's narrative. But only eight pages used as lining papers in another book have survived the passage of time because a limited number of copies was printed and because the text was so popular it was read to shreds. Therefore, critics must choose from the other three editions published in 1682 or come up with their own copy text.

While the first appearance of a narrative might seem like the one to opt for, a later version might be fuller or more accurate, as in the case of Cotton Mather's last published version of Hannah Dustan's story and the second edition of Sarah F. Wakefield's *Six Weeks in the Sioux Tepees* (1864). Therefore, I have chosen the best available edition of each narrative on an individual, not standardized, basis. Owing to the impossibility, in many cases, of establishing a definitive edition, I do not make any further textual changes. Thus all the narratives appear as they were printed in the sources from which I took them without modernized punctuation, spelling, or orthography except the removal of the long "s," the correction of glaring typographical errors, and a few alterations for clarity.

Many captivity narratives appeared with extensive supplementary material in the form of prefaces to and appendixes after the main text. It has not been possible to publish all this material in the present edition. However, in three important instances I have reproduced prefatory material: "The Preface to the Reader," signed "Per Amicum," in front of Rowlandson's narrative; James E. Seaver's preface and introduction to his *Narrative of the Life of Mrs. Mary Jemison*; and Sarah F. Wakefield's brief but powerful preface to *Six Weeks in the Sioux Tepees*.

One last observation: The general and individual introductions indicate that assigning authorship or assessing editorial intervention in the narratives is often difficult. However, it is sometimes easier simply to use the purported author's name than to avoid it altogether. Thus, for example, I might refer to "Hanson's narrative" even though Elizabeth Hanson did not compose her own story.

The texts in this edition, arranged in chronological order of publication, are as follows:

Rowlandson, Mary. *A True History of the Captivity and Restoration of Mrs. Mary Rowlandson.* London: Joseph Poole, 1682.

Mather, Cotton. *Magnalia Christi Americana: Or, the Ecclesiastical History of New-England.* London: Thomas Parkhurst, 1702.

*God's Mercy Surmounting Man's Cruelty, Exemplified in the Captivity and Redemption of Elizabeth Hanson.* Philadelphia: Samuel Keimer, 1728.

Panther, Abraham [pseud.]. *A Surprising Account of the Discovery of a Lady Who Was Taken by the Indians in the Year 1777, and After Making Her Escape, She Retired to a Lonely Cave, Where She Lived Nine Years.* In *Bickerstaff's Almanac, for the Year of Our Lord, 1788.* Norwich, Conn.: John Trumbull, 1787.

Gay, Bunker. *A Genuine and Correct Account of the Captivity, Sufferings and Deliverance of Mrs. Jemima Howe.* Boston: Belknap and Young, 1792.

Kollock, Shepard. *A True Narrative of the Sufferings of Mary Kinnan.* Elizabethtown, N.J.: Shepard Kollock, 1795.

Seaver, James E. *A Narrative of the Life of Mrs. Mary Jemison.* Canandaigua, N.Y.: J. D. Bemis, 1824.

*An Authentic Narrative of the Seminole War; and of the Miraculous Escape of Mary Godfrey and Her Four Female Children.* New York: Daniel F. Blanchard, 1836.

Wakefield, Sarah F. *Six Weeks in the Sioux Tepees: A Narrative of Indian Captivity.* Shakopee, Minn.: Argus, 1864.

Fuller, Emeline L. *Left by the Indians: Story of My Life.* Mt. Vernon, Iowa: Hawk-Eye, 1892. Rpt. New York: Edward Eberstadt, 1936.

# WOMEN'S
# INDIAN CAPTIVITY
# NARRATIVES

# MARY
# ROWLANDSON

First published in 1682 under the title *The Soveraignty and Goodness of God*, Mary Rowlandson's (c. 1637–1710/11) Indian captivity narrative went through four editions that year and sold more than a thousand copies combined in America and England, qualifying it as a contemporary best-seller. By the nineteenth century, it was well on its way to becoming a colonial classic, and since then it has been regularly republished. Currently, it holds the status of a touchstone text in early American literature. But we should not forget that it is also a *woman's* text charting the emotions and experiences of a relatively affluent, socially prominent, well-educated Puritan woman.

Mary White Rowlandson was born about 1637 in England to John and Joan White, middle-class Puritans who emigrated to Massachusetts in 1639. While John White amassed land first in Wenham and then in Nashaway (renamed Lancaster), his wife was active and vocal in church affairs in both communities, to the extent allowed a Puritan woman. The marriage between Mary White and Joseph Rowlandson, who was pastor of the Lancaster church when the Whites moved there in the mid-1650s, benefited both families. The Whites were wealthy pillars of the community but despite their land holdings had insufficient social status, and the Rowlandsons were poor and litigation-prone, but their son, Joseph, in his elevated position as minister, was the only Lancaster resident allowed the prestigious title of "Mister" rather than the lowly "Goodman" (Rowlandson, ed. Salisbury, pp. 15–19). Thus Mary brought respectability and material comfort to the marriage, and Joseph, education and social prestige. When Metacom's (King Philip's) War extended to Lancaster in 1676, Mary Rowlandson became its most important political prisoner, the one that the authorities tried hardest to ransom, and the first actually to be released (Rowlandson, ed. Salisbury, p. 43).

Metacom's War erupted in 1675 as Wampanoag, Narragansett, and Nipmuck Indians, who had lived alongside the New England colonists for decades, rebelled against increasing European expansionism, discrimination, and enforced conversion to Christianity. Surprised by the Indians' flexible military strategies and guerrilla attacks,

3

initially the English fared badly. However, they rallied and took advantage of the Indian alliance's food shortage. Rowlandson's captive status from February to May 1676 coincided first with the nadir then, three months later, the resurgence of English domination.

As a colonist and a Puritan minister's wife with the title Mistress—a counterpart to her husband's "Mister"—Rowlandson was far more used to exerting power over the Indians than having them exert it over her. Nonetheless, as a captive, she realized very quickly that the status quo had changed and her captors had the upper hand.

Rowlandson documents in her narrative how the traumatic attack and capture jolted her worldview. She realized that outside of her own culture, her social standing meant nothing, and the powerful "squaw sachem," or female leader of the Pocassets, Weetamoo, was the real mistress (here, the female equivalent of "master") in this situation. Additionally, Rowlandson realized that her family unit was not fixed, as seen in her separation from her two eldest children and the deaths of her sister and her youngest child. Although her comfortable house with its extensive library was fortified and used as one of the garrisons in time of attack, it proved to be as impermanent as her family structure and went up in flames. She also found her assumption that the English military forces would prevail continually challenged, and for a Puritan, defeat appeared to indicate God's disfavor. But she came to understand that affliction was a way to test, strain, and ultimately recharge her own personal spiritual complacency. Finally, the last paragraphs of the narrative show Rowlandson's acceptance that her return to Puritan culture did not mean it would be possible to resume life as it was before the attack on Lancaster.

Indeed, in the next few years, Rowlandson experienced more turbulence and change. In spring 1677, after depending on the charity of friends for about a year, the Rowlandsons moved to Wethersfield, Connecticut, where Joseph accepted a call to be minister. But in November 1678, he died suddenly. Like many other colonial women, Rowlandson was not a widow for long; in August 1679, she married Captain Samuel Talcott, a respected community leader. Widowed a second time in 1691, Mary Talcott continued to live in Wethersfield until her death in January 1710/11.

Rowlandson's only literary work is her autobiographical narrative, *A True History*, which reveals the physical, psychological, and spiritual terrain she traversed while she was a captive. Internal evidence suggests that Rowlandson composed her narrative within a year or so of her release in May 1676; however, it was not published until 1682. Most extant seventeenth-century editions of the narrative also include the last sermon of her husband, Joseph Rowlandson, preached in 1678 (though in addition the captivity narrative and the sermon were printed and distributed separately). In these editions, the narrative appears second in a sequence of four texts: 1) "The Preface to the Reader," in front of Mary Rowlandson's account; 2) Rowlandson's captivity narrative; 3) "To the Courteous Reader," prefacing Joseph Rowlandson's sermon; and 4) "The Possibility of God's Forsaking a People," the title of Rev. Rowlandson's final sermon.

The influential Puritan minister and author Increase Mather almost certainly sponsored Rowlandson's captivity narrative, wrote its preface, and arranged for its publication. Very likely, Rev. John Woodbridge, Jr., who succeeded Joseph in the pulpit at Wethersfield, Connecticut, arranged for his predecessor's last sermon to be published and asked his own brother, Rev. Benjamin Woodbridge, to write the sermon's preface, which is signed "B. W." Thus we have the known involvement of four prominent Puritan ministers: Joseph Rowlandson, Increase Mather, and the Woodbridge brothers. What cannot be confirmed, however, is whether or not they edited Mary's narrative before it was printed. Yet it seems naive to assume that at least her husband or her senior spiritual adviser, Mather, would not have had some input, which might well have included editorial additions and revisions; indeed, several aspects of Rowlandson's story recall sermon stylistics and ministerial retellings of other captivities. In the absence of more definitive proof, scholars assign authorship of Rowlandson's text to her alone, but it seems almost certain that it was mediated to some extent.

A True History is one of those rare texts that engenders multiple readings and renews its significance over time. Like The Diary of Anne Frank, Rowlandson's Indian captivity narrative transcends the historical and cultural circumstances that produced it and, by combining stark details, honesty, and exquisite style, brings the experience of war and suffering to a personal and accessible level.

The text is that of the fourth edition: Mary Rowlandson, A True History of the Captivity and Restoration of Mrs. Mary Rowlandson. London: Joseph Poole, 1682.

## SUGGESTIONS FOR FURTHER READING

*PRIMARY WORKS*

Diebold; Rowlandson, ed. Salisbury.

*SECONDARY WORKS*

Armstrong and Tennenhouse; Breitwieser; Burnham, *Captivity* and "Journey"; Castiglia; Davis; Derounian; "Publication" and "Puritan Orthodoxy"; Derounian-Stodola, "Indian Captivity Narratives"; Derounian-Stodola and Levernier; Dietrich; Downing; Ebersole; Fitzpatrick; Greene; Henwood; Howe; Kolodny, *Land*; Leach; Logan; Mott; Namias; Sieminski; Slotkin; Stanford; Toulouse, "Mary Rowlandson" and " 'My Own Credit.' "

# A True History of the Captivity and
# Restoration of Mrs. Mary Rowlandson

## THE PREFACE TO THE READER

IT *was on* Tuesday *Feb.* 1. 1675.[1] *in the afternoon, when the* Nar-rhagansets *Quarters (in or toward the* Nipmug *Country, whither they were now retired for fear of the* English *Army lying in their own Country) were the second time beaten up by the Forces of the United Colonies;*[2] *who thereupon soon betook themselves to flight, and were all the next day pursued by the* English, *some overtaken and destroyed. But on* Thursday *Feb.* 3. *the* English *having now been six days on their March, from their Head-quarters at* Wickford, *in the* Narrhaganset *Country, toward, and after the Enemy, and Provision grown exceeding short; insomuch that they were fain to kill some Horses for the supply, especially of their* Indian *Friends, they were necessitated to consider what was best to be done; and about noon (having hitherto followed the Chase as hard as they might) a Council was called, and though some few were of another mind, yet it was concluded by far the greater part of the Council of War, that the Army should desist the pursuit, and retire: The Forces of* Plimouth *and the* Bay *to the next Town of the* Bay, *and* Connecticut *Forces to their own next Towns: which determination was immediately put in execution. The consequent whereof, as it was not difficult to be foreseen by those that knew the causeless enmity of these* Barbarians *against the* English, *and the malicious and revengeful spirit of these* Heathen; *so it soon proved dismal.*

*The* Narrhagansets *were now driven quite from their own Country, and all their Provisions there hoarded up, to which they durst not at present return, and being so numerous as they were, soon devoured those to whom they went,*[3] *whereby both the one and the other were now reduced to extream straits, and so necessitated to take the first and best opportunity for supply, and very glad no doubt of such an opportunity as this, to provide for themselves, and make spoile of the* English *at once; and seeing themselves thus discharged of their pursuers, and a little refreshed after their flight, the very next week on* Thursday Feb. 10. *they fell with mighty force and fury upon*

Lancaster: *which small Town, remote from aid of others, and not being Garrison'd as it might, the Army being now come in, and as the time indeed required (the design of the* Indians *against that place being known to the English some time before)*[4] *was not able to make effectual resistance; but notwithstanding the utmost endeavour of the Inhabitants, most of the buildings were turned into ashes; many People (Men, Women and Children) slain, and others captivated. The most solemn and remarkable part of this Tragedy, may that justly be reputed, which fell upon the Family of that Reverend Servant of God, Mr.* Joseph Rowlandson, *the faithful Pastor of the Church of Christ in that place, who being gon down to the Council of the* Massachusets, *to seek aid for the defence of the place; at his return found the Town in flames, or smoke, his own house being set on fire by the Enemy, through the disadvantage of a defective Fortification and all in it consumed: His precious yoke-fellow, and dear Children, wounded and captivated (as the issue evidenced, and the following Narrative declares) by these cruel and barbarous Salvages. A sad Catastrophe! Thus all things come alike to all: None knows either love or hatred by all that is before him. 'Tis no new thing for Gods precious ones to drink as deep as others, of the Cup of common Calamity: take just* Lot *(yet captivated) for instance, beside others.*[5] *But it is not my business to dilate on these things, but only in few words introductively to preface to the following script, which is a Narrative of the wonderfully awful, wise, holy, powerful, and gracious providence of God, toward that worthy and precious Gentlewoman, the dear Consort of the said Reverend Mr.* Rowlandson, *and her Children with her, as in casting of her into such a waterless pit, so in preserving, supporting, and carrying through so many such extream hazards, unspeakable difficulties and disconsolateness, and at last delivering her out of them all, and her surviving Children also. It was a strange and amazing dispensation, that the Lord should so afflict his precious Servant, and Hand-maid: It was as strange, if not more, that he should so bear up the spirits of his Servant under such bereavements, and of his Hand-maid under such Captivity, travels, and hardships (much too hard for flesh and blood) as he did, and at length deliver and restore. But he was their Saviour, who hath said,* When thou passest through the Waters, I will be with thee, and through the Rivers, they shall not overflow thee: when thou walkest through the Fire, thou shalt not be burnt, nor shall the flame kindle upon thee, *Isai. 43. Ver. 3. and again,* He woundeth, and his hands make whole, He shall deliver thee in six troubles, yea in seven there shall no evil touch thee: In Famine he shall redeem thee from death; and in War from the power of the sword, *Job. 5. 18, 19, 20. Methinks this dispensation doth bear some resemblance to those of Joseph, David and Daniel, yea and of the three Children too,[6] the stories whereof do represent us with the excellent textures of divine providence, curious pieces of divine work: And truly so doth this, and therefore not to be forgotten, but worthy to be exhibited to, and viewed, and pondered by all, that disdain not to consider the operation of his hands.*

*The works of the Lord (not only of Creation, but of Providence also, especially those that do more peculiarly concern his dear ones, that are as the apple of his eye, as the signet upon his hand, the delight of his eyes, and the object of his tenderest care) are great, sought out of all those that have pleasure therein. And of these, verily this is none of the least.*

*This Narrative was Penned by this Gentlewoman her self, to be to her a Memorandum of Gods dealing with her, that she might never forget, but remember the same, and the several circumstances thereof, all the daies of her life. A pious scope, which deserves both commendation and imitation. Some Friends having obtained a sight of it, could not but be so much affected with the many passages of working providence discovered therein, as to judge it worthy of publick view, and altogether unmeet that such works of God should be hid from present and future Generation: and therefore though this Gentlewomans modesty would not thrust it into the Press, yet her gratitude unto God, made her not hardly perswadable to let it pass, that God might have his due glory, and others benefit by it as well as her selfe.*

*I hope by this time none will cast any reflection upon this Gentlewoman, on the score of this publication of her Affliction and Deliverance. If any should, doubtless they may be reckoned with the nine Lepers, of whom it is said,* Were there not ten cleansed, where are the nine?[7] *but one returning to give God thanks. Let such further know, that this was a dispensation of publick note, and of Universal concernment; and so much the more, by how much the nearer this Gentlewoman stood related to that faithful Servant of God whose capacity and employment was publick, in the House of God, and his Name on that account of a very sweet saviour in the Churches of Christ. Who is there of a true Christian spirit, that did not look upon himself much concerned in this bereavement, this Captivity in the time thereof, and in this deliverance when it came, yea more than in many others? and how many are there to whom, so concerned, it will doubtless be a very acceptable thing, to see the way of God with this Gentlewoman in the aforesaid dispensation, thus laid out and pourtrayed before their eyes.*

To conclude, *Whatever any coy phantasies may deem, yet it highly concerns those that have so deeply tasted how good the Lord is, to enquire with* David, What shall I render to the Lord for all his benefits to me? *Psal.* 116. 12. *He thinks nothing too great: yea, being sensible of his own disproportion to the due praises of God, he calls in help;* O magnifie the Lord with me, let us exalt his Name together, Psal. 34. 3. *And it is but reason, that our praises should hold proportion with our prayers; and that as many have helped together by prayer for the obtaining of this mercy, so praises should be returned by many on this behalf; and forasmuch as not the general but particular knowledge of things makes deepest impression upon the affections, this Narrative particularizing the several passages of this providence, will not a little conduce thereunto: and therefore holy* David, *in order to the attainment of that end, accounts himself concerned to declare what God had done for his Soul,* Psal. 66. 16. Come and hear, all ye that fear God, and I will declare what God hath done for my Soul, *i. e.* for his Life: *See Ver.* 9, 10. He holdeth our soul in life, and suffers not our feet to be moved; for thou our God hast proved us: thou hast tried us, as silver is tried. *Life-mercies are heart-affecting-mercies; of great impression and force, to enlarge pious hearts in the praises of God, so that such know not how but to talk of Gods acts, and to speak of and publish his wonderful works. Deep troubles, when the waters come in unto the Soul, are wont to produce vows: Vows must be paid,* It is better not vow, than to vow and not pay.[8] *I may say, that as none knows what it is to fight and pursue such an enemy as this, but they that have fought and pursued them: so none can imagine, what it is to be captivated, and enslaved to such Atheistical, proud, wild, cruel, barbarous, brutish, (in one word) diabolical Creatures as these, the worst of the heathen; nor what difficulties, hardships, hazards, sorrows, anxieties, and perplexities, do unavoidably wait upon such a condition, but those that have tried it. No serious spirit then (especially knowing any thing of this Gentlewomans Piety) can imagine but that the vows of God are upon her. Excuse her then if she come thus into the publick, to pay those Vows. Come and hear what she hath to say.*

I am confident that no Friend of divine Providence, will ever re-

*pent his time and pains spent in reading over these sheets; but will judge them worth perusing again and again.*

Here Reader, *you may see an instance of the Soveraignty of God, who doth what he will with his own as well as others; and who may say to him,* what dost thou?[9] *here you may see an instance of the Faith and Patience of the Saints, under the most heart-sinking Tryals: here you may see, the Promises are breasts full of Consolation, when all the World besides is empty, and gives nothing but sorrow. That God is indeed the supream Lord of the World: ruling the most unruly, weakening the most cruel and salvage: granting his People mercy in the sight of the most unmerciful: curbing the lusts of the most filthy, holding the hands of the violent, delivering the prey from the mighty, and gathering together the out-casts of Israel. Once and again, you have heard, but here you may see, that power belongeth unto God: that our God is the God of Salvation: and to him belong the issues from Death. That our God is in the Heavens, and doth what ever pleases him. Here you have* Samsons *Riddle exemplified, and that great promise,* Rom. 8. 28. *verified:* Out of the Eater comes forth meat, and sweetness out of the strong;[10] *The worst of evils working together for the best good. How evident is it that the Lord hath made this Gentlewoman a gainer by all this Affliction, that she can say, 'tis good for her, yea better that she hath been, than she should not have been, thus afflicted.*

*Oh how doth God shine forth in such things as these!*

Reader, *if thou gettest no good by such a Declaration as this, the fault must needs be thine own. Read therefore, peruse, ponder, and from hence lay up something from the experience of another, against thine own turn comes: that so thou also through patience and consolation of the Scripture mayest have hope,*

*PER AMICUM.*[11]

# A Narrative of the Captivity
## and Restoration of Mrs. *Mary Rowlandson.*

On the tenth of *February*, 1675. came the *Indians* with great numbers upon *Lancaster*. Their first coming was about Sun-rising. Hearing the noise of some Guns, we looked out; several Houses were burning, and the Smoke ascending to Heaven. There were five Persons taken in one House, the Father, and the Mother, and a sucking Child they knock'd on the head; the other two they took, and carried away alive. There were two others, who being out of their Garrison upon some occasion, were set upon; one was knock'd on the head, the other escaped. Another there was who running along was shot and wounded, and fell down; he begged of them his Life, promising them Money (as they told me); but they would not hearken to him, but knock'd him on the head, stripped him naked, and split open his Bowels. Another seeing many of the *Indians* about his Barn, ventured and went out, but was quickly shot down. There were three others belonging to the same Garrison who were killed. The *Indians* getting up upon the Roof of the Barn, had advantage to shoot down upon them over their Fortification. Thus these murtherous Wretches went on, burning and destroying before them.

At length they came and beset our own House, and quickly it was the dolefullest day that ever mine eyes saw. The House stood upon the edge of a Hill; some of the *Indians* got behind the Hill, others into the Barn, and others behind any thing that would shelter them: from all which Places they shot against the House, so that the Bullets seemed to fly like Hail: and quickly they wounded one Man among us, then another, and then a third. About two Hours (according to my observation in that amazing time) they had been about the House, before they could prevail to fire it, (which they did with Flax and Hemp which they brought out of the Barn, and there being no Defence about the House, onely two Flankers,[12] at two opposite Corners, and one of them not finished.) They fired it once, and one ventured out and quenched it; but they quickly fired it again, and that took. Now is that dreadful Hour come, that I have often heard of, (in the time of the War, as it was the Case of others) but now mine Eyes see it. Some in our House were fighting for their Lives, others wallowing in their Blood; the House on fire over our Heads, and the bloody Heathen ready to knock us on the Head if we stirred out. Now might we hear Mothers and Children crying out for themselves, and one another, *Lord, what shall we do!* Then I took my Children[13] (and one of my Sisters, hers)[14] to go forth and leave the House: But as soon as we came to the Door and appeared, the *Indians* shot so thick; that the Bullets ratled against the House, as if one had taken an handful of Stones and threw them; so that we were fain to give back. We had six stout Dogs belonging to our Garrison, but none of them would stir, though another time, if an *Indian* had come to the Door, they were ready to fly upon him, and tear him down. The Lord hereby would make us the more to acknowledge his Hand, and to see that our Help is always in him. But out we must go, the Fire increasing, and coming along behind us roaring, and the *Indians* gaping before us with their Guns, Spears, and Hatchets, to devour us. No sooner were we out of the House, but my Brother-in-Law (being before wounded (in defending the House) in or near the Throat) fell down dead, whereat the *Indians* scornfully shouted, and hallowed, and were presently upon him, stripping off his Clothes. The Bullets flying thick, one went thorow my Side, and the same (as would seem) thorow the Bowels and Hand of my dear Child in my Arms.[15] One of my eldest Sisters Children (named *William*) had then his Leg broken, which the *Indians* perceiving, they knock'd him on the head. Thus were we butchered by those merciless Heathen, standing amazed, with the Blood running down to our Heels. My elder Sister[16] being yet in the House, and seeing those woful Sights, the Infidels haling Mothers one way, and Children another, and some wallowing in their Blood, and her elder son telling her that (her Son) *William* was dead, and my self was wounded; she said, And *Lord, let me die with them*: Which was no sooner said, but she was struck with a Bullet, and fell down dead over the Threshold. I hope she is reaping the Fruit of her good Labours, being faithful to the Service of God in her Place. In her younger years she lay under much trouble upon Spiritual accounts, till it pleased God to make that precious Scripture take hold of her Heart, 2 *Cor.* 12. 9. *And he said unto me, My grace is sufficient for thee*. More than twenty years after I have heard her tell, how sweet and comfortable that Place was to her. But to return: The *Indians* laid hold of us, pulling me one way, and the

Children another, and said, *Come, go along with us:* I told them, they would kill me: They answered, *If I were willing to go along with them, they would not hurt me.*

O the doleful Sight that now was to behold at this House! *Come, behold the Works of the Lord, what desolation he has made in the Earth.*[17] Of thirty seven Persons who were in this one House, none escaped either present Death, or a bitter Captivity, save onely one, who might say as he, *Job* 1. 15. *And I onely am escaped alone to tell the News.* There were twelve killed, some shot, some stabb'd with their Spears, some knock'd down with their Hatchets. When we are in prosperity, Oh the Little that we think of such dreadful Sights, and to see our dear Friends and Relations lie bleeding out their Heart-blood upon the Ground! There was one who was chopp'd into the Head with a Hatchet, and stripp'd naked, and yet was crawling up and down. It is a solemn Sight to see so many Christians lying in their Blood, some here, and some there, like a company of Sheep torn by Wolves. All of them stript naked by a company of hell-hounds, roaring, singing, ranting and insulting, as if they would have torn our very hearts out, yet the Lord by his Almighty power, pre-served a number of us from death, for there were twenty four of us taken alive: and carried Captive.

I had often before this said, that if the *Indians* should come, I should chuse rather to be killed by them, than taken alive: but when it came to the trial my mind changed: their glittering Weapons so daunted my Spirit, that I chose rather to go along with those (as I may say) ravenous Bears, than that moment to end my daies. And that I may the better declare what happened to me during that griev-ous Captivity, I shall particularly speak of the several Removes we had up and down the Wilderness.

*The first Remove.*[18] Now away we must go with those Barbarous Creatures, with our bodies wounded and bleeding, and our hearts no less than our bodies. About a mile we went that night; up upon a hill within sight of the Town where they intended to lodge. There was hard by a vacant house (deserted by the English before, for fear of the *Indians*) I asked them whether I might not lodge in the house that night? to which they answered, what will you love *English-men* still? this was the dolefullest night that ever my eyes saw. Oh the roaring, and singing, and dancing, and yelling of those black crea-tures in the night, which made the place a lively resemblance of hell: And as miserable was the waste that was there made, of Horses,

Cattle, Sheep, Swine, Calves, Lambs, Roasting Pigs, and Fowls (which they had plundered in the Town) some roasting, some lying and burning, and some boyling, to feed our merciless Enemies; who were joyful enough though we were disconsolate. To add to the dolefulness of the former day, and the dismalness of the present night, my thoughts ran upon my losses and sad bereaved condition. All was gone, my Husband gone (at least separated from me, he being in the Bay;[19] and to add to my grief, the *Indians* told me they would kill him as he came homeward) my Children gone, my Relations and Friends gone, our house and home, and all our comforts within door, and without, all was gone (except my life) and I knew not but the next moment that might go too.

There remained nothing to me but one poor wounded Babe, and it[20] seemed at present worse than death, that it was in such a pitiful condition, bespeaking Compassion, and I had no refreshing for it, nor suitable things to revive it. Little do many think, what is the savageness and bruitishness of this barbarous Enemy! even those that seem to profess more than others among them, when the *English* have fallen into their hands.

Those seven that were killed at *Lancaster* the summer before upon a Sabbath day, and the one that was afterward killed upon a week day, were slain and mangled in a barbarous manner, by one-ey'd *John*,[21] and *Marlberough's* Praying *Indians*,[22] which Capt. *Mosely*[23] brought to *Boston*, as the *Indians* told me.

*The second Remove.* But now (the next morning) I must turn my back upon the Town, and travel with them into the vast and desolate Wilderness, I know not whither. It is not my tongue, or pen can express the sorrows of my heart, and bitterness of my spirit, that I had at this departure: But God was with me, in a wonderful manner, carrying me along, and bearing up my Spirit, that it did not quite fail. One of the *Indians* carried my poor wounded Babe upon a horse: it went moaning all a long, I shall die, I shall die. I went on foot after it, with sorrow that cannot be exprest. At length I took it off the Horse, and carried it in my arms, till my strength failed, and *I* fell down with it. Then they set me upon a horse, with my wounded Child in my lap, and there being no Furniture[24] upon the horse back; as we were going down a steep hill, we both fell over the horses head, at which they like inhuman creatures laught, and rejoiced to see it, though I thought we should there have ended our dayes, as overcome with so many difficulties. But the Lord renewed my strength still, and carried me along, that I might see more of his power, yea, so much that *I* could never have thought of, had *I* not experienced it.

After this it quickly began to Snow, and when night came on, they stopt: and now down I must sit in the Snow, (by a little fire, and a few boughs behind me) with my sick Child in my lap; and calling much for water, being now (thorough the wound) fallen into a violent Fever. (My own wound also growing so stiff, that I could scarce sit down or rise up) yet so it must be, that I must sit all this cold winter night, upon the cold snowy ground, with my sick Child in my arms, looking that every hour would be the last of its life; and having no Christian Friend near me, either to comfort or help me. Oh I may see the wonderful power of God, that my Spirit did not utterly sink under my affliction; still the Lord upheld me with his gracious and merciful Spirit, and we were both alive to see the light of the next morning.

*The third Remove.* The morning being come, they prepared to go on their way: one of the *Indians* got up upon a horse, and they set me up behind him with my poor sick Babe in my lap. A very wearisome and tedious day I had of it; what with my own wound, and my Childs being so exceeding sick, and in a lamentable Condition with her wound. It may easily be judged what a poor feeble condition we were in, there being not the least crumb of refreshing that came within either of our mouths, from Wednesday night to Saturday night, except only a little cold water. This day in the afternoon, about an hour by Sun, we came to the place where they intended, *viz.* an *Indian Town* called *Wenimesset*, Northward of *Quabaug*. When we were come, Oh the Number of *Pagans* (now merciless Enemies) that there came about me, that I may say as *David*, Psal. 27. 13. *I had fainted, unless I had believed*, &c. The next day was the Sabbath: I then remembred how careless I had been of Gods holy time: how many Sabbaths I had lost and mispent, and how evilly I had walked in Gods sight; which lay so close upon my Spirit, that it was easie for me to see how righteous it was with God to cut off the threed of my life, and cast me out of his presence for ever. Yet the Lord still shewed mercy to me, and upheld me; and as he wounded me with one hand, so he healed me with the other. This day there came to me one *Robert Pepper*[25] (a Man belonging to *Roxbury*,) who was taken in Capt. *Beers* his fight; and had been now a considerable time with the *Indians*; and up with them almost as far as *Albany* to see King *Philip*, as he told me, and was now very lately come with them into these parts. Hearing I say that I was in this *Indian* Town he obtained leave to come and see me. He told me he himself was wounded in the Leg at Capt. *Beers* his fight; and was not able sometime to go, but as they carried him, and that he took oaken leaves and laid to his wound, and through the blessing of God, he was able to travel again. Then I took Oaken leaves and laid to my side, and with the blessing of God it cured me also; yet before the cure was wrought, I may say as it is in *Psal.* 38. 5, 6. *My wounds stink and are corrupt, I am troubled, I am bowed down greatly, I go mourning all the day long.* I sate much alone with a poor wounded Child in my lap, which moaned night and day, having nothing to revive the body, or chear the Spirits of her: but instead of that, sometimes one Indian would come and tell me, one hour, and your Master will knock your Child in the head, and then a second, and then a third, your Master will quickly knock your child in the head.

This was the Comfort I had from them; miserable comforters are ye all, as he said.[26] Thus nine dayes I sat upon my knees, with my babe in my lap, till my flesh was raw again: my child being even ready to depart this sorrowful world, they bad me carry it out, to another Wigwam: (I suppose because they would not be troubled with such spectacles.) Whither I went with a very heavy heart, and down I sate with the picture of death in my lap. About two hours in the Night, my sweet Babe like a Lamb departed this life, on *Feb.* 18. 1675. it being about six years and five months old. It was nine dayes (from the first wounding) in this Miserable condition, without any refreshing of one nature or other, except a little cold water. I cannot but take notice, how at another time I could not bear to be in the room where any dead person was, but now the case is changed: I must and could lye down by my dead Babe, side by side, all the night after. I have thought since of the wonderful goodness of God to me, in preserving me so in the use of my reason and senses, in that distressed time, that I did not use wicked and violent means to end my own miserable life. In the morning, when they understood that my child was dead, they sent for me home to my Masters Wigwam: (by my Master in this writing must be understood *Quannopin*,[27] who was a Saggamore and married King *Philips* wives Sister;[28] not that he first took me, but I was sold to him by another *Narrhaganset Indian*, who took me when first I came out of the Garrison) I went to take up my dead Child in my arms to carry it with me, but they bid me let it alone: there was no resisting, but go I must and leave it. When I had been a while at my Masters wigwam, I took the first opportunity I could get, to go look after my dead child: when I came I asked them what they had done with it? they told me it was upon the hill: then they went and shewed me where it was, where I saw the ground was newly digged, and there they told me they had buried it, there I left that child in the Wilderness, and must commit it, and my self also in this Wilderness condition, to him who is above all. God having taken away this dear child, I went to see my daughter *Mary*, who was at this same *Indian Town*, at a Wigwam not very far off, though we had little liberty or opportunity to see one another: she was about ten years old, and taken from the door at first by a Praying *Indian*, and afterward sold for a gun. When I came in sight she would fall a weeping; at which they were provoked, and would not let me come near her, but bade me be gone: which was a heart-cutting word to me. I had one child dead, another in the wilderness, I knew not where, the third they would not let me come near to: *Me* (as he said) *have ye bereaved of my Children, Joseph is not, and Simeon is not, and ye will take Benjamin also, all these things are against me.*[29] I could not sit still in this condition, but kept walking from one place to another. And as I was going along, my heart was even overwhelmed with the thoughts of my condition, and that I should have Children, and a Nation which I knew not ruled over them. Whereupon I earnestly intreated the Lord, that he would consider my low estate, and shew me a token for good, and if it were his blessed will, some sign and hope of some relief. And indeed quickly the Lord answered, in some measure, my poor Prayer: For as I was going up and down mourning and lamenting my condition, my Son came to me, and asked me how I did? I had not seen him before, since the destruction of the Town: and I knew not where he was, till I was informed by himself, that he was amongst a smaller parcel of *Indians*, whose place was about six miles off, with tears in his eyes, he asked me whether his Sister *Sarah* was dead? and told me he had seen his Sister *Mary*; and prayed me, that I would not be troubled in reference to himself. The occasion of his coming to see me at this time was this: There was, as I said, about six miles from us, a small Plantation of *Indians*, where it seems he had been during his Captivity: and at this time, there were some Forces of the *Indians* gathered out of our company, and some also from them (amongst whom was my Sons Master) to go to assault and burn *Medfield*: in this time of the absence of his Master, his Dame brought him to see me. I took this to be some gracious Answer, to my earnest and un-feigned desire. The next day, *viz.* to this, the *Indians* returned from

*Medfield*: (all the Company, for those that belonged to the other smaller company, came thorow the Town that now we were at) But before they came to us, Oh the outragious roaring and hooping that there was! They began their din about a mile before they came to us. By their noise and hooping they signified how many they had destroyed: (which was at that time twenty three) Those that were with us at home, were gathered together as soon as they heard the hooping, and every time that the other went over their number, these at home gave a shout, that the very Earth rang again. And thus they continued till those that had been upon the expedition were come up to the Saggamores Wigwam; and then Oh the hideous insulting and triumphing that there was over some *English-men*s Scalps, that they had taken (as their manner is) and brought with them. *I* cannot but take notice of the wonderful mercy of God to me in those afflictions, in sending me a Bible: one of the *Indians* that came from *Medfield* fight and had brought some plunder; came to me, and asked me, if I would have a Bible, he had got one in his Basket, I was glad of it, and asked him, whether he thought the *Indians* would let me read? he answered yes: so I took the Bible, and in that melancholly time, it came into my mind to read first the 28 *Chapter* of *Deuteronomie*, which I did, and when I had read it, my dark heart wrought on this manner, that there was no mercy for me, that the blessings were gone, and the curses came in their room, and that I had lost my opportunity. But the Lord helped me still to go on reading, till I came to *Chap.* 30. the seven first verses: where I found there was mercy promised again, if we would return to him, by repentance: and though we were scattered from one end of the earth to the other, yet the Lord would gather us together, and turn all those curses upon our Enemies. I do not desire to live to forget this Scripture, and what comfort it was to me.

Now the *Indians* began to talk of removing from this place, some one way, and some another. There were now besides my self nine *English* Captives in this place (all of them Children, except one Woman) I got an opportunity to go and take my leave of them; they being to go one way, and I another. I asked them whether they were earnest with God for deliverance; they all told me, they did as they were able; and it was some comfort to me, that the Lord stirred up Children to look to him. The Woman, *viz.* Goodwife *Joslin*[30] told me, she should never see me again, and that she could find in her heart to run away: I wisht her not to run away by any means, for we were near thirty miles from any *English* Town, and she very big with Child and had but one week to reckon: and another Childe, in her Arms, two years old, and bad rivers there were to go over, and we were feeble with our poor and course entertainment. I had my Bible with me, I pulled it out, and asked her, whether she would read; we opened the Bible, and lighted on *Psal.* 27. in which Psalm we especially took notice of that, *ver. ult.*[31] *Wait on the Lord, be of good courage, and he shall strengthen thine Heart, wait I say on the Lord.*

*The fourth Remove.* And now must I part with that little company that I had. Here I parted from my daughter *Mary,* (whom I never saw again till I saw her in *Dorchester,* returned from Captivity) and from four little Cousins and Neighbours, some of which *I* never saw afterward, the Lord only knows the end of them. Amongst them also was that poor woman before mentioned, who came to a sad end, as some of the company told me in my travel: she having much grief upon her Spirit, about her miserable condition, being so near her time, she would be often asking the *Indians* to let her go home; they not being willing to that, and yet vexed with her importunity, gathered a great company together about her, and stript her naked, and set her in the midst of them: and when they had sung and danced about her (in their hellish manner) as long as they pleased: they knockt her on the head, and the child in her arms with her: when they had done that, they made a fire and put them both into it: and told the other Children that were with them, that if they attempted to go home they would serve them in like manner: The Children said she did not shed one tear, but prayed all the while. But to return to my own Journey: we travelled about half a day or a little more, and came to a desolate place in the Wilderness; where there were no Wigwams or Inhabitants before: we came about the middle of the afternoon to this place; cold, and wet, and snowy, and hungry, and weary, and no refreshing (for man) but the cold ground to sit on, and our poor *Indian cheer.*

Heart-aking thoughts here I had about my poor Children, who were scattered up and down amongst the wild Beasts of the Forest: my head was light and dizzy (either through hunger, or hard lodging, or trouble, or all together) my knees feeble, my body raw by sitting double night and day, that *I* cannot express to man the affliction that lay upon my Spirit, but the Lord helped me at that time to express it to himself. I opened my Bible to read, and the Lord brought that precious Scripture to me, *Jer.* 31. 16. *Thus saith the Lord, refrain thy voice from weeping, and thine eyes from tears, for thy work shall be rewarded, and they shall come again from the land of the Enemy.*

This was a sweet Cordial to me, when *I* was ready to faint; many and many a time, have *I* sate down and wept swetely over this Scripture. At this place we continued about four days.

*The fifth Remove.* The occasion (as I thought) of their moving at this time, was, the *English Army* its being near and following them: For they went as if they had gone for their lives, for some considerable way; and then they made a stop, and chose out some of their stoutest men, and sent them back to hold the *English* Army in play whilst the rest escaped; and then like *Jehu* they marched on furiously,[32] with their old, and with their young: some carried their old decrepit Mothers, some carried one, and some another. Four of them carried a great *Indian* upon a Bier:[33] but going through a thick Wood with him they were hindered, and could make no haste; whereupon they took him upon their backs, and carried him, one at a time, till we came to *Bacquaug* River. Upon a Fryday a little after noon we came to this River. When all the Company was come up, and were gathered together, I thought to count the number of them, but they were so many, and being somewhat in motion, it was beyond my skill. In this Travel, because of my wound, *I* was somewhat favoured in my load; I carried only my knitting-work, and two quarts of parched Meal: Being very faint I asked my Mistress[34] to give me one spoonful of the Meal, but she would not give me a taste. They quickly fell to cutting dry trees, to make rafts to carry them over the River: and soon my turn came to go over: By the advantage of some brush which they had laid upon the Raft to sit on; I did not wet my foot, (when many of themselves at the other end were mid-leg-deep) which cannot but be acknowledged as a favour of God to my weakned body, it being a very cold time. I was not before acquainted with such kind of doings or dangers. *When thou passest through the waters I will be with thee, and through the rivers they shall not overflow thee.* Isai. 43. 2. A certain number of us got over the river that night, but it was the night after the Sabbath before all the company was got over. On the Saturday they boyled an old Horses leg (which they had got) and so we drank of the broth; as soon as they thought it was ready, and when it was almost all gone, they filled it up again.

The first week of my being among them, *I* hardly ate any thing; the second week I found my stomach grow very faint for want of something; and yet 'twas very hard to get down their filthy trash: but the third week (though I could think how formerly my stomach would turn against this or that, and *I* could starve and die before *I* could eat such things, yet) they were pleasant and savoury to my taste. *I* was at this time knitting a pair of white Cotton Stockins for my Mistriss: and *I* had not yet wrought upon the Sabbath day: when the Sabbath came they bad me go to work; *I* told them it was Sabbath-day, and desired them to let me rest, and told them *I* would do as much more to morrow: to which they answered me, they would break my face. And here I cannot but take notice of the strange providence of God in preserving the Heathen: They were many hundreds, old and young, some sick and some lame, many had *Papooses* at their backs, the greatest number (at this time with us) were *Squaws*: and they travelled with all they had, bag and baggage, and yet they got over this River aforesaid: and on Monday they set their Wigwams on fire, and away they went: on that very day came the *English* Army after them to this River, and saw the smoke of their Wigwams; and yet this River put a stop to them. God did not give them courage or activity to go over after us: we were not ready for so great a mercy as victory and deliverance: if we had been, God would have found out a way for the *English* to have passed this River, as well as for the *Indians* with their *Squaws* and *Children*, and all their *Luggage*. *Oh that my people had hearkened to me, and Israel had walked in my wayes, I should soon have subdued their Enemies, and turned my hand against their Adversaries*, Psal. 81. 13, 14.

*The sixth Remove.* On Monday (as I said) they set their Wigwams on fire, and went away. It was a cold morning; and before us was a great Brook with Ice on it: some waded through it, up to the knees and higher: but others went till they came to a Beaver-Dam, and I amongst them, where thorough the good providence of God, I did not wet my foot. I went along that day, mourning and lamenting, leaving farther my own Countrey, and travelling into the vast and howling Wilderness; and I understood something of *Lots* Wife's Temptation,[35] when she looked back: we came that day to a great Swamp; by the side of which we took up our lodging that night. When I came to the brow of the hill, that looked toward the Swamp, I thought we had been come to a great *Indian Town*, (though there were none but our own Company) the *Indians* were as thick as the Trees; it seemed as if there had been a thousand Hatchets going at once: if one looked before one, there was nothing but *Indians*, and behind one, nothing but *Indians*; and so on either hand: I my self in the midst, and no Christian Soul near me, and yet how hath the Lord preserved me in safety! Oh the experience that I have had of the goodness of God, to me and mine!

*The seventh Remove.* After a restless and hungry night there, we had a wearisome time of it the next day. The Swamp by which we lay, was as it were, a deep Dungeon, and an exceeding high and steep hill before it. Before I got to the top of the hill, I thought my heart and legs and all would have broken, and failed me. What through faintness and soreness of Body, it was a grievous day of Travel to me. As we went along, I saw a place where *English* Cattle had been: that was a comfort to me, such as it was: quickly after that we came to an *English* path, which so took with me, that I thought I could there have freely lyen down and died. That day, a little after noon, we came to *Squaukheag*; where the *Indians* quickly spread themselves over the deserted *English* Fields, gleaning what they could find; some pickt up Ears of Wheat, that were crickled down;[36] some found ears of *Indian Corn*; some found Ground-nuts, and others sheaves of Wheat, that were frozen together in the Shock, and went to threshing of them out. My self got two Ears of *Indian Corn*, and whilst I did but turn my back, one of them was stollen from me, which much troubled me. There came an *Indian* to them at that time, with a Basket of *Horse-liver*: I asked him to give me a piece: what (sayes he) can you eat Horse-liver? I told him, I would try, if he would give a piece; which he did: and I laid it on the coals to rost; but before it was half ready, they got half of it away from me; so that I was fain to take the rest and eat it as it was with the blood about my mouth, and yet a savoury bit it was to me: For to the hungry Soul every bitter thing is sweet.[37] A solemn sight methought it was, to see whole fields of Wheat, and Indian Corn forsaken and spoiled: and the remanders of them to be food for our merciless Enemies. That night we had a mess of Wheat for our supper.

*The eighth Remove.* On the morrow morning we must go over the River, *i.e. Connecticot*, to meet with King *Philip*,[38] two Cannoos full, they had carried over, the next turn I my self was to go; but as my foot was upon the Cannoo to step in, there was a sudden outcry among them, and I must step back: and instead of going over the River, I must go four or five miles up the River farther northward. Some of the *Indians* ran one way, and some another. The cause of this rout was as I thought their espying some *English* Scouts, who were thereabout.

In this travel up the River; about noon the Company made a stop, and sate down; some to eat, and others to rest them. As I sate amongst them, musing of things past, my Son *Joseph* unexpectedly came to me: we asked of each others welfare; bemoaning our doleful condition, and the change that had come upon us: we had Husband

and Father, and Children and Sisters, and Friends and Relations, and House, and Home, and many Comforts of this life: but now we might say as *Job, Naked came I out of my mothers womb, and naked shall I return, The Lord gave, and the Lord hath taken away, blessed be the Name of the Lord*. I asked him whether he would read? he told me, he earnestly desired it. I gave him my Bible, and he lighted upon that comfortable Scripture, *Psal*. 118. 17, 18. *I shall not die but live, and declare the works of the Lord: The Lord hath chastened me sore, yet he hath not given me over to death*. Look here *Mother*, (sayes he) did you read this? And here I may take occasion to mention one principal ground of my setting forth these few Lines; even as the Psalmist says, To declare the works of the Lord, and his wonderful power in carrying us along, preserving us in the Wilderness, while under the Enemies hand, and returning of us in safety again. And his goodness in bringing to my hand so many comfortable and suitable Scriptures in my distress. But to Return: We travelled on till night; and in the morning we must go over the River to *Philip*'s Crew. When I was in the Cannoo, I could not but be amazed at the numerous Crew of Pagans, that were on the Bank on the other side. When I came ashore, they gathered all about me, I sitting alone in the midst: I observed they asked one another Questions, and laughed, and rejoyced over their Gains and Victories. Then my heart began to faile: and I fell a weeping; which was the first time to my remembrance, that I wept before them. Although I had met with so much Affliction, and my heart was many times ready to break, yet could I not shed one tear in their sight; but rather had been all this while in a maze, and like one astonished; but now I may say, as *Psal*. 137. 1. *By the Rivers of* Babylon, *there we sate down, yea, we wept when we remembred Zion*. There one of them asked me, why I wept; I could hardly tell what to say; yet I answered, they would kill me: No, said he, none will hurt you. Then came one of them, and gave me two spoonfuls of Meal (to comfort me) and another gave me half a pint of Pease, which was more worth than many Bushels at another time. Then I went to see King *Philip*; he bade me come in, and sit down, and asked me whether I would smoak it (an usual Complement now a days amongst Saints and Sinners.) But this no way suited me. For though I had formerly used Tobacco, yet I had left it ever since I was first taken. *It seems to be a Bait the Devil layes to make men lose their precious time*: I remember with shame, how formerly, when I had taken two or three Pipes, I was presently ready for another, such a bewitching thing it is: But I thank God, he has now given me power over it; surely there are many who may be better imployed, than to lye sucking a stinking Tobacco-pipe.

Now the *Indians* gather their Forces to go against *North-hampton*: over night one went about yelling and hooting to give notice of the design. Whereupon they fell to boyling of Ground Nuts, and parching of Corn, (as many as had it) for their Provision: and in the morning away they went. During my abode in this place *Philip* spake to me to make a shirt for his Boy, which I did; for which he gave me a shilling; I offered the money to my Master, but he bade me keep it: and with it I bought a piece of Horse-flesh. Afterwards I made a Cap for his Boy, for which he invited me to Dinner: I went, and he gave me a Pancake, about as big as two fingers; it was made of parched Wheat, beaten and fryed in Bears-grease, but I thought I never tasted pleasanter meat in my life. There was a Squaw who spake to me to make a shirt for her Sannup;[39] for which she gave me a piece of Bear. Another asked me to knit a pair of Stockins, for which she gave me a quart of Pease. I Boyled my Pease and Bear together, and invited my Master and Mistress to Dinner: but the proud Gossip, because I served them both in one Dish, would eat nothing, except one bit that he gave her upon the point of his Knife. Hearing that my Son was come to this place, I went to see him, and found him lying flat upon the ground: I asked him how he could sleep so? he answered me, that he was not asleep, but at Prayer; and lay so, that they might not observe what he was doing. I pray God, he may remember these things now he is returned in safety. At this place (the Sun now getting higher) what with the beams and heat of the Sun, and the smoak of the Wigwams, I thought I should have been blind: I could scarce discern one Wigwam from another. There was here one *Mary Thurston*[40] of *Medfield*, who seeing how it was with me, lent me a Hat to wear; but as soon as I was gone, the Squaw (who owned that *Mary Thurston*) came running after me, and got it away again. Here there was a Squaw who gave me one spoonful of Meal, I put it in my Pocket to keep it safe: yet notwithstanding some body stole it, but put five *Indian Corns* in the room of it: which Corns were the greatest Provision I had in my travel for one day.

The *Indians* returning from *North-hampton*, brought with them some Horses and Sheep, and other things which they had taken; I desired them, that they would carry me to *Albany* upon one of those Horses, and sell me for Powder; for so they had sometimes discoursed. I was utterly hopeless of getting home on foot, the way that I came. I could hardly bear to think of the many weary steps I had taken, to come to this place.

*The ninth Remove.* But instead of going either to *Albany* or homeward we must go five miles up the River, and then go over it. Here we abode a while. Here lived a sorry *Indian*, who spake to me to make him a shirt, when I had done it, he would pay me nothing. But he living by the River side, where I often went to fetch water, I would often be putting him in mind, and calling for my pay: at last, he told me, if I would make another shirt, for a Papoos not yet born, he would give me a knife, which he did, when I had done it. I carried the knife in, and my Master asked me to give it him, and I was not a little glad that I had any thing that they would accept of, and be pleased with. When we were at this place my Masters Maid came home, she had been gone three Weeks into the *Narrhaganset Country*, to fetch Corn, where they had stored up some in the ground: she brought home about a peck and half of Corn. This was about the time that their great Captain (*Naananto*)[41] was killed in the *Narrhaganset* Country.

My Son being now about a mile from me, I asked liberty to go and see him, they bade me go, and away I went; but quickly lost my self, travelling over Hills and through Swamps, and could not find the way to him. And I cannot but admire at the wonderful power and goodness of God to me, in that though I was gone from home, and met with all sorts of *Indians*, and those I had no knowledge of, and there being no *Christian Soul* near me; yet not one of them offered the least imaginable miscarriage to me. I turned homeward again, and met with my Master; he shewed me the way to my Son. When I came to him I found him not well; and withal he had a Boyl on his side, which much troubled him: we bemoaned one another a while, as the Lord helped us, and then I returned again. When I was returned, I found my self as unsatisfied as I was before. I went up and down moaning and lamenting: and my spirit was ready to sink, with the thoughts of my poor Children: my Son was ill, and I could not but think of his mournful looks: and no *Christian Friend* was near him, to do any office of love for him, either for Soul or Body. And my poor Girl, I knew not where she was, nor whether she was sick, or well, or alive, or dead. I repaired under these thoughts to my Bible (my great comforter in that time) and that Scripture came to my hand, *Cast thy burden upon the Lord and he shall sustain thee*, Psal. 55. 22.

But I was fain to go and look after something to satisfie my hunger: and going among the Wigwams, I went into one, and there found a Squaw who shewed her self very kind to me, and gave me a piece of Bear. I put it into my pocket, and came home; but could not find an opportunity to broil it, for fear they would get it from me, and there it lay all that day and night in my stinking pocket. In the morning I went again to the same Squaw, who had a Kettle of Ground-nuts boyling: I asked her to let me boyle my piece of Bear in her Kettle, which she did, and gave me some Ground-nuts to eat with it, and I cannot but think how pleasant it was to me. I have seen Bear baked very handsomly amongst the *English*, and some liked it, but the thoughts that it was Bear, made me tremble: but now that was savoury to me that one would think was enough to turn the stomach of a bruit-Creature.

One bitter cold day, I could find no room to sit down before the fire: I went out, and could not tell what to do, but I went into another Wigwam where they were also sitting round the fire: but the Squaw laid a skin for me, and bid me sit down; and gave me some Ground-nuts, and bade me come again; and told me they would buy me if they were able; and yet these were Strangers to me that I never knew before.

*The tenth Remove.* That day a small part of the Company removed about three quarters of a mile, intending farther the next day. When they came to the place where they intended to lodge, and had pitched their Wigwams; being hungry, *I* went again back to the place we were before at, to get something to eat: being incouraged by the Squaws kindness, who bade me come again; when I was there, there came an *Indian* to look after me: who when he had found me, kickt me all along: I went home and found Venison roasting that night, but they would not give me one bit of it. Sometimes I met with Favour, and sometimes with nothing but Frowns.

*The eleventh Remove.* The next day in the morning they took their Travel, intending a dayes journey up the River, I took my load at my back, and quickly we came to wade over a River: and passed over tiresome and wearisome Hills. One Hill was so steep, that I was fain to creep up, upon my knees: and to hold by the twigs and bushes to keep my self from falling backward. My head also was so light, that I usually reeled as I went, but I hope all those wearisome steps that I have taken, are but a forwarding of me to the Heavenly rest. *I know, O Lord, that thy Judgments are right, and that thou in faithfulness hast afflicted me,* Psal. 119. 75.

*The twelfth Remove.* It was upon a Sabbath day morning, that they prepared for their Travel. This morning, I asked my Master whether he would sell me to my Husband? he answered *Nux*:[42] which did much rejoyce my spirit. My Mistriss, before we went, was gone to the burial of a *Papoos*; and returning, she found me sitting, and reading in my Bible: she snatched it hastily out of my hand, and threw it out of doors; I ran out, and catcht it up, and put it into my pocket, and never let her see it afterward. Then they packed up their things to be gone, and gave me my load, I complained it was too heavy, whereupon she gave me a slap in the face, and bade me go: I lifted up my heart to God, hoping the Redemption was not far off: and the rather because their insolency grew worse and worse.

But the thoughts of my going homeward (for so we bent our course) much cheared my Spirit, and made my burden seem light, and almost nothing at all. But (to my amazement and great perplexity) the scale was soon turned: for when we had gone a little way, on a sudden my Mistriss gives out, she would go no further, but turn back again, and said I must go back again with her, and she called her Sannup, and would have had him gone back also, but he would not, but said, he would go on, and come to us again in three dayes. My Spirit was upon this (I confess) very impatient and almost outragious.[43] I thought I could as well have died as went back. I cannot declare the trouble that I was in about it: but yet back again I must go. As soon as I had an opportunity, I took my Bible to read, and that quieting Scripture came to my hand, *Psal.* 46. 10. *Be still, and know that I am God*; which stilled my spirit for the present: but a sore time of trial I concluded I had to go through. My Master being gone, who seemed to me the best Friend that I had of an *Indian*, both in cold and hunger, and quickly so it proved. Down I sat, with my Heart as full as it could hold, and yet so hungry that I could not sit neither: but going out to see what I could find, and walking among the Trees, I found six Acorns and two Chesnuts, which were some refreshment to me. Towards night I gathered me some sticks for my own comfort, that I might not lye a Cold: but when we came to lye down, they bade me go out and lye somewhere else, for they had company (they said) come in more than their own: I told them I could not tell where to go, they bade me go look: I told them, if I went to another *Wigwam* they would be angry, and send me home again. Then one of the Company drew his Sword, and told me he would run me through if I did not go presently. Then was I fain to stoop to this rude fellow, and to go out in the Night, I knew not whither.

Mine eyes have seen that Fellow afterwards walking up and down in *Boston*, under the appearance of a *Friend-Indian*: and several others of the like Cut. I went to one *Wigwam*, and they told me they had no room. Then I went to another, and they said the same: at last an old *Indian* bade me come to him, and his Squaw gave me some Ground-nuts: she gave me also something to lay under my Head, and a good Fire we had: and through the good Providence of God, I had a comfortable lodging that Night. In the morning another *Indian* bade me come at night, and he would give me six Ground-nuts, which I did. We were at this place and time about two miles from *Connecticut River*. We went in the morning (to gather Ground-nuts) to the River, and went back again at Night. I went with a great load at my back (for they when they went, though but a little way, would carry all their trumpery with them) I told them the skin was off my back, but I had no other comforting answer from them than this, that it would be no matter if my Head were off too.

*The thirteenth Remove.* Instead of going toward the Bay (which was that I desired) I must go with them five or six miles down the River, into a mighty Thicket of Brush: where we abode almost a fortnight. Here one asked me to make a shirt for her Papoos, for which she gave me a mess of Broth, which was thickened with meal made of the Bark of a Tree: and to make it the better she had put into it about a handful of Pease, and a few rosted Ground-nuts. I had not seen my Son a pretty while, and here was an *Indian* of whom I made inquiry after him, and asked him when he saw him? he answered me that such a time his Master roasted him; and that himself did eat a piece of him, as big as his two fingers, and that he was very good meat: but the Lord upheld my Spirit, under his discouragement; and I considered their horrible addictedness to lying, and that there is not one of them that makes the least conscience of speaking the truth. In this place on a cold night as I lay by the fire, I removed a stick which kept the heat from me, a Squaw moved it down again, at which I lookt up, and she threw an handful of ashes in my eyes; I thought I should have been quite blinded and have never seen more: but lying down, the Water run out of my eyes, and carried the dirt with it, that by the morning, I recovered my sight again. Yet upon this, and the like occasions, I hope it is not too much to say with *Job, Have pity upon me, have pity upon me, Oh ye my Friends, for the hand of the Lord has touched me*.[44] And here I cannot but remember how many times sitting in their Wigwams, and musing on things past, I should suddenly leap up and run out, as if I had been at home, forgetting where I was, and what my condition was: But when I was without, and saw nothing but Wilderness, and Woods, and a company of barbarous Heathen; my mind quickly returned to me, which made me think of that, spoken concerning *Sampson*, who said, *I will go out and shake my self as at other times, but he wist not that the Lord was departed from him.*[45] About this time, I began to think that all my hopes of Restoration would come to nothing. I thought of the *English* Army, and hoped for their coming, and being retaken by them, but that failed. I hoped to be carried to *Albany*, as the *Indians* had discoursed, but that failed also. I thought of being sold to my Husband, as my Master spake; but instead of that, my Master himself was gone, and I left behind: so that my spirit was now quite ready to sink. *I* asked them to let me go out, and pick up some sticks, that *I* might get alone, and pour out my heart unto the Lord. Then also *I* took my Bible to read, but *I* found no comfort here neither: yet *I* can say, that in all my sorrows and afflictions, God did not leave me to have my impatience work towards himself, as if his ways were unrighteous; but *I* knew that he laid upon me less then *I* deserved. Afterward, before this doleful time ended with me, I was turning the leaves of my Bible, and the Lord brought to me some Scriptures, which did a little revive me, as that *Isai.* 55. 8. *For my thoughts are not your thoughts, neither are your ways my ways, saith the Lord.* And also that, *Ps.* 37. 5. *Commit thy way unto the Lord, trust also in him, and he shall bring it to pass.*

About this time they came yelping from *Hadly*, having there killed three *English-men*, and brought one Captive with them, *viz. Thomas Read.*[46] They all gathered about the poor Man, asking him many Questions. I desired also to go and see him; and when I came he was crying bitterly: supposing they would quickly kill him. Whereupon I asked one of them, whether they intended to kill him? he answered me, they would not: He being a little cheared with that, *I* asked him about the welfare of my Husband, he told me he saw him such a time in the *Bay*, and he was well, but very Melancholly. By which I certainly understood (though I suspected it before) that whatsoever the *Indians* told me respecting him, was vanity and lies. Some of them told me, he was dead, and they had killed him: some said he was Married again, and that the Governour wished him to Marry; and told him he should have his choice, and that all perswaded him I was dead. So like were these barbarous creatures to him who was a liar from the beginning.

As *I* was sitting once in the Wigwam here, *Philips* Maid came in

with the Child in her arms, and asked me to give her a piece of my
Apron, to make a flap for it, I told her I would not: then my Mistress
bad me give it, but still I said no. The Maid told me, if I would not
give her a piece, she would tear a piece off it: I told her I would tear
her Coat then: with that my Mistress rises up: and takes up a stick
big enough to have killed me, and struck at me with it, but I stept
out, and she struck the stick into the Mat of the Wigwam. But while
she was pulling of it out, I ran to the Maid and gave her all my
Apron, and so that storm went over.

Hearing that my Son was come to this place, I went to see him,
and told him his Father was well, but very melancholly: he told me
he was as much grieved for his Father as for himself; I wondred at
his speech, for I thought I had enough upon my spirit in reference to
my self, to make me mindless of my Husband and every one else:
they being safe among their Friends. He told me also, that a while
before, his Master (together with other *Indians*) were going to the
*French* for Powder; but by the way the *Mohawks*[47] met with them,
and killed four of their Company, which made the rest turn back
again: for which I desire that my self and he may bless the Lord; for
it might have been worse with him, had he been sold to the *French*,
than it proved to be in his remaining with the *Indians*.[48]

I went to see an *English* Youth in this place, one *John Gilberd*[49]
of *Springfield*. I found him lying without doors, upon the ground; I
asked him how he did? he told me was very sick of a flux,[50] with
eating so much blood. They had turned him out of the Wigwam, and
with him an *Indian Papoos*, almost dead (whose Parents had been
killed) in a bitter cold day, without fire or clothes: the young man
himself had nothing on, but his shirt and wastcoat: This sight was
enough to melt a heart of flint. There they lay quivering in the Cold,
the youth round like a dog; the *Papoos* stretcht out, with his eyes,
and nose, and mouth full of dirt, and yet alive, and groaning. I advised *John* to go and get to some fire: he told me he could not stand,
but I perswaded him still, lest he should ly there and die. And with
much ado I got him to a fire, and went my self home. As soon as I
was got home, his Masters Daughter came after me, to know what
I had done with the *English-man*? I told her I had got him to a fire
in such a place. Now had I need to pray *Pauls* prayer, 2 *Thess*. 3. 2.
*That we may be delivered from unreasonable and wicked men.* For
her satisfaction I went along with her, and brought her to him; but
before I got home again, it was noised about, that I was running
away, and getting the *English* youth along with me: that as soon as

I came in, they began to rant and domineer: asking me where I had been? and what I had been doing? and saying they would knock me in the head: I told them, I had been seeing the *English Youth*: and that I would not run away: they told me I lied, and taking up a Hatchet, they came to me, and said, they would knock me down if I stirred out again: and so confined me to the Wigwam. Now may I say with *David, 2 Sam.* 24. 14. *I am in a great strait.* If I keep in, I must dye with hunger, and if I go out, I must be knockt in the head. This distressed condition held that day, and half the next; and then the Lord remembred me, whose mercies are great. Then came an *Indian* to me, with a pair of Stockins which were too big for him; and he would have me ravel them out, and knit them fit for him. I shewed my self willing, and bid him ask my Mistress, if I might go along with him a little way: She said yes, I might, but I was not a little refresht with that news, that I had my liberty again. Then I went along with him, and he gave me some roasted Ground-nuts, which did again revive my feeble stomach.

Being got out of her sight, I had time and liberty again to look into my Bible: which was my guide by day, and my Pillow by night. Now that comfortable Scripture presented it self to me, *Isai.* 54. 7. *For a small moment have I forsaken thee: but with great mercies will I gather thee.* Thus the Lord carried me along from one time to another: and made good to me this precious promise, and many others. Then my Son came to see me, and I asked his Master to let him stay a while with me: that I might comb his head, and look over him for he was almost overcome with lice. He told me, when I had done, that he was very hungry, but I had nothing to relieve him; but bid him go into the Wigwams as he went along, and see if he could get any thing among them. Which he did, and (it seems) tarried a little too long; for his Master was angry with him, and beat him, and then sold him. Then he came running to tell me he had a new Master, and that he had given him some Ground-nuts already. Then I went along with him to his new Master, who told me he loved him: and he should not want. So his Master carried him away, and I never saw him afterward: till I saw him at *Pascataqua* in *Portsmouth*.

That night they bade me go out of the Wigwam again: my Mistresses *Papoos* was sick, and it died that night; and there was one benefit in it, that there was more room. I went to a Wigwam, and they bad me come in, and gave me a skin to lye upon, and a mess of Venison and Ground-nuts; which was a choice Dish among them. On the morrow they buried the *Papoos*: and afterward, both morning and evening, there came a company to mourn and howl with her: though I confess, I could not much condole with them. Many sorrowful days I had in this place: often getting alone; *like a Crane or a Swallow so did I chatter; I did mourn as a Dove, mine eyes fail with looking upward. Oh Lord I am oppressed, undertake for me*, Isai. 38. 14. I could tell the Lord, as *Hezechiah*, ver. 3. *Remember now, O Lord, I beseech thee, how I have walked before thee in truth.*[51] Now had I time to examine all my wayes: my Conscience did not accuse me of unrighteousness toward one or other: yet I saw how in my walk with God, I had been a careless creature. As *David* said, *Against thee, thee only have I sinned*: and I might say with the poor Publican, *God be merciful unto me a sinner.*[52] On the Sabbath days I could look upon the Sun, and think how People were going to the house of God, to have their Souls refresht; and then home, and their Bodies also: but I was destitute of both; and might say as the poor Prodigal, *he would fain have filled his belly with the husks that the Swine did eat, and no man gave unto him*, Luke 15. 16. For I must say with him, *Father I have sinned against Heaven, and in thy sight*, ver. 21. I remembred how on the night before and after the Sabbath, when my Family was about me, and Relations and Neighbours with us, we could pray and sing, and then refresh our bodies with the good creatures of God: and then have a comfortable Bed to ly down on: but instead of all this, I had only a little Swill for the body, and then like a Swine, must ly down on the Ground: I cannot express to man the sorrow that lay upon my Spirit, the Lord knows it. Yet that comfortable Scripture would often come to my mind, *For a small moment have I forsaken thee, but with great mercies I will gather thee.*[53]

*The fourteenth Remove.* Now must we pack up and be gone from this Thicket, bending our course towards the Bay-Towns. I having nothing to eat by the way this day, but a few crumbs of Cake, that an *Indian* gave my Girl, the same day we were taken. She gave it me, and I put it into my pocket: there it lay till it was so mouldy (for want of good baking) that one could not tell what it was made of; it fell all to crumbs, and grew so dry and hard, that it was like little flints; and this refreshed me many times, when I was ready to faint. It was in my thoughts when I put it into my mouth, that if ever I returned, I would tell the World, what a blessing the Lord gave to such mean food. As we went along, they killed a *Deer*, with a young one in her: they gave me a piece of the *Fawn*, and it was so young and tender, that one might eat the bones as well as the flesh, and yet I thought it very good. When night came on we sate down, it rained, but they quickly got up a Bark Wigwam, where I lay dry that night. I looked out in the morning, and many of them had lain in the rain all night, I saw by their Reeking. Thus the Lord dealt mercifully with me many times: and I fared better than many of them. In the morning they took the blood of the *Deer*, and put it into the Paunch, and so boiled it I could eat nothing of that, though they ate it sweetly. And yet they were so nice[54] in other things, that when I had fetcht water, and had put the Dish I dipt the water with, into the Kittle of water which I brought, they would say, they would knock me down; for they said, it was a sluttish trick.

*The fifteenth Remove.* We went on our travel. I having got one handful of Ground-nuts, for my support that day: they gave me my load, and I went on cheerfully (with the thoughts of going home-ward) having my burden more on my back than my spirit: we came to *Baquaug* River again that day, near which we abode a few days. Sometimes one of them would give me a Pipe, another a little To-bacco, another a little Salt: which I would change for a little Victuals. I cannot but think what a Wolvish appetite persons have in a starving condition: for many times when they gave me that which was hot, I was so greedy, that I should burn my mouth, that it would trouble me hours after; and yet I should quickly do the same again. And after I was throughly hungry, I was never again satisfied. For though some-times it fell out, that I got enough, and did eat till I could eat no more, yet I was as unsatisfied as I was when I began. And now could I see that Scripture verified (there being many Scriptures which we do not take notice of, or understand till we are afflicted) *Mic.* 6. 14. *Thou shalt eat and not be satisfied*. Now might I see more than ever before, the miseries that sin hath brought upon us. Many times I should be ready to run out against the Heathen, but that Scripture would quiet me again, *Amos* 3. 6. *Shall there be evil in the City, and the Lord hath not done it*? The Lord help me to make a right im-provement of his word, and that I might learn that great lesson, *Mic.* 6. 8, 9. *He hath shewed thee, O Man, what is good; and what doth the Lord require of thee, but to do justly, and love mercy, and walk humbly with thy God? Hear ye the rod, and who hath appointed it.*

*The sixteenth Remove.* We began this Remove with wading over *Baquaug* River. The Water was up to the knees, and the stream very swift, and so cold that I thought it would have cut me in sunder. I was so weak and feeble, that I reeled as I went along, and thought there I must end my days at last, after my bearing and getting through so many difficulties. The *Indians* stood laughing to see me staggering along, but in my distress the Lord gave me experience of the truth and goodness of that promise, *Isai.* 43. 2. *When thou passest thorough the waters, I will be with thee, and thorough the Rivers, they shall not overflow thee.* Then I sate down to put on my stockins and shoes, with the tears running down my eyes, and many sorrowful thoughts in my heart: but I gat up to go along with them. Quickly there came up to us an *Indian*, who informed them, that I must go to *Wachuset* to my Master: for there was a Letter come from the Council to the *Saggamores*,[55] about redeeming the Captives, and that there would be another in fourteen days, and that I must be there ready. My heart was so heavy before that I could scarce speak, or go in the path; and yet now so light, that I could run. My strength seemed to come again, and to recruit my feeble knees, and aking heart: yet it pleased them to go but one mile that night, and there we stayed two days. In that time came a company of *Indians* to us, near thirty, all on Horse back. My heart skipt within me, thinking they had been *English-men* at the first sight of them: for they were dressed in *English* Apparel, with Hats, white Neck-cloths, and Sashes about their wasts, and Ribbons upon their shoulders: but when they came near, there was a vast difference between the lovely Faces of *Christians*, and the foul looks of those *Heathens*: which much damped my spirit again.

*The seventeenth Remove.* A comfortable Remove it was to me, because of my hopes. They gave me my pack, and along we went cheerfully: but quickly my Will proved more than my strength; having little or no refreshing my strength failed, and my spirits were almost quite gone. Now may I say as *David, Psal.* 109. 22, 23, 24. *I am poor and needy, and my heart is wounded within me. I am gone like the shadow when it declineth: I am tossed up and down like the Locust: my knees are weak through fasting, and my flesh faileth of fatness.* At night we came to an *Indian Town*, and the *Indians* sate down by a Wigwam discoursing, but I was almost spent, and could scarce speak. I laid down my load, and went into the Wigwam, and there sate an *Indian* boiling of *Horses feet*: (they being wont to eat the flesh first, and when the feet were old and dried, and they had nothing else, they would cut off the feet and use them) I asked him to give me a little of his Broth, or Water they were boiling in: he took a Dish, and gave me one spoonful of Samp,[56] and bid me take as much of the Broth as I would. Then I put some of the hot water to the Samp, and drank it up, and my spirit came again. He gave me also a piece of the Ruffe or Ridding[57] of the small Guts, and I broiled it on the coals; and now may I say with *Jonathan, See I pray you how mine eyes have been enlightned, because I tasted a little of this honey*, 1 Sam. 14. 29. Now is my Spirit revived again: though means be never so inconsiderable, yet if the Lord bestow his blessing upon them, they shall refresh both Soul and Body.

*The eighteenth Remove.* We took up our packs, and along we went. But a wearisome day I had of it. As we went along, I saw an *English-man* strip naked, and lying dead upon the ground, but knew not who it was. Then we came to another *Indian Town*, where we stayed all night. In this Town, there were four *English Children*, Captives: and one of them my own Sisters. I went to see how she did, and she was well, considering her Captive condition. I would have tarried that night with her, but they that owned her would not suffer it. Then I went to another Wigwam, where they were boiling Corn and Beans, which was a lovely sight to see, but I could not get a taste thereof. Then I went into another Wigwam, where there were two of the *English Children:* The Squaw was boiling horses feet, then she cut me off a little piece, and gave one of the *English Children* a piece also. Being very hungry, I had quickly eat up mine: but the Child could not bite it, it was so tough and sinewy, but lay sucking, gnawing, chewing, and slobbering it in the Mouth and Hand, then I took it of the Child, and eat it my self; and savoury it was to my taste.

That I may say as *Job, Chap.* 6. 7. *The things that my Soul refused to touch, are as my sorrowful meat.* Thus the Lord made that pleasant and refreshing, which another time would have been an Abomination. Then I went home to my Mistresses Wigwam: and they told me I disgraced My Master with begging: and if I did so any more, they would knock me on the Head: I told them, they had as good knock me on the Head, as starve me to death.

*The nineteenth Remove.* They said, when we went out, that we must travel to *Wachuset* this day. But a bitter weary day I had of it; travelling now three dayes together, without resting any day between. At last, after many weary steps, I saw *Wachuset* hills, but many miles off. Then we came to a great Swamp, through which we travelled up to the knees in mud and water, which was heavy going to one tried before. Being almost spent, I thought I should have sunk down at last, and never got out; but I may say, as in *Psal.* 94. 18. *When my foot slipped, thy mercy, O Lord, held me up.* Going along, having indeed my life, but little Spirit, *Philip*, (who was in the Company) came up, and took me by the hand, and said, *Two weeks more, and you shall be Mistriss again.* I asked him if he speak true? he answered, Yes, and quickly you shall come to your Master again: who had been gone from us three weeks. After many weary steps we came to *Wachuset*, where he was; and glad I was to see him. He asked me, when I washt me? I told him not this moneth; then he fetch me some water himself, and bid me wash, and gave me the Glass to see how I lookt, and bid his Squaw give me something to eat. So she gave me a mess of Beans and meat, and a little Ground-nut Cake. I was wonderfully revived with this favour shewed me, *Psal.* 106. 46. *He made them also to be pitied of all those that carried them Captives.*

My Master had three Squaws: living sometimes with one, and sometimes with another. One, this old Squaw at whose Wigwam I was, and with whom my Master had been those three weeks. Another was *Wettimore*, with whom I had lived and served all this while. A severe and proud Dame she was; bestowing every day in dressing her self near as much time as any of the Gentry of the land: powdering her hair and painting her face, going with her Neck-laces, with Jewels in her ears, and bracelets upon her hands. When she had dressed her self, her Work was to make Girdles of Wampom and Beads. The third Squaw was a younger one, by whom he had two Papooses. By that time I was refresht by the old Squaw, with whom my Master was, *Wettimores* Maid came to call me home, at which I fell a weeping; then the old Squaw told me, to encourage me, that if I wanted victuals, I should come to her, and that I should lye there in her Wigwam. Then I went with the Maid, and quickly came again and lodged there. The Squaw laid a Mat under me, and a good Rugg over me; the first time I had any such Kindness shewed me. I understood that *Wettimore* thought, that if she should let me go and serve with the old Squaw, she would be in danger to lose not only my service but the redemption-pay also. And I was not a little glad to hear this; being by it raised in my hopes, that in Gods due time there would be an end of this sorrowful hour. Then came an *Indian*, and asked me to knit him three pair of Stockins, for which I had a Hat, and a silk Handkerchief. Then another asked me to make her a shift, for which she gave me an Apron.

Then came *Tom* and *Peter*,[58] with the second Letter from the Council, about the Captives. Though they were *Indians*, I gat them by the hand, and burst out into Tears; my heart was so full that I could not speak to them: but recovering my self, I asked them how my Husband did? and all my Friends and Acquaintance? they said, they were well, but very Melancholy. They brought me two Biskets, and a pound of Tobacco. The Tobacco I quickly gave away: when it was all gone, one asked me to give him a pipe of Tobacco, I told him all was gone; then began he to rant and threaten; I told him when my Husband came, I would give him some: Hang him Rogue (says he) I will knock out his brains, if he comes here. And then again in the same breath, they would say, that if there should come an hundred without Guns they would do them no hurt. So unstable and like mad men they were: So that fearing the worst, I durst not send to my Husband; though there were some thoughts of his coming to Redeem and fetch me, not knowing what might follow; for there was little more trust to them than to the Master they served. When the Letter was come, the Saggamores met to consult about the Captives, and called me to them to enquire how much my Husband would give to redeem me: When I came, I sate down among them, as I was wont to do, as their manner is: Then they bade me stand up, and said, they were the *General Court*. They bid me speak what I thought he would give. Now knowing that all we had was destroyed by the *Indians*, I was in a great strait. I thought if I should speak of but a little, it would be slighted, and hinder the matter; if of a great Sum, I knew not where it would be procured: yet at a venture, I said *Twenty pounds*,[59] yet desired them to take less: but they would not hear of that, but sent that message to *Boston*, that for *twenty pounds* I should be redeemed. It was a Praying *Indian* that wrote their Letter for them.[60] There was another Praying *Indian*, who told me, that he had a Brother, that would not eat Horse; his Conscience was so tender and scrupulous, (though as large as Hell, for the destruction of poor *Christians*). Then he said, he read that Scripture to him, 2 *King.* 6. 25. *There was a Famine in* Samaria, *and behold they besieged it, until an Asses head was sold for four-score pieces of silver, and the fourth part of a Kab*[61] *of Doves dung, for five pieces of silver.* He expounded this place to his Brother, and shewed him that it was lawful to eat that in a Famine, which is not at another time. And now, says he, he will eat Horse with any *Indian* of them all. There was another Praying *Indian*, who when he had done all the Mischief that he could, betrayed his own Father into the *Englishes* hands, thereby to purchase his own Life. Another Praying *Indian* was at *Sudbury* Fight,[62] though, as he deserved, he was afterward hanged for it. There was another Praying *Indian*, so wicked and cruel, as to wear a string about his neck, strung with *Christian* Fingers. Another Praying *Indian*, when they went to *Sud-*

*bury* Fight, went with them, and his Squaw also with him, with her Papoos at her back: before they went to that Fight, they got a company together to *Powaw*:[63] the manner was as followeth. There was one that kneeled upon a *Deer-skin*, with the Company round him in a Ring, who kneeled, striking upon the Ground with their hands, and with sticks, and muttering or humming with their Mouths. Besides him who kneeled in the Ring, there also stood one with a Gun in his hand: Then he on the Deer-skin made a speech, and all manifested assent to it; and so they did many times together. Then they bade him with the Gun go out of the Ring, which he did; but when he was out they called him in again; but he seemed to make a stand; then they called the more earnestly, till he returned again. Then they all sang. Then they gave him two Guns, in either hand one. And so he on the Deer-skin began again; and at the end of every Sentence in his speaking, they all assented, humming or muttering with their Mouthes, and striking upon the Ground with their Hands. Then they bade him with the two Guns go out of the Ring again: which he did a little way. Then they called him in again, but he made a stand, so they called him with greater earnestness: but he stood reeling and wavering, as if he knew not whether he should stand or fall, or which way to go. Then they called him with exceeding great vehemency, all of them, one and another: after a little while, he turned in, staggering as he went, with his Arms stretched out; in either hand a Gun. As soon as he came in, they all sang and rejoyced exceedingly a while. And then he upon the Deer-skin, made another speech, unto which they all assented in a rejoycing manner: and so they ended their business, and forthwith went to *Sudbury* Fight. To my thinking they went without any scruple but that they should prosper and gain the Victory. And they went out not so rejoycing, but that they came home with as great a Victory. For they said they had killed two Captains, and almost an hundred men. One *Englishman* they brought alive with them; and he said it was too true, for they had made sad work at *Sudbury*; as indeed it proved. Yet they came home without that rejoycing and triumphing over their Victory, which they were wont to shew at other times: but rather like Dogs, (as they say) which have lost their Ears. Yet I could not perceive that it was for their own loss of Men: they said they had not lost above five or six: and I missed none, except in one Wigwam. When they went, they acted as if the Devil had told them that they should gain the Victory: and now they acted, as if the Devil had told them that they should have a fall. Whether it were so or no, I cannot tell, but so it proved: for quickly they began to fall, and so held on that Summer, till they came to utter ruine. They came home on a Sabbath day, and the Powaw[64] that kneeled upon the Deer-skin, came home (I may say without any abuse) as black as the Devil. When my Master came home, he came to me and bid me make a shirt for his Papoos of a Hollandlaced Pillowbeer.[65] About that time there came an *Indian* to me, and bade me come to his *Wigwam* at night, and he would give me some Pork and Ground-nuts. Which I did, and as I was eating, another *Indian* said to me, he seems to be your good Friend, but he killed two *English-men* at *Sudbury*, and there lye their Cloaths behind you: I looked behind me, and there I saw bloody-Cloathes, with Bullet-holes in them: yet the Lord suffered not this Wretch to do me any hurt. Yea, instead of that, he many times refresht me: five or six times did he and his Squaw refresh my feeble Carcass. If I went to their *Wigwam* at any time, they would always give me something, and yet they were strangers that I never saw before. Another *Squaw* gave me a piece of fresh Pork, and a little Salt with it: and lent me her Frying pan to fry it in: and I cannot but remember what a sweet, pleasant and delightful relish that bit had to me, to this day. So little do we prize common mercies, when we have them to the full.

*The twentieth Remove.* It was their usual manner to remove, when they had done any mischeif, lest they should be found out: and so they did at this time. We went about three or four miles, and there they built a great *Wigwam*, big enough to hold an hundred *Indians*, which they did in preparation to a great day of Dancing. They would say now amongst themselves, that the *Governour* would be so angry for his loss at *Sudbury*, that he would send no more about the Captives, which made me grieve and tremble. My Sister[66] being not far from the place where we now were, and hearing that I was here, desired her Master let her come and see me, and he was willing to it, and would go with her; but she being ready before him, told him she would go before, and was come within a Mile or two of the place: Then he overtook her, and began to rant as if he had been mad, and made her go back again in the Rain; so that I never saw her till I saw her in *Charlstown*. But the Lord requited many of their ill-doings, for this *Indian*, her Master, was hanged after at *Boston*. The *Indians* now began to come from all quarters against the merry dancing day. Amongst some of them came one Goodwife *Kettle*:[67] I told her that my Heart was so heavy that it was ready to break: so is mine too, said she, but yet said, *I* hope we shall hear some good news shortly. *I* could hear how earnestly my Sister desired to see me, and *I* as earnestly desired to see her; and yet neither of us could get an opportunity. My Daughter was also now but about a Mile off: and I had not seen her in nine or ten Weeks, as I had not seen my Sister since our first taking. *I* earnestly desired them to let me go and see them: yea, *I* intreated, begged, and perswaded them, but to let me see my Daughter: and yet so hard-hearted were they, that they would not suffer it. They made use of their Tyrannical Power whilst they had it: but through the Lords wonderful mercy, their time was now but short.

On a Sabbath-day, the Sun being about an hour high, in the Afternoon, came Mr. *John Hoar*,[68] (the Council permitting him, and his own forward spirit inclining him) together with the two forementioned *Indians*, *Tom* and *Peter*, with the third Letter from the Council. When they came near, I was abroad; though I saw them not, they presently called me in, and bade me sit down, and not stir. Then they catched up their Guns, and away they ran, as if an Enemy had been at hand: and the Guns went off apace. I manifested some great trouble, and they asked me what was the matter? I told them *I* thought they had killed the *English-man* (for they had in the mean time informed me that an *English-man* was come) they said No; they shot over his Horse, and under, and before his Horse; and they pusht him this way and that way, at their pleasure: shewing what they could do. Then they let them come to their Wigwams. I begged of them to let me see the *English-man*, but they would not. But there was I fain to sit their pleasure. When they had talked their fill with him, they suffered me to go to him. We asked each other of our welfare, and how my Husband did? and all my Friends? he told me they were all well, and would be glad to see me. Amongst other things which my Husband sent me, there came a pound of *Tobacco*: which I sold for nine shillings in Money: for many of the *Indians* for want of *Tobacco*, smoked *Hemlock*, and *Ground-Ivy*. It was a great mistake in any, who thought I sent for *Tobacco*: for through the favour of God, that desire was overcome. I now asked them, whether I should go home with Mr. *Hoar*? they answered No, one and another of them: and it being Night, we lay down with that Answer: in the Morning Mr. *Hoar* invited the *Saggamores* to Dinner: but when we went to get it ready, we found that they had stollen the greatest part of the Provision Mr. *Hoar* had brought out of his Bags in the Night. And we may see the wonderful power of God, in that one passage, in that when there was such a great number of the *Indians* together, and so greedy of a little good Food; and no *English* there, but Mr. *Hoar*, and my self: that there they did not knock us in the Head, and take what we had: there being not only some Provision, but also Trading Cloth, a part of the twenty pounds agreed upon: But instead of doing us any mischief, they seemed to be ashamed of the Fact, and said, it were some *Matchit*[69] *Indians* that did it. O that we could believe that there is nothing too hard for God! God shewed his power over the Heathen in this, as he did over the hungry Lions when *Daniel* was cast into the Den. Mr. *Hoar* called them betime to Dinner; but they ate very little, they being so busie in dressing themselves, and getting ready for their Dance: which was carried on by eight of them; four Men and four Squaws: my Master and Mistriss being two. He was dressed in his Holland Shirt, with great Laces sewed at the tail of it; he had his silver Buttons, his white Stockings, his Garters were hung round with Shillings, and he had Girdles of Wampon upon his Head and Shoulders. She had a Kersey Coat,[70] and covered with Girdles of Wampom from the Loins and upward. Her Arms from her Elbows to her Hands were covered with Bracelets; there were handfuls of Neck-laces about her Neck, and several sorts of Jewels in her Ears. She had fine red Stockins, and white Shoos, her Hair powdered, and her Face painted Red, that was always before Black. And all the Dancers were after the same manner. There were two other singing and knocking on a Kettle for their Musick. They kept hopping up and down one after another, with a Kettle of Water in the midst, standing warm upon some Embers, to drink of when they were a dry. They held on, till it was almost night, throwing out Wampom to the standers by. At night I asked them again, if I should go home? they all as one said no, except my Husband would come for me. When we were lain down, my Master went out of the Wigwam, and by and by sent in an *Indian*, called *James*, the *PRINTER*, who told Mr. *Hoar*, that my Master would let me go home to morrow, if he would let him have one pint of *Liquors*. Then Mr. *Hoar* called his own *Indians*, *Tom* and *Peter*: and bid them all go, and see whether he would promise it before them three: and if he would, he should have it; which he did, and had it. Then *Philip* smelling the business, called me to him, and asked me what I would give him, to tell me some good news, and to speak a good word for me, that I might go home to morrow? I told him I could not tell what to give him; I would give any thing I had, and asked him what he would have? He said two Coats, and twenty shillings in Money, and half a bushel of Seed-Corn, and some Tobacco. I thanked him for his love: but I knew the good news as well as that crafty Fox. My Master, after he had

had his Drink, quickly came ranting into the Wigwam again, and called for Mr. *Hoar*, drinking to him, and saying he was a good man; and then again he would say, Hang him Rogue. Being almost drank, he would drink to him, and yet presently say he should be hanged. Then he called for me; I trembled to hear him, yet I was fain to go to him; and he drunk to me, shewing no incivility. He was the first *Indian*, I saw drunk all the while that I was amongst them. At last his Squaw ran out, and he after her, round the Wigwam, with his money gingling at his knees: but she escaped him; but having an old Squaw, he ran to her: and so through the Lords mercy, we were no more troubled with him that night. Yet I had not a comfortable nights rest: for I think I can say, I did not sleep for three nights together. The night before the Letter came from the Council, I could not rest, I was so full of fears and troubles (God many times leaving us most in the dark, when deliverance is nearest) yea at this time I could not rest night nor day. The next night I was over-joyed, Mr. *Hoar* being come, and that with such good Tydings. The third night I was even swallowed up with the thoughts of things; *viz.* that ever I should go home again: and that I must go, leaving my Children behind me in the Wilderness; so that sleep was now almost departed from mine eyes.

On *Tuesday* morning[71] they called their General Court (as they stiled it) to consult and determine, whether I should go home or no: And they all as one man did seemingly consent to it, that I should go home: except *Philip*, who would not come among them.[72]

But before I go any further, I would take leave to mention a few remarkable passages of Providence; which I took special notice of in my afflicted time.

1. Of the fair opportunity lost in the long March, a little after the Fort-fight,[73] when our *English* Army was so numerous, and in pursuit of the Enemy; and so near as to overtake several, and destroy them: and the Enemy in such distress for Food, that our men might track them by their rooting in the Earth for Ground-nuts, whilst they were flying for their lives: I say, that then our Army should want Provision, and be forced to leave their pursuit, and return homeward: and the very next week the Enemy came upon our Town, like Bears bereft of their whelps, or so many ravenous Wolves, rending us and our Lambs to death. But what shall I say? God seemed to leave his People to themselves; and ordered all things for his own holy ends. *Shall there be evil in the City and the Lord hath not done it? They are not grieved for the affliction of Joseph, therefore they shall go Captive,*

*with the first that go Captive. It is the Lords doing, and it should be marvellous in our Eyes.*[74]

2. I cannot but remember, how the *Indians* derided the slowness, and dulness of the *English* Army, in its setting out. For after the desolations at *Lancaster* and *Medfield*, as I went along with them, they asked me when I thought the *English* Army would come after them? I told them I could not tell: it may be they will come in *May*, said they. Thus did they scoffe at us, as if the *English* would be a quarter of a Year getting ready.

3. Which also I have hinted before; when the *English* Army with new supplies were sent forth to pursue after the Enemy, and they understanding it; fled before them till they came to *Baquaug River*, where they forthwith went over safely: that that River should be impassable to the *English*, I cannot but admire to see the wonderful providence of God in preserving the Heathen for farther affliction to our poor Country. They could go in great numbers over, but the *English* must stop: God had an over-ruling hand in all those things.

4. It was thought, if their Corn were cut down, they would starve and die with hunger: and all their Corn that could be found, was destroyed, and they driven from that little they had in store, into the Woods, in the midst of Winter; and yet how to admiration did the Lord preserve them for his holy ends, and the destruction of many still amongst the *English*! strangely did the Lord provide for them: that I did not see (all the time I was among them) one Man, or Woman, or Child, die with Hunger.[75]

Though many times they would eat that, that a Hog or a Dog would hardly touch: yet by that God strengthened them to be a scourge to his People.

Their chief and commonest food was Ground-nuts: they eat also Nuts, and Acorns, Hartychoaks,[76] Lilly-roots, Ground-beans, and several other weeds and roots that I know not.

They would pick up old bones, and cut them in pieces at the joynts, and if they were full of worms and magots, they would scald them over the fire to make the vermine come out; and then boyle them, and drink up the Liquor, and then beat the great ends of them in a Morter, and so eat them. They would eat Horses guts and ears, and all sorts of wild birds which they could catch: Also Bear, Venison, Beavers, Tortois, Frogs, Squirils, Dogs, Skunks, Rattle-snakes: yea, the very Barks of Trees; besides all sorts of Creatures, and provision which they plundered from the *English*. I cannot but stand in admiration to see the wonderful power of God, in providing for such a vast number of our Enemies in the Wilderness, where there was nothing to be seen, but from hand to mouth. Many times in the morning, the generality of them, would eat up all they had, and yet have some farther supply against they wanted. It is said, *Psal.* 81. 13. 14. *Oh that my people had hearkened to me, and Israel had walked in my wayes; I should soon have subdued their Enemies, and turned my hand against their adversaries.* But now our perverse and evil carriages in the sight of the Lord, have so offended him; that instead of turning his hand against them, the Lord feeds and nourishes them up to be a scourge to the whole Land.

5. Another, thing that I would observe is, the strange providence of God in turning things about when the *Indians were at the highest*, and the *English at the lowest*. I was with the Enemy eleven weeks and five days; and not one Week passed without the fury of the Enemy, and some desolation by fire and sword upon one place or other. They mourned (with their black faces) for their own losses: yet triumphed and rejoyced in their inhumane (and many times devillish cruelty) to the *English*. They would boast much of their Victories; saying, that in two hours time, they had destroyed such a Captain, and his Company, in such a place; and such a Captain, and his Company, in such a place; and such a Captain, and his Company, in such a place: and boast how many Towns they had destroyed, and then scoff, and say, they had done them a good turn, to send them to Heaven so soon. Again they would say, this Summer they would knock all the Rogues in the head, or drive them into the Sea, or make them flie the Country: thinking surely, *Agag-like, The bitterness of Death is past.*[77] Now the *Heathen* begin to think that all is their own, and the poor *Christians* hopes to fail (as to man) and now their eyes are more to God, and their hearts sigh heaven-ward: and to say in good earnest, *Help Lord, or we perish;*[78] when the Lord had brought his People to this, that they saw no help in any thing but himself; then he takes the quarrel into his own hand: and though they had made a pit (in their own imaginations) as deep as hell for the *Christians* that Summer; yet the Lord hurll'd themselves into it. And the Lord had not so many wayes before, to preserve them, but now he hath as many to destroy them.

But to return again to my going home: where we may see a remarkable change of providence: at first they were all against it, except my Husband would come for me; but afterwards they assented to it, and seemed much to rejoyce in it: some asking me to send them some Bread, others some Tobacco, others shaking me by the hand, offering

me a Hood and Scarf to ride in; not one moving hand or tongue
against it. Thus hath the Lord answered my poor desires, and the
many earnest requests of others put up unto God for me. In my
Travels an *Indian* came to me, and told me, if I were willing, he and
his Squaw would run away, and go home along with me. I told him,
No, I was not willing to run away, but desired to wait Gods time,
that I might go home quietly, and without fear. And now God hath
granted me my desire. O the wonderful power of God that I have
seen, and the experiences that I have had! I have been in the midst
of those roaring Lions, and Salvage Bears, that feared neither God,
nor Man, nor the Devil, by night and day, alone and in company,
sleeping all sorts together; and yet not one of them ever offered the
least abuse of unchastity to me, in word or action.[79] Though some
are ready to say, I speak it for my own credit; but I speak it in the
presence of God, and to his Glory. Gods power is as great now, and
as sufficient to save, as when he preserved *Daniel* in the Lions Den,
or the three Children in the Fiery Furnace. I may well say, as he,
*Psal.* 107. 1, 2. *Oh give thanks unto the Lord, for he is good, for
his mercy endureth for ever. Let the Redeemed of the Lord say so,
whom he hath redeemed from the hand of the Enemy*; especially that
I should come away in the midst of so many hundreds of Enemies,
quietly and peaceably, and not a Dog moving his tongue. So I took
my leave of them, and in coming along my heart melted into Tears,
more than all the while I was with them, and I was almost swallowed
up with the thoughts that ever I should go home again. About the
Suns going down, Mr. *Hoar*, and my self, and the two *Indians* came
to *Lancaster*, and a solemn sight it was to me. There had I lived
many comfortable years amongst my Relations and Neighbours; and
now not one *Christian* to be seen, nor one House left standing. We
went on to a Farm-house that was yet standing, where we lay all
night; and a comfortable lodging we had, though nothing but straw
to lye on. The Lord preserved us in safety that night, and raised us
up again in the morning, and carried us along, that before noon we
came to *Concord*. Now was I full of joy, and yet not without sorrow:
joy, to see such a lovely sight, so many *Christians* together, and some
of them my Neighbours: There I met with my Brother, and my
Brother in Law, who asked me, if I knew where his Wife was? poor
heart! he had helped to bury her, and knew it not; she being shot
down by the house, was partly burnt: so that those who were at
*Boston* at the desolation of the Town, and came back afterward, and
buried the dead, did not know her. Yet I was not without sorrow,

to think how many were looking and longing, and my own Children
amongst the rest, to enjoy that deliverance that I had now received;
and I did not know whether ever I should see them again. Being
recruited with Food and Raiment, we went to *Boston* that day, where
I met with my dear Husband, but the thoughts of our dear Children,
one being dead, and the other we could not tell where, abated our
comfort each in other. I was not before so much hem'd in with the
merciless and cruel *Heathen*, but now as much with pitiful, tender-
hearted, and compassionate *Christians*. In that poor, and distressed,
and beggarly condition, I was received in, I was kindly entertained
in several houses: so much love I received from several, (some of
whom I knew, and others I knew not) that *I* am not capable to
declare it. But the Lord knows them all by name: the Lord reward
them seven-fold into their bosoms of his spirituals for their tempor-
als. The twenty pounds, the price of my Redemption, was raised by
some *Boston* Gentlewomen, and M. *Usher*,[80] whose bounty and religious charity I would not forget to make mention of. Then Mr.
*Thomas Shepherd*[81] of *Charlstown* received us into his House, where
we continued eleven weeks; and a Father and Mother they were unto
us. And many more tender-hearted Friends we met with in that place.
We were now in the midst of love, yet not without much and frequent
heaviness of heart, for our poor Children, and other Relations, who
were still in affliction.

The week following, after my comming in, the Governour[82] and
Council sent forth to the *Indians* again; and that not without success:
for they brought in my Sister, and Goodwife *Kettle*: Then not knowing where our Children were, was a sore trial to us still, and yet we
were not without secret hopes that we should see them again. That
which was dead lay heavier upon my spirit than those which were
alive amongst the *Heathen*: thinking how it suffered with its wounds,
and I was no way able to relieve it: and how it was buried by the
*Heathen* in the Wilderness, from amongst all *Christians*. We were
hurried up and down in our thoughts; sometimes we should hear a
report that they were gone this way, and sometimes that: and that
they were come in, in this place or that: we kept inquiring and
listning to hear concerning them, but no certain news as yet. About
this time the Council had ordered a day of publick *Thanks-giving*:
though I thought I had still cause of mourning; and being unsettled
in our minds, we thought we would ride toward the Eastward, to
see if we could hear any thing concerning our Children. And as we
were riding along (God is the wise disposer of all things) between

*Ipswich* and *Rowly* we met with Mr *William Hubbard*,[83] who told us our Son *Joseph* was come in to Major *Waldrens*,[84] and another with him, which was my Sisters Son. I asked him how he knew it? he said the Major himself told me so. So along we went till we came to *Newbury*; and their Minister being absent, they desired my Husband to Preach the *Thanks-giving* for them; but he was not willing to stay there that night, but would go over to *Salisbury*, to hear farther, and come again in the morning; which he did: and Preached there that day. At night, when he had done, one came and told him that his Daughter was come in at *Providence*: here was mercy on both hands. Now hath God fulfilled that precious Scripture, which was such a comfort to me in my distressed condition. When my heart was ready to sink into the Earth (my Children being gone I could not tell whither) and my knees trembled under me, and I was walking through the valley of the shadow of death: then the Lord brought, and now has fulfilled that reviving word unto me: *Thus saith the Lord, Refrain thy voice from weeping, and thy eyes from tears, for thy work shall be rewarded, saith the Lord, and they shall come again from the Land of the Enemy.*[85] Now we were between them, the one on the East, and the other on the West: our Son being nearest, we went to him first, to *Portsmouth*; where we met with him, and with the Major also: who told us he had done what he could, but could not redeem him under seven pounds, which the good People thereabouts were pleased to pay. The Lord reward the Major, and all the rest, though unknown to me, for their labour of love. My Sisters Son was redeemed for four pounds, which the Council gave order for the payment of. Having now received one of our Children, we hastened towards the other: going back through *Newbury*, my Husband preached there on the Sabbath day: for which they rewarded him manifold.

On Monday we came to *Charlstown*; where we heard that the Governour of *Road-Island*[86] had sent over for our Daughter, to take care of her, being now within his Jurisdiction: which should not pass without our acknowledgments. But she being nearer *Rehoboth* than *Road-Island*, Mr. *Newman*[87] went over, and took care of her, and brought her to his own house. And the goodness of God was admirable to us in our low estate; in that he raised up compassionate Friends on every side to us; when we had nothing to recompence any for their love. The *Indians* were now gone that way, that it was apprehended dangerous to go to her: but the Carts which carried

Provision to the *English* Army, being guarded, brought her with them to *Dorchester*, where we received her safe: blessed be the Lord for it, *for great is his power, and he can do whatsoever seemeth him good*. Her coming in was after this manner: she was travelling one day with the *Indians*, with her basket at her back: the company of *Indians* were got before her, and gone out of sight, all except one Squaw: she followed the Squaw till night, and then both of them lay down: having nothing over them but the Heavens; nor under them but the Earth. Thus she travelled three days together, not knowing whither she was going: having nothing to eat or drink but water, and green *Hirtleberries*.[88] At last they came into *Providence*, where she was kindly entertained by several of that Town. The *Indians* often said, that I should never have her under twenty pounds: but now the Lord hath brought her in upon free cost, and given her to me the second time. The Lord make us a blessing indeed, each to others. Now have I seen that Scripture also fulfilled, *Deut. 30. 4, 7. If any of thine be driven out to the utmost parts of heaven, from thence will the Lord thy God gather thee, and from thence will he fetch thee. And the Lord thy God will put all these curses upon thine enemies, and on them which hate thee, which persecuted thee*. Thus hath the Lord brought me and mine out of that horrible pit, and hath set us in the midst of tender-hearted and compassionate Christians. 'Tis the desire of my soul that we may walk worthy of the mercies received, and which we are receiving.

Our Family being now gathered together (those of us that were living) the South Church in *Boston* hired an house for us: then we removed from Mr. *Shepards* (those cordial Friends) and went to *Boston*, where we continued about three quarters of a year: Still the Lord went along with us, and provided graciously for us. I thought it somewhat strange to set up House-keeping with bare walls, but, as *Solomon* says, *Money answers all things*:[89] and that we had through the benevolence of *Christian* friends, some in this Town, and some in that, and others, and some from *England*, that in a little time we might look, and see the house furnished with love. The Lord hath been exceeding good to us in our low estate, in that when we had neither house nor home, nor other necessaries, the Lord so moved the hearts of these and those towards us; that we wanted neither food, nor rayment, for our selves or ours, Prov. 18. 24. *There is a Friend which sticketh closer than a Brother*. And how many such Friends have we found, and now living amongst! and truly such a Friend have we found him to be unto us, in whose house we lived, *viz.* Mr. *James Whitcomb*,[90] a Friend unto us near hand, and afar off.

I can remember the time, when I used to sleep quietly without workings in my thoughts, whole nights together: but now it is otherwise with me. When all are fast about me, and no eye open, but his who ever waketh, my thoughts are upon things past, upon the awful dispensations of the Lord towards us: upon his wonderful power and might in carrying us through so many difficulties, in returning us in safety, and suffering none to hurt us. I remember in the night season, how the other day I was in the midst of thousands of enemies, and nothing but death before me: it was then hard work to perswade my self that ever I should be satisfied with bread again. But now we are fed with the finest of the Wheat, and (as I may so say) with honey out of the rock:[91] instead of the husks, we have the fatted Calf:[92] the thoughts of these things in the particulars of them, and of the love and goodness of God towards us, make it true of me, what *David* said of himself, *Psal.* 6. 6. *I water my Couch with my tears*. Oh the wonderful power of God that mine eyes have seen, affording matter enough for my thoughts to run in, that when others are sleeping mine eyes are weeping.

I have seen the extream vanity of this World: one hour I have been in health, and wealth, wanting nothing: but the next hour in sickness, and wounds, and death, having nothing but sorrow and affliction.

Before I knew what affliction meant, I was ready sometimes to wish for it. When I lived in prosperity; having the comforts of this World about me, my Relations by me, and my heart chearful: and taking little care for any thing; and yet seeing many (whom I preferred before my self) under many trials and afflictions, in sickness, weakness, poverty, losses, crosses, and cares of the World, I should be sometimes jealous least I should have my portion in this life; and that Scripture would come to my mind, *Heb.* 12. 6. *For whom the Lord loveth he chasteneth, and scourgeth every Son whom he receiveth*: but now I see the Lord had his time to scourge and chasten me. The portion of some is to have their Affliction by drops, now one drop and then another: but the dregs of the Cup, the wine of astonishment, like a sweeping rain that leaveth no food, did the Lord prepare to be my portion. Affliction I wanted, and Affliction I had, full measure (I thought) pressed down and running over: yet I see when God calls a person to any thing, and through never so many difficulties, yet he is fully able to carry them through, and make them see and say they have been gainers thereby. And I hope I can say in some measure, as *David* did, *It is good for me that I have been afflicted.*[93] The Lord hath shewed me the vanity of these outward things, that they are the *Vanity of vanities, and vexation of spirit;*[94] that they are but a shadow, a blast, a bubble, and things of no continuance; that we must rely on God himself, and our whole dependance must be upon him. If trouble from smaller matters begin to arise in me, I have something at hand to check my self with, and say when I am troubled, It was but the other day, that if I had had the world, I would have given it for my Freedom, or to have been a Servant to a *Christian.* I have learned to look beyond present and smaller troubles, and to be quieted under them, as *Moses* said, *Exod.* 14. 13. *Stand still, and see the salvation of the Lord.*

# HANNAH
# DUSTAN

Hannah Dustan (1657–1736; the name is variously spelled *Dustan, Duston*, and *Dustin*) and her family were not just famous but infamous even before she was captured by Abenaki Indians in 1697. Hannah's father, Michael Emerson, was constantly in trouble with the Massachusetts authorities for abuse toward his family and neighbors. But in 1693, the family became a household name when Hannah's unmarried sister Elizabeth was accused of infanticide, found guilty, and hanged. Cotton Mather preached the execution sermon and chastised Elizabeth for tainting the community; the accused protested that she was innocent of killing her newborn twins, but admitted that she was guilty of rebellious behavior (Ulrich, p. 201). Yet only four years later, Mather preached another sermon praising Hannah's equally—if not more—violent act as a communal providence.

On March 15, 1697, less than a week after Dustan had given birth to a baby girl, Abenakis, encouraged by French bounty offers for English prisoners and scalps, attacked her house in Haverhill. Thomas Dustan was able to shepherd his seven other children to safety, but his wife and the midwife, Mary Neff, were captured and marched toward Canada. The Abenakis killed the baby, and a dozen or so other prisoners, shortly after the initial raid. An Indian family of twelve kept Dustan, Neff, and Samuel Leonardson (an English boy taken eighteen months earlier) as prisoners on what is now called Dustin Island, near Penacook. Hearing that she would be forced to run the gauntlet, Dustan masterminded a plan with her fellow captives to kill their captors and succeeded in slaying ten of them; the two surviving Indians escaped.

Now free to canoe to safety, why did Dustan, Neff, and Leonardson take up time scalping the Abenakis? Various theories have been advanced including revenge, righteousness, and fear that others would not believe their story. However, one incentive was probably greed. In 1694, the Massachusetts Bay Colony had established the enormous bounty of fifty pounds per Indian scalp, reduced the bounty to twenty-five pounds in 1695, and repealed it entirely in 1696, several months before Dustan's capture. Despite the bounty's expiration, Thomas Dustan successfully petitioned the Legislature to offer his wife and her accomplices a suitable reward. In recognition of Hannah's central role—and perhaps as partial compensation for financial losses after the raid—she received twenty-five pounds and Neff and Leonardson twelve and a half pounds each. The settlement came in June 1697, three months after Mather had delivered his sermon on Dustan's capture and escape. It was only one of many gifts showered on Dustan in recognition of her actions.

Many hostages stay in the public eye for a short time after their release and then slip back into obscurity. However, a fascinating document written decades after her captivity provides us with Dustan's own commentary on her experiences. Although Dustan was a forty-year-old woman in 1697 when she sat in the congregation at Cotton Mather's North Church in Boston and heard him preach her own story, she was not technically a church member then. Only at the age of sixty-seven, in 1724, did she formally apply for admission to the church at Haverhill by submitting a brief conversion narrative. Quite likely Dustan dictated this document (which survives) but did not write it down herself. In the conversion account, she recalled her captivity as the central event of her life, but she prudently stressed its role in strengthening her faith rather than in lining her pockets: "I am Thankful for my Captivity," she says, "twas the Comfortablest time that ever I had" (quoted in Kilgore, p. 13). By "Comfortablest," the writer intended a now archaic meaning of the word as morally or spiritually strengthening. Indeed, according to Puritan belief, not only did God use Dustan as His instrument to kill the Indians, but He allowed her to withstand the Indians' pressure on her to renounce Puritanism and adopt Roman Catholicism.

While initially victimized in the raid, Hannah Dustan as fashioned by Mather was the model of the captive woman as victor since she proved herself physically, intellectually, and spiritually superior by killing, outwitting, and exemplifying Puritanism's power over the Indians. Mather's intuitive sense of the mythic resonance of Dustan's basic story has been borne out in many retellings since, even when other writers interpret her significance differently than Mather.

Mather published three texts in 1697, 1699, and 1702 that dramatize the incident. Historian Thomas Hutchinson's *The History of Massachusetts* (1795) continues in Mather's mold but pairs Dustan with another woman, Thomas's ancestor Anne Hutchinson, to make the story a study of two strong Puritan heroines. Leverett Saltonstall, in his 1816 "Sketch of Haverhill," and Timothy Dwight, in his *Travels in New England and New York* (1821–22), consolidate the Dustan story as local legend and regional history, but Dwight has more difficulty melding Dustan's roles as deviant vigilante and exemplary frontierswoman (Carroll, " 'Taken,' " p. 69). These earlier histories all provide sources for three short nineteenth-century prose recastings by John Greenleaf Whittier (1831), Nathaniel Hawthorne (1836), and Henry Thoreau (1849), which convert history into historical romance (Carroll, " 'Taken,' " p. 76). The fictionalizations by Whittier, Hawthorne, and Thoreau focus on the essential immorality of Dustan's act and see her, rather than the Indians, as evil, thus completing a chronological circle that began with Mather's fact-based depiction of Dustan as heroic.

As a last note, Dustan has been literally and figuratively recast in two nineteenth-century statues. The first permanent statue to a woman in the United States is the 25-foot granite memorial to Dustan at Boscawen—on the island she escaped from—which was unveiled in 1874. It shows Dustan as Amazon, with a hatchet in her right hand and the Indian scalps ominously dangling from her left. The other statue, in Haverhill, is a 15-foot bronze completed in 1879 to replace an earlier figure and depicts a militant Dustan whose right hand grips a tomahawk but whose upraised left hand is empty. Both statues present Dustan as forbidding and heroic yet still matronly.

The text is from Cotton Mather, *Magnalia Christi Americana: Or, the Ecclesiastical History of New-England*. London: Thomas Parkhurst, 1702.

## SUGGESTIONS FOR FURTHER READING

*BIBLIOGRAPHY*

Vail.

*PRIMARY WORK*

"Bloody Escape."

*SECONDARY WORKS*

Arner; Carroll, " 'My Outward' " and " 'Taken' "; Derounian-Stodola and Levernier; Ebersole; Fiedler; Namias; Ramsey; Ulrich; Whitford.

# A Notable Exploit; wherein, Dux Faemina Facti[1] from *Magnalia Christi Americana*

On *March* 15. 1697. the *Salvages* made a Descent upon the Skirts of *Haverhil*, Murdering and Captiving about Thirty-nine Persons, and Burning about half a Dozen Houses. In this Broil, one *Hannah Dustan* having lain-in about a Week, attended with her Nurse, *Mary Neff*,[2] a Widow, a Body of terrible *Indians* drew near unto the House where she lay, with Designs to carry on their Bloody Devastations. Her Husband[3] hastened from his Employments abroad unto the relief of his Distressed Family; and first bidding *Seven* of his *Eight* Children (which were from *Two* to *Seventeen* Years of Age) to get away as fast as they could unto some Garrison in the Town, he went in to inform his Wife of the horrible Distress come upon them. E'er she could get up, the fierce *Indians* were got so near, that utterly despairing to do her any Service, he ran out after his Children; resolving that on the Horse which he had with him, he would Ride away with *That* which he should in this Extremity find his Affections to pitch most upon, and leave the rest unto the Care of the Divine Providence. He overtook his Children about Forty Rod[4] from his Door; but then such was the *Agony* of his Parental Affections, that he found it impossible for him to distinguish any one of them from the rest; wherefore he took up a Courageous Resolution to Live and Die with them all. A Party of *Indians* came up with him; and now though they Fired at him, and he Fired at them, yet he Manfully kept at the Reer of his *Little Army* of Unarmed Children, while they Marched off with the Pace of a Child of Five Years Old; until, by the Singular Providence of God, he arrived safe with them all unto a Place of Safety about a Mile or two from his House. But his House must in the mean time have more dismal *Tragedies* acted at it. The *Nurse* trying to escape with the New-born Infant, fell into the Hands of the Formidable *Salvages;* and those furious Tawnies coming into the House, bid poor *Dustan* to rise immediately. Full of Astonishment she did so; and sitting down in the Chimney with an Heart full of most fearful *Expectation*, she saw the raging Dragons rifle all that they could carry away, and set the House on Fire. About Nineteen or

Twenty *Indians* now led these away, with about half a Score other *English Captives;* but e'er they had gone many Steps, they dash'd out the Brains of the *Infant* against a Tree; and several of the other *Captives,* as they began to Tire in their sad *Journey,* were soon sent unto their *Long Home;*[5] the *Salvages* would presently Bury their Hatchets in their Brains, and leave their Carcasses on the Ground for Birds and Beasts to Feed upon. However, *Dustan* (with her Nurse) notwithstanding her present Condition, Travelled that Night about a Dozen Miles, and then kept up with their New Masters in a long Travel of an Hundred and Fifty Miles, more or less, within a few Days Ensuing, without any sensible Damage in their Health, from the Hardships of their *Travel,* their *Lodging,* their *Diet,* and their many other Difficulties. These Two poor Women were now in the Hands of those whose *Tender Mercies are Cruelties;* but the good God, who hath all *Hearts in his own Hands,* heard the Sighs of these *Prisoners,* and gave them to find unexpected Favour from the *Master* who laid claim unto them. That *Indian Family* consisted of Twelve Persons; Two Stout Men, Three Women, and Seven Children; and for the Shame of many an *English Family,* that has the Character of *Prayerless* upon it, I must now Publish what these poor Women assure me: 'Tis this, in Obedience to the Instructions which the *French* have given them,[6] they would have *Prayers* in their Family no less than Thrice every Day; in the *Morning,* at *Noon,* and in the *Evening;* nor would they ordinarily let their Children *Eat or Sleep* without first saying their *Prayers.* Indeed these *Idolaters* were like the rest of their whiter Brethren *Persecutors,* and would not endure that these poor Women should retire to their *English Prayers,* if they could hinder them. Nevertheless, the poor Women had nothing but Fervent Prayers to make their Lives Comfortable or Tolerable; and by being daily sent out upon Business, they had Opportunities together and asunder to do like another *Hannah,* in *Pouring out their Souls before the Lord:* Nor did their praying Friends among our selves forbear to *Pour out* Supplications for them. Now they could not observe it without some Wonder, that their *Indian* Master sometimes when he saw them dejected would say unto them, *What need you Trouble your self? If your God will have you delivered, you shall be so!* And it seems our God would have it so to be. This *Indian Family* was now Travelling with these Two Captive Women, (and an *English* Youth[7] taken from *Worcester* a Year and half before,) unto a Rendezvouz of *Salvages,* which they call a *Town* somewhere beyond *Penacook;*[8] and they still told these poor Women, that when they came to this

Town they must be Stript, and Scourg'd, and Run the *Gantlet*[9] through the whole Army of *Indians*. They said this was the *Fashion* when the Captives first came to a Town; and they derided some of the Faint-hearted *English,* which they said, fainted and swoon'd away under the *Torments* of this Discipline. But on *April* 30. while they were yet, it may be, about an Hundred and Fifty Miles from the *Indian* Town, a little before break of Day, when the whole Crew was in a *Dead Sleep,* (Reader, see if it prove not so!) one of these Women took up a Resolution to intimate the Action of *Jael*[10] upon *Sisera;* and being where she had not her own *Life* secured by any *Law* unto her, she thought she was not forbidden by any *Law* to take away the *Life* of the *Murderers,* by whom her *Child* had been Butchered. She heartened the *Nurse* and the *Youth* to assist her in this Enter-prize; and all furnishing themselves with *Hatchets* for the purpose, they struck such home Blows upon the Heads of their *Sleeping Oppressors,* that e'er they could any of them struggle into any effectual resistance, *at the Feet* of those poor Prisoners, *they bow'd, they fell, they lay down; at their Feet they bowed, they fell; where they bowed, there they fell down Dead.* Only one *Squaw* escaped sorely Wounded from them in the Dark; and one *Boy,* whom they reserved asleep, intending to bring him away with them, suddenly wak'd and Scuttled away from this Desolation. But cutting off the *Scalps* of the *Ten Wretches,* they came off, and received *Fifty Pounds* from the General Assembly of the Province, as a Recompence of their Action; besides which, they received many *Presents of Congratulation* from their more private Friends; but none gave 'em a greater Taste of Bounty than Colonel *Nicholson,*[11] the Governour of *Maryland,* who hearing of their Action, sent 'em a very generous Token of his Favour.

ELIZABETH
HANSON

Elizabeth Hanson (1684–1737), a Quaker farmer's wife, was captured with four of her children and a woman servant on August 27, 1724 in New Hampshire. On the march to Canada, the hostage group was divided, and Hanson, her infant, and her six-year-old son were left with the head of the raiding party (probably Abenakis). The three were bought by a Frenchman who ransomed them to Hanson's husband six months after the attack. John Hanson also succeeded in obtaining the release of his younger daughter and the maid, but not his elder daughter, Sarah. The family returned to New Hampshire in September 1725, and a year and a half later, John Hanson traveled back to Canada to try once again to obtain Sarah's release, but he died en route. Sarah attracted the attention of a French officer who proposed marriage and thus secured her release from captivity since the Indians were more willing to trade with the French than with the British. She and her husband remained in Canada.

This is the plot outline of one of the most frequently reprinted and rewritten eighteenth-century captivities. One could point to its affecting portrayal of a passive, victimized heroine and its use of a spare style and precise details to explain its popularity, but in fact it stayed in print largely because it was authorized by a group of influential male Quakers who controlled all British and American imprints from the Society of Friends. While Hanson, who was not well educated, dictated her story, it is not clear who wrote it. The American editions of 1728 and 1754 are signed "E. H.," and the title pages say that the "Substance" of Hanson's story "was taken from her own Mouth," but it does not say by whom. The English editions ascribe authorship to Samuel Bownas, a well-known English Quaker missionary and preacher who met Hanson in New Hampshire in 1727 and who included a one-page account of her story in his autobiography. Though inconclusive, external evidence suggests that he was not the author of the longer book publication (Vail, pp. 217–18); perhaps his name recognition in England explains the attribution. The narrative most likely was written and edited by one or more male Friends and then sponsored by the Quaker publishing establishment.

A number of critics have discussed Hanson's extraordinary passivity and stoicism in describing, and often rationalizing, her hardships. During the attack on her home, when Indians killed her
hysterical four-year-old son, she comments that she dared not "appear disturb'd, or shew much Uneasiness" in case they killed her six-
year-old son, but adds that she wished the boys—who had been
outside—had stayed away until the Indians had left. Though recovering from the birth of her baby two weeks previously and scarcely
able to maintain the pace of the forced march, she notes frequently
and gratefully that her Indian master sometimes carried her baby,
despite his own heavy load, or led her by the hand over rough terrain.
Hanson's most surprising psychological displacement concerns her
rationalization of her master's frequent threats and physical abuse:
that he was at his worst when he could not find enough food. In
addition, Hanson often interrupts the narrative flow to explain Indian customs, defining a wigwam and scalping, for example, and
commenting on the Native American practice of communal property.

Hanson's seeming detachment may indicate her acculturation to
Indian ways, her attempt to understand her unpredictable master,
her new role as ethnographer, or her inability to confront her traumatic experiences. Or, as Carroll persuasively argues, these narrative
disjunctions may "signal the intervention of a shaping hand who
shifts the tone from personal suffering to impersonal observation"
(" 'Taken,' " p. 119). By 1728, the Quaker committee overseeing the
Hanson narrative's production wanted to realign the role of women's
affliction from the early female evangelists' public assertiveness to a
more private submissiveness of which Hanson became an ideal
model. Carroll compares Hanson's narrative with *God's Protecting
Providence* (1699), by Jonathan Dickinson, the only other first-
person captivity narrative published by the Society of Friends between 1699 and 1728, although Hanson and Dickinson were by no
means the only Quaker captives during the same time period. While
both Hanson and Dickinson submit to divine providence in their
texts, Dickinson is allowed to retain "an assertive personal agency"
as a male Friend that Hanson, as a female, is denied (Carroll,
" 'Taken,' " p. 123).

Yet modern readers of Hanson's story can access its underlying
poignancy by filling in its emotional gaps for themselves and reflecting on questions like the following. Wasn't Hanson traumatized by
the deaths of her two children? How did she really feel about her
brutal Indian master? Did she brood on the irony of her husband's

death while trying to obtain Sarah's release? How did she come to terms with the realization that Sarah could escape Indian captivity only by converting to Catholicism—which Quakers abhorred—and remaining permanently in Canada among the French?

One final piece of information outside the narrative reveals further ironies regarding Hanson's capture and her husband's repeated attempts to ransom Sarah. A contemporary document describes John Hanson as "a stiff quaker" who refused to garrison his family in 1724 though warned of impending Indian hostilities (quoted in Coleman, vol. 2, p. 162). When his home was attacked, he and his eldest daughter were away at the weekly meeting and were spared. Unharmed and unable to protect his wife and younger children, he must have felt deeply guilty and willing belatedly to do whatever was necessary to get his family back.

The text is that of the first American edition: *God's Mercy Surmounting Man's Cruelty*. Philadelphia: Samuel Keimer, 1728.


## SUGGESTIONS FOR FURTHER READING

*BIBLIOGRAPHY*

Vail.

*SECONDARY WORKS*

Carroll, " 'Taken' "; Derounian-Stodola and Levernier; Scheick; Ulrich.

# God's Mercy Surmounting Man's Cruelty, Exemplified in the Captivity and Redemption of Elizabeth Hanson

REmarkable and many have been the Providences of God, towards his People for their Deliverance in a Time of Trouble, by which we may behold as in lively Characters, the Truth of that Saying, That *he is a God nigh at hand, and always ready to help and assist those that fear him, and put their Confidence in him.*

The Sacred Writings give us Instances of the Truth hereof, in Days of Old, as in the Case of the *Israelites, Job, David, Daniel, Paul, Silas,* and many others. Besides which, our modern Histories have plentifully abounded with Instances of God's Fatherly Care over his People, in their sharpest Trials, deepest Distresses, and sorest Exercises by which we may know he is *a God that changeth not, but is the same Yesterday, to Day and for ever.*[1]

Among the many modern Instances, I think, I have not met with a more singular One, of the Mercy and preserving Hand of God, than in the Case of *Elizabeth Hanson,* Wife of *John Hanson* of *Knox-marsh* in *Kecheachey,* in *Dover*-Township, in *New-England,* who was taken into Captivity the 27th Day of the 6th Month,[2] call'd *August,* 1724, and carried away with four Children,[3] and a Servant, by the *Indians;* which Relation, as it was taken from her own Mouth, by a Friend, differs very little from the Original Copy, but is even almost in her own Words (what small Alteration is made being partly owing to the Mistake of the Transcriber) which take as follows,

As soon as[4] they discovered themselves (having as we understood by their Discourse, been sculking in the Fields some Days, watching their Opportunity when my dear Husband with the rest of our Men, were gone out of the Way) two of these barbarous Salvages came in upon us, next Eleven more, all naked, with their Guns and Tomahauks came into the House in a great Fury upon us, and killed one Child immediately, as soon as they entred the Door, thinking thereby to strike in us the greater Terror, and to make us more fearful of them.

Then in as great Fury the Captain came up to me; but at my Request, he gave me Quarter;[5] there being with me our Servant, and Six of our Children, two of the little Ones being at Play about the Orchard, and my youngest Child but Fourteen Days old, whether in Cradle or Arms, I now mind not: Being in that Condition, I was very unfit for the Hardships I after met with, which are briefly contained in the following Pages.

They next go to rifling the House in a great Hurry, (fearing, as I suppose, a Surprize from our People it being late in the Afternoon.) and packed up some Linnen, Woollen, and what other Things pleased them best; and when they had done what they would, they turned out of the House immediately, and being at the Door, Two of my younger Children, One Six, and the other Four Years old, came in Sight, and being under a great Surprize, cryed aloud, upon which one of the *Indians* running to them, takes one under each Arm, and brings them to us. My Maid prevailed with the biggest to be quiet and still; but the other could by no Means be prevailed with, but continued screaking[6] and crying very much, in the Fright, and the *Indians* to ease themselves of the Noise, and to prevent the Danger of a Discovery that might arise from it, immediately before my Face, knockt its Brains out. I bore this as well as I could, nor daring to appear disturb'd, or shew much Uneasiness, lest they should do the same to the other: But should have been exceeding glad they had kept out of Sight till we had been gone from our House.

Now having kill'd two of my Children, they scalp'd 'em (a Practice common with these People, which is, when-ever they kill any *English* People, they cut the Skin off from the Crown of their Heads, and carry it with them for a Testimony and Evidence that they have kill'd so many, receiving sometimes a Reward of a Sum of Money for every Scalp) and then put forward to leave the House in great Haste, without doing any other Spoil than taking what they had pack'd together, with my self and little Babe Fourteen Days old, the Boy Six, and two Daughters, the one about Fourteen, and the other about Sixteen Years, with my Servant Girl.

It must be considered that I having lain-in but 14 Days, and being but very tender and weakly, being removed now out of a good Room well accommodated with Fire, Bedding, and other Things suiting a Person in my Condition, it made these Hardships to me greater than if I had been in a strong and healthy Frame; yet for all this, I must go or die. There was no Resistance.

In the Condition aforesaid we left the House, each *Indian* having something; and I with my Babe and three Children that could go of themselves. The Captain, tho' he had as great a Load as he could well carry, and was helped up with it, did for all that, carry my Babe for me in his Arms, which I took to be a Favour from him. Thus we went thro' several Swamps and some Brooks, they carefully avoiding all Paths of any Track like a Road, lest by our Footsteps we should be followed.

We got that Night, I suppose, not quite ten Miles from our House, on a direct Line; then taking up their Quarters, lighted a Fire, some of them lying down while others kept Watch; I being both wet and weary, and lying on the cold Ground in the open Woods, took but little Rest.

However, early in the Morning, we must go just as Day appeared, travelling very hard all that Day thro' sundry Rivers, Brooks and Swamps, they as before, carefully avoiding all Paths, for the Reason already assign'd: At Night I was both wet and tyred exceedingly, having the same Lodging on the cold Ground in the open Woods. Thus for 26 Days, Day by Day, we travelled very hard, sometimes a little by Water over Lakes and Ponds; and in this Journey we went up some very high Mountains so steep, that I was forc'd to creep up on my Hands and Knees, under which Difficulty the *Indian* my Master, would mostly carry my Babe for me, which I took as a great Favour of God that his Heart was so tenderly inclined to assist me, tho' he had, as is said, a very heavy Burden of his own; nay, he would sometimes take my very Blanket, so that I had nothing to do, but take my little Boy by the Hand for his Help, and assist him as well as I could, taking him up in my Arms a little at Times, because so small, and when we came at very bad Places, he would lend me his Hand, or coming behind, would push me up before him: In all which, he shewed some Humanity and Civility more than I could have expected: For which Privilege I was secretly thankful to God as the moving Cause thereof.

Next to this, we had some very great Runs of Water and Brooks to wade thro', in which at Times, we met with much Difficulty, wading often to our middle, and sometimes our Girls were up to their Shoulders and Chin, the *Indians* carrying my Boy on their Shoulders. At the Side of one of these Runs or Rivers, the *Indians* would have

my eldest Daughter *Sarah* to sing them a Song: Then was brought
into her Remembrance that Passage in the 137th Psalm, *By the Rivers
of Babylon there we sat down, yea we wept when we remember'd
Zion; we hanged our Harps on the Willows in the midst thereof; for
there they that carryed us away captive required of us a Song, and
they that wasted us, required of us Mirth.* When my poor Child had
given me this Account, it was very affecting, and my Heart was very
full of Trouble, yet on my Child's Account, I was glad that she had
so good an Inclination, which she yet further manifested in longing
for a Bible, that we might have the Comfort in reading the Holy
Text, at vacant Times, for our Spiritual Comfort under our present
Affliction.

Next to the Difficulties of the Rivers, were the prodigious Swamps
and Thickets, very difficult to pass thro'; in which Places my Master
would sometimes lead me by the Hand a great Way together, and
give me what Help he was capable of under the Straits we went thro';
and we passing one after another, the first made it pretty passable
for the hindmost.

But the greatest Difficulty that deserves the first to be named, was
Want of Food, having at Times nothing to eat but Pieces of old
Beaver-Skin-Match Coats,[7] which the *Indians* having hid (for they
came naked as is said before) which in their going back again they
took with them, and they were used more for Food than Rayment:
Being cut out in long narrow Straps, they gave us little Pieces, which
by the *Indians* Example we laid on the Fire till the Hair was singed
away, and then we eat them as a sweet Morsel, experimentally knowing, that *to the hungry Soul every bitter thing is sweet.*[8]

It's to be consider'd further, that of this poor Dyet we had but
very scanty Allowance; so that we were in no Danger of being over-
charged. But that which added to my Trouble, was the Complaints
of my poor Children, especially the little Boy. Sometimes the *Indians*
would catch a Squirrel, or a Beaver, and at other Times, we met with
Nutts, Berries and Roots they digg'd out of the Ground, with the
Bark of some Trees: But we had no Corn for a great while together,
tho' some of the younger *Indians* went back, and brought some Corn
from the *English* Inhabitants, the Harvest not being gathered, of
which we had a little allowed us: But when they caught a Beaver, we
liv'd high while it lasted, they allowing me the Guts and Garbage for
my self and Children: But not allowing us to clean and wash them
as they ought, made the Food very irksome to us, in the Conceit of

our Minds, to feed upon, and nothing besides pinching Hunger could have made it any way tolerable to be born. But *that makes every bitter Thing sweet.*

The next Difficulty was no less hard to me; for my daily Travel and hard Living made my Milk dry almost quite up, and how to preserve my poor Babe's Life was no small Care on my Mind, having no other Sustenance for it, many Times, but cold Water, which I took in my Mouth, and let it fall on my Breast, (when I gave it the Teat,) to suck in, with what it could get from the Breast; and when I had any of the Broth of the Beaver, or other Guts, I fed my Babe with it, as well as I could: By which Means, thro' Care to keep it as warm as I could, I preserved its Life till I got to *Canada,* and then I had some other Food, of which more in its Place.

Having by this Time got considerably on the Way, the *Indians* part; and we must be divided amongst them. This was a sore Grief to us all: But we must submit, and no Way to help our selves. My eldest Daughter was first taken away, and carryed to another Part of the Country far distant from us, where for the present, we must take Leave of her, tho' with a heavy Heart.

We did not travel far after this, before they divided again, taking my second Daughter and Servant Maid from me, into another Part of the Country: So, I having now only my Babe at my Breast, and little Boy six Years old, we remained with the Captain still: But my Daughter and Servant underwent great Hardships after they were parted from me, travelling three Days, without any Food, taking nothing for Support, but cold Water; and the third Day, what with the Cold, the Wet, and Hunger, the Servant fell down as dead in a Swoon, being both very cold and wet, at which the *Indians* with whom they were, were surpriz'd, shewing some Kind of Tenderness, being unwilling then to lose them by Death, having got them so near home, hoping if they lived, by their Ransom to make considerable Profit by them.

In a few Days after this, they got near their Journey's End, where they had more Plenty of Corn and other Food: But Flesh often fell very short, having no other Way to depend on for it, but hunting; and when that failed, they had very short Commons.[9] It was not long ere my Daughter and Servant were likewise parted; and my Daughter's Master being sick, was not able to hunt for Flesh: Neither had they any Corn in that Place, but were forced to eat Bark of Trees for a whole Week.

Being almost famished in this Distress, Providence so ordered that some other *Indians* hearing of their Misery and Want, came to visit them; (these People being very kind and helpful to one another, which is very commendable) and brought unto them the Guts and Liver of a Beaver, which afforded them a good Repast, being but Four in Number, the *Indian,* his Wife and Daughter, and my Daughter.

By this Time my Master and our Company got to our Journey's End, where we were better fed at Times, having some Corn and Venison, and wild Fowl, or what they could catch by hunting in the Woods; and my Master having a large Family, being Fifteen in Number, we had at Times very short Commons, more especially when Game was scarce.

But here our Lodging was still on the cold Ground in a poor Wigwam, (which is a kind of little Shelter made with the Rinds of Trees and Mats for a Covering, something like a Tent.) These are so easily set up and taken down, that they oft remove them from one Place to another: Our Shoes and Stockings being done, and our other Cloaths wore out in that long Journey thro' the Bushes and Swamps, and the Weather coming in very hard, we were poorly defended from the Cold, for Want of Necessaries; which caused one of my Feet, one of the little Babe's, and both the little Boys to freeze, and this was no small Exercise, yet thro' Mercy, we all did well.

Now tho' we got to our Journey's End, we were never long in one Place, but very often moved from one Place to another, carrying their Wigwams with them which they could do, without much Difficulty. This being for the Conveniency of Hunting, made our Accommodations much more unpleasant than if we had continued in one Place, by reason the Coldness and Dampness of the Ground, where our Wigwams were pitched, made it very unwholesome and unpleasant Lodging.

Being now got to the *Indian* Fort, many of the *Indians* came to visit us, and in their Way welcom'd my Master home; and held a great Rejoycing, with Dancing, Firing Guns, Beating on hollow Trees, instead of Drums, shouting, drinking and Feasting after their Manner, in much Excess for several Days together, which I suppose, in their Thoughts, was a Kind of Thanks to God put up for their safe Return and good Success: But while they were in their Jollitry and Mirth, my Mind was greatly exercised towards the Lord, that I, with my dear Children separated from me, might be preserved from repining against God, under our Affliction on the one Hand, and on the other, we might have our Dependance on him who rules the

Hearts of Men, and can do what pleases in the Kingdoms of the Earth, knowing that his Care is over them who put their Trust in him; but I found it very hard to keep my Mind as I ought, under the Resignation which is proper to be in, under such Afflictions and sore Trials, as at that Time I suffer'd, in being under various Fears and Doubts concerning my Children, that were separated from me, which helpt to add to, and greatly encrease my Troubles: And herein I may truly say, my Afflictions are not to be set forth in Words to the Extent of them.

We had not been long at home ere my Master went a hunting, and was absent about a Week, he ordering me in his Absence to get in Wood, gather Nuts, &c. I was very diligent, cutting the Wood, and putting it in Order, not having very far to carry it: But when he returned, having got no Prey, he was very much out of Humour, and the Disappointment was so great, that he could not forbear revenging it on us poor Captives. However he allowed me a little boyled Corn for self and Child, but with a very angry Look threw a Stick or Corn-Cob at me, with such Violence as did bespeak he grudged our Eating. At this his Squaw and Daughter broke out in a great Crying. This made me fear Mischief was hatching against us: And on it, I imme-diately went out of his Presence into another Wigwam; upon which he comes after me, and in great Fury tore my Blanket off my Back, and took my little Boy from me and struck him down as he went along before him; But the poor Child not being hurted, only frighted in the Fall, he started up and ran away, without crying; then the *Indian* my Master left me; but his Wife's Mother came and sat down by me, and told me, *I must sleep there that Night*. She then going from me a little Time, came back with a small Skin to cover my Feet withal, informing, that my Master intended now to kill us; and I being desirous to know the Reason, expostulated, that *in his Absence I had been diligent to do as I was ordered by him.* Thus, as well as I could, I made her sensible how unreasonable he was. Now, tho' she could not understand me, nor I her, but by Signs, we reasoned as well as we could: She therefore makes Signs that I must die, ad-vising me, by pointing up with her Fingers, in her Way, to pray to God, endeavouring by her Signs and Tears to instruct me in that which was most needful, *viz.* to prepare for Death, which now threatned me; the poor old Squaw was so very kind and tender, that she would not leave me all that Night, but laid her self down at my Feet, designing what she could to asswage her Son-in-law's Wrath, who had conceived Evil against me, chiefly as I understood, because the Want of Victuals urged him to it. My Rest was little this Night, my poor Babe sleeping sweetly by me.

I dreaded the tragical Design of my Master, looking every Hour for his coming to execute his bloody Will upon us: But he being weary with his Hunting and Travel in the Woods, (having toyled for nothing) went to Rest, and forgot it. Next Morning he applied himself again to hunting in the Woods; but I dreaded his returning empty, and prayed secretly in my Heart, that he might catch some Food to satisfy his Hunger, and cool his ill Humour. He had been gone but a little Time till he returned with Booty, having shot some wild Duck; and now he appeared in a better Temper, ordering the Fowls to be dress'd with Speed; for these kind of People, when they have Plenty, spend it as freely as they get it; spending in Gluttony and Drunkenness in two Days Time, as much, as with prudent Management might serve a Week.[10] Thus do they live, for the most Part, either in Excess of Gluttony and Drunkenness, or under great Straits for Want of Necessaries. However in this plentiful Time I felt the Comfort of it in Part with the Family, having a Portion sent for me and my little ones, which was very acceptable. Now, I thinking to my self the Bitterness of Death was over for this Time, my Spirits were a little easier.

Not long after this, he got into the like ill Humour again, threatning to take away my Life. But I always observed when-ever he was in such a Temper, he wanted Food, and was pinched with Hunger. But when he had Success in hunting, to take either Bears, Beavers, Bucks or Fowls, on which he could fill his Belly, he was better humoured, tho' he was naturally of a very hot and passionate Temper, throwing Sticks, Stones, or whatever lay in his Way, on every slight Occasion. This made me in continual Danger of my Life: But That God whose Providence is over all his Works, so preserved me, that I never received any Damage from him that was of any great Consequence to me; for which I ever desire to be thankful to my Maker.

When Flesh was scarce, we had only the Guts and Garbage allowed to our Part; and not being permitted to cleanse the Guts any otherwise than emptying the Dung, without so much as washing them, as before is noted, in that filthy Pickle we must boil them, and eat them, which was very unpleasant: But Hunger made up that Difficulty, so that this Food which was very often our Lot, became pretty tolerable to a sharp Appetite, which otherwise by no Means could have been dispensed with. Thus I consider'd, none knows what they can undergo, till they are tryed: For what I had thought in my own

Family, nor fit for Food, would here have been a Dainty-Dish and a sweet Morsel.

By this Time, what with Fatigue of Spirits, hard Labour, mean Diet, and often Want of Natural Rest, I was brought so low, that my Milk was dryed up, my Baby very poor and weak, just Skin and Bone; for I could perceive all its Joynts from one End of the Babe's Back to the other; and how to get what would suit its weak Appetite, I was at a Loss; on which one of the *Indian* Squaws perceiving my Uneasiness about my Child, began some Discourse with me, in which she advised me to take the Kernels of Walnuts, and clean them, and beat them with a little Water, which I did, and when I had so done, the Water look'd like Milk; then she advised me to add to this Water, a little of the finest of the *Indian* Corn Meal, and boyl it a little together. I did so, and it became palatable, and was very nourishing to the Babe, so that it began to thrive and look well; which was before more like to die than live. I found that with this kind of Diet the *Indians* did often nurse their Infants. This was no small Comfort to me: But this Comfort was soon mixed with Bitterness and Trouble, which thus happen'd; My Master taking Notice of my dear Babe's thriving Condition, would often look upon it, and say, *when it was fat enough, it should be killed, and he would eat it;* and pursuant to his Pretence, at a certain Time, he made me to fetch him a Stick that he had prepared for a Spit, to roast the Baby upon, as he said, which when I had done, he made me sit down by him, and undress the Infant. When the Child was naked, he felt its Arms, Legs, and Thighs, and told me, *It was not fat enough yet; I must dress it again until it was better in Case.*

Now tho' he thus acted, I could not perswade my self, that he intended to do as he pretended; but only to aggravate and afflict me: Neither ever could I think but our Lives would be preserved from his barbarous Hands, by the over-ruling Power of him in whose Providence I put my Trust, both Day and Night.

A little Time after this my Master fell sick, and in his sickness, as he lay in his Wigwam, he order'd his own Son to beat my Son: But the old Squaw, the *Indian* Boy's Grandmother, would not suffer him to do it: Then his Father, my Master, being provoked, catches up a Stick very sharp at one End, and with great Violence threw it from him, at my Son, and hit him on the Breast, with which my Child was much bruised, and the Pain, with the Surprize, made him turn as pale as Death; I entreating him not to cry, and the Boy tho' but Six Years old, bore it with wonderful Patience, not so much as in the least complaining, so that the Child's Patience asswaged the Barbarity of his hard Heart: who, no Doubt, would have carryed his Passion and Resentment higher, had the Child cryed, as always Complaining did aggravate his Passion, and his Anger grew hotter upon it. Some little Time after, on the same Day he got upon his Feet, but far from being well. However, tho' he was sick, his Wife and Daughter let me know, he intended to kill us, and I was under a Fear, unless Providence now intercepted, how it would end, I therefore put down my Child, and going out of his Presence, went to cut Wood for the Fire, as I used to do, hoping that would in Part, allay his Passion; but withal ere I came to the Wigwam again, I expected my Children would be killed in this mad Fit, having no other Way but to cast my Care upon God, who had hitherto helped and cared for me and mine.

Under this great Feud, the old Squaw, my Master's Mother-in-law left him; but my Mistress and her Daughter abode in the Wigwam with my Master; and when I came with my Wood, the Daughter came to me, whom I asked, if her Father had kill'd my Children, and she made me a Sign, *No*, with a Countenance that seem'd pleas'd it was so; for instead of his further venting his Passion on me and my Children, the Lord, in whom I trusted, did seasonably interpose, and I took it as a merciful Deliverance from him, and the *Indian* was under some Sense of the same as himself did confess to them about him afterwards.

Thus it was a little after he got up on his Feet, the Lord struck him with great Sickness, and a violent Pain, as appeared by the Complaint he made in a doleful and hideous Manner; which when I understood, not having yet seen him, I went to another Squaw, that was come to see my Master, which could both speak and understand *English,* and enquired of her if my Mistress (for so I always called her, and him Master) thought that Master would die? She answer'd *Yes, it was very likely he would, being worse and worse:* Then I told her, *He struck my Boy a dreadful Blow without any Provocation at all, and had threatned to kill us all in his Fury and Passion;* upon which the Squaw told me, *My Master had confessed the Abuse he offered my Child, and that the Mischief he had done, was the Cause why God afflicted him with that Sickness and Pain; and he had promised never to abuse us in such Sort more:* And after this he soon recovered, but was not so passionate; nor do I remember he ever after struck either me or Children, so as to hurt us, or with that mischievous Intent as before he used to do. This I took as the Lord's Doing, and it was marvellous in my Eyes.

Some few Weeks after this, my Master made another Remove,[11] having, as before, made several: But this was the longest ever he made, it being two Day's Journey, and mostly upon the Ice. The first Day's Journey the Ice was bare, but the next Day some Snow falling, made it troublesome, very tedious and difficult travelling; and I took much Damage in often falling, having the Care of my Babe, that added not a little to my Uneasiness; and the last Night, when we came to encamp, it being in the Night, I was ordered to fetch Water: But having sate a while on the cold Ground, I could neither go nor stand; but crawling on my Hands and Knees, a young *Indian* Squaw came to see our People, being of another Family, in Compassion took the Kettle, and knowing where to go, which I did not, fetcht the Water for me. This I took as a great Kindness and Favour, that her Heart was inclined to do me this Service.

I now saw the Design of this Journey; my Master being, as I suppose, weary to keep us, was willing to make what he could of our Ransom; therefore he went further towards the *French,* and left his Family in this Place, where they had a great Dance, sundry other *Indians* coming to our People. This held some Time, and while they were in it, I got out of their Way in a Corner of the Wigwam as well as I could: But every Time they came by me, in their Dancing, they would bow my Head towards the Ground, and frequently kick me with as great Fury as they could bear, being sundry of them barefoot, and others having *Indian* Mocossons: This Dance held some Time, and they made (in their Manner) great rejoycings and Noise.

It was not many Days ere my Master returned from the *French;* but he was in such a Humour, when he came back, he would not suffer me in his Presence. Therefore I had a little Shelter made with some Boughs, they having digg'd thro' the Snow to the Ground, the Snow being pretty deep. In this Hole, I and my poor Children were put to lodge, the Weather being very sharp, and hard Frost in the Month called *January,* made it more tedious to me and poor Babes. Our Stay not being long in this Place, he took me to the *French,* in Order for a Chapman;[12] and when we came among them, I was exposed to Sale, and he asked for me 800 Livres: But the *French* not complying with his Demand, put him in a great Rage, offering him but 600, he said in a great Passion, *If he could not have his Demand, he would make a great Fire, and burn me and the Babe in the View of the City,* which was named *Port-Royal.* The *Frenchman* bid the *Indian* make his Fire, *and I will,* says he, *help you, if you think that will do you more Good than 600 Livres,* calling my Master *Fool,* and speaking roughly to him, bid him be gone. But at the same Time, the *Frenchman* was very civil to me; and for my Encouragement, *bid me be of good Cheer, for I should be redeemed, and not go back with them again.*

Retiring now with my Master for this Night, the next Day I was redeemed for 600 Livres, and in treating with my Master, the *Frenchman* queried, *Why he asked so much for the Babe's Ransom,* urging, *when it had its Bellyful, it would die;* My Master said, No, *it would not die, having already lived 26 Days on nothing but Water,* believing the Babe to be a Devil. The *Frenchman* told him, No, *the Child is order'd for longer Life; and it has pleased God to preserve it to Admiration.* My Master said, No *it was a Devil, and he believed it would not die, unless they took a Hatchet, and beat its Brains out.* Thus ended their Discourse, and I was, as aforesaid, with my Babe, ransomed for 600 Livres, my little Boy, likewise at the same Time, for an additional Sum of Livres, was redeemed also.

I now having changed my Landlord, my Table and Diet, as well as my Lodging, the *French* were civil beyond what I could either desire or expect. But the next Day after I was redeemed, the *Romish* Priests took my Babe from me, and according to their Custom, they baptized it (urging if it died before That, it would be damned, like some of our modern pretended reformed Priests) and they gave it a Name as pleased them best; which was *Mary Ann Frossways*,[13] telling me, *My Child, if it now died, would be saved, being baptized;* and my Landlord speaking to the Priest that baptized it, said, *It would be well now* Frossways *was baptized, for it to die, being now in a State to be saved.* But the Priest said, No, *the Child having been so miraculously preserved thro' so many Hardships, it may be designed by God for some great Work, and by its Life being still continued, may much more glorify God than if it should now die.* A very sensible Remark, and I wish it may prove true.

I having been about five Months amongst the *Indians,* in about one Month after I got amongst the *French,* my dear Husband, to my unspeakable Comfort and Joy, came to me, who was now himself concerned to redeem his Children, two of our Daughters being still Captives, and only my self and two little ones redeemed; and thro' great Difficulty and Trouble he recover'd the younger Daughter: But the eldest we could by no Means obtain from their Hands, for the Squaw, to whom she was given, had a Son which she intended my Daughter should in Time be prevailed with to marry; the *Indians* being very civil toward their captive Women, not offering any Incivility by any indecent Carriage (unless they be much overgone in Liquor, which is commendable in them so far).

However the Affections they had for my Daughter, made them refuse all Offers and Terms of Ransom; so that after my poor Husband had waited, and made what Attempts and Endeavours he could, to obtain his Child, and all to no Purpose, we were forced to make homeward, leaving our Daughter to our great Grief, behind us, amongst the *Indians,* and set forwards over the Lake, with Three of our Children, and Servant-Maid, in Company with sundry others, and by the Kindness of Providence we got well home on the first Day of the Seventh Month, 1725. From which it appears I had been from home amongst the *Indians* and *French,* about Twelve Months, and Six Days.

In the Series of which Time, the many Deliverances and wonderful Providences of God unto us, and over us, have been, and I hope will so remain to be as a continued Obligation on my Mind ever to live in that Fear, Love and Obedience to God, duly regarding, by his Grace, with Meekness and Wisdom, to approve myself by his Spirit, in all Holiness of Life, and Godliness of Conversation, to the Praise of him that hath called me, who is God blessed forever.

But my dear Husband, poor Man! could not enjoy himself in Quiet with us, for Want of his dear Daughter Sarah, that was left behind; and not willing to omit any thing for her redemption which lay in his Power, he could not be easy without making a second Attempt; in order to which, he took his Journey about the nineteenth Day of the Second Month, 1727, in company with a Kinsman and his Wife, who went to redeem some of their Children, and were so happy as to obtain what they went about: But my dear Husband being taken sick on the way, grew worse and worse, as we were informed, and was sensible he should not get over it; telling my Kinsman, that, if it was the Lord's Will he must die in the Wilderness, he was freely given up to it. He was under a good Composure of mind, and sensible to the last Moment, and died, as near as we can guess, in about the Half-way between Albany and Canada, in my Kinsman's Arms, and is at rest, I hope in the Lord: And though my own Children's loss is very great; yet I doubt not but his gain is much more; I therefore desire and pray that the Lord will enable me patiently to submit to his will in all things he is pleased to suffer to my lot while here, earnestly supplicating the God and Father of all our mercies, to be a Father to my fatherless Children, and give unto them that Blessing which maketh truly rich, and adds no sorrow to it; that as they grow in years they may grow in Grace, and experience the Joy of his Salvation, which is come by Jesus Christ, our Lord and Savior. Amen.

Now though my Husband died, by reason of which his Labor was ended, yet my Kinsman prosecuted the thing, and left no Stone unturned that he thought, or could be advised, was proper to the obtaining my daughter's Freedom; but could by no means prevail; for as is before said (she being in another part of the Country distant from where I was) and given to an old Squaw, who intended to marry her in time to her Son, using what persuading she could to effect her end, sometimes by fair Means, and sometimes by severe. In the mean time a Frenchman interposed and they, by persuasion enticed my Child to marry, in order to obtain her Freedom, by reason that those Captives married by the French, are by that Marriage made free among them, the Indians having then no pretence longer to keep them as Captives, she therefore was prevailed upon, for the reasons afore assigned, to marry, and she was accordingly married to the Frenchman.[14]

Thus, as well, and as near as I can from my memory, (not being capable of keeping a Journal) I have given a short, but a true Account of some of the remarkable Trials and wonderful Deliverances, which I never purposed to expose; but that I hope thereby the merciful Kindness and Goodness of God may be magnified, and the Reader hereof provoked with more care and fear to serve him in Righteousness and Humility and then my designed End and Purpose will be answered.

E. H.

# "PANTHER CAPTIVITY"

Between 1787 and 1814, the "Panther Captivity" was published more than twenty times, mostly as separate pamphlets in large and small Northeastern locales including New York; Windsor, Putney, and Rutland, Vermont; Leominster, Massachusetts; and Fryeburgh, Maine. While the titles varied somewhat, they all ran along the lines of "An Account of a Beautiful Young Lady . . . ," "A Surprising Account of the Discovery . . . ," or, the title used most frequently, "A Very Surprising Narrative . . .".

Frontier fiction featuring American men, wilderness exploits, and encounters with Indians was extremely popular in almanacs, pamphlets, and longer publications (witness the sales of John Filson's *Discovery . . . of Kentucke*, published in 1784, whose famous and much-plagiarized appendix contained the adventures of Daniel Boone). The "Panther Captivity" not only drew on these elements but added the central character of an axe-wielding woman whose feminine exterior masked an inner violence usually associated with the masculine. In this way, the heroine of the "Panther Captivity" became part of a genealogy of women whose violent exploits have passed into American popular mythology, including her historical ancestor, Hannah Dustan, and her successor, Lizzie Borden.

The "Panther Captivity" is written in the form of a letter from the pseudonymous Abraham Panther to an unnamed male recipient describing a hunting expedition Panther and a friend undertook in 1786. After two weeks, the men were stunned to hear a woman singing at the entrance to a cave in the middle of the wilderness. The unnamed lady (the story refers to her as a lady rather than as just a woman) fainted, then offered the men hospitality and told her story in her own voice. Born to a good family in Albany, she had eloped in 1777 with her lover when her father refused his consent for them to marry. They were attacked by Indians, and her lover was killed, but the lady managed to escape and live off the land. The worst threat came when she encountered a gigantic figure who made sexual advances; however, the lady outwitted him, then ritually decapitated him with an axe and quartered his body. Although she had lived alone for nine years and seemed reluctant to return to "civilization," she accompanied the men back and inherited a large fortune when her guilt-stricken father died shortly after her return.

The story is laden with implications regarding gender roles in urban and rural/wilderness environments in post-Revolutionary America. As a representative woman in the new republic, the lady of the story exhibits surprising resourcefulness and independence in leaving her home and adapting to the wilderness, finding and growing (but not hunting) food, killing the giant, and living alone. Even when she returns to American society, she maintains a certain independence because of her inheritance. The hunters, too, undertake their own journey but reach a very different conclusion about the wilderness: they discover that the woman has already begun to cultivate and domesticate land they imagined was virgin territory for men.

The other character that commands attention is the giant that the lady overcomes. He is a mythic figure tied both to Native American lore about the ritual killing of a fertility god and also to the Green Giant in the fourteenth-century classic, *Sir Gawain and the Green Knight*. In this early version of the "Panther Captivity," the figure is not identified as an Indian, but he certainly possesses Indian attributes; for example, he speaks a different language, eats Indian cake, has bows and arrows in the cave, and lies down on animal skins. Later editions of the "Panther Captivity" completed the implication by specifically identifying him as an Indian.

The "Panther Captivity" lends itself to a host of interpretations including mythic/historical, Freudian, and feminist. A mythic/historical reading sees the narrative as dramatizing the dilemma facing America as an independent republic with two models to choose from: the Europeans' world (signified by the story's ties to the Puritan captivity narrative form) and the American Indians' world (signified by the wilderness locale). In a Freudian interpretation, the independent woman brandishing an axe and a knife becomes every red-blooded (white) male's nightmare: she is woman as castrator. In the right circumstances, this lady—indeed, any woman—can become defeminized and thus no longer under male control. One among many feminist interpretations recognizes that as women really did move westwards with their families in the eighteenth and nineteenth centuries, the new environment accommodated not only the male wilderness hunter, but also the female wilderness cultivator, of which the lady in the "Panther Captivity" was a model. But America did not seem to be ready for the figure of the white woman in the wilderness, so the hunter model—found most clearly in Filson's portrayal of Daniel Boone, which was almost certainly one of the "Panther Captivity" 's sources—eventually prevailed.

We do not know the real person behind the pseudonym Abraham Panther, though critics have long assumed the author is male. Certainly the use of pen names in the eighteenth century was widespread for both men and women to protect an individual's true identity and to impart a sense of authenticity. Given the possibility of the narrative's feminist subtext, it is tempting to speculate that the masculine-sounding Abraham Panther could just as easily have been a female, as a male, writer.

The text is Abraham Panther, *A Surprising Account of the Discovery of a Lady Who Was Taken by the Indians in the Year 1777, and After Making Her Escape, She Retired to a Lonely Cave, Where She Lived Nine Years*. In *Bickerstaff's Almanac, for . . . 1788*. Norwich, Conn.: John Trumbull, 1787.


## SUGGESTIONS FOR FURTHER READING

*BIBLIOGRAPHY*

Vail.

*SECONDARY WORKS*

Derounian-Stodola and Levernier; Kolodny, "Turning the Lens"; Namias; Slotkin.

*A surprising account of the Discovery of a Lady
who was taken by the Indians in the year 1777,
and after making her escape, she retired to a
lonely Cave, where she lived nine years*

SIR,
Having returned from the Westward, I now sit down agreeable to
your request to give you an account of my journey. Two days after
you left my house Mr. Isaac Camber and myself, after providing
ourselves with provisions, begun our journey; determining to penetrate the Western wilderness as far as prudence and safety would
permit. We travelled for thirteen days in a westerly direction, without
meeting any thing uncommon or worthy description, except the very
great variety of birds and wild beasts, which would frequently start
before us, and as we had our muskets contributed not a little to our
amusement and support. The land we found exceeding rich and fertile, every where well watered, and the variety of berries, nuts,
ground-nuts, &c. afforded us very comfortable living.

On the 14th day of our travels, while we were observing a high
hill, at the foot of which ran a beautiful stream, which passing
through a small plain, after a few windings lost itself in a thicket,
and observing the agreeable picturesque prospect which presented
itself on all sides, we were surprised at the sound of a voice which
seemed at no great distance. At first we were uncertain whether the
voice was a human one, or that of some bird as many extraordinary
ones inhabited these wilds. After listening some time the voice ceased,
and we then determined to proceed up the hill, from whence we
judged the sound to come, that we might if possible discover what
voice it was that had so much astonished us. Accordingly crossing
the brook we proceeded up the hill, and having arrived near the
summit we again distinctly heard a voice singing in our own language
a mournful song. When the voice ceased we observed a small foot
path which we followed, and arriving at the top of the hill, passed
round a large rock, then through a thicket of bushes at the end of
which was a large opening; upon our arival here, to our inexpressible
amazement, we beheld a most beautiful young LADY sitting near the

mouth of a cave. She not observing us begun again to sing. We now attempted to approach her, when a dog which we had not before observed, sprung up and began to bark at us, at which she started up and seeing us, gave a scream and swooned away. We ran to her assistance and having lifted her up, she soon recovered; and looking wildly at us exclaimed, Heavens! Where am I? and who, and from whence are you? We desired her to be under no uneasiness, told her we were travellers, that we came only to view the country but that in all our travels we had not met with any thing that had surprised us so much as her extraordinary appearance, in a place which we imagined totally unfrequented.

After a little conversation, having convinced her of our peaceable dispositions, she invited us into the cave where she refreshed us with some ground nuts, a kind of apples, some Indian cake and excellent water. We found her to be an agreeable, sensible lady, and after some conversation we requested to know who she was and how she came to this place, she very readily complied with this request and begun her story as follows.[1] "Strangers, your appearance and conversation intitle you to my confidence, and though my story cannot be very interesting or entertaining, yet it may possibly excite your pity, while it gratifies your curiosity. I was born near Albany[2] in the year 1760. My father was a man of some consequence and of considerable estate in the place where he lived, I was his only child. In the 15th year of my age my father received into his family a young gentleman of education as his clerk—he had not been long with us before he conceived an unfortunate passion for me, and as he had frequent opportunities of conversing with me, his insinuating address, added to his sensible, engaging conversation, soon found way to my heart. After this we spent together many happy evenings, vowing unalterable love, and fondly anticipating future happiness. We were however obliged to conceal our attachment from my father, who as he was excessively eager in pursuit of riches, we had no reason to suppose he would countenance our loves or consent to my marriage with a man destitute of fortune. It happened one evening while we were discoursing by ourselves in a little garden adjoining our house, that we were overheard by my father. Next morning my father with an angry countenance upbraided my lover with treacherously engaging his daughters affections, and after calling him many hard names, dismissed him with peremptory order never again to enter his house. By means however of an old servant, long attached to my lover, we found means to carry on a correspondence, and in about a month after we so contrived matters that I had an interview with my lover: I then agreed to quit my father's house and retire into the country, to a little hut, my father enraged at my elopement, had hired several men to search the country in pursuit of us, that he threatened vengeance to us both, and declared that he would be the death of the man who had carried off his daughter. In order to elude the search of those who were in pursuit of us, we proposed to move further back into the country, and there to wait till time should calm my father's rage, or effectually cool his resentment.

We accordingly left the hut and travelled at an easy rate for four days, determining to avoid being taken. But O! how shall I relate the horred scene that followed?—Towards the evening of the fourth day we were surrounded and made prisoners by a party of Indians, who led us about two miles and then barbarously murdered my lover, cutting and mangling him in a most inhuman manner after tying him to a stake they kindled a fire round him, and while he burnt they run round singing and dancing, rejoicing in their brutal cruelty. I was at a few rods[3] distance during this transaction, and this scene had well nigh deprived me of life. I fainted away and lay some time motionless on the ground, when I recovered my senses, I perceived that my guard had joined his companions, some of whom were seated round in rings, and others continued singing and dancing. Seeing them all engaged I withdrew by degrees into the bushes, and being out of their sight I got up and run for about an hour: I then sat down by the side of a tree and being overcome by fatigue and the sight I had seen, I either fainted or fell asleep, and knew nothing till next morning about 7 o'clock. 'Tis impossible for me to describe my feelings—or for you to conceive a situation more wretched than mine, at this time. Surrounded, as I supposed, on all sides by danger—I knew not what to do, without a guide to direct, or friend to protect me.

At length I got up, and after walking some time I resolved to seek some place of shelter where I might be secure from storms by day and from beasts by night, where I might dwell till a period should be put to my miserable existence.—With this view I wandered about for 14 days without knowing whether I went. By day the spontaneous produce of the earth supplied me with food, by night the ground was my couch, and the canopy of heaven my only covering. In the afternoon of the fifteenth day I was surprized at seeing a man of a gigantic figure walking towards me—to run I knew would be vain, and no less vain to attempt to hide. He soon came up with me and accosted me in a language I did not understand, and after surveying me for some time he took me by the hand and led me to this cave, having entered he pointed to a stone seat on which I sat down, he then gave me to eat some nuts and some Indian cake, after which he stretched himself out upon a long stone covered with skins which he used as a bed, and several times motioned to me to lay myself beside him; I declined his offer, and at length he rose in a passion and went into another apartment of the cave and brought forth a sword and hatchet. He then motioned to me that I must either accept of his bed or expect death for my obstinacy; I still declined his offer, and was resolved to die rather than comply with his desire. He then brought a walnut bark, and having bound me pointed to the east, intimating that he left me till next morning to consider his proposal, he then returned to his bed and happily for me soon fell asleep. Having the liberty of my mouth I soon made out to bite the bark in two with which he bound me, by which I found means to liberate myself while he continued sleeping. As I considered this as the only opportunity I should have of freeing myself from him,—as I expected that he would use violence when he awaked, to make me partake of his bed, and as I knew I could not escape him by flight I did not long deliberate, but took up the hatchet he had brought, and summoning resolution I with three blows effectually put an end to his existence. I then cut off his head, and next day having cut him into quarters drew him out of the cave about half a mile distance, when after covering him with leaves and bushes I returned to this place. I now found myself alone in possession of this cave in which are several apartments. I found here a kind of Indian corn which I planted, and have yearly raised a small quantity, here I contented myself as well as my wretched situation would permit—here have I existed for nine long years, in all which time this faithful dog which I found in the cave has been my only companion, and you are the only human beings who ever heard me tell my tale.[4]" Here she finished her narration, and after shedding a plentiful shower of tears and a little conversation she requested us to take rest, which request we willingly complied with.

Next morning she conducted us through the cave, in which were four appartments, one of which appeared to be dug pretty deep in the earth, in which was a spring of excellent water—in the other three were nothing remarkable, except four skulls, which we supposed were of persons murdered by the owner of the cave, or of his former companions. We found also three hatchets, four bows and several arrows, one large tinder box, one sword, one old gun and a number of skins of dead beasts, and a few clothes. The bows, some arrows, the sword and one hatchet we brought away, which are now in my possession. After continuing in the cave five days we proposed returning home, and requested the lady to accompany us—at first she refused to quit her cave; but after some persuasion she consented. We together left the cave on the morning of the sixth day after our arrival in it, and travelling the way we went, arrived at my house in 17 days. After resting about a week we accompanied the Lady, agreeable to her desire, to her father's house: the old man did not at first recognize his daughter, but being told who she was—he looked at her for some time and then tenderly embraced her crying, O! my child, my long lost child, do I once more fold thee in my arms—He then fainted away. We with difficulty brought him to life; but the scene had overcome him; he opened his eyes and being recovered, a little requested to know where she had lived so long, and what had happened to her since her leaving his house. We desired him to wait till he should be better recovered—but he beged to be satisfied immediately, observing that he had but a few moments to live. She then briefly related what had happened to her and the tragical death of her lover—he seemed much affected, and when she had finished, he took her by the hand and affectionately squeezed it, acknowledged he had been unjustly cruel to her, asked her forgiveness and attempted to say something more, but immediately fainted—all our endeavours to recover him were in vain.—he lay about seven hours and then expired. He left a handsome fortune to his daughter, who, notwithstanding his cruelty, was deeply affected at his sudden death. This adventure, the most singular and extraordinary of my life, I have communicated agreeable to your desire, as it really happened, without addition or diminition, and am Sir, yours, &c.

ABRAHAM PANTHER.

# JEMIMA HOWE

On July 27, 1755, Jemima Howe (c. 1715–1805) was captured for ransom during an Abenaki raid on Hinsdale, New Hampshire, with two daughters from her first marriage, Mary and Submit Phipps, and five sons from her second marriage, aged from eight years to six months. Her husband, Caleb, was killed as he was farming outside the fort. The Indians gave Submit to the French governor, de Vaudreuil, and sold Howe to a Frenchman named Saccapee. Saccapee and his son became infatuated with Howe and harassed her until a benefactor of Howe's asked the governor to intervene. Through the auspices of "several gentlemen of note," Howe, Submit Phipps, and all Howe's sons except the baby, who had died, were ransomed and returned. In 1760, the governor went back to France, took Mary Phipps with him, and married her to a French gentleman. Howe was married and widowed a third time but, despite her traumatic experiences, did not die until 1805, aged around ninety.

Thirty years after her captivity, Howe's story appeared in three men's works between 1788 and 1792 in a complex series of textual appropriations: David Humphreys's *An Essay on the Life of . . . Israel Putnam* (1788), volumes two and three of Jeremy Belknap's *The History of New-Hampshire* (1791–92), and Rev. Bunker Gay's *A Genuine and Correct Account* (1792). Generally, the earliest edition of a captivity will be the most authentic and least embroidered; in Howe's case, however, the reverse is true.

Humphreys set out to write an idealized biography of Israel Putnam—the Revolutionary War hero and friend of George Washington—whom Col. Schuyler rescued from captivity by the French. Schuyler also ransomed Howe, and at Schuyler's quarters, Putnam and Howe met. From a melodramatic and romantic rendition of Putnam's captivity (and entire life), Humphreys proceeds to an equally romanticized version of Howe's captivity. Humphreys depicts Howe as the heroine of a novel of seduction, "a Canadian Clarissa" (Carroll, " 'Taken,' " p. 169), and plays her against the villainous Saccapees—father and son—and the heroic Putnam, who escorted Howe back from Canada.

In 1790, the historian and writer Jeremy Belknap sent out a broadside request for verifiable incidents that he could use in a history of New Hampshire that he was compiling. The Rev. Bunker Gay of Hinsdale—Howe's home—sent a first-person account of her captivity framed by his own comments in a letter to Belknap. For reasons that are unclear, in volume two of his history, Belknap decided not to use Gay's version but to refer readers to Humphreys's patently overwrought and inaccurate retelling of 1788; however, he did include Gay's entire manuscript in an appendix to volume three (Carroll, " 'Taken,' " pp. 170–73).

Perhaps recognizing the marketability of Howe's own story via Bunker Gay, Belknap gave his permission for Gay's manuscript letter to be extracted from *The History of New-Hampshire* and issued as a separate pamphlet. In an interesting example of marketing and intertextuality, Gay's title page claims to correct the mistakes of the Humphreys publication. The first several pages are in Gay's voice, but then he quotes Howe's first-person account until a couple of pages before the end, when his voice resumes. Gay's voice castigates Humphreys for depicting Howe in a "romantick and extravagant" way. Gay's ministerial status presumably confers authority on Howe's portion, which indeed is far more muted than Humphreys's rendering. Also, instead of focusing only on her own story of beset womanhood, Howe writes the narratives of three captive women: herself and her two daughters.

All three stories focus on the commodification of women as a result of captivity. If women had little power in eighteenth-century New England as mothers, wives, sisters, and daughters, they often had even less choice about their fate while they were hostages of either Indians or the French. After holding Howe for almost a year, her moody Indian master sold her to Saccapee for very little money (it was all he could get). Initially, this seemed like freedom compared to her previous state until she realized Saccapee viewed her as his property and she had to fend off both father and son. In the Gay version that follows, Howe's narrative voice is almost lighthearted as she tells how the men became "excessively fond of my company" and how Schuyler and de Vaudreuil commanded "the young and amorous Saccapee, then an officer in the French army, from the field of Venus to the field of Mars" and ordered Saccapee père to leave her alone. Thus male authority figures with more power than the Saccapees allow Howe to maintain the role of mother rather than that of would-be wife.

But Howe adopts a much more serious tone when discussing the dangers surrounding her adolescent daughters. The Indians saw Submit as the most marketable of the three and tried to sell her first to the French. Unable to find a buyer, they gave her to de Vaudreuil, who placed her in a convent. She stayed there for several years and would have gone with the nuns to France had not Howe insisted that her daughter be released into her care. But Submit had acculturated to Catholic life and to the sisterhood of the convent, so that she left extremely reluctantly. From the seventeenth-century onwards, many captive English girls like Submit were placed in Canadian convents, converted to Catholicism, became nuns, and did not wish to leave.

Meanwhile, the Abenakis had kept Mary and intended to marry her to an Indian. Horrified, Howe prevailed on de Vaudreuil who sent Mary to the same convent as her sister, saying that they should both be considered his "adopted children." In 1760, de Vaudreuil took Mary with him when he returned to France and married her off; whether this was with either Howe's or Mary's consent is unknown.

Thus the narrative explores the powerlessness of women as mothers, daughters, sisters, and even authors. If Howe and Submit were able to return to New England, it was only because powerful men like Schuyler and De Vaudreuil intervened; maybe Mary was better off married to a French officer than to an Abenaki, but Mary did not seem to have much say in the decision; and maybe the version of Howe's story that follows really does incorporate her authentic first-person account, but if so, it was only because Gay allowed her to speak in between his commentary.

The text is Bunker Gay, *A Genuine and Correct Account of the Captivity, Sufferings and Deliverance of Mrs. Jemima Howe*. Boston: Belknap and Young, 1792.


## SUGGESTIONS FOR FURTHER READING

*BIBLIOGRAPHY*

Vail.

*SECONDARY WORKS*

Carroll, " 'Taken' "; Castiglia; Coleman; Derounian-Stodola and Levernier.

# A Genuine and Correct Account of the Captivity, Sufferings and Deliverance of Mrs. Jemima Howe

## JULY 27, 1758.

As Messrs. Caleb Howe, Hilkiah Grout, and Benjamin Gaffield, who had been hoeing corn in the meadow, west of the river, were returning home, a little before sunset, to a place called Bridgman's Fort, they were fired upon by twelve Indians, who had ambushed their path. Howe was on horseback, with two young lads, his children, behind him. A ball, which broke his thigh, brought him to the ground. His horse ran a few rods and fell likewise, and both the lads were taken. The Indians in their savage manner, coming up to Howe, pierced his body with a spear, tore off his scalp, stuck a hatchet in his head, and left him in this forlorn condition. He was found alive the morning after, by a party of men from Fort Hinsdale; and being asked by one of the party whether he knew him, he answered, yes, I know you all. These were his last words, though he did not expire until after his friends had arrived with him at Fort Hinsdale. Grout was so fortunate as to escape unhurt. But Gaffield, in attempting to wade through the river, at a certain place which was indeed fordable at that time, was unfortunately drowned. Flushed with the success they had met with here, the savages went directly to Bridgman's Fort. There was no man in it, and only three women and some children,[1] viz. Mrs. Jemima Howe, Mrs. Submit Grout, and Mrs. Eunice Gaffield. Their husbands, I need not mention again, and their feelings at this juncture I will not attempt to describe. They had heard the enemies guns, but knew not what had happened to their friends. Extremely anxious for their safety, they stood longing to embrace them, until at length, concluding from the noise they heard without that some of them were come, they unbarred the gate in a hurry to receive them; when lo! to their inexpressible disappointment and surprise, instead of their husbands, in rushed a number of hideous Indians, to whom they and their tender offspring became an easy prey; and from whom they had nothing to expect, but either an immediate death, or a long and doleful captivity. The latter of these, by the favor of Providence, turned out to be the lot of these unhappy women and

their still more unhappy, because more helpless, children. Mrs. Gaffield had but one, Mrs. Grout had three, and Mrs. Howe seven. The
eldest of Mrs. Howe's was eleven years old, and the youngest but six
months. The two eldest were daughters, which she had by her first
husband, Mr. William Phipps,[2] who was also slain by the Indians, of
which, I doubt not but you have seen an account in Mr. Doolittle's
history.[3] It was from the mouth of this woman that I lately received
the foregoing account. She also gave me, I doubt not, a true, though
to be sure, a very brief and imperfect history of her captivity, which
I here insert for your perusal. It may perhaps afford you some amusement, and can do no harm; if after it has undergone your critical
inspection, you should not think it (or an abreviation of it) worthy
to be preserved among the records you are about to publish.

'The Indians[4] (she says) having plundered and put fire to the Fort,
we marched as near as I could judge, a mile and a half into the
woods, where we encamped that night. When the morning came, and
we had advanced as much farther, six Indians were sent back to the
place of our late abode, who collected a little more plunder, and
destroyed some other effects that had been left behind; but they did
not return until the day was so far spent, that it was judged best to
continue where we were, through the night. Early the next morning
we set off for Canada, and continued our march eight days successively, until we had reached the place where the Indians had left their
canoes, about fifteen miles from Crown Point. This was a long and
tedious march; but the captives, by divine assistance, were enabled
to endure it with less trouble and difficulty, than they had reason to
expect. From such savage masters, in such indigent circumstances,
we could not rationally hope for kinder treatment than we received.
Some of us, it is true, had a harder lot than others; and, among the
children, I thought my son Squire had the hardest of any. He was
then only four years old, and when we stopped to rest our weary
limbs, and he sat down on his master's pack, the savage monster
would often knock him off; and sometimes too, with the handle of
his hatchet. Several ugly marks, indented in his head by the cruel
Indians, at that tender age, are still plainly to be seen.

At length we arrived at Crown Point, and took up our quarters
there, for the space of near a week. In the mean time some of the
Indians went to Montreal, and took several of the weary captives
along with them, with a view of selling them to the French. They did
not succeed, however, in finding a market for any of them. They
gave my youngest daughter, Submit Phipps, to the Governor, de Vau-

dreuil,[5] had a drunken frolick, and returned again to Crown Point, with the rest of their prisoners. From hence we set off for St. John's, in four or five canoes, just as night was coming on, and were soon surrounded with darkness. A heavy storm hung over us. The sound of the rolling thunder was very terrible upon the waters, which at every flash of expansive lightning, seemed to be all in a blaze. Yet to this we were indebted for all the light we enjoyed. No object could we discern any longer than the flashes lasted. In this posture we failed in our open tottering canoes, almost the whole of that dreary night. The morning indeed had not yet begun to dawn, when we all went ashore; and having collected a heap of sand and gravel for a pillow, I laid myself down, with my tender infant by my side, not knowing where any of my other children were, or what a miserable condition they might be in. The next day, however, under the wing of that ever present and all-powerful Providence, which had preserved us through the darkness, and imminent dangers of the preceding night, we all arrived in safety at St. Johns.

Our next movement was to St. Francois,[6] the metropolis, if I may so call it, to which the Indians, who led us captive, belonged. Soon after our arrival at their wretched capital, a council, consisting of the chief Sachem, and some principal warriors of the St. Francois tribe, was convened; and after the ceremonies usual on such occasions, were over, I was conducted and delivered to an old squaw, whom the Indians told me, I must call my mother. My infant still continuing to be the property of its original Indian owners. I was nevertheless permitted to keep it with me a while longer, for the sake of saving them the trouble of looking after it, and of maintaining it with my milk. When the weather began to grow cold, shuddering at the prospect of approaching winter, I acquainted my new mother that I did not think it would be possible for me to endure it, if I must spend it with her, and fare as the Indians did. Listening to my repeated and earnest solicitations, that I might be disposed of among some of the French inhabitants of Canada, she, at length, set off with me and my infant, attended by some male Indians, upon a journey to Montreal, in hopes of finding a market for me there. But the attempt proved unsuccessful, and the journey tedious indeed. Our provisions were so scanty as well as insipid and unsavory, the weather was so cold, and the travelling so very bad, that it often seemed as if I must have perished on the way. The lips of my poor child were sometimes so benumbed, that when I put it to my breast, it could not, till it grew warm, imbibe the nourishment requisite for its support. While we

were at Montreal, we went into the house of a certain French gentleman, whose lady, being sent for, and coming into the room where I
was, to examine me, seeing I had an infant, exclaimed suddenly in
this manner, 'Damn it, I will not buy a woman that has a child to
look after.' There was a swill-pail standing near me, in which I observed some crusts and crumbs of bread swimming on the surface of
the greasy liquor it contained: Sorely pinched with hunger, I skimmed
them off with my hands and eat them; and this was all the refreshment which the house afforded me. Some where in the course of this
visit to Montreal, my Indian mother was so unfortunate as to catch
the small pox, of which distemper she died, soon after our return,
which was by water, to St. Francois.

And now came on the season when the Indians begun to prepare
for a winter's hunt. I was ordered to return my poor child to those
of them, who still claimed it as their property. This was a severe trial.
The babe clung to my bosom with all its might; but I was obliged to
pluck it thence, and deliver it, shrieking and screaming, enough to
penetrate a heart of stone, into the hands of those unfeeling wretches
whose tender mercies may be termed cruel. It was soon carried off
by a hunting party of those Indians, to a place called Messiskow,[7] at
the lower end of Lake Champlain, whither, in about a month after,
it was my fortune to follow them. I had preserved my milk, in hopes
of seeing my beloved child again. And here I found it, it is true, but
in a condition that afforded me no great satisfaction; it being greatly
emaciated, and almost starved. I took it in my arms, put its face to
mine, and it instantly bit me with such violence, that it seemed as if
I must have parted with a piece of my cheek. I was permitted to
lodge with it that, and the two following nights; but every morning
that intervened, the Indians, I suppose on purpose to torment me,
sent me away to another wigwam, which stood at a little distance,
though not so far from the one in which my distressed infant was
confined, but that I could plainly hear its incessant cries, and heart
rending lamentations. In this deplorable condition I was obliged to
take my leave of it, on the morning of the third day after my arrival
at the place. We moved down the Lake several miles the same day;
and the night following was remarkable on account of the *great
earthquake*[8] which terribly shook that howling wilderness. Among
the islands hereabouts we spent the winter season, often shifting our
quarters, and roving about from one place to another; our family
consisting of three persons only, besides myself, viz. my late mother's
daughter, whom therefore I called my sister, her sanhop,[9] and a pap-

poose. They once left me alone two dismal nights; and when they returned to me again, perceiving them smile at each other, I asked what is the matter? They replied, that two of my children were no more: One of which, they said, died a natural death, and the other was knocked on the head. I did not utter many words, but my heart was sorely pained within me, and my mind exceedingly troubled with strange and awful ideas. I often imagined, for instance, that I plainly saw the naked carcases of my deceased children hanging upon the limbs of the trees, as the Indians are wont to hang the raw hides of those beasts which they take in hunting. It was not long, however, before it was so ordered by kind Providence, that I should be relieved in a good measure from those horrid imaginations; for as I was walking one day upon the ice, observing a smoke at some distance upon the land, it must proceed, thought I, from the fire of some Indian hut, and who knows but some one of my poor children may be there. My curiosity, thus excited, led me to the place, and there I found my son Caleb, a little boy between two and three years old, whom I had lately buried, in sentiment at least; or rather imagined to have been deprived of life, and perhaps also denied a decent grave. I found him likewise in tolerable health and circumstances, under the protection of a fond Indian mother; and moreover had the happiness of lodging with him in my arms one joyful night. Again we shifted our quarters, and when we had travelled eight or ten miles upon the snow and ice, came to a place where the Indians manufactured sugar which they extracted from the maple trees. Here an Indian came to visit us, whom I knew, and could speak English. He asked me why I did not go to see my son Squire. I replied that I had lately been informed that he was dead. He assured me that he was yet alive, and but two or three miles off, on the opposite side of the Lake. At my request he gave me the best directions he could to the place of his abode. I resolved to embrace the first opportunity that offered of endeavoring to search it out. While I was busy in contemplating this affair, the Indians obtained a little bread, of which they gave me a small share. I did not taste a morsel of it myself, but saved it all for my poor child, if I should be so lucky as to find him. At length, having obtained of my keepers leave to be absent for one day, I set off early in the morning, and steering, as well as I could, according to the directions which the friendly Indian had given me, I quickly found the place, which he had so accurately marked out. I beheld, as I drew nigh, my little son without the camp; but he looked, thought I, like a starved and mangy puppy, that had been wallowing in the ashes.

I took him in my arms, and he spoke to me these words, in the Indian tongue: 'Mother, are you come?' I took him into the wigwam with me, and observing a number of Indian children in it, I distributed all the bread which I had reserved for my own child, among them all, otherwise I should have given great offence. My little boy appeared to be very fond of his new mother, kept as near me as possible while I staid, and when I told him I must go, he fell as though he had been knocked down with a club. But having recommended him to the care of Him that made him, when the day was far spent, and the time would permit me to stay no longer, I departed, you may well suppose, with a heavy load at my heart. The tidings I had received of the death of my youngest child had, a little before, been confirmed to me beyond a doubt, but I could not mourn so heartily for the deceased, as for the living child.

When the winter broke up, we removed to St. John's; and, through the ensuing summer, our principal residence was at no great distance from the fort at that place. In the mean time, however, my sister's husband having been out with a scouting party to some of the English settlements, had a drunken frolick at the fort, when he returned. His wife, who never got drunk, but had often experienced the ill effects of her husband's intemperance, fearing what the consequence might prove, if he should come home in a morose and turbulent humour, to avoid his insolence, proposed that we should both retire, and keep out of the reach of it, until the storm abated. We absconded accordingly, but so it happened, that I returned, and ventured into his presence, before his wife had presumed to come nigh him. I found him in his wigwam, and in a surly mood; and not being able to revenge upon his wife, because she was not at home, he laid hold of me, and hurried me to the fort; and, for a trifling consideration, sold me to a French gentleman, whose name was Saccapee. 'Tis an ill wind certainly that blows no body any good. I had been with the Indians a year lacking fourteen days; and, if not for my sister, yet for me, 'twas a lucky circumstance indeed, which thus at last, in an unexpected moment, snatched me out of their cruel hands, and placed me beyond the reach of their insolent power.

After my Indian master had disposed of me in the manner related above, and the moment of sober reflection had arrived, perceiving that the man who bought me had taken the advantage of him in an unguarded hour, his resentments begun to kindle, and his indignation rose so high, that he threatened to kill me if he should meet me alone, or if he could not revenge himself thus, that he would set fire to the

fort. I was therefore secreted in an upper chamber, and the fort carefully guarded, until his wrath had time to cool. My service in the
family to which I was now advanced, was perfect freedom, in com-
parison of what it had been among the barbarous Indians. My new
master and mistress were both as kind and generous towards me as
I could any ways expect. I seldom asked a favor of either of them,
but it was readily granted: In consequence of which I had it in my
power, in many instances, to administer aid and refreshment to the
poor prisoners of my own nation, who were brought into St. John's
during my abode in the family of the above-mentioned benevolent
and hospitable Saccapee. Yet even in this family such trials awaited
me as I had little reason to expect, but stood in need of a large stock
of prudence, to enable me to encounter them. Must I tell you then,
that even the good old man himself, who considered me as his property, and likewise a warm and resolute son of his, at that same time,
and under the same roof, became both excessively fond of my company; so that between these two rivals, the father and the son, I found
myself in a very critical situation indeed, and was greatly embar-
rassed and perplexed, hardly knowing many times, how to behave
in such a manner as at once to secure my own virtue, and the good
esteem of the family in which I resided, and upon which I was wholly
dependent for my daily support. At length, however, through the
tender compassion of a certain English gentleman,[10] the Governor de
Vaudreuil being made acquainted with the condition I had fallen
into, immediately ordered the young and amorous Saccapee, then an
officer in the French army, from the field of Venus to the field of
Mars, and at the same time also wrote a letter to his father, enjoining
it upon him, by no means to suffer me to be abused, but to make
my situation and service in his family as easy and delightful as possible. I was moreover under unspeakable obligations to the Governor
upon another account. I had received intelligence from my daughter
Mary, the purport of which was, that there was a prospect of her
being shortly married to a young Indian of the tribe of Saint Francois,
with which tribe she had continued from the beginning of her captivity. These were heavy tidings, and added greatly to the poignancy
of my other afflictions. However, not long after I had heard this
melancholy news, an opportunity presented, of acquainting that humane and generous gentleman, the commander in chief, and my il-
lustrious benefactor, with this affair also, who in compassion for my
sufferings, and to mitigate my sorrows, issued his orders in good

time, and had my daughter taken away from the Indians, and conveyed to the same nunnery where her sister was then lodged, with
his express injunction, that they should both of them together, be
well looked after, and carefully educated, as his adopted children. In
this school of superstition and bigotry,[11] they continued while the
war in those days between France and Great-Britain lasted. At the
conclusion of which war, the Governor went home to France, took
my oldest daughter along with him, and married her then to a French
gentleman, whose name is Cron Lewis. He was at Boston with the
fleet under Count de Estaing,[12] [1778] and one of his Clerks. My
other daughter still continuing in the nunnery, a considerable time
had elapsed after my return from captivity, when I made a journey
to Canada, resolving to use my best endeavours not to return without
her. I arrived just in time to prevent her being sent to France. She
was to have gone in the next vessel that sailed for that place. And I
found it extremely difficult to prevail with her to quit the nunnery
and go home with me. Yea, she absolutely refused, and all the per-
suasions and arguments I could use with her, were to no effect, until
after I had been to the Governor, and obtained a letter from him to
the superintendant of the nuns, in which he threatened, if my daughter should not be immediately delivered into my hands, or could not
be prevailed with to submit to my parental authority, that he would
send a band of soldiers to assist me in bringing her away. Upon
hearing this she made no farther resistance. But so extremely bigoted
was she to the customs and religion of the place, that after all, she
left it with the greatest reluctance, and the most bitter lamentations,
which she continued as we passed the streets, and wholly refused to
be comforted. My good friend, Major Small, whom we met with on
the way, tried all he could to console her; and was so very kind and
obliging as to bear us company, and carry my daughter behind him
on horseback.

But I have run on a little before my story, for I have not yet
informed you of the means and manner of my own redemption, to
the accomplishing of which, the recovery of my daughter just mentioned, and the ransoming of some of my other children, several
gentlemen of note, contributed not a little; to whose goodness, therefore, I am greatly indebted, and sincerely hope I shall never be so
ungrateful as to forget. Col. Schuyler in particular was so very kind
and generous as to advance 2700 livres to procure a ransom for
myself and three of my children. He accompanied and conducted us

from Montreal to Albany, and entertained us in the most friendly and hospitable manner a considerable time, at his own house, and I believe entirely at his own expense.

I have spun[13] out the above narrative to a much greater length than I at first intended, and shall conclude it with referring you, for a more ample and *brilliant* account of the captive heroine, who is the subject of it, to Col. Humphrey's history of the life of Gen. Israel Putnum, together with some remarks upon a few clauses in it. I never indeed had the pleasure of perusing the whole of said history, but remember to have seen, some time ago, an extract from it in one of the Boston newspapers, in which the Colonel has extolled the beauty and good sense, and rare accomplishments of Mrs. Howe, the person whom he endeavors to paint in the most lively and engaging colours, perhaps a little too highly, and in a style, that may appear to those who are acquainted with her at this day, romantick and extravagant. And the Colonel must needs have been misinformed with respect to some particulars that he has mentioned in her story. Indeed, when I read the extract from his history to Mrs. Tute,[14] (which name she has derived from a third husband, whose widow she now remains) she seemed to be well pleased, and said, at first, it was all true, but soon after contradicted the circumstance of her lover's being so bereft of his senses when he saw her moving off in a boat at some distance from the shore, as to plunge into the water after her, in consequence of which he was seen no more. It is true, she said, that as she was returning from Montreal to Albany, she met with young Saccapee on the way, that she was in a boat with Col. Schuyler, that the French officer came on board the boat, made her some handsome presents, took his final leave of her, and departed, to outward appearance, in tolerable good humour.

She moreover says, that when she went to Canada for her daughter, she met with him again, that he showed her a lock of her hair, and her name likewise, printed with vermilion on his arm. As to her being chosen agent to go to Europe,[15] in behalf of the people of Hinsdale, when Col. Howard obtained from the government of New-York a patent of their lands on the west-side of Connecticut river, it was never once thought of by Hinsdale people until the above-mentioned extract arrived among them, in which the author has inserted it as a matter of undoubted fact.

# MARY KINNAN

Traditionally, *A True Narrative of the Sufferings of Mary Kinnan* is considered a prime example of the eighteenth-century Indian captivity narrative as an editorially embellished text, still based loosely in fact, but lacking the spirituality of the early captivities and resisting the wholesale secularism and fictionalization of the later ones. Scholars point to its excessive melodrama and stylization, for example in the description of Kinnan's dead baby and husband and in the quotations from *King Lear*, *Macbeth*, and *Hamlet*. But viewing this narrative as merely sensational is too simple; greater attention to the historical record and to the printer's role indicates a more complicated scenario.

Although the narrative's sentimentality obscures its factual information, Mary Kinnan (1763–1848) was, as she says, captured by Shawnees on May 13, 1791, from her home in Tygarts Valley, Virginia (now West Virginia). Encouraged by the British, the Shawnees launched raids on the Ohio River settlements from 1791 to 1794. Of the household of eleven, three died (including Kinnan's husband and baby daughter), seven fled (including her two sons and her brother, Jacob Lewis), and only Kinnan herself was taken. In July 1791, a Delaware woman bought Kinnan from the Shawnees to be her servant. In 1793, still hopeful for release, Kinnan told her story to an Indian trader and urged him to get word to her family in Basking Ridge, New Jersey. He recounted it to one William Hindman, who wrote a letter to Basking Ridge using the first person as if Kinnan were writing it herself. Eventually, the letter got through, and members of the village Presbyterian Church raised money for Jacob Lewis to bring his sister back. Kinnan escaped to a meeting point, where she was reunited with Lewis. They returned safely to Basking Ridge in October 1794, three and a half years after the attack, and Kinnan remained there until her death in 1848 (Stutler, pp. 39–43).

Although it is buried in the drama, a surprising amount of historical, geographical, and even military information can be obtained from *A True Narrative*. Additionally, textual information regarding Kinnan's frame of mind during her captivity provides clues that can be paralleled in the historical record. The vague emotionalism of such lines as "Spare me the pain of describing my feelings at this scene

. . . which racked my agonizing heart" and "The picture of my life was deeply, too deeply dashed with shade" seems insincere. Yet Hindman's letter, using information from the Indian trader, refers several times to Kinnan's being discouraged and depressed.

What can we tell about the narrative's authorship and the writer's rationale in overlaying the basic story with propaganda, sentimentality, and religious moralizing? First, it is worth noting that no one assigns authorship of this narrative to Mary Kinnan herself. Kinnan's niece, who knew her aunt well, stated that *A True Narrative* was written by Shepard Kollock, the man named on the title page as the printer (Voorhees, p. 154). The multitalented Kollock was a journalist, soldier, patriot, judge, and publisher of some importance: the British called him "the rebel printer." By the time he moved his printing shop to Elizabethtown, New Jersey, in 1785, most of his imprints were religious books (he was a Presbyterian), and he was always on the lookout for a profitable venture, since one talent he lacked was holding on to his money.

Thus Kollock certainly possessed the credentials to ghostwrite Kinnan's tale and cast it in the mold of his patriotism and religious beliefs while taking stylistic advantage of sentimental fiction's growing popularity. Given this information, we can reassess this propagandist comment, "O Britain! how heavy will be the weight of thy crimes at the last great day!" and this providential plea, "I breathed out a fervent prayer to heaven, and relied on the beneficence of the Father of All." Not merely empty emotional rhetoric, such statements reflect Kollock's hatred of the British and his strong religious beliefs. Since Kinnan returned to New Jersey in October 1794 and *A True Narrative* appeared in 1795, Kollock was apparently also cashing in on the currency of the returned hostage and the propagandistic use of her story in maintaining support for General Wayne's campaign.

The text is Shepard Kollock, *A True Narrative of the Sufferings of Mary Kinnan.* Elizabethtown, N.J.: Shepard Kollock, 1795.

## SUGGESTIONS FOR FURTHER READING

*BIBLIOGRAPHY*
   Vail.

*SECONDARY WORKS*
   J. R. Anderson; Derounian-Stodola and Levernier; Stutler; Voorhees.

# A True Narrative of the Sufferings of Mary Kinnan

Whilst the tear of sensibility so often flows at the unreal tale of woe, which glows under the pen of the poet and the novelist, shall our hearts refuse to be melted with sorrow at the unaffected and unvarnished tale of a female, who has surmounted difficulties and dangers, which on a review appear romantic, even to herself.

Her history will not, perhaps, be without its use. It will display the supporting arm of a Divine Providence: it will point to the best and surest support under danger and adversity: and "it will teach the repiner at little evils to be juster to his God and to himself."

It would be[1] unnecessary and tedious to describe the first part of my life, as it exhibited nothing which is not daily observed in the common walks of mankind. Suffice it to say, that, blest with the affections of the best of husbands, and the love and esteem of the most dutiful of children, my days passed sweetly on, and I had scarcely one single wish ungratified. Happiness smiled on our cottage;—content spread her influence around;—the voice of grief was not heard;—and old age crept imperceptibly on. Alas! how soon was my horizon obscured by the dark clouds of misfortune!—how doubly poignant were rendered succeeding miseries by the recollection of such exalted happiness!

The thirteenth day of May, 1791, will never be effaced from my mind. Although since that memorable period, four years have almost rolled their ample round, still at the recollection, my bosom heaves impetuous; the cold sweat of fear stands on my brow; and the burning tear of anguish glistens in my eye. Our house was situated in a beautifully romantic and agreeable place, called Tiger's Valley,[2] in Randolph County, State of Virginia. Here I would mark nature progressing, and the revolutions of the seasons; and from these would turn to contemplate the buds of virtue and of genius, sprouting in the bosoms of my children. Employed in such a pleasing occupation, on that evening, I was startled by the bursting open of the door: I turned my affrighted eyes, and leapt with terror at the sight of three armed Indians. I saw the flash of the musket!—I heard the groan of my husband! Quick as thought, I seized my youngest child: fear added wings to my flight, and I ran with the swiftness of the wind.

Alas! scarcely had I time to congratulate myself on my good fotune, before I was again caught; desperation gave me strength, and I again broke loose. I scarcely touched the ground as I coursed over the plain, when the cry of my child, supplicating me for help, arrested my ear. The yearnings of maternal affection extinguished my prudence; forgetting my imbecility,[3] I flew to assist her, and was taken. A third time I attempted to escape, but was knocked to the ground with a tomahawk; I then made signs of submission, and was carried to the house. Gracious God! what a scene presented itself to me! My child, scalped and slaughtered, smiled even then; my husband, scalped and weltering in his blood, fixed on me his dying eye, which, though languid, still expressed an apprehension for my safety, and sorrow at his inability to assist me; and accompanied the look with a groan that went through my heart. Spare me the pain of describing my feelings at this scene, this mournful scene, which racked my agonizing heart, and precipitated me to the verge of madness.

In happier times, I should have thought that my heart would cease to beat, and my pulse forget to throb under such an accumulated weight of misery. But the soul often acquires vigor from misfortune, and by adversity is led to the exertion of faculties, which till then were not possessed, or at least lay dormant. Thus it was with me; I have supported *in reality* what, *in idea,* had appeared impossible.

After plundering the house of the most valuable articles, and pinioning my arms behind me, they departed; with them I too was forced to go. Under the most favorable circumstances, this journey would have been painful: how much more so was it now, when the arrow of calamity was rankling in my bosom; when I was faint through loss of blood; and without refreshment, without rest. Nature too seemed to conspire against me: the rain descended in torrents; the lightnings flashed dreadfully, and almost without intermission; whilst the thunder rolled awfully on high. We rested not during the whole of that night,

"Wherein the cub-drawn bear would couch,
"The lion and the belly-pinched wolf
"Keep their fur dry."[4]

It was on Friday night that I was taken; on Saturday night they rested, and trimmed their scalps.[5] Ah! what did I not feel at the sight of these memorials of savage cruelty. I became indifferent to my existence; I was willing to bid adieu to that world, whence all the lovely relatives of life were borne before me; and, had I not been restrained by the spirit of Christianity, I had terminated my existence by my

own hand. I appeared, as it were, insulated to the civilized world—
nay, worse than insulated, for the poor lonely mariner, who is ship-
wrecked on some desart coast, has far greater cause to rejoice than
I then had.

The next day we continued our march over the most rugged rocks
and mountains, wet and slippery with the rain which had so lately
fallen. Nature was now so far exhausted, that I could not advance,
except in a very slow manner, when, instead of compassionating my
sufferings, my weariness and misfortunes, I was beaten severely for
not performing impossibilities. About this time they frequently
threatened me with death; though I recked not[6] his approach in genuine form, yet, I must confess, my soul shrunk from him, when thus
cloathed in vengeance, too much for man to bear.

In this manner we continued our journey, sorrow and fatigue still
making increased ravages on my constitution, when one of the Indians was bitten by a snake. We were obliged to stay nineteen days,
before he was cured and able to proceed: during this period I again
recovered spirits and health sufficient to follow my savage conduc-
tors. In this accident I beheld and blest the good providence of God,
thus eminently exerted in rescuing me from that world, "from whose
bourn no traveller returns."[7]

In a few days after this we arrived at the Ohio. Dark and rainy
was the night in which we formed a raft, and crossed the river: dangerous as was the passage, we arrived in safety at the opposite bank;
—the period of my misfortunes had not yet arrived; many bitter
calamities were yet to be felt.

After this we travelled for two days through the gloomy ridges of
pine. Although their extreme wetness subjected us to many incon-
veniencies, not to say dangers, yet the Indians were fearful of being
discovered, if they made a fire, and, of consequence, remained without one. From these we passed into a fine country, where we had
plenty of venison, and other game; nevertheless so deeply was I afflicted that I cared not for the food, which was absolutely necessary
to preserve life, and I was compelled by their threats of death, in its
most horrid form, to eat those victuals for which I had no relish.

On the 29th of June we approached the Shawanee towns; when
we arrived within about half a mile of them they fired their guns,
stripped the bark from five trees, painted themselves and me in a
most horrid manner, and commenced the scalp-whoop: never did I
hear a sound so calculated to inspire terror: my blood curdled within
me at the sound, and fear took possession of all my faculties. This

they repeated five times:[8] they then seated themselves, until a vast number of people, attracted by the well-known and pleasing sound, came from the town and shook hands with them: each person then struck me with great violence over the head and face, till I could not see, and till I finally dropt down senseless.[9] They then recovered me and assisted me to walk into the town; having previously explained to me, that all the abuse which had been so liberally bestowed upon me, was to welcome me amongst them.

During my journey, the sense of present danger blunted the remembrance of past misery, and prevented me from indulging in gloomy anticipations of future woe;—but now the whole weight of my affliction pressed heavily on my heart. The picture of my life was deeply, too deeply dashed with shade, and but a few faint strokes of light were intermingled with the numerous touches of the *sombre* pencil. But when my spirits were surcharged with sorrow's dew, I breathed out a fervent prayer to heaven, and relied on the beneficence of the Father of All. Uniformly my efforts were successful, and a calm resignation diffused itself through my frame, or the rays of hope danced sweetly round my heart.

I lived during four days with the sister of the savage who tore me from my peaceful home, and often contemplated with a sigh the depth of degradation, of which the human character is capable. On the third of July I was bought by a Delaware squaw, and by her was put to the most menial and laborious offices.

One of the principal objects of my attention, whilst I lived amongst the Indians, was the humiliating condition of their women. Here the female sex, instead of polishing and improving the rough manners of the men, are equally ferocious, cruel, and obdurate. Instead of that benevolent disposition and warm sensibility to the sufferings of others, which marks their characters in more civilized climes, they quaff with extatic pleasure the blood of the innocent prisoner, writhing with agony under the inhuman torments inflicted upon him—whilst his convulsive groans speak music to their souls.

With my new mistress I continued until the defeat of St. Clair;[10] then another scene was presented to me, which opened afresh the sluices of sorrow. The numerous scalps of my unfortunate countrymen, which were then exhibited to my view—the rejoicings which took place on that lamentable occasion—and the brutal scenes which were then transacted, sorely wounded my bosom, already pierced so deeply by misfortune's shaft.—Still my sufferings were not alleviated; fed in a very scanty manner, I was forced, nevertheless, to chop and carry wood to a considerable distance: in this occupation I had my feet frozen, and this added one more to my already long list of woes.

In the spring, for fear of my countrymen, the Indians removed from the Miami towns to Grand Glaize,[11] a most beautiful place. Here my sufferings became still more aggravated, although they had before appeared at their highest possible height. A new piece of ground was now to be cleared, and my heart grew more heavy in proportion as I was separated from my beloved country.

About this time there were prospects of peace. Hope, at all times easily enkindled, blazed forth at this prospect, and gilded my solitary footsteps: but the year passed away, and the devastations of war still continued. At this time an Indian trader engaged to convey a letter from me to my friends in New Jersey, which he did by my direction, and this was the first news they had heard of me since my captivity, and, in the end, was the means of procuring my escape.[12]

The succeeding year commissioners came from the United States to conclude a treaty: they departed, however, without attaining their object. The Indians, finding peace was not to be expected, turned out very generally for war, and left me, a prey to all the gloomy horrors of despair. In a short time they returned, bringing with them some horses and two prisoners; one of whom, Peter Tuttle, was afterwards redeemed—the other was killed by one of their chiefs.

In November the Indians began to be weary of war, and, in the beginning of January, sent in a talk to General Wayne[13] by a Robert Wilson, an Indian trader, together with three Indians. General Wayne insisted, as a preliminary article, that all the prisoners should be delivered up: accordingly they came home, and collected a great number of us, unfortunate sufferers, and prepared to set out the next day to General Wayne at Fort Jefferson. But previously to our departure, one of the British agents came to them, and persuaded them, that perfidy was a leading trait in the character of the people of the United States; that they had placed ambuscades for them; and that they would never return alive. By these and other arts, they persuaded the Indians to persevere in their warfare, and we were again dismissed to our laborious occupations.

O Britain! how heavy will be the weight of thy crimes at the last great day! Instigated by thee, the Indian murderer plunges his knife into the bosom of innocence, of piety, and of virtue; and drags thousands into a captivity, worse than death. The cries of widows, and the groans of orphans daily ascend, like a thick cloud, before the judgment-seat of heaven, and

"Plead like angels, trumpet-tongued,
"For your damnation:
"And pity, like a naked, new-born babe,
"Striding the blast, or heav'n's cherubin, hors'd
"Upon the sightless couriers of the air,
"Shall blow your horrid deeds in every eye,
"That tears shall drown the wind."[14]

I had by this time witnessed so many disappointments, that I yielded myself up entirely to despondency, and endeavored to stifle the few scattered rays of hope, which faintly twinkled, like the glimmerings of a lamp just ready to expire.—In consequence of these impressions, I fell dangerously ill of a fever, which was accompanied by an excessive pain over my whole frame. The Indians now abated, in some degree, of the rough treatment which I had before experienced: but what contributed principally to my recovery was a letter, which I received from my brother, Jacob Lewis, mentioning that he was at Detroit, but that he dared not at present come to assist me because of the antipathy which the Indians evidenced against him, on account of his being a native of the United States.[15] To know that I was not immured beyond the knowledge of my friends and relatives; that they still entertained for me a warm, impassioned affection, was a delicious cordial to my drooping spirits. In return to this letter I wrote, that as it would be in the highest degree dangerous to come to the place where I then was, I advised him still to continue at Detroit, and if it were possible by any means to ameliorate my condition, I made no doubt he would exert himself to the utmost of his power. For six months, we enjoyed the pleasure of each other's correspondence, being but one hundred and forty miles distant, and enjoying a constant communication by means of the Indian traders. In the darkest and most gloomy seasons, his letters inspired me with comfort; and whilst I traced in them with joy the sentiment of friendship, and the warmth of fraternal affection, I would for a time forget my griefs in the extacy of delight.

On the first day of August, 1793, we heard of the approach of General Wayne's army. Fearful and perturbed, they immediately started for the Rapids of the Miami; taking only those things with which they could not dispense, and hiding or burying the rest. On the tenth I had resolved to make my escape; my plan was thoroughly matured, and I waited with impatience the approach of night to put it in execution. But how frail and uncertain are the schemes of mankind! how easily are even their best projects overturned! Going out on that day to get a tent-pole, I accidentally cut my foot in a most dangerous manner; this being at the distance of eighteen miles from the Rapids and being unable to walk, I was obliged to be carried thither on a horse.

Soon after I arrived I heard from my brother who had joined a party of British traders, and was coming down to the Rapids that he might see and perhaps assist me to escape. He sent a Frenchman to me, who behaving in a manner which displeased the Indians, I requested him not to come again. He returned, and in a short time my brother came himself. As he was passing through the Indian camp I accidentally saw him: my joy was so great that I involuntarily gave a scream of pleasure:—the Indian who was with me, surprized at this singular behaviour, viewed me with an inquisitive eye; I fully comprehended the meaning of his look, and excused myself in a manner which, I believe, dissipated his apprehensions.

In order to concert some means of escape, my brother sent a friend to exchange bread for milk. After performing this errand he opened to me his real business, and appointed a tree where I might meet my brother that night. According to these directions I went, and how great was my surprize and disappointment to find nobody there. But the person who had previously appointed the tree as a place to meet, explained to me the next day the reason why we missed of each other, we having gone to different trees. The next night, however, the Indians having fallen asleep, I stole out about eleven o'clock. I found the brother of my heart anxiously expecting my arrival: after those congratulations which might be expected from two so dear to each other, who had been so long seperated, we started and ran two miles to the British camp. I then, with a beating, fearful heart, crept into a brush-heap, where I lay during all that night, and on the next day my brother came and carried me from the place where I was lodged on board a vessel, which was about to descend the Miami river, the captain of which he had interested in my behalf—having previously drest me in one of his own suits of clothes and tied an handkerchief over my eyes, in order, as much as possible, to conceal my features. When we came to the mouth of the river, we anchored in full view of the Indians, who had come to the Lake, as well to avoid General Wayne, as to receive their provision, which was given them at this place. In this situation I remained some time, fearful of being recognized and re-claimed by some of the Indians: but finally, I prevailed with the master of a batteau, who was going to Turtle Island in Lake Erie, to carry me thither with him. When we arrived there we went

on board a ship which was then lying at anchor there, bearing twelve
guns, and were strictly examined by a Commodore Grant,[16] who,
when informed of my sufferings, used his interest to have me taken
on board a brig going to Detroit. Having arrived at this last-
mentioned place, I was so overcome by the joy which I felt at my
delivery and the fatigue which attended it, that I continued unwell
and unable to proceed for eight days. At the expiration of this period,
I crossed Lake Erie and came to Niagara, where I was again examined, and having produced the pass given us by Commodore Grant,
obtained another from Simcoe[17] to the United States. We descended
in a batteau to the Genesee river, and thence travelled to New Jersey,
where I arrived amongst my friends on the eleventh day of October,
1794.

If my history has been marked with woe-worn incidents;—if I
have been in a peculiar manner the child of misfortune;—if my cup
of life has been deeply mixed with gall;—if despair has brooded over
my soul, with all its horrors;—and finally, if I have been obliged
to dismiss even dear delusive hope, having so often felt "what kind
of sickness of the heart that was, which proceeds from hope deferred:"[18]—yet, by these very woes, I have been led to place my
dependence on the beneficent dispenser of good and evil, and to with-
draw my affections from that world, where the ties by which mankind are in general so firmly bound are indissolubly broken. Since
the consequences of my affliction have been so beneficial, I repine
not at it; ye, who are pierced by the darts of misfortune, imitate
my example, and like me recline on the bosom of your Father and
your God.

MARY JEMISON

Mary Jemison's (1742/43–1833) Scottish-Irish parents came to Pennsylvania in 1742 or 1743 and settled in the western part of the state. There, on April 5, 1758, a Shawnee and French raiding party attacked the family farm. Jemison's mother, father, and three siblings died, but Mary—who was about fifteen—was captured and taken to Fort Duquesne, where she was given to two Seneca women to replace a lost family member.

As a Seneca, Jemison was called Dehgewanus, which means "Two Falling Voices" or "The Sound of Two Voices Falling." She also continued to use her British name when appropriate and gave her children British names, too, ironically following the matrilinear Seneca tradition of naming. The binary names of Mary Jemison/ Dehgewanus and of the "Two Falling Voices" rhetorically contained within "Dehgewanus" signified that while she certainly transculturated to Indian life and considered herself a Seneca, she could not completely evade her culture of origin and its continued impact on her life.

This dualism is evident, for example, in several episodes detailed in the text where the issue of her returning to white culture arose because she herself considered it, because other Indians threatened to take her back for the reward, or because her immediate Seneca family resisted her removal. In one instance, in 1763, when the Seven Years' War ended, Jemison might have been handed back with other English captives, and indeed she was taken as far as Fort Pitt. However, her Seneca sisters, who were with her, thwarted this effort by whisking her away from the fort and back to the Indian camp.

Marriage (first to the youthful Sheninjee, who died about four years after they wed, and second to the older, better established Hiokatoo, with whom she stayed for some fifty years) and then motherhood cemented Jemison's identity as a Seneca woman and made a return to white society less desirable or even viable. After the Revolution, she declined another offer to go back because she realized both she and her children would be ostracized. At the end of the narrative, Jemison reiterates her position as matriarch within Seneca culture and revalidates her decision to stay by referring to her family network of three living children (of the eight she had given birth to), thirty-nine grandchildren, and fourteen great-grand-children.

Jemison's dualism was also signified by her physical appearance, language, and cultural mannerisms. Her light brown hair, blue eyes, and Irish-accented English marked her European origins, but her behavior among whites was that of an Indian woman as seen when her editor, Seaver, points out that she would not look at him directly and when he describes in detail her Seneca dress.

Comfortable and secure in her identity among the Senecas, Jemison had no reason to deny her white birth, but her lack of knowledge about any remaining British relatives and her sense of loyalty towards any family members—whether European American or Native American—made her vulnerable to at least one con man claiming to be her cousin. This was a poor white who called himself George Jemison and whom Jemison supported for eight years, until he inveigled her into signing a document giving him ten times more land than she had agreed to. From then on, Jemison took care to check documents and conduct important affairs through a trusted white neighbor more familiar with the legal system, Thomas Clute. Thus she shrewdly used one white man, Clute, to ensure the honesty of others in the white community.

Clute accompanied Jemison when she agreed to be interviewed by James Everett Seaver, and Seaver says in his introduction that without Clute there as witness, Jemison would probably have told a good deal less. Seaver was a local doctor who had been hired by antiquarians to write a book about Jemison. To give credibility to the narrative proper, Seaver constructed an elaborate apparatus: 1) an "Author's Preface" including his observations on the nature of biography and on his methodology; 2) an "Author's Introduction," containing historical background, information on how the three-day interview with Jemison came about, and a detailed description of his impressions of the eighty-year-old Seneca woman; 3) the narrative itself, written in the first person; and 4) a lengthy appendix of other source material.

Yet while Seaver's story contains many examples of his own editorialization and interpolation, it also retains surprising instances of Jemison's textual manipulation. Indeed, according to one scholar, the narrative is marked "by preliterate Seneca traditions of self-telling that differ significantly from Western autobiographic modes" (Walsh, p. 51). Jemison preselected events or people for Seaver either to dignify and ennoble the Senecas or to discredit the whites. The *Narrative* contains, for example, an entire chapter on Ebenezer Allen, a Tory who soon proved himself also a bigamist, thief, murderer, and outlaw. Seaver may have included this chapter because he thought his readers would lap up the adventures of a rogue. But Jemison's detailed information suggests she herself aims to critique white culture as a whole through the acts of one man by using the Indian "oral tradition of the self-vindication narrative" (Walsh, p. 60).

Jemison is by no means the only transculturated captive whose story became popular. Other famous women who exchanged the white for the Native American world include Eunice Williams (A'ongote), who became a Kahnawake; Cynthia Ann Parker (Preloch), who became a Comanche; and Frances Slocum (We-let-a-wash), who became a Delaware and Miami. Yet these other transculturated women's voices do not seem to have penetrated their editorialized narratives as strongly as Jemison's, which makes her text particularly significant.

The first edition of 1824 was a best-seller, and throughout the nineteenth century especially *A Narrative of the Life of Mrs. Mary Jemison* was regularly reprinted and reedited. It continues to fascinate. The surface text concerns a white woman who chose to live with the Senecas despite continued exposure to European-American ways, and white readers have been intrigued, often for ethnocentric reasons, by that story of her dualism. Yet perhaps they have been even more captivated by the narrative's subtext—that Jemison was so thoroughly a Seneca woman that she learned to manipulate and maneuver white cultural practices in order to privilege herself and her adopted culture.

The text is that of the first edition: James Everett Seaver, *A Narrative of the Life of Mrs. Mary Jemison.* Canandaigua, N.Y.: J. D. Bemis, 1824. The appendixes have been omitted.

## SUGGESTIONS FOR FURTHER READING

*PRIMARY SOURCE*

Seaver, ed. Namias; Seaver, ed. Vail.

*SECONDARY SOURCES*

Berkhofer; Castiglia; Derounian-Stodola and Levernier; Heard, *White*; Namias; Walsh.

# A Narrative of the Life of Mrs. Mary Jemison

PREFACE

THAT to biographical writings we are indebted for the greatest and best field in which to study mankind, or human nature, is a fact duly appreciated by a well-informed community. In them we can trace the effects of mental operations to their proper sources; and by comparing our own composition with that of those who have excelled in virtue, or with that of those who have been sunk in the lowest depths of folly and vice, we are enabled to select a plan of life that will at least afford self-satisfaction, and guide us through the world in paths of morality.

Without a knowledge of the lives of the vile and abandoned, we should be wholly incompetent to set an appropriate value upon the charms, the excellence and the worth of those principles which have produced the finest traits in the character of the most virtuous.

Biography is a telescope of life, through which we can see the extremes and excesses of the varied properties of the human heart. Wisdom and folly, refinement and vulgarity, love and hatred, tenderness and cruelty, happiness and misery, piety and infidelity, commingled with every other cardinal virtue or vice, are to be seen on the variegated pages of the history of human events, and are eminently deserving the attention of those who would learn to walk in the "paths of peace."

The brazen statue and the sculptured marble, can commemorate the greatness of heroes, statesmen, philosophers, and blood-stained conquerors, who have risen to the zenith of human glory and popularity, under the influence of the mild sun of prosperity: but it is the faithful page of biography that transmits to future generations the poverty, pain, wrong, hunger, wretchedness and torment, and every nameless misery that has been endured by those who have lived in obscurity, and groped their lonely way through a long series of unpropitious events, with but little help besides the light of nature. While the gilded monument displays in brightest colors the vanity of pomp, and the emptiness of nominal greatness, the biographical page, that lives in every line, is giving lessons of fortitude in time of danger, patience in suffering, hope in distress, invention in necessity, and resignation to unavoidable evils. Here also may be learned, pity for the bereaved, benevolence for the destitute, and compassion for the helpless; and at the same time all the sympathies of the soul will be naturally excited to sigh at the unfavorable result, or to smile at the fortunate relief.

In the great inexplicable chain which forms the circle of human events, each individual link is placed on a level with the others, and performs an equal task; but, as the world is partial, it is the situation that attracts the attention of mankind, and excites the unfortunate vociferous eclat of elevation, that raises the pampered parasite to such an immense height in the scale of personal vanity, as, generally, to deprive him of respect, before he can return to a state of equilibrium with his fellows, or to the place whence he started.

Few great men have passed from the stage of action, who have not left in the history of their lives indelible marks of ambition or folly, which produced insurmountable reverses, and rendered the whole a mere caricature, that can be examined only with disgust and regret. Such pictures, however, are profitable, for "by others' faults wise men correct their own."

The following is a piece of biography, that shows what changes may be effected in the animal and mental constitution of man; what trials may be surmounted; what cruelties perpetrated, and what pain endured, when stern necessity holds the reins, and drives the car of fate.

As books of this kind are sought and read with avidity, especially by children, and are well calculated to excite their attention, inform their understanding, and improve them in the art of reading, the greatest care has been observed to render the style easy, the language comprehensive, and the description natural. Prolixity has been studiously avoided. The line of distinction between virtue and vice has been rendered distinctly visible; and chastity of expression and sentiment have received due attention. Strict fidelity has been observed in the composition: consequently, no circumstance has been intentionally exaggerated by the paintings of fancy, nor by fine flashes of rhetoric: neither has the picture been rendered more dull than the original. Without the aid of fiction, what was received as matter of fact, only has been recorded.

It will be observed that the subject of this narrative has arrived at least to the advanced age of eighty years; that she is destitute of education; and that her journey of life, throughout its texture, has been interwoven with troubles, which ordinarily are calculated to impair the faculties of the mind; and it will be remembered, that there are but few old people who can recollect with precision the circumstances of their lives, (particularly those circumstances which transpired after middle age.) If, therefore, any error shall be discovered in the narration in respect to time, it will be overlooked by the kind reader, or charitably placed to the narrator's account, and not imputed to neglect, or to the want of attention in the compiler.

The appendix is principally taken from the words of Mrs. Jemison's statements. Those parts which were not derived from her, are deserving equal credit, having been obtained from authentic sources.

For the accommodation of the reader, the work has been divided into chapters, and a copious table of contents affixed. The introduction will facilitate the understanding of what follows; and as it contains matter that could not be inserted with propriety in any other place, will be read with interest and satisfaction.

Having finished my undertaking, the subsequent pages are cheerfully submitted to the perusal and approbation or animadversion of a candid, generous and indulgent public. At the same time it is fondly hoped that the lessons of distress that are pourtrayed, may have a direct tendency to increase our love of liberty; to enlarge our views of the blessings that are derived from our liberal institutions; and to excite in our breasts sentiments of devotion and gratitude to the great Author and finisher of our happiness.

THE AUTHOR.
*Pembroke, March* 1, 1824.

# Introduction

THE Peace of 1783,[1] and the consequent cessation of Indian hostilities and barbarities, returned to their friends those prisoners, who had escaped the tomahawk, the gauntlet, and the savage fire, after their having spent many years in captivity, and restored harmony to society.

The stories of Indian cruelties which were common in the new settlements, and were calamitous realities previous to that propitious event; slumbered in the minds that had been constantly agitated by them, and were only roused occasionally, to become the fearful topic of the fireside.

It is presumed that at this time there are but few native Americans that have arrived to middle age, who cannot distinctly recollect of sitting in the chimney corner when children, all contracted with fear, and there listening to their parents or visitors, while they related stories of Indian conquests, and murders, that would make their flaxen hair nearly stand erect, and almost destroy the power of motion.

At the close of the Revolutionary war; all that part of the State of New-York that lies west of Utica was uninhabited by white people, and few indeed had ever passed beyond Fort Stanwix, except when engaged in war against the Indians, who were numerous, and occupied a number of large towns between the Mohawk river and lake Erie. Sometime elapsed after this event, before the country about the lakes and on the Genesee river was visited, save by an occasional land speculator, or by defaulters who wished by retreating to what in those days was deemed almost the end of the earth, to escape the force of civil law.

At length, the richness and fertility of the soil excited emigration, and here and there a family settled down and commenced improvements in the country which had recently been the property of the aborigines. Those who settled near the Genesee river, soon became acquainted with "The White Woman," as Mrs. Jemison is called, whose history they anxiously sought, both as a matter of interest and curiosity. Frankness characterized her conduct, and without reserve she would readily gratify them by relating some of the most important periods of her life.

Although her bosom companion was an ancient Indian warrior, and notwithstanding her children and associates were all Indians, yet it was found that she possessed an uncommon share of hospitality, and that her friendship was well worth courting and preserving. Her house was the stranger's home; from her table the hungry were refreshed;—she made the naked as comfortable as her means would admit of; and in all her actions, discovered so much natural goodness of heart, that her admirers increased in proportion to the extension of her acquaintance, and she became celebrated as the friend of the distressed. She was the protectress of the homeless fugitive, and made welcome the weary wanderer. Many still live to commemorate her benevolence towards them, when prisoners during the war, and to ascribe their deliverance to the mediation of "The White Woman."

The settlements increased, and the whole country around her was inhabited by a rich and respectable people, principally from New-England, as much distinguished for their spirit of inquisitiveness as for their habits of industry and honesty, who had all heard from one source and another a part of her life in detached pieces, and had obtained an idea that the whole taken in connection would afford instruction and amusement.

Many gentlemen of respectability, felt anxious that her narrative might be laid before the public, with a view not only to perpetuate the remembrance of the atrocities of the savages in former times, but to preserve some historical facts which they supposed to be intimately connected with her life, and which otherwise must be lost.

Forty years had passed since the close of the Revolutionary war, and almost seventy years had seen Mrs. Jemison with the Indians, when Daniel W. Banister, Esq. at the instance of several gentlemen, and prompted by his own ambition to add something to the accumulating fund of useful knowledge, resolved, in the autumn of 1823, to embrace that time, while she was capable of recollecting and reciting the scenes through which she had passed, to collect from herself, and to publish to the world, an accurate account of her life.

I was employed to collect the materials, and prepare the work for the press; and accordingly went to the house of Mrs. Jennet Whaley in the town of Castile, Genesee co. N. Y. in company with the publisher, who procured the interesting subject of the following narrative, to come to that place (a distance of four miles) and there repeat the story of her eventful life. She came on foot in company with Mr. Thomas Clute,[2] whom she considers her protector, and tarried almost three days, which time was busily occupied in taking a sketch of her narrative as she recited it.

Her appearance was well calculated to excite a great degree of sympathy in a stranger, who had been partially informed of her origin, when comparing her present situation with what it probably would have been, had she been permitted to have remained with her friends, and to have enjoyed the blessings of civilization.

In stature she is very short, and considerably under the middle size, and stands tolerably erect, with her head bent forward, apparently from her having for a long time been accustomed to carrying heavy burdens in a strap placed across her forehead. Her complexion is very white for a woman of her age, and although the wrinkles of fourscore years are deeply indented in her cheeks, yet the crimson of youth is distinctly visible. Her eyes are light blue, a little faded by age, and naturally brilliant and sparkling. Her sight is quite dim, though she is able to perform her necessary labor without the assistance of glasses. Her cheek bones are high, and rather prominent, and her front teeth, in the lower jaw, are sound and good. When she looks up and is engaged in conversation her countenance is very expressive; but from her long residence with the Indians, she has acquired the habit of peeping from under eye-brows as they do with the head inclined downwards. Formerly her hair was of a light chestnut brown—it is now quite grey, a little curled, of middling length and tied in a bunch behind. She informed me that she had never worn a cap nor a comb.

She speaks English plainly and distinctly, with a little of the Irish emphasis, and has the use of words so well as to render herself intelligible on any subject with which she is acquainted. Her recollection and memory exceeded my expectation. It cannot be reasonably supposed, that a person of her age has kept the events of seventy years in so complete a chain as to be able to assign to each its proper time and place; she, however, made her recital with as few obvious mistakes as might be found in that of a person of fifty.

She walks with a quick step without a staff, and I was informed by Mr. Clute, that she could yet cross a stream on a log or pole as steadily as any other person.

Her passions are easily excited. At a number of periods in her narration, tears trickled down her grief worn cheek, and at the same time a rising sigh would stop her utterance.

Industry is a virtue which she has uniformly practised from the day of her adoption to the present. She pounds her samp, cooks for herself, gathers and chops wood, feeds her cattle and poultry, and performs other laborious services. Last season she planted, tended and gathered corn—in short, she is always busy.

Her dress at the time I saw her, was made and worn after the Indian fashion, and consisted of a shirt, short gown, petticoat, stockings, moccasins, a blanket and a bonnet. The shirt was of cotton and made at the top, as I was informed, like a man's without collar or sleeves—was open before and extended down about midway of the hips.—The petticoat was a piece of broadcloth with the list at the top and bottom and the ends sewed together. This was tied on by a string that was passed over it and around the waist, in such a manner as to let the bottom of the petticoat down half way between the knee and ankle and leave one-fourth of a yard at the top to be turned down over the string—the bottom of the shirt coming a little below, and on the outside of the top of the fold so as to leave the list and two or three inches of the cloth uncovered. The stockings, were of blue broadcloth, tied, or pinned on, which reached from the knees, into the mouth of the moccasins.—Around her toes only she had some rags, and over these her buckskin moccasins. Her gown was of undressed flannel, colored brown. It was made in old yankee style, with long sleeves, covered the top of the hips, and was tied before in two places with strings of deer skin. Over all this, she wore an Indian blanket. On her head she wore a piece of old brown woollen cloth made somewhat like a sun bonnet.

Such was the dress that this woman was contented to wear, and habit had rendered it convenient and comfortable. She wore it not as a matter of necessity, but from choice, for it will be seen in the sequel, that her property is sufficient to enable her to dress in the best fashion, and to allow her every comfort of life.

Her house, in which she lives, is 20 by 28 feet; built of square timber, with a shingled roof, and a framed stoop. In the centre of the house is a chimney of stones and sticks, in which there are two fire places. She has a good framed barn, 26 by 36, well filled, and owns a fine stock of cattle and horses. Besides the buildings above mentioned, she owns a number of houses that are occupied by tenants, who work her flats upon shares.

Her dwelling, is about one hundred rods[3] north of the Great Slide, a curiosity that will be described in its proper place, on the west side of the Genesee river.

Mrs. Jemison, appeared sensible of her ignorance of the manners of the white people, and for that reason, was not familiar, except with those with whom she was intimately acquainted. In fact she was (to appearance) so jealous of her rights, or that she should say something that would be injurious to herself or family, that if Mr. Clute had not been present, we should have been unable to have obtained her history. She, however, soon became free and unembarrassed in her conversation, and spoke with a degree of mildness, candor and simplicity, that is calculated to remove all doubts as to the veracity of the speaker. The vices of the Indians, she appeared disposed not to aggravate, and seemed to take pride in extoling their virtues. A kind of family pride inclined her to withhold whatever would blot the character of her descendants, and perhaps induced her to keep back many things that would have been interesting.

For the life of her last husband, we are indebted to her cousin, Mr. George Jemison,[4] to whom she referred us for information on that subject generally. The thoughts of his deeds, probably chilled her old heart, and made her dread to rehearse them, and at the same time she well knew they were no secret, for she had frequently heard him relate the whole, not only to her cousin, but to others.

Before she left us she was very sociable, and she resumed her naturally pleasant countenance, enlivened with a smile.

Her neighbors speak of her as possessing one of the happiest tempers and dispositions, and give her the name of never having done a censurable act to their knowledge.

Her habits, are those of the Indians—she sleeps on skins without a bedstead, sits upon the floor or on a bench, and holds her victuals on her lap, or in her hands.

Her ideas of religion, correspond in every respect with those of the great mass of the Senecas. She applauds virtue, and despises vice. She believes in a future state, in which the good will be happy, and the bad miserable; and that the acquisition of that happiness, depends primarily upon human volition, and the consequent good deeds of the happy recipient of blessedness. The doctrines taught in the Christian religion, she is a stranger to.

Her daughters are said to be active and enterprizing women, and her grandsons, who arrived to manhood, are considered able, decent and respectable men in their tribe.

Having in this cursory manner, introduced the subject of the following pages, I proceed to the narration of a life that has been viewed with attention, for a great number of years by a few, and which will be read by the public with the mixed sensations of pleasure and pain, and with interest, anxiety and satisfaction.

# Life of Mary Jemison

## CHAPTER I

*Nativity of her Parents.—Their removal to America.—Her Birth.—Parents settle in Pennsylvania.—Omen of her Captivity.*

ALTHOUGH I may have frequently heard the history of my ancestry, my recollection is too imperfect to enable me to trace it further back than to my father and mother, whom I have often heard mention the families from whence they originated, as having possessed wealth and honorable stations under the government of the country in which they resided.

On the account of the great length of time that has elapsed since I was separated from my parents and friends, and having heard the story of their nativity only in the days of my childhood, I am not able to state positively, which of the two countries, Ireland or Scotland, was the land of my parents' birth and education. It, however, is my impression, that they were born and brought up in Ireland.

My Father's name was Thomas Jemison, and my mother's, before her marriage with him, was Jane Erwin. Their affection for each other was mutual, and of that happy kind which tends directly to sweeten the cup of life; to render connubial sorrows lighter; to assuage every discontentment; and to promote not only their own comfort, but that of all who come within the circle of their acquaintance. Of their happiness I recollect to have heard them speak; and the remembrance I yet retain of their mildness and perfect agreement in the government of their children, together with their mutual attention to our common education, manners, religious instruction and wants, renders it a fact in my mind, that they were ornaments to the married state, and examples of connubial love, worthy of imitation. After my remembrance, they were strict observers of religious duties; for it was the daily practice of my father, morning and evening, to attend, in his family, to the worship of God.

Resolved to leave the land of their nativity, they removed from their residence to a port in Ireland, where they lived but a short time before they set sail for this country, in the year 1742 or 3, on board the ship Mary William, bound to Philadelphia, in the state of Pennsylvania.

The intestine divisions, civil wars, and ecclesiastical rigidity and domination that prevailed in those days, were the causes of their leaving their mother country, to find a home in the American wilderness, under the mild and temperate government of the descendants of William Penn;[5] where, without fear, they might worship God, and perform their usual avocations.

In Europe my parents had two sons and one daughter, whose names were John, Thomas and Betsey; with whom, after having put their effects on board, they embarked, leaving a large connexion of relatives and friends, under all those painful sensations, which are only felt when kindred souls give the parting hand and last farewell to those to whom they are endeared by every friendly tie.

In the course of their voyage I was born, to be the sport of fortune and almost an outcast to civil society; to stem the current of adversity through a long chain of vicissitudes, unsupported by the advice of tender parents, or the hand of an affectionate friend; and even without the enjoyment, from others, of any of those tender sympathies that are adapted to the sweetening of society, except such as naturally flow from uncultivated minds, that have been calloused by ferocity.

Excepting my birth, nothing remarkable occurred to my parents on their passage, and they were safely landed at Philadelphia. My father being fond of rural life, and having been bred to agricultural pursuits, soon left the city, and removed his family to the then frontier settlements of Pennsylvania, to a tract of excellent land lying on Marsh creek. At that place he cleared a large farm, and for seven or eight years enjoyed the fruits of his industry. Peace attended their labors; and they had nothing to alarm them, save the midnight howl of the prowling wolf, or the terrifying shriek of the ferocious panther, as they occasionally visited their improvements, to take a lamb or a calf to satisfy their hunger.

During this period my mother had two sons, between whose ages there was a difference of about three years: the oldest was named Matthew, and the other Robert.

Health presided on every countenance, and vigor and strength characterized every exertion. Our mansion was a little paradise. The morning of my childish, happy days, will ever stand fresh in my remembrance, notwithstanding the many severe trials through which I have passed, in arriving at my present situation, at so advanced an age. Even at this remote period, the recollection of my pleasant home at my father's, of my parents, of my brothers and sister, and of the manner in which I was deprived of them all at once, affects me so powerfully, that I am almost overwhelmed with grief, that is seemingly insupportable. Frequently I dream of those happy days: but, alas! they are gone: they have left me to be carried through a long life, dependent for the little pleasures of nearly seventy years, upon the tender mercies of the Indians! In the spring of 1752, and through the succeeding seasons, the stories of Indian barbarities inflicted upon the whites in those days, frequently excited in my parents the most serious alarm for our safety.

The next year the storm gathered faster; many murders were committed; and many captives were exposed to meet death in its most frightful form, by having their bodies stuck full of pine splinters, which were immediately set on fire, while their tormentors, exulting in their distress, would rejoice at their agony!

In 1754, an army for the protection of the settlers, and to drive back the French and Indians, was raised from the militia of the colonial governments, and placed (secondarily) under the command of Col. George Washington. In that army I had an uncle, whose name was John Jemison, who was killed at the battle at the Great Meadows, or Fort Necessity. His wife had died some time before this, and left a young child, which my mother nursed in the most tender manner, till its mother's sister took it away, a few months after my uncle's death. The French and Indians, after the surrender of Fort Necessity by Col. Washington, (which happened the same season, and soon after his victory over them at that place,) grew more and more terrible. The death of the whites, and plundering and burning their property, was apparently their only object: But as yet we had not heard the death-yell, nor seen the smoke of a dwelling that had been lit by an Indian's hand.

The return of a new-year's day found us unmolested; and though we knew that the enemy was at no great distance from us, my father concluded that he would continue to occupy his land another season: expecting (probably from the great exertions which the government was then making) that as soon as the troops could commence their operations in the spring, the enemy would be conquered and compelled to agree to a treaty of peace.

In the preceding autumn my father either moved to another part of his farm, or to another neighborhood, a short distance from our former abode. I well recollect moving, and that the barn that was on the place we moved to was built of logs, though the house was a good one.

The winter of 1754–5 was as mild as a common fall season, and the spring presented a pleasant seed time, and indicated a plenteous harvest. My father, with the assistance of his oldest sons, repaired his farm as usual, and was daily preparing the soil for the reception of the seed. His cattle and sheep were numerous, and according to the best idea of wealth that I can now form, he was wealthy.

But alas! how transitory are all human affairs! how fleeting are riches! how brittle the invisible thread on which all earthly comforts are suspended! Peace in a moment can take an immeasurable flight; health can lose its rosy cheeks; and life will vanish like a vapor at the appearance of the sun! In one fatal day our prospects were all blasted; and death, by cruel hands, inflicted upon almost the whole of the family.

On a pleasant day in the spring of 1755,[6] when my father was sowing flax-seed, and my brothers driving the teams, I was sent to a neighbor's house, a distance of perhaps a mile, to procure a horse and return with it the next morning. I went as I was directed. I was out of the house in the beginning of the evening, and saw a sheet wide spread approaching towards me, in which I was caught (as I have ever since believed) and deprived of my senses! The family soon found me on the ground, almost lifeless, (as they said,) took me in, and made use of every remedy in their power for my recovery, but without effect till day-break, when my senses returned, and I soon found myself in good health, so that I went home with the horse very early in the morning.

The appearance of that sheet, I have ever considered as a forerunner of the melancholy catastrophe that so soon afterwards happened to our family: and my being caught in it, I believe, was ominous of my preservation from death at the time we were captured.

CHAPTER II

*Her Education.—Captivity.—Journey to Fort Pitt.—Mother's Farewell Address.—Murder of her Family.—Preparation of the Scalps.—Indian Precautions.—Arrival at Fort Pitt, &c.*

MY education had received as much attention from my parents, as their situation in a new country would admit of. I had been at school some, where I learned to read in a book that was about half as large as a Bible; and in the Bible I had read a little. I had also learned the Catechism, which I used frequently to repeat to my parents, and every night, before I went to bed, I was obliged to stand up before my mother and repeat some words that I suppose was a prayer.

My reading, Catechism and prayers, I have long since forgotten; though for a number of the first years that I lived with the Indians, I repeated the prayers as often as I had an opportunity. After the revolutionary war, I remembered the names of some of the letters when I saw them; but have never read a word since I was taken prisoner. It is but a few years since a Missionary kindly gave me a Bible, which I am very fond of hearing my neighbors read to me, and should be pleased to learn to read it myself; but my sight has been for a number of years, so dim that I have not been able to distinguish one letter from another.

As I before observed, I got home with the horse very early in the morning, where I found a man that lived in our neighborhood, and his sister-in-law who had three children, one son and two daughters. I soon learned that they had come there to live a short time; but for what purpose I cannot say. The woman's husband, however, was at that time in Washington's army, fighting for his country; and as her brother-in-law had a house she had lived with him in his absence. Their names I have forgotten.

Immediately after I got home, the man took the horse to go to his house after a bag of grain, and took his gun in his hand for the purpose of killing game, if he should chance to see any.—Our family, as usual, was busily employed about their common business. Father was shaving an axe-helve at the side of the house; mother was making preparations for breakfast;—my two oldest brothers were at work near the barn; and the little ones, with myself, and the woman and her three children, were in the house.

Breakfast was not yet ready, when we were alarmed by the discharge of a number of guns, that seemed to be near. Mother and the women before mentioned, almost fainted at the report, and every one trembled with fear. On opening the door, the man and horse lay dead near the house, having just been shot by the Indians.

I was afterwards informed, that the Indians discovered him at his own house with his gun, and pursued him to father's, where they shot him as I have related. They first secured my father, and then rushed into the house, and without the least resistance made prisoners of my mother, Robert, Matthew, Betsey, the woman and her three children, and myself, and then commenced plundering.

My two brothers, Thomas and John, being at the barn, escaped and went to Virginia, where my grandfather Erwin then lived, as I was informed by a Mr. Fields, who was at my house about the close of the revolutionary war.

The party that took us consisted of six Indians and four Frenchmen, who immediately commenced plundering, as I just observed, and took what they considered most valuable; consisting principally of bread, meal and meat. Having taken as much provision as they could carry, they set out with their prisoners in great haste, for fear of detection, and soon entered the woods. On our march that day, an Indian went behind us with a whip, with which he frequently lashed the children to make them keep up. In this manner we travelled till dark without a mouthful of food or a drop of water; although we had not eaten since the night before. Whenever the little children cried for water, the Indians would make them drink urine or go thirsty. At night they encamped in the woods without fire and without shelter, where we were watched with the greatest vigilance. Extremely fatigued, and very hungry, we were compelled to lie upon the ground supperless and without a drop of water to satisfy the cravings of our appetites. As in the day time, so the little ones were made to drink urine in the night if they cried for water. Fatigue alone brought us a little sleep for the refreshment of our weary limbs; and at the dawn of day we were again started on our march in the same order that we had proceeded on the day before. About sunrise we were halted, and the Indians gave us a full breakfast of provision that they had brought from my father's house. Each of us being very hungry, partook of this bounty of the Indians, except father, who was so much overcome with his situation—so much exhausted by anxiety and grief, that silent despair seemed fastened upon his countenance, and he could not be prevailed upon to refresh his sinking nature by the use of a morsel of food. Our repast being finished, we again resumed our march, and before noon passed a small fort that I heard my father say was called Fort Canagojigge.

That was the only time that I heard him speak from the time we were taken till we were finally separated the following night.

Towards evening we arrived at the border of a dark and dismal swamp, which was covered with small hemlocks, or some other evergreen, and other bushes, into which we were conducted; and having gone a short distance we stopped to encamp for the night.

Here we had some bread and meat for supper: but the dreariness of our situation, together with the uncertainty under which we all labored, as to our future destiny, almost deprived us of the sense of hunger, and destroyed our relish for food.

Mother, from the time we were taken, had manifested a great degree of fortitude, and encouraged us to support our troubles without complaining; and by her conversation seemed to make the distance and time shorter, and the way more smooth. But father lost all his ambition in the beginning of our trouble, and continued apparently lost to every care—absorbed in melancholy. Here, as before, she insisted on the necessity of our eating; and we obeyed her, but it was done with heavy hearts.

As soon as I had finished my supper, an Indian took off my shoes and stockings and put a pair of moccasins on my feet, which my mother observed; and believing that they would spare my life, even if they should destroy the other captives, addressed me as near as I can remember in the following words:—

"My dear little Mary, I fear that the time has arrived when we must be parted forever Your life, my child, I think will be spared; but we shall probably be tomahawked here in this lonesome place by the Indians. O! how can I part with you my darling? What will become of my sweet little Mary? Oh! how can I think of your being continued in captivity without a hope of your being rescued? O that death had snatched you from my embraces in your infancy; the pain of parting then would have been pleasing to what it now is; and I should have seen the end of your troubles!—Alas, my dear! my heart bleeds at the thoughts of what awaits you; but, if you leave us, remember my child your own name, and the name of your father and mother. Be careful and not forget your English tongue. If you shall have an opportunity to get away from the Indians, don't try to escape; for if you do they will find and destroy you. Don't forget, my little daughter, the prayers that I have learned you—say them often; be a good child, and God will bless you. May God bless you my child, and make you comfortable and happy."

During this time, the Indians stripped the shoes and stockings from the little boy that belonged to the woman who was taken with us, and put moccasins on his feet, as they had done before on mine. I was crying. An Indian took the little boy and myself by the hand, to lead us off from the company, when my mother exclaimed, "Don't cry Mary—don't cry my child. God will bless you! Farewell—farewell!"

The Indian led us some distance into the bushes, or woods, and there lay down with us to spend the night. The recollection of parting with my tender mother kept me awake, while the tears constantly flowed from my eyes. A number of times in the night the little boy begged of me earnestly to run away with him and get clear of the Indians; but remembering the advice I had so lately received, and knowing the dangers to which we should be exposed, in travelling without a path and without a guide, through a wilderness unknown to us, I told him that I would not go, and persuaded him to lie still till morning.

Early the next morning the Indians and Frenchmen that we had left the night before, came to us; but our friends were left behind. It is impossible for any one to form a correct idea of what my feelings were at the sight of those savages, whom I supposed had murdered my parents and brothers, sister, and friends, and left them in the swamp to be devoured by wild beasts! But what could I do? A poor little defenceless girl; without the power or means of escaping; without a home to go to, even if I could be liberated; without a knowledge of the direction or distance to my former place of residence; and without a living friend to whom to fly for protection, I felt a kind of horror, anxiety, and dread, that, to me, seemed insupportable. I durst not cry—I durst not complain; and to inquire of them the fate of my friends (even if I could have mustered resolution) was beyond my ability, as I could not speak their language, nor they understand mine. My only relief was in silent stifled sobs.

My suspicions as to the fate of my parents proved too true; for soon after I left them they were killed and scalped, together with Robert, Matthew, Betsey, and the woman and her two children, and mangled in the most shocking manner.

Having given the little boy and myself some bread and meat for breakfast, they led us on as fast as we could travel, and one of them went behind and with a long staff, picked up all the grass and weeds that we trailed down by going over them. By taking that precaution they avoided detection; for each weed was so nicely placed in its natural position that no one would have suspected that we had passed that way. It is the custom of Indians when scouting, or on private expeditions, to step carefully and where no impression of their feet can be left—shunning wet or muddy ground. They seldom take hold of a bush or limb, and never break one; and by observing those precautions and that of setting up the weeds and grass which they necessarily lop, they completely elude the sagacity of their pursuers, and escape that punishment which they are conscious they merit from the hand of justice.

After a hard day's march we encamped in a thicket, where the Indians made a shelter of boughs, and then built a good fire to warm and dry our benumbed limbs and clothing; for it had rained some through the day. Here we were again fed as before. When the Indians had finished their supper they took from their baggage a number of scalps and went about preparing them for the market, or to keep without spoiling, by straining them over small hoops which they prepared for that purpose, and then drying and scraping them by the fire. Having put the scalps, yet wet and bloody, upon the hoops, and stretched them to their full extent, they held them to the fire till they were partly dried and then with their knives commenced scraping off the flesh; and in that way they continued to work, alternately drying and scraping them, till they were dry and clean. That being done they combed the hair in the neatest manner, and then painted it and the edges of the scalps yet on the hoops, red. Those scalps I knew at the time must have been taken from our family by the color of the hair. My mother's hair was red; and I could easily distinguish my father's and the children's from each other. That sight was most appalling; yet, I was obliged to endure it without complaining.

In the course of the night they made me to understand that they should not have killed the family if the whites had not pursued them.

Mr. Fields, whom I have before mentioned, informed me that at the time we were taken, he lived in the vicinity of my father; and that on hearing of our captivity, the whole neighborhood turned out in pursuit of the enemy, and to deliver us if possible: but that their efforts were unavailing. They however pursued us to the dark swamp, where they found my father, his family and companions, stripped and mangled in the most inhuman manner: That from thence the march of the cruel monsters could not be traced in any direction; and that they returned to their homes with the melancholy tidings of our misfortunes, supposing that we had all shared in the massacre.

The next morning we went on; the Indian going behind us and setting up the weeds as on the day before. At night we encamped on the ground in the open air, without a shelter or fire.

In the morning we again set out early, and travelled as on the two former days, though the weather was extremely uncomfortable, from the continual falling of rain and snow.

At night the snow fell fast, and the Indians built a shelter of boughs, and a fire, where we rested tolerably dry through that and the two succeeding nights.

When we stopped, and before the fire was kindled, I was so much fatigued from running, and so far benumbed by the wet and cold, that I expected that I must fail and die before I could get warm and comfortable. The fire, however, soon restored the circulation, and after I had taken my supper I felt so that I rested well through the night.

On account of the storm, we were two days at that place. On one of those days, a party consisting of six Indians who had been to the frontier settlements, came to where we were, and brought with them one prisoner, a young white man who was very tired and dejected. His name I have forgotten.

Misery certainly loves company. I was extremely glad to see him, though I knew from his appearance, that his situation was as deplorable as mine, and that he could afford me no kind of assistance. In the afternoon the Indians killed a deer, which they dressed, and then roasted it whole; which made them a full meal. We were each allowed a share of their venison, and some bread, so that we made a good meal also.

Having spent three nights and two days at that place, and the storm having ceased, early in the morning the whole company, consisting of twelve Indians, four Frenchmen, the young man, the little boy and myself, moved on at a moderate pace without an Indian behind us to deceive our pursuers.

In the afternoon we came in sight of Fort Pitt (as it is now called,) where we were halted while the Indians performed some customs upon their prisoners which they deemed necessary. That fort was then occupied by the French and Indians, and was called Fort Du Quesne. It stood at the junction of the Monongahela, which is said to signify, in some of the Indian languages, the Falling-in-Banks,* and the Alleghany† rivers, where the Ohio river begins to take its name. The word O-hi-o, signifies bloody.

At the place where we halted, the Indians combed the hair of the

---

*Navigator.

†The word Alleghenny, was derived from an ancient race of Indians called "Tallegnwe." The Delaware Indians, instead of saying "Alleghenny," say "Allegawe," or "Allegawenink."

Western Tour—p. 455.

young man, the boy and myself, and then painted our faces and hair red, in the finest Indian style. We were then conducted into the fort, where we received a little bread, and were then shut up and left to tarry alone through the night.

## CHAPTER III

*She is given to two Squaws.—Her Journey down the Ohio.—Passes a Shawanee town where white men had just been burnt.—Arrives at the Seneca town.—Her Reception.—She is adopted.—Ceremony of Adoption.—Indian Custom.—Address.—She receives a new name.—Her Employment.—Retains her own and learns the Seneca Language.—Situation of the Town, &c.—Indians go on a Hunting Tour to Sciota and take her with them.—Returns.—She is taken to Fort Pitt, and then hurried back by her Indian Sisters.—Her hopes of Liberty destroyed.—Second Tour to Sciota.—Return to Wiishto, &c. —Arrival of Prisoners.—Priscilla Ramsay.—Her Chain.—Mary marries a Delaware.—Her Affection for him.—Birth and Death of her first Child.—Her Sickness and Recovery.—Birth of Thomas Jemison.*

THE night was spent in gloomy forebodings. What the result of our captivity would be, it was out of our power to determine or even imagine.—At times we could almost realize the approach of our masters to butcher and scalp us;—again we could nearly see the pile of wood kindled on which we were to be roasted; and then we would imagine ourselves at liberty: alone and defenceless in the forest, surrounded by wild beasts that were ready to devour us. The anxiety of our minds drove sleep from our eyelids; and it was with a dreadful hope and painful impatience that we waited for the morning to determine our fate.

The morning at length arrived, and our masters came early and let us out of the house, and gave the young man and boy to the French, who immediately took them away. Their fate I never learned; as I have not seen nor heard of them since.

I was now left alone in the fort, deprived of my former companions, and of every thing that was near or dear to me but life. But it was not long before I was in some measure relieved by the appearance of two pleasant looking squaws of the Seneca tribe, who came and examined me attentively for a short time, and then went out. After a few minutes absence they returned with my former masters, who gave me to them to dispose of as they pleased.

The Indians by whom I was taken were a party of Shawanees, if I remember right, that lived, when at home, a long distance down the Ohio.

My former Indian masters, and the two squaws, were soon ready to leave the fort, and accordingly embarked; the Indians in a large canoe, and the two squaws and myself in a small one, and went down the Ohio.

When we set off, an Indian in the forward canoe took the scalps of my former friends, strung them on a pole that he placed upon his shoulder, and in that manner carried them, standing in the stern of the canoe, directly before us as we sailed down the river, to the town where the two squaws resided.

On our way we passed a Shawanee town, where I saw a number of heads, arms, legs, and other fragments of the bodies of some white people who had just been burnt. The parts that remained were hanging on a pole which was supported at each end by a crotch stuck in the ground, and were roasted or burnt black as a coal. The fire was yet burning; and the whole appearances afforded a spectacle so shocking, that, even to this day, my blood almost curdles in my veins when I think of them!

At night we arrived at a small Seneca Indian town, at the mouth of a small river, that was called by the Indians, in the Seneca language, She-nan-jee,* where the two Squaws to whom I belonged resided. There we landed, and the Indians went on; which was the last I ever saw of them.

Having made fast to the shore, the Squaws left me in the canoe while they went to their wigwam or house in the town, and returned with a suit of Indian clothing, all new, and very clean and nice. My clothes, though whole and good when I was taken, were now torn in pieces, so that I was almost naked. They first undressed me and

---

*That town, according to the geographical description given by Mrs. Jemison, must have stood at the mouth of Indian Cross creek, which is about 76 miles by water, below Pittsburgh; or at the mouth of Indian Short creek, 87 miles below Pittsburgh, where the town of Warren now stands: But at which of those places I am unable to determine.

Author.

threw my rags into the river; then washed me clean and dressed me in the new suit they had just brought, in complete Indian style; and then led me home and seated me in the center of their wigwam.

I had been in that situation but a few minutes, before all the Squaws in the town came in to see me. I was soon surrounded by them, and they immediately set up a most dismal howling, crying bitterly, and wringing their hands in all the agonies of grief for a deceased relative.

Their tears flowed freely, and they exhibited all the signs of real mourning. At the commencement of this scene, one of their number began, in a voice somewhat between speaking and singing, to recite some words to the following purport, and continued the recitation till the ceremony was ended; the company at the same time varying the appearance of their countenances, gestures and tone of voice, so as to correspond with the sentiments expressed by their leader:

"Oh our brother! Alas! He is dead—he has gone; he will never return! Friendless he died on the field of the slain, where his bones are yet lying unburied! Oh, who will not mourn his sad fate? No tears dropped around him; oh, no! No tears of his sisters were there! He fell in his prime, when his arm was most needed to keep us from danger! Alas! he has gone! and left us in sorrow, his loss to bewail: Oh where is his spirit? His spirit went naked, and hungry it wanders, and thirsty and wounded it groans to return! Oh helpless and wretched, our brother has gone! No blanket nor food to nourish and warm him; nor candles to light him, nor weapons of war:—Oh, none of those comforts had he! But well we remember his deeds!—The deer he could take on the chase! The panther shrunk back at the sight of his strength! His enemies fell at his feet! He was brave and courageous in war! As the fawn he was harmless: his friendship was ardent: his temper was gentle: his pity was great! Oh! our friend, our companion is dead! Our brother, our brother, alas! he is gone! But why do we grieve for his loss? In the strength of a warrior, undaunted he left us, to fight by the side of the Chiefs! His war-whoop was shrill! His rifle well aimed laid his enemies low: his tomahawk drank of their blood: and his knife flayed their scalps while yet covered with gore! And why do we mourn? Though he fell on the field of the slain, with glory he fell, and his spirit went up to the land of his fathers in war! Then why do we mourn? With transports of joy they received him, and fed him, and clothed him, and welcomed him there! Oh friends, he is happy; then dry up your tears! His spirit has seen our distress, and sent us a helper whom with pleasure we greet. Dickewamis[7] has come: then let us receive her with joy! She is handsome and pleasant! Oh! she is our sister, and gladly we welcome her here. In the place of our brother she stands in our tribe. With care we will guard her from trouble; and may she be happy till her spirit shall leave us."

In the course of that ceremony, from mourning they became serene—joy sparkled in their countenances, and they seemed to rejoice over me as over a long lost child. I was made welcome amongst them as a sister to the two Squaws before mentioned, and was called Dickewamis; which being interpreted, signifies a pretty girl, a handsome girl, or a pleasant, good thing. That is the name by which I have ever since been called by the Indians.

I afterwards learned that the ceremony I at that time passed through, was that of adoption. The two squaws had lost a brother in Washington's war,[8] sometime in the year before, and in consequence of his death went up to Fort Pitt, on the day on which I arrived there, in order to receive a prisoner or an enemy's scalp, to supply their loss.

It is a custom of the Indians, when one of their number is slain or taken prisoner in battle, to give to the nearest relative to the dead or absent, a prisoner, if they have chanced to take one, and if not, to give him the scalp of an enemy. On the return of the Indians from conquest, which is always announced by peculiar shoutings, demonstrations of joy, and the exhibition of some trophy of victory, the mourners come forward and make their claims. If they receive a prisoner, it is at their option either to satiate their vengeance by taking his life in the most cruel manner they can conceive of; or, to receive and adopt him into the family, in the place of him whom they have lost. All the prisoners that are taken in battle and carried to the encampment or town by the Indians, are given to the bereaved families, till their number is made good. And unless the mourners have but just received the news of their bereavement, and are under the operation of a paroxysm of grief, anger and revenge; or, unless the prisoner is very old, sickly, or homely, they generally save him, and treat him kindly. But if their mental wound is fresh, their loss so great that they deem it irreparable, or if their prisoner or prisoners do not meet their approbation, no torture, let it be ever so cruel, seems sufficient to make them satisfaction. It is family, and not national, sacrifices amongst the Indians, that has given them an indelible stamp as barbarians, and identified their character with the idea which is generally formed of unfeeling ferocity, and the most abandoned cruelty.

It was my happy lot to be accepted for adoption; and at the time of the ceremony I was received by the two squaws, to supply the place of their brother in the family; and I was ever considered and treated by them as a real sister, the same as though I had been born of their mother.

During my adoption, I sat motionless, nearly terrified to death at the appearance and actions of the company, expecting every moment to feel their vengeance, and suffer death on the spot. I was, however, happily disappointed, when at the close of the ceremony the company retired, and my sisters went about employing every means for my consolation and comfort.

Being now settled and provided with a home, I was employed in nursing the children, and doing light work about the house. Occasionally I was sent out with the Indian hunters, when they went but a short distance, to help them carry their game. My situation was easy; I had no particular hardships to endure. But still, the recollection of my parents, my brothers and sisters, my home, and my own captivity, destroyed my happiness, and made me constantly solitary, lonesome and gloomy.

My sisters would not allow me to speak English in their hearing; but remembering the charge that my dear mother gave me at the time I left her, whenever I chanced to be alone I made a business of repeating my prayer, catechism, or something I had learned in order that I might not forget my own language. By practising in that way I retained it till I came to Genesee flats, where I soon became acquainted with English people with whom I have been almost daily in the habit of conversing.

My sisters were diligent in teaching me their language; and to their great satisfaction I soon learned so that I could understand it readily, and speak it fluently. I was very fortunate in falling into their hands; for they were kind good natured women; peaceable and mild in their dispositions; temperate and decent in their habits, and very tender and gentle towards me. I have great reason to respect them, though they have been dead a great number of years.

The town where they lived was pleasantly situated on the Ohio, at the mouth of the Shenanjee: the land produced good corn; the woods furnished a plenty of game, and the waters abounded with fish. Another river emptied itself into the Ohio, directly opposite the mouth of the Shenanjee. We spent the summer at that place, where we planted, hoed, and harvested a large crop of corn, of an excellent quality.

About the time of corn harvest, Fort Pitt was taken from the French by the English.*

The corn being harvested, the Indians took it on horses and in canoes, and proceeded down the Ohio, occasionally stopping to hunt a few days, till we arrived at the mouth of Sciota river; where they established their winter quarters, and continued hunting till the ensuing spring, in the adjacent wilderness. While at that place I went with the other children to assist the hunters to bring in their game. The forests on the Sciota were well stocked with elk, deer, and other large animals; and the marshes contained large numbers of beaver, muskrat, &c. which made excellent hunting for the Indians; who depended, for their meat, upon their success in taking elk and deer; and for ammunition and clothing, upon the beaver, muskrat, and other furs that they could take in addition to their peltry.

The season for hunting being passed, we all returned in the spring to the mouth of the river Shenanjee, to the houses and fields we had left in the fall before. There we again planted our corn, squashes, and beans, on the fields that we occupied the preceding summer.

About planting time, our Indians all went up to Fort Pitt, to make peace with the British, and took me with them.† We landed on the opposite side of the river from the fort, and encamped for the night. Early the next morning the Indians took me over to the fort to see the white people that were there. It was then that my heart bounded to be liberated from the Indians and to be restored to my friends and

---

*The above statement is apparently an error; and is to be attributed solely to the treachery of the old lady's memory; though she is confident that that event took place at the time above mentioned. It is certain that Fort Pitt was not evacuated by the French and given up to the English, till sometime in November, 1758. It is possible, however, that an armistice was agreed upon, and that for a time, between the spring of 1755 and 1758, both nations visited that post without fear of molestation. As the succeeding part of the narrative corresponds with the true historical chain of events, the public will overlook this circumstance, which appears unsupported by history.

AUTHOR.

†History is silent as to any treaty having been made between the English, and French and Indians, at that time; though it is possible that a truce was agreed upon, and that the parties met for the purpose of concluding a treaty of peace.

my country. The white people were surprized to see me with the Indians, enduring the hardships of a savage life, at so early an age, and with so delicate a constitution as I appeared to possess. They asked me my name; where and when I was taken—and appeared very much interested on my behalf. They were continuing their inquiries, when my sisters became alarmed, believing that I should be taken from them, hurried me into their canoe and recrossed the river—took their bread out of the fire and fled with me, without stopping, till they arrived at the river Shenanjee. So great was their fear of losing me, or of my being given up in the treaty, that they never once stopped rowing till they got home.

Shortly after we left the shore opposite the fort, as I was informed by one of my Indian brothers, the white people came over to take me back; but after considerable inquiry, and having made diligent search to find where I was hid, they returned with heavy hearts. Although I had then been with the Indians something over a year, and had become considerably habituated to their mode of living, and attached to my sisters, the sight of white people who could speak English inspired me with an unspeakable anxiety to go home with them, and share in the blessings of civilization. My sudden departure and escape from them, seemed like a second captivity, and for a long time I brooded the thoughts of my miserable situation with almost as much sorrow and dejection as I had done those of my first sufferings. Time, the destroyer of every affection, wore away my unpleasant feelings, and I became as contented as before.

We tended our cornfields through the summer; and after we had harvested the crop, we again went down the river to the hunting ground on the Sciota, where we spent the winter, as we had done the winter before.

Early in the spring we sailed up the Ohio river, to a place that the Indians called Wiishto,* where one river emptied into the Ohio on one side, and another on the other. At that place the Indians built a town, and we planted corn.

We lived three summers at Wiishto, and spent each winter on the Sciota.

The first summer of our living at Wiishto, a party of Delaware Indians came up the river, took up their residence, and lived in com-

*Wiishto I suppose was situated near the mouth of Indian Guyundal, 327 miles below Pittsburgh, and 73 above Big Sciota; or at the mouth of Swan creek, 307 miles below Pittsburgh.

mon with us. They brought five white prisoners with them, who by their conversation, made my situation much more agreeable, as they could all speak English. I have forgotten the names of all of them except one, which was Priscilla Ramsay. She was a very handsome, good natured girl, and was married soon after she came to Wiishto to Capt. Little Billy's uncle, who went with her on a visit to her friends in the states. Having tarried with them as long as she wished to, she returned with her husband to Can-a-ah-tun, where he died. She, after his death, married a white man by the name of Nettles, and now lives with him (if she is living) on Grand River, Upper Canada.

Not long after the Delawares came to live with us, at Wiishto, my sisters told me that I must go and live with one of them, whose name was She-nin-jee. Not daring to cross them, or disobey their commands, with a great degree of reluctance I went; and Sheninjee and I were married according to Indian custom.

Sheninjee[9] was a noble man; large in stature; elegant in his appearance; generous in his conduct; courageous in war; a friend to peace, and a great lover of justice. He supported a degree of dignity far above his rank, and merited and received the confidence and friendship of all the tribes with whom he was acquainted. Yet, Sheninjee was an Indian. The idea of spending my days with him, at first seemed perfectly irreconcilable to my feelings: but his good nature, generosity, tenderness, and friendship towards me, soon gained my affection; and, strange as it may seem, I loved him!—To me he was ever kind in sickness, and always treated me with gentleness; in fact, he was an agreeable husband, and a comfortable companion. We lived happily together till the time of our final separation, which happened two or three years after our marriage, as I shall presently relate.

In the second summer of my living at Wiishto, I had a child at the time that the kernels of corn first appeared on the cob. When I was taken sick, Sheninjee was absent, and I was sent to a small shed, on the bank of the river, which was made of boughs, where I was obliged to stay till my husband returned. My two sisters, who were my only companions, attended me, and on the second day of my confinement my child was born; but it lived only two days. It was a girl: and notwithstanding the shortness of the time that I possessed it, it was a great grief to me to lose it.

After the birth of my child, I was very sick, but was not allowed to go into the house for two weeks; when, to my great joy, Sheninjee returned, and I was taken in and as comfortably provided for as our situation would admit of. My disease continued to increase for a number of days; and I became so far reduced that my recovery was despaired of by my friends, and I concluded that my troubles would soon be finished. At length, however, my complaint took a favorable turn, and by the time that the corn was ripe I was able to get about. I continued to gain my health, and in the fall was able to go to our winter quarters, on the Sciota, with the Indians.

From that time, nothing remarkable occurred to me till the fourth winter of my captivity, when I had a son born, while I was at Sciota: I had a quick recovery, and my child was healthy. To commemorate the name of my much lamented father, I called my son Thomas Jemison.[10]

## CHAPTER IV

*She leaves Wiishto for Fort Pitt, in company with her Husband.—Her feelings on setting out.—Contrast between the labor of the white and Indian Women.—Deficiency of Arts amongst the Indians.—Their former Happiness.—Baneful effects of Civilization, and the introduction of ardent Spirits amongst them, &c.—Journey up the River.—Murder of three Traders by the Shawnees.—Her Husband stops at a Trading House.—Wantonness of the Shawnees.—Moves up the Sandusky.—Meets her Brother from Ge-nish-a-u.—Her Husband goes to Wiishto, and she sets out for Genishau in company with her Brothers.—They arrive at Sandusky.— Occurrences at that place.—Her Journey to Genishau, and Reception by her Mother and Friends.*

IN the spring, when Thomas was three or four moons [months] old, we returned from Sciota to Wiishto, and soon after set out to go to Fort Pitt, to dispose of our fur and skins, that we had taken in the winter, and procure some necessary articles for the use of our family.

I had then been with the Indians four summers and four winters, and had become so far accustomed to their mode of living, habits and dispositions, that my anxiety to get away, to be set at liberty, and leave them, had almost subsided. With them was my home; my family was there, and there I had many friends to whom I was warmly attached in consideration of the favors, affection and friendship with which they had uniformly treated me, from the time of my adoption. Our labor was not severe; and that of one year was exactly similar, in almost every respect, to that of the others, without that endless variety that is to be observed in the common labor of the white people. Notwithstanding the Indian women have all the fuel and bread to procure, and the cooking to perform, their task is probably not harder than that of white women, who have those articles provided for them; and their cares certainly are not half as numerous, nor as great. In the summer season, we planted, tended and harvested our corn, and generally had all our children with us; but had no master to oversee or drive us, so that we could work as leisurely as we pleased. We had no ploughs on the Ohio; but performed the whole process of planting and hoeing with a small tool that resembled, in some respects, a hoe with a very short handle.

Our cooking consisted in pounding our corn into samp or hommany, boiling the hommany, making now and then a cake and baking it in the ashes, and in boiling or roasting our venison. As our cooking and eating utensils consisted of a hommany block and pestle, a small kettle, a knife or two, and a few vessels of bark or wood, it required but little time to keep them in order for use.

Spinning, weaving, sewing, stocking knitting, and the like, are arts which have never been practised in the Indian tribes generally. After the revolutionary war, I learned to sew, so that I could make my own clothing after a poor fashion; but the other domestic arts I have been wholly ignorant of the application of, since my captivity. In the season of hunting, it was our business, in addition to our cooking, to bring home the game that was taken by the Indians, dress it, and carefully preserve the eatable meat, and prepare or dress the skins. Our clothing was fastened together with strings of deer skin, and tied on with the same.

In that manner we lived, without any of those jealousies, quarrels, and revengeful battles between families and individuals, which have been common in the Indian tribes since the introduction of ardent spirits amongst them.

The use of ardent spirits amongst the Indians and the attempts which have been made to civilize and christianize them by the white people, has constantly made them worse and worse; increased their vices, and robbed them of many of their virtues; and will ultimately produce their extermination. I have seen, in a number of instances, the effects of education upon some of our Indians, who were taken when young, from their families, and placed at school before they had had an opportunity to contract many Indian habits, and there kept till they arrived to manhood, but I have never seen one of those but what was an Indian in every respect after he returned. Indians must and will be Indians, in spite of all the means that can be used for their cultivation in the sciences and arts.

One thing only marred my happiness, while I lived with them on the Ohio; and that was the recollection that I had once had tender parents and a home that I loved. Aside from that consideration, or, if I had been taken in infancy, I should have been contented in my situation. Notwithstanding all that has been said against the Indians, in consequence of their cruelties to their enemies—cruelties that I have witnessed, and had abundant proof of—it is a fact that they are naturally kind, tender and peaceable towards their friends, and strictly honest; and that those cruelties have been practised, only upon their enemies, according to their idea of justice.

At the time we left Wiishto, it was impossible for me to suppress a sigh of regret on parting with those who had truly been my friends—with those whom I had every reason to respect. On account of a part of our family living at Genishau, we thought it doubtful whether we should return directly from Pittsburgh, or go from thence on a visit to see them.

Our company consisted of my husband, my two Indian brothers, my little son and myself. We embarked in a canoe that was large enough to contain ourselves and our effects, and proceeded on our voyage up the river.

Nothing remarkable occurred to us on our way, till we arrived at the mouth of a creek which Sheninjee and my brothers said was the outlet of Sandusky lake; where, as they said, two or three English traders in fur and skins had kept a trading house but a short time before, though they were then absent. We had passed the trading house but a short distance, when we met three white men floating down the river, with the appearance of having been recently murdered by the Indians. We supposed them to be the bodies of the traders, whose store we had passed the same day. Sheninjee being alarmed for fear of being apprehended as one of the murderers, if he should go on, resolved to put about immediately, and we accordingly returned to where the traders had lived, and there landed.

At the trading house we found a party of Shawnee Indians, who had taken a young white man prisoner, and had just begun to torture him for the sole purpose of gratifying their curiosity in exulting at his distress. They at first made him stand up, while they slowly pared his ears and split them into strings; they then made a number of slight incisions in his face; and then bound him upon the ground, rolled him in the dirt, and rubbed it in his wounds: some of them at the same time whipping him with small rods! The poor fellow cried for mercy and yelled most piteously.

The sight of his distress seemed too much for me to endure: I begged of them to desist—I entreated them with tears to release him. At length they attended to my intercessions, and set him at liberty. He was shockingly disfigured, bled profusely, and appeared to be in great pain: but as soon as he was liberated he made off in haste, which was the last I saw of him.

We soon learned that the same party of Shawnees had, but a few hours before, massacred the three white traders whom we saw in the river, and had plundered their store. We, however, were not molested by them, and after a short stay at that place, moved up the creek about forty miles to a Shawnee town, which the Indians called Gaw-gush-shaw-ga, (which being interpreted signifies a mask or a false face.) The creek that we went up was called Candusky.

It was now summer; and having tarried a few days at Gawgush-shawga, we moved on up the creek to a place that was called Yis-kah-wa-na, (meaning in English open mouth.)

As I have before observed, the family to which I belonged was part of a tribe of Seneca Indians, who lived, at that time, at a place called Genishau,[11] from the name of the tribe, that was situated on a river of the same name which is now called Genesee. The word Genishau signifies a shining, clear or open place. Those of us who lived on the Ohio, had frequently received invitations from those at Genishau, by one of my brothers, who usually went and returned every season, to come and live with them, and my two sisters had been gone almost two years.

While we were at Yiskahwana, my brother arrived there from Genishau, and insisted so strenuously upon our going home (as he called it) with him, that my two brothers concluded to go, and to take me with them.

By this time the summer was gone, and the time for harvesting corn had arrived. My brothers, for fear of the rainy season setting in early, thought it best to set out immediately that we might have good travelling. Sheninjee consented to have me go with my brothers; but concluded to go down the river himself with some fur and skins which he had on hand, spend the winter in hunting with his friends, and come to me in the spring following.

That was accordingly agreed upon, and he set out for Wiishto; and my three brothers and myself, with my little son on my back, at the same time set out for Genishau. We came on to Upper Sandusky, to an Indian town that we found deserted by its inhabitants, in consequence of their having recently murdered some English traders, who resided amongst them. That town was owned and had been occupied by Delaware Indians, who, when they left it, buried their provision in the earth, in order to preserve it from their enemies, or to have a supply for themselves if they should chance to return. My brothers understood the customs of the Indians when they were obliged to fly from their enemies; and suspecting that their corn at least must have been hid, made diligent search, and at length found a large quantity of it, together with beans, sugar and honey, so carefully buried that it was completely dry and as good as when they left it. As our stock of provision was scanty, we considered ourselves extremely fortunate in finding so seasonable a supply, with so little trouble. Having caught two or three horses, that we found there, and furnished ourselves with a good store of food, we travelled on till we came to the mouth of French Creek, where we hunted two days, and from thence came on to Conowongo Creek, where we were obliged to stay seven or ten days, in consequence of our horses having left us and straying into the woods. The horses, however, were found, and we again prepared to resume our journey. During our stay at that place the rain fell fast, and had raised the creek to such a height that it was seemingly impossible for us to cross it. A number of times we ventured in, but were compelled to return, barely escaping with our lives. At length we succeeded in swimming our horses and reached the opposite shore; though I but just escaped with my little boy from being drowned. From Sandusky the path that we travelled was crooked and obscure; but was tolerably well understood by my oldest brother, who had travelled it a number of times, when going to and returning from the Cherokee wars. The fall by this time was considerably advanced, and the rains, attended with cold winds, continued daily to increase the difficulties of travelling. From Conowongo we came to a place, called by the Indians Che-ua-shung-gau-tau, and from that to U-na-waum-gwa, (which means an eddy, not strong,) where the early frosts had destroyed the corn so that the Indians were in danger of starving for the want of bread. Having rested ourselves two days at that place, we came on to Caneadea and stayed one day, and then continued our march till we arrived at Genishau. Genishau at that time was a large Seneca town, thickly inhabited, lying on Genesee river, opposite what is now called the Free Ferry, adjoining Fall-Brook, and about south west of the present village of Geneseo, the county seat for the county of Livingston, in the state of New-York.

Those only who have travelled on foot the distance of five or six hundred miles, through an almost pathless wilderness, can form an idea of the fatigue and sufferings that I endured on that journey. My clothing was thin and illy calculated to defend me from the continually drenching rains with which I was daily completely wet, and at night with nothing but my wet blanket to cover me, I had to sleep on the naked ground, and generally without a shelter, save such as nature had provided. In addition to all that, I had to carry my child, then about nine months old, every step of the journey on my back, or in my arms, and provide for his comfort and prevent his suffering, as far as my poverty of means would admit. Such was the fatigue that I sometimes felt, that I thought it impossible for me to go through, and I would almost abandon the idea of even trying to proceed. My brothers were attentive, and at length, as I have stated, we reached our place of destination, in good health, and without having experienced a day's sickness from the time we left Yiskah-wana.

We were kindly received by my Indian mother and the other members of the family, who appeared to make me welcome; and my two sisters, whom I had not seen in two years, received me with every expression of love and friendship, and that they really felt what they expressed, I have never had the least reason to doubt. The warmth of their feelings, the kind reception which I met with, and the continued favors that I received at their hands, rivetted my affection for them so strongly that I am constrained to believe that I loved them as I should have loved my own sister had she lived, and I had been brought up with her.

## CHAPTER V

*Indians march to Niagara to fight the British.—Return with*
*two Prisoners, &c.—Sacrifice them at Fall-Brook.—Her In-*
*dian Mother's Address to her Daughter.—Death of her*
*Husband.—Bounty offered for the Prisoners taken in the last*
*war.—John Van Sice attempts to take her to procure her*
*Ransom.—Her Escape.—Edict of the Chiefs.—Old King of*
*the tribe determines to have her given up.—Her brother threat-*
*ens her Life.—Her narrow Escape.—The old King goes off.—*
*Her brother is informed of the place of her concealment, and*
*conducts her home.—Marriage to her second Husband.—*
*Names of her Children.*

WHEN we arrived at Genishau, the Indians of that tribe were making
active preparations for joining the French, in order to assist them in
retaking Fort Ne-a-gaw (as Fort Niagara was called in the Seneca
language) from the British, who had taken it from the French in the
month preceding.[12] They marched off the next day after our arrival,
painted and accoutred in all the habiliments of Indian warfare, determined on death or victory; and joined the army in season to assist
in accomplishing a plan that had been previously concerted for the
destruction of a part of the British army. The British feeling themselves secure in the possession of Fort Neagaw, and unwilling that
their enemies should occupy any of the military posts in that quarter,
determined to take Fort Schlosser, lying a few miles up the river from
Neagaw, which they expected to effect with but little loss. Accordingly a detachment of soldiers, sufficiently numerous, as was supposed, was sent out to take it, leaving a strong garrison in the fort,
and marched off, well prepared to effect their object. But on their
way they were surrounded by the French and Indians, who lay in
ambush to receive them, and were driven off the bank of the river
into a place called the "Devil's Hole," together with their horses,
carriages, artillery, and every thing pertaining to the army. Not a
single man escaped being driven off, and of the whole number one
only was fortunate enough to escape with his life. Our Indians were
absent but a few days, and returned in triumph, bringing with them
two white prisoners, and a number of oxen. Those were the first meat
cattle that were ever brought to the Genesee flats.

The next day after their return to Genishau, was set apart as a day of feasting and frolicing, at the expence of the lives of their two unfortunate prisoners, on whom they purposed to glut their revenge, and satisfy their love for retaliation upon their enemies. My sister was anxious to attend the execution, and to take me with her, to witness the customs of the warriors, as it was one of the highest kind of frolics ever celebrated in their tribe, and one that was not often attended with so much pomp and parade as it was expected that would be. I felt a kind of anxiety to witness the scene, having never attended an execution, and yet I felt a kind of horrid dread that made my heart revolt, and inclined me to step back rather than support the idea of advancing. On the morning of the execution she made her intention of going to the frolic, and taking me with her, known to our mother, who in the most feeling terms remonstrated against a step at once so rash and unbecoming the true dignity of our sex:

"How, my daughter, (said she, addressing my sister,) how can you even think of attending the feast and seeing the unspeakable torments that those poor unfortunate prisoners must inevitably suffer from the hands of our warriors? How can you stand and see them writhing in the warriors' fire, in all the agonies of a slow, a lingering death? How can you think of enduring the sound of their groanings and prayers to the Great Spirit for sudden deliverance from their enemies, or from life? And how can you think of conducting to that melancholy spot your poor sister Dickewamis, (meaning myself,) who has so lately been a prisoner, who has lost her parents and brothers by the hands of the bloody warriors, and who has felt all the horrors of the loss of her freedom, in lonesome captivity? Oh! how can you think of making her bleed at the wounds which now are but partially healed? The recollection of her former troubles would deprive us of Dickewamis, and she would depart to the fields of the blessed, where fighting has ceased, and the corn needs no tending—where hunting is easy, the forests delightful, the summers are pleasant, and the winters are mild!—O! think once, my daughter, how soon you may have a brave brother made prisoner in battle, and sacrificed to feast the ambition of the enemies of his kindred, and leave us to mourn for the loss of a friend, a son and a brother, whose bow brought us venison, and supplied us with blankets!—Our task is quite easy at home, and our business needs our attention. With war we have nothing to do: our husbands and brothers are proud to defend us, and their hearts beat with ardor to meet our proud foes. Oh! stay then, my daughter; let our warriors alone perform on their victims their customs of war!"

This speech of our mother had the desired effect; we stayed at home and attended to our domestic concerns. The prisoners, however, were executed by having their heads taken off, their bodies cut in pieces and shockingly mangled, and then burnt to ashes!—They were burnt on the north side of Fall-brook, directly opposite the town which was on the south side, some time in the month of November, 1759.

I spent the winter comfortably, and as agreeably as I could have expected to, in the absence of my kind husband. Spring at length appeared, but Sheninjee was yet away; summer came on, but my husband had not found me. Fearful forebodings haunted my imagination; yet I felt confident that his affection for me was so great that if he was alive he would follow me and I should again see him. In the course of the summer, however, I received intelligence that soon after he left me at Yiskahwana he was taken sick and died at Wiishto. This was a heavy and an unexpected blow. I was now in my youthful days left a widow, with one son, and entirely dependent on myself for his and my support. My mother and her family gave me all the consolation in their power, and in a few months my grief wore off and I became contented.

In a year or two after this, according to my best recollection of the time, the King of England offered a bounty to those who would bring in the prisoners that had been taken in the war, to some military post where they might be redeemed and set at liberty.

John Van Sice, a Dutchman, who had frequently been at our place, and was well acquainted with every prisoner at Genishau, resolved to take me to Niagara, that I might there receive my liberty and he the offered bounty. I was notified of his intention; but as I was fully determined not to be redeemed at that time, especially with his assistance, I carefully watched his movements in order to avoid falling into his hands. It so happened, however, that he saw me alone at work in a corn-field, and thinking probably that he could secure me easily, ran towards me in great haste. I espied him at some distance, and well knowing the amount of his errand, run from him with all the speed I was mistress of, and never once stopped till I reached Gardow.*[13] He gave up the chase, and returned: but I, fearing that he might be lying in wait for me, stayed three days and three nights in an old cabin at Gardow, and then went back trembling at every

---

*I have given this orthography, because it corresponds with the popular pronunciation.

step for fear of being apprehended. I got home without difficulty; and soon after, the chiefs in council having learned the cause of my elopement, gave orders that I should not be taken to any military post without my consent; and that as it was my choice to stay, I should live amongst them quietly and undisturbed. But, notwithstanding the will of the chiefs, it was but a few days before the old king of our tribe told one of my Indian brothers that I should be redeemed, and he would take me to Niagara himself. In reply to the old king, my brother said that I should not be given up; but that, as it was my wish, I should stay with the tribe as long as I was pleased to. Upon this a serious quarrel ensued between them, in which my brother frankly told him that sooner than I should be taken by force, he would kill me with his own hands!—Highly enraged at the old king, my brother came to my sister's house, where I resided, and informed her of all that had passed respecting me; and that, if the old king should attempt to take me, as he firmly believed he would, he would immediately take my life, and hazard the consequences. He returned to the old king. As soon as I came in, my sister told me what she had just heard, and what she expected without doubt would befal me. Full of pity, and anxious for my preservation, she then directed me to take my child and go into some high weeds at no great distance from the house, and there hide myself and lay still till all was silent in the house, for my brother, she said, would return at evening and let her know the final conclusion of the matter, of which she promised to inform me in the following manner: If I was to be killed, she said she would bake a small cake and lay it at the door, on the outside, in a place that she then pointed out to me. When all was silent in the house, I was to creep softly to the door, and if the cake could not be found in the place specified, I was to go in: but if the cake was there, I was to take my child and go as fast as I possibly could to a large spring on the south side of Samp's Creek, (a place that I had often seen,) and there wait till I should by some means hear from her.

Alarmed for my own safety, I instantly followed her advice, and went into the weeds, where I lay in a state of the greatest anxiety, till all was silent in the house, when I crept to the door, and there found, to my great distress, the little cake! I knew my fate was fixed, unless I could keep secreted till the storm was over; and accordingly crept back to the weeds, where my little Thomas lay, took him on my back, and laid my course for the spring as fast as my legs would carry me. Thomas was nearly three years old, and very large and heavy. I got to the spring early in the morning, almost overcome with fatigue, and at the same time fearing that I might be pursued and taken, I felt my life an almost insupportable burthen. I sat down with my child at the spring, and he and I made a breakfast of the little cake, and water of the spring, which I dipped and supped with the only implement which I possessed, my hand.

In the morning after I fled, as was expected, the old King came to our house in search of me, and to take me off; but, as I was not to be found, he gave me up, and went to Niagara with the prisoners he had already got into his possession.

As soon as the old King was fairly out of the way, my sister told my brother where he could find me. He immediately set out for the spring, and found me about noon. The first sight of him made me tremble with the fear of death; but when he came near, so that I could discover his countenance, tears of joy flowed down my cheeks, and I felt such a kind of instant relief as no one can possibly experience, unless when under the absolute sentence of death he receives an unlimited pardon. We were both rejoiced at the event of the old King's project; and after staying at the spring through the night, set out together for home early in the morning. When we got to a cornfield near the town, my brother secreted me till he could go and ascertain how my case stood; and finding that the old King was absent, and that all was peaceable, he returned to me, and I went home joyfully.

Not long after this, my mother went to Johnstown, on the Mohawk river, with five prisoners, who were redeemed by Sir William Johnson,[14] and set at liberty.

When my son Thomas was three or four years old, I was married to an Indian, whose name was Hiokatoo, commonly called Gardow,[15] by whom I had four daughters and two sons. I named my children, principally, after my relatives, from whom I was parted, by calling my girls Jane, Nancy, Betsey and Polly, and the boys John and Jesse. Jane died about twenty-nine years ago, in the month of August, a little before the great Council at Big-Tree, aged about fifteen years. My other daughters are yet living, and have families.

## CHAPTER VI

*Peace amongst the Indians.—Celebrations.—Worship. Exercises.—Business of the Tribes.—Former Happiness of the Indians in time of peace extolled.—Their Morals; Fidelity; Honesty; Chastity; Temperance. Indians called to German Flats.—Treaty with Americans.—They are sent for by the British Commissioners, and go to Oswego.—Promises made by those Commissioners.—Greatness of the King of England. Reward that was paid them for joining the British. They make a Treaty.—Bounty offered for Scalps. Return richly dressed and equipped.—In 1776 they kill a man at Cautega to provoke the Americans. Prisoners taken at Cherry Valley, brought to Beard's-Town; redeemed, &c.—Battle at Fort Stanwix.—Indians suffer a great loss.—Mourning at Beard's Town.—Mrs. Jemison's care of and services rendered to Butler and Brandt.*

AFTER the conclusion of the French war, our tribe had nothing to trouble it till the commencement of the Revolution. For twelve or fifteen years the use of the implements of war was not known, nor the war-whoop heard, save on days of festivity, when the achievements of former times were commemorated in a kind of mimic warfare, in which the chiefs and warriors displayed their prowess, and illustrated their former adroitness, by laying the ambuscade, surprizing their enemies, and performing many accurate manœuvres with the tomahawk and scalping knife; thereby preserving and handing to their children, the theory of Indian warfare. During that period they also pertinaciously observed the religious rites of their progenitors, by attending with the most scrupulous exactness and a great degree of enthusiasm to the sacrifices, at particular times, to appease the anger of the evil deity, or to excite the commisseration and friendship of the Great Good Spirit, whom they adored with reverence, as the author, governor, supporter and disposer of every good thing of which they participated.

They also practised in various athletic games, such as running, wrestling, leaping, and playing ball, with a view that their bodies might be more supple, or rather that they might not become enervated, and that they might be enabled to make a proper selection of Chiefs for the councils of the nation and leaders for war.

While the Indians were thus engaged in their round of traditionary performances, with the addition of hunting, their women attended to agriculture, their families, and a few domestic concerns of small consequence, and attended with but little labor.

No people can live more happy than the Indians did in times of peace, before the introduction of spirituous liquors amongst them. Their lives were a continual round of pleasures. Their wants were few, and easily satisfied; and their cares were only for to-day; the bounds of their calculations for future comfort not extending to the incalculable uncertainties of to-morrow. If peace ever dwelt with men, it was in former times, in the recesses from war, amongst what are now termed barbarians. The moral character of the Indians was (if I may be allowed the expression) uncontaminated. Their fidelity was perfect, and became proverbial; they were strictly honest; they despised deception and falsehood; and chastity was held in high veneration, and a violation of it was considered sacrilege. They were temperate in their desires, moderate in their passions, and candid and honorable in the expression of their sentiments on every subject of importance.

Thus, at peace amongst themselves, and with the neighboring whites, though there were none at that time very near, our Indians lived quietly and peaceably at home, till a little before the breaking out of the revolutionary war, when they were sent for, together with the Chiefs and members of the Six Nations generally, by the people of the States, to go to the German Flats, and there hold a general council, in order that the people of the states might ascertain, in good season, who they should esteem and treat as enemies, and who as friends, in the great war which was then upon the point of breaking out between them and the King of England.

Our Indians obeyed the call, and the council was holden, at which the pipe of peace was smoked, and a treaty made, in which the Six Nations solemnly agreed that if a war should eventually break out, they would not take up arms on either side; but that they would observe a strict neutrality. With that the people of the states were satisfied, as they had not asked their assistance, nor did not wish it. The Indians returned to their homes well pleased that they could live on neutral ground, surrounded by the din of war, without being engaged in it.

About a year passed off, and we, as usual, were enjoying ourselves in the employments of peaceable times, when a messenger arrived from the British Commissioners, requesting all the Indians of our tribe to attend a general council which was soon to be held at Oswego. The council convened, and being opened, the British Commissioners informed the Chiefs that the object of calling a council of the Six Nations, was, to engage their assistance in subduing the rebels, the people of the states, who had risen up against the good King, their master, and were about to rob him of a great part of his possessions and wealth, and added that they would amply reward them for all their services.

The Chiefs then arose, and informed the Commissioners of the nature and extent of the treaty which they had entered into with the people of the states, the year before, and that they should not violate it by taking up the hatchet against them.

The Commissioners continued their entreaties without success, till they addressed their avarice, by telling our people that the people of the states were few in number, and easily subdued; and that on the account of their disobedience to the King, they justly merited all the punishment that it was possible for white men and Indians to inflict upon them; and added, that the King was rich and powerful, both in money and subjects: That his rum was as plenty as the water in lake Ontario: that his men were as numerous as the sands upon the lake shore:—and that the Indians, if they would assist in the war, and persevere in their friendship to the King, till it was closed, should never want for money or goods. Upon this the Chiefs concluded a treaty with the British Commissioners, in which they agreed to take up arms against the rebels, and continue in the service of his Majesty till they were subdued, in consideration of certain conditions which were stipulated in the treaty to be performed by the British government and its agents.

As soon as the treaty was finished, the Commissioners made a present to each Indian of a suit of clothes, a brass kettle, a gun and tomahawk, a scalping knife, a quantity of powder and lead, a piece of gold, and promised a bounty on every scalp that should be brought in. Thus richly clad and equipped, they returned home, after an absence of about two weeks, full of the fire of war, and anxious to encounter their enemies. Many of the kettles which the Indians received at that time are now in use on the Genesee Flats.

Hired to commit depredations upon the whites, who had given them no offence, they waited impatiently to commence their labor, till sometime in the spring of 1776, when a convenient opportunity offered for them to make an attack. At that time, a party of our

Indians were at Cau-te-ga, who shot a man that was looking after his horse, for the sole purpose, as I was informed by my Indian brother, who was present, of commencing hostilities.

In May following, our Indians were in their first battle with the Americans; but at what place I am unable to determine. While they were absent at that time, my daughter Nancy[16] was born.

The same year, at Cherry Valley, our Indians took a woman and her three daughters prisoners, and brought them on, leaving one at Canandaigua, one at Honeoy, one at Cattaraugus, and one (the woman) at Little Beard's Town, where I resided. The woman told me that she and her daughters might have escaped, but that they expected the British army only, and therefore made no effort. Her husband and sons got away. Sometime having elapsed, they were redeemed at Fort Niagara by Col. Butler, who clothed them well, and sent them home.

In the same expedition, Joseph Smith was taken prisoner at or near Cherry Valley, brought to Genesee, and detained till after the revolutionary war. He was then liberated, and the Indians made him a present, in company with Horatio Jones, of 6000 acres of land lying in the present town of Leicester, in the county of Livingston.

One of the girls just mentioned, was married to a British officer at Fort Niagara, by the name of Johnson, who at the time she was taken, took a gold ring from her finger, without any compliments or ceremonies. When he saw her at Niagara he recognized her features, restored the ring that he had so impolitely borrowed, and courted and married her.

Previous to the battle at Fort Stanwix,[17] the British sent for the Indians to come and see them whip the rebels; and, at the same time stated that they did not wish to have them fight, but wanted to have them just sit down, smoke their pipes, and look on. Our Indians went, to a man; but contrary to their expectation, instead of smoking and looking on, they were obliged to fight for their lives, and at the end of the battle were completely beaten, with a great loss in killed and wounded. Our Indians alone had thirty-six killed, and a great number wounded. Our town exhibited a scene of real sorrow and distress, when our warriors returned and recounted their misfortunes, and stated the real loss they had sustained in the engagement. The mourning was excessive, and was expressed by the most doleful yells, shrieks, and howlings, and by inimitable gesticulations.

During the revolution, my house was the home of Col's Butler and Brandt,[18] whenever they chanced to come into our neighborhood as they passed to and from Fort Niagara, which was the seat of their military operations. Many and many a night I have pounded samp for them from sun-set till sun-rise, and furnished them with necessary provision and clean clothing for their journey.

## CHAPTER VII

*Gen. Sullivan with a large army arrives at Canandaigua.—Indians' troubles.—Determine to stop their march.—Skirmish at Connessius Lake.—Circumstances attending the Execution of an Oneida warrior. Escape of an Indian Prisoner.—Lieut. Boyd and another man taken Prisoners.—Cruelty of Boyd's Execution.—Indians retreat to the woods.—Sullivan comes on to Genesee Flats and destroys the property of the Indians.—Returns.—Indians return.—Mrs. Jemison goes to Gardow.—Her Employment there.—Attention of an old Negro to her safety, &c.—Severe Winter.—Sufferings of the Indians.—Destruction of Game.—Indians' Expedition to the Mohawk.—Capture old John O'Bail, &c.—Other Prisoners taken, &c.*

FOR four or five years we sustained no loss in the war, except in the few who had been killed in distant battles; and our tribe, because of the remoteness of its situation from the enemy, felt secure from an attack. At length, in the fall of 1779, intelligence was received that a large and powerful army of the rebels, under the command of General Sullivan,[19] was making rapid progress towards our settlement, burning and destroying the huts and corn-fields; killing the cattle, hogs and horses, and cutting down the fruit trees belonging to the Indians throughout the country.

Our Indians immediately became alarmed, and suffered every thing but death from fear that they should be taken by surprise, and totally destroyed at a single blow. But in order to prevent so great a catastrophe, they sent out a few spies who were to keep themselves at a short distance in front of the invading army, in order to watch its operations, and give information of its advances and success.

Sullivan arrived at Canandaigua Lake, and had finished his work of destruction there, and it was ascertained that he was about to march to our flats when our Indians resolved to give him battle on the way, and prevent, if possible, the distresses to which they knew we should be subjected, if he should succeed in reaching our town. Accordingly they sent all their women and children into the woods a little west of Little Beard's Town, in order that we might make a good retreat if it should be necessary, and then, well armed, set out to face the conquering enemy. The place which they fixed upon for their battle ground lay between Honeoy Creek and the head of Connessius Lake.

At length a scouting party from Sullivan's army arrived at the spot selected, when the Indians arose from their ambush with all the fierceness and terror that it was possible for them to exercise, and directly put the party upon a retreat. Two Oneida Indians were all the prisoners that were taken in that skirmish. One of them was a pilot of Gen. Sullivan, and had been very active in the war, rendering to the people of the states essential services. At the commencement of the revolution he had a brother older than himself, who resolved to join the British service, and endeavored by all the art that he was capable of using to persuade his brother to accompany him; but his arguments proved abortive. This went to the British, and that joined the American army. At this critical juncture they met, one in the capacity of a conqueror, the other in that of a prisoner; and as an Indian seldom forgets a countenance that he has seen, they recognized each other at sight. Envy and revenge glared in the features of the conquering savage, as he advanced to his brother (the prisoner) in all the haughtiness of Indian pride, heightened by a sense of power, and addressed him in the following manner:

"Brother, you have merited death! The hatchet or the war-club shall finish your career!—When I begged of you to follow me in the fortunes of war, you was deaf to my cries—you spurned my entreaties!

"Brother! you have merited death and shall have your deserts! When the rebels raised their hatchets to fight their good master, you sharpened your knife, you brightened your rifle and led on our foes to the fields of our fathers!—You have merited death and shall die by our hands! When those rebels had drove us from the fields of our fathers to seek out new homes, it was you who could dare to step forth as their pilot, and conduct them even to the doors of our wigwams, to butcher our children and put us to death! No crime can be greater!—But though you have merited death and shall die on this spot, my hands shall not be stained in the blood of a brother! *Who will strike?*"

Little Beard, who was standing by, as soon as the speech was ended, struck the prisoner on the head with his tomahawk, and despatched him at once!

Little Beard then informed the other Indian prisoner that as they were at war with the whites only, and not with the Indians, they would spare his life, and after a while give him his liberty in an honorable manner. The Oneida warrior, however, was jealous of Little Beard's fidelity; and suspecting that he should soon fall by his hands, watched for a favorable opportunity to make his escape; which he soon effected. Two Indians were leading him, one on each side, when he made a violent effort, threw them upon the ground, and ran for his life towards where the main body of the American army was encamped. The Indians pursued him without success; but in their absence they fell in with a small detachment of Sullivan's men, with whom they had a short but severe skirmish, in which they killed a number of the enemy, took Capt. or Lieut. William Boyd[20] and one private, prisoners, and brought them to Little Beard's Town, where they were soon after put to death in the most shocking and cruel manner. Little Beard, in this, as in all other scenes of cruelty that happened at his town, was master of ceremonies, and principal actor. Poor Boyd was stripped of his clothing, and then tied to a sapling, where the Indians menaced his life by throwing their tomahawks at the tree, directly over his head, brandishing their scalping knives around him in the most frightful manner, and accompanying their ceremonies with terrific shouts of joy. Having punished him sufficiently in this way, they made a small opening in his abdomen, took out an intestine, which they tied to the sapling, and then unbound him from the tree, and drove him round it till he had drawn out the whole of his intestines. He was then beheaded, his head was stuck upon a pole, and his body left on the ground unburied. Thus ended the life of poor William Boyd, who, it was said, had every appearance of being an active and enterprizing officer, of the first talents. The other prisoner was (if I remember distinctly) only beheaded and left near Boyd.

This tragedy being finished, our Indians again held a short council on the expediency of giving Sullivan battle, if he should continue to advance, and finally came to the conclusion that they were not strong enough to drive him, nor to prevent his taking possession of their fields: but that if it was possible they would escape with their own lives, preserve their families, and leave their possessions to be overrun by the invading army.

The women and children were then sent on still further towards Buffalo, to a large creek that was called by the Indians Catawba, accompanied by a part of the Indians, while the remainder secreted themselves in the woods back of Beard's Town, to watch the movements of the army.

At that time I had three children who went with me on foot, one who rode on horse back, and one whom I carried on my back.

Our corn was good that year; a part of which we had gathered and secured for winter.

In one or two days after the skirmish at Connissius lake, Sullivan and his army arrived at Genesee river, where they destroyed every article of the food kind that they could lay their hands on. A part of our corn they burnt, and threw the remainder into the river. They burnt our houses, killed what few cattle and horses they could find, destroyed our fruit trees, and left nothing but the bare soil and timber. But the Indians had eloped and were not to be found.

Having crossed and recrossed the river, and finished the work of destruction, the army marched off to the east. Our Indians saw them move off, but suspecting that it was Sullivan's intention to watch our return, and then to take us by surprize, resolved that the main body of our tribe should hunt where we then were, till Sullivan had gone so far that there would be no danger of his returning to molest us.

This being agreed to, we hunted continually till the Indians concluded that there could be no risk in our once more taking possession of our lands. Accordingly we all returned; but what were our feelings when we found that there was not a mouthful of any kind of sustenance left, not even enough to keep a child one day from perishing with hunger.

The weather by this time had become cold and stormy; and as we were destitute of houses and food too, I immediately resolved to take my children and look out for myself, without delay. With this intention I took two of my little ones on my back, bade the other three follow, and the same night arrived on the Gardow flats, where I have ever since resided.

At that time, two negroes, who had run away from their masters sometime before, were the only inhabitants of those flats. They lived in a small cabin and had planted and raised a large field of corn, which they had not yet harvested. As they were in want of help to secure their crop, I hired to them to husk corn till the whole was harvested.

I have laughed a thousand times to myself when I have thought of the good old negro, who hired me, who fearing that I should get taken or injured by the Indians, stood by me constantly when I was husking, with a loaded gun in his hand, in order to keep off the enemy, and thereby lost as much labor of his own as he received from me, by paying good wages. I, however, was not displeased with his attention; for I knew that I should need all the corn that I could earn, even if I should husk the whole. I husked enough for them, to gain for myself, at every tenth string, one hundred strings of ears, which were equal to twenty-five bushels of shelled corn. This seasonable supply made my family comfortable for samp and cakes through the succeeding winter, which was the most severe that I have witnessed since my remembrance. The snow fell about five feet deep, and remained so for a long time, and the weather was extremely cold; so much so indeed, that almost all the game upon which the Indians depended for subsistence, perished, and reduced them almost to a state of starvation through that and three or four succeeding years. When the snow melted in the spring, deer were found dead upon the ground in vast numbers; and other animals, of every description, perished from the cold also, and were found dead, in multitudes. Many of our people barely escaped with their lives, and some actually died of hunger and freezing.

But to return from this digression: Having been completely routed at Little Beard's Town, deprived of a house, and without the means of building one in season, after I had finished my husking, and having found from the short acquaintance which I had had with the negroes, that they were kind and friendly, I concluded, at their request, to take up my residence with them for a while in their cabin, till I should be able to provide a hut for myself. I lived more comfortable than I expected to through the winter, and the next season made a shelter for myself.

The negroes continued on my flats two or three years after this, and then left them for a place that they expected would suit them much better. But as that land became my own in a few years, by virtue of a deed from the Chiefs of the Six Nations, I have lived there from that to the present time.

My flats were cleared before I saw them; and it was the opinion of the oldest Indians that were at Genishau, at the time that I first went there, that all the flats on the Genesee river were improved before any of the Indian tribes ever saw them. I well remember that soon after I went to Little Beard's Town, the banks of Fall-Brook were washed off, which left a large number of human bones uncovered. The Indians then said that those were not the bones of Indians, because they had never heard of any of their dead being buried there; but that they were the bones of a race of men who a great many moons before, cleared that land and lived on the flats.

The next summer after Sullivan's campaign, our Indians, highly incensed at the whites for the treatment they had received, and the sufferings which they had consequently endured, determined to obtain some redress by destroying their frontier settlements. Corn Planter,[21] otherwise called John O'Bail, led the Indians, and an officer by the name of Johnston commanded the British in the expedition. The force was large, and so strongly bent upon revenge and vengeance, that seemingly nothing could avert its march, nor prevent its depredations. After leaving Genesee they marched directly to some of the head waters of the Susquehannah river, and Schoharie Creek, went down that creek to the Mohawk river, thence up that river to Fort Stanwix, and from thence came home. In their route they burnt a number of places; destroyed all the cattle and other property that fell in their way; killed a number of white people, and brought home a few prisoners.

In that expedition, when they came to Fort Plain, on the Mohawk river, Corn Planter and a party of his Indians took old John O'Bail, a white man, and made him a prisoner. Old John O'Bail, in his younger days had frequently passed through the Indian settlements that lay between the Hudson and Fort Niagara, and in some of his excursions had become enamored with a squaw, by whom he had a son that was called Corn Planter.

Corn Planter, was a chief of considerable eminence; and having been informed of his parentage and of the place of his father's residence, took the old man at this time, in order that he might make an introduction leisurely, and become acquainted with a man to whom, though a stranger, he was satisfied that he owed his existence.

After he had taken the old man, his father, he led him as a prisoner ten or twelve miles up the river, and then stepped before him, faced about, and addressed him in the following terms:—

"My name is John O'Bail, commonly called Corn Planter. I am your son! you are my father! You are now my prisoner, and subject to the customs of Indian warfare: but you shall not be harmed; you need not fear. I am a warrior! Many are the scalps which I have taken! Many prisoners I have tortured to death! I am your son! I am a warrior! I was anxious to see you, and to greet you in friendship. I went to your cabin and took you by force! But your life shall be spared. Indians love their friends and their kindred, and treat them

with kindness. If now you choose to follow the fortune of your yellow son, and to live with our people, I will cherish your old age with
plenty of venison, and you shall live easy: But if it is your choice to
return to your fields and live with your white children, I will send a
party of my trusty young men to conduct you back in safety. I respect
you, my father; you have been friendly to Indians, and they are your
friends."

Old John chose to return. Corn Planter, as good as his word,
ordered an escort to attend him home, which they did with the
greatest care.

Amongst the prisoners that were brought to Genesee, was William
Newkirk, a man by the name of Price, and two negroes.

Price lived a while with Little Beard, and afterwards with Jack
Berry, an Indian. When he left Jack Berry he went to Niagara, where
he now resides.

Newkirk was brought to Beard's Town, and lived with Little
Beard and at Fort Niagara about one year, and then enlisted under
Butler, and went with him on an expedition to the Monongahela.

## CHAPTER VIII

*Life of Ebenezer Allen, a Tory.—He comes to Gardow.—His
intimacy with a Nanticoke Squaw.—She gives him a Cap.—
Her Husband's jealousy.—Cruelty to his Wife.—Hiokatoo's
Mandate.—Allen supports her.—Her Husband is received into
favor.—Allen labors.—Purchases Goods.—Stops the Indian
War.—His troubles with the Indians.—Marries a Squaw.—Is
taken and carried to Quebec.—Acquitted.—Goes to Phila-
delphia.—Returns to Genesee with a Store of Goods, &c.—
Goes to Farming.—Moves to Allen's Creek.—Builds Mills at
Rochester.—Drowns a Dutchman.—Marries a white Wife.—
Kills an old Man.—Gets a Concubine.—Moves to Mt.
Morris.—Marries a third Wife and gets another Concubine.—
Receives a tract of Land.—Sends his Children to other States,
&c.—Disposes of his Land.—Moves to Grand River, where
he dies.—His Cruelties.*

SOMETIME near the close of the revolutionary war, a white man by
the name of Ebenezer Allen,[22] left his people in the state of Pennsylvania on the account of some disaffection towards his countrymen,
and came to the Genesee river, to reside with the Indians. He tarried

at Genishau a few days, and came up to Gardow, where I then resided.—He was, apparently, without any business that would support him; but he soon became acquainted with my son Thomas, with whom he hunted for a long time, and made his home with him at my house; winter came on, and he continued his stay.

When Allen came to my house, I had a white man living on my land, who had a Nanticoke squaw for his wife, with whom he had lived very peaceably; for he was a moderate man commonly, and she was a kind, gentle, cunning creature. It so happened that he had no hay for his cattle; so that in the winter he was obliged to drive them every day, perhaps half a mile from his house, to let them feed on rushes, which in those days were so numerous as to nearly cover the ground.

Allen having frequently seen the squaw in the fall, took the opportunity when her husband was absent with his cows, daily to make her a visit; and in return for his kindnesses she made and gave him a red cap finished and decorated in the highest Indian style.

The husband had for some considerable length of time felt a degree of jealousy that Allen was trespassing upon him with the consent of his squaw; but when he saw Allen dressed in so fine an Indian cap, and found that his dear Nanticoke had presented it to him, his doubts all left him, and he became so violently enraged that he caught her by the hair of her head, dragged her on the ground to my house, a distance of forty rods, and threw her in at the door. Hiokatoo, my husband, exasperated at the sight of so much inhumanity, hastily took down his old tomahawk, which for awhile had lain idle, shook it over the cuckold's head, and bade him jogo (i.e. go off.) The enraged husband, well knowing that he should feel a blow if he waited to hear the order repeated, instantly retreated, and went down the river to his cattle. We protected the poor Nanticoke woman, and gave her victuals; and Allen sympathized with her in her misfortunes till spring, when her husband came to her, acknowledged his former errors, and that he had abused her without a cause, promised a reformation, and she received him with every mark of a renewal of her affection. They went home lovingly, and soon after removed to Niagara.

The same spring, Allen commenced working my flats, and continued to labor there till after the peace in 1783. He then went to Philadelphia on some business that detained him but a few days, and returned with a horse and some dry goods, which he carried to a place that is now called Mount Morris, where he built or bought a small house.

The British and Indians on the Niagara frontier, dissatisfied with the treaty of peace, were determined, at all hazards, to continue their depredations upon the white settlements which lay between them and Albany. They actually made ready, and were about setting out on an expedition to that effect, when Allen (who by this time understood their customs of war) took a belt of wampum, which he had fraudulently procured, and carried it as a token of peace from the Indians to the commander of the nearest American military post.

The Indians were soon answered by the American officer that the wampum was cordially accepted; and, that a continuance of peace was ardently wished for. The Indians, at this, were chagrined and disappointed beyond measure; but as they held the wampum to be a sacred thing, they dared not to go against the import of its meaning, and immediately buried the hatchet as it respected the people of the United States; and smoked the pipe of peace. They, however, resolved to punish Allen for his officiousness in meddling with their national affairs, by presenting the sacred wampum without their knowledge, and went about devising means for his detection. A party was accordingly despatched from Fort Niagara to apprehend him; with orders to conduct him to that post for trial, or for safe keeping, till such time as his fate should be determined upon in a legal manner.

The party came on; but before it arrived at Gardow, Allen got news of its approach, and fled for safety, leaving the horse and goods that he had brought from Philadelphia, an easy prey to his enemies. He had not been long absent when they arrived at Gardow, where they made diligent search for him till they were satisfied that they could not find him, and then seized the effects which he had left, and returned to Niagara. My son Thomas, went with them, with Allen's horse, and carried the goods.

Allen, on finding that his enemies had gone, came back to my house, where he lived as before; but of his return they were soon notified at Niagara, and Nettles (who married Priscilla Ramsay) with a small party of Indians came on to take him. He, however, by some means found that they were near, and gave me his box of money and trinkets to keep safely, till he called for it, and again took to the woods.

Nettles came on determined at all events to take him before he went back; and, in order to accomplish his design, he, with his Indians, hunted in the day time and lay by at night at my house, and in that way they practised for a number of days. Allen watched the motion of his pursuers, and every night after they had gone to rest, came home and got some food, and then returned to his retreat. It was in the fall, and the weather was cold and rainy, so that he suffered extremely. Some nights he sat in my chamber till nearly daybreak, while his enemies were below, and when the time arrived I assisted him to escape unnoticed.

Nettles at length abandoned the chase—went home, and Allen, all in tatters, came in. By running in the woods his clothing had become torn into rags, so that he was in a suffering condition, almost naked. Hiokatoo gave him a blanket, and a piece of broadcloth for a pair of trowsers. Allen made his trowsers himself, and then built a raft, on which he went down the river to his own place at Mount Morris.

About that time he married a squaw, whose name was Sally.

The Niagara people finding that he was at his own house, came and took him by surprize when he least expected them, and carried him to Niagara. Fortunately for him, it so happened that just as they arrived at the fort, a house took fire and his keepers all left him to save the building, if possible. Allen had supposed his doom to be nearly sealed; but finding himself at liberty he took to his heels, left his escort to put out the fire, and ran to Tonnawanta. There an Indian gave him some refreshment, and a good gun, with which he hastened on to Little Beard's Town, where he found his squaw. Not daring to risk himself at that place for fear of being given up, he made her but a short visit, and came immediately to Gardow.

Just as he got to the top of the hill above the Gardow flats, he discovered a party of British soldiers and Indians in pursuit of him; and in fact they were so near that he was satisfied that they saw him, and concluded that it would be impossible for him to escape. The love of liberty, however, added to his natural swiftness, gave him sufficient strength to make his escape to his former castle of safety. His pursuers came immediately to my house, where they expected to have found him secreted, and under my protection. They told me where they had seen him but a few moments before, and that they were confident that it was within my power to put him into their hands. As I was perfectly clear of having had any hand in his escape, I told them plainly that I had not seen him since he was taken to Niagara, and that I could give them no information at all respecting him. Still unsatisfied, and doubting my veracity, they advised my

Indian brother to use his influence to draw from me the secret of his concealment, which they had an idea that I considered of great importance, not only to him but to myself. I persisted in my ignorance of his situation, and finally they left me.

Although I had not seen Allen, I knew his place of security, and was well aware that if I told them the place where he had formerly hid himself, they would have no difficulty in making him a prisoner.

He came to my house in the night, and awoke me with the greatest caution, fearing that some of his enemies might be watching to take him at a time when, and in a place where it would be impossible for him to make his escape. I got up and assured him that he was then safe; but that his enemies would return early in the morning and search him out if it should be possible. Having given him some victuals, which he received thankfully, I told him to go, but to return the next night to a certain corner of the fence near my house where he would find a quantity of meal that I would have well prepared and deposited there for his use.

Early the next morning, Nettles and his company came in while I was pounding the meal for Allen, and insisted upon my giving him up. I again told them that I did not know where he was, and that I could not, neither would I, tell them any thing about him. I well knew that Allen considered his life in my hands; and although it was my intention not to lie, I was fully determined to keep his situation a profound secret. They continued their labor and examined (as they supposed) every crevice, gully, tree and hollow log in the neighboring woods, and at last concluded that he had left the country, and gave him up for lost, and went home.

At that time Allen lay in a secret place in the gulph a short distance above my flats, in a hole that he accidentally found in the rock near the river. At night he came and got the meal at the corner of the fence as I had directed him, and afterwards lived in the gulph two weeks. Each night he came to the pasture and milked one of my cows, without any other vessel in which to receive the milk than his hat, out of which he drank it. I supplied him with meal, but fearing to build a fire he was obliged to eat it raw and wash it down with the milk. Nettles having left our neighborhood, and Allen considering himself safe, left his little cave and came home. I gave him his box of money and trinkets, and he went to his own house at Mount Morris. It was generally considered by the Indians of our tribe, that Allen was an innocent man, and that the Niagara people were persecuting him without a just cause. Little Beard, then about to go to the eastward on public business, charged his Indians not to meddle with Allen, but to let him live amongst them peaceably, and enjoy himself with his family and property if he could. Having the protection of the chief, he felt himself safe, and let his situation be known to the whites from whom he suspected no harm. They, however, were more inimical than our Indians and were easily bribed by Nettles to assist in bringing him to justice. Nettles came on, and the whites, as they had agreed, gave poor Allen up to him. He was bound and carried to Niagara, where he was confined in prison through the winter. In the spring he was taken to Montreal or Quebec for trial, and was honorably acquitted. The crime for which he was tried was, for his having carried the wampum to the Americans, and thereby putting too sudden a stop to their war.

From the place of his trial he went directly to Philadelphia, and purchased on credit, a boat load of goods which he brought by water to Conhocton, where he left them and came to Mount Morris for assistance to get them brought on. The Indians readily went with horses and brought them to his house, where he disposed of his dry goods; but not daring to let the Indians begin to drink strong liquor, for fear of the quarrels which would naturally follow, he sent his spirits to my place and we sold them. For his goods he received ginseng roots, principally, and a few skins. Ginseng at that time was plenty, and commanded a high price. We prepared the whole that he received for the market, expecting that he would carry them to Philadelphia. In that I was disappointed; for when he had disposed of, and got pay for all his goods, he took the ginseng and skins to Niagara, and there sold them and came home.

Tired of dealing in goods, he planted a large field of corn on or near his own land, attended to it faithfully, and succeeded in raising a large crop, which he harvested, loaded into canoes and carried down the river to the mouth of Allen's Creek, then called by the Indians Gin-is-a-ga, where he unloaded it, built him a house, and lived with his family.

The next season he planted corn at that place and built a grist and saw mill on Genesee Falls, now called Rochester.

At the time Allen built the mills, he had an old German living with him by the name of Andrews, whom he sent in a canoe down the river with his mill irons. Allen went down at the same time; but before they got to the mills Allen threw the old man overboard and drowned him, as it was then generally believed, for he was never seen or heard of afterwards.

In the course of the season in which Allen built his mills, he became acquainted with the daughter of a white man, who was moving to Niagara. She was handsome, and Allen soon got into her good graces, so that he married and took her home, to be a joint partner with Sally, the squaw, whom she had never heard of till she got home and found her in full possession; but it was too late for her to retrace the hasty steps she had taken, for her father had left her in the care of a tender husband and gone on. She, however, found that she enjoyed at least an equal half of her husband's affections, and made herself contented. Her father's name I have forgotten, but her's was Lucy.

Allen was not contented with two wives, for in a short time after he had married Lucy he came up to my house, where he found a young woman who had an old husband with her. They had been on a long journey, and called at my place to recruit and rest themselves. She filled Allen's eye, and he accordingly fixed upon a plan to get her into his possession. He praised his situation, enumerated his advantages, and finally persuaded them to go home and tarry with him a few days at least, and partake of a part of his comforts. They accepted his generous invitation and went home with him. But they had been there but two or three days when Allen took the old gentleman out to view his flats; and as they were deliberately walking on the bank of the river, pushed him into the water. The old man, almost strangled, succeeded in getting out; but his fall and exertions had so powerful an effect upon his system that he died in two or three days, and left his young widow to the protection of his murderer. She lived with him about one year in a state of concubinage and then left him.

How long Allen lived at Allen's Creek I am unable to state; but soon after the young widow left him, he removed to his old place at Mount Morris, and built a house, where he made Sally, his squaw, by whom he had two daughters, a slave to Lucy, by whom he had had one son; still, however, he considered Sally to be his wife.

After Allen came to Mt. Morris at that time, he married a girl by the name of Morilla Gregory, whose father at the time lived on Genesee Flats. The ceremony being over, he took her home to live in common with his other wives; but his house was too small for his family; for Sally and Lucy, conceiving that their lawful privileges would be abridged if they received a partner, united their strength and whipped poor Morilla so cruelly that he was obliged to keep her in a small Indian house a short distance from his own, or lose her entirely. Morilla, before she left Mt. Morris, had four children.

One of Morilla's sisters lived with Allen about a year after Morilla was married, and then quit him.

A short time after they all got to living at Mt. Morris, Allen prevailed upon the Chiefs to give to his Indian children, a tract of land four miles square, where he then resided. The Chiefs gave them the land, but he so artfully contrived the conveyance, that he could apply it to his own use, and by alienating his right, destroy the claim of his children.

Having secured the land, in that way, to himself, he sent his two Indian girls to Trenton, (N. J.) and his white son to Philadelphia, for the purpose of giving each of them a respectable English education.

While his children were at school, he went to Philadelphia, and sold his right to the land which he had begged of the Indians for his children to Robert Morris. After that, he sent for his daughters to come home, which they did.

Having disposed of the whole of his property on the Genesee river, he took his two white wives and their children, together with his effects, and removed to a Delaware town on the river De Trench, in Upper Canada. When he left Mt. Morris, Sally, his squaw, insisted upon going with him, and actually followed him, crying bitterly, and praying for his protection some two or three miles, till he absolutely bade her leave him, or he would punish her with severity.

At length, finding her case hopeless, she returned to the Indians.

At the great treaty at Big Tree, one of Allen's daughters claimed the land which he had sold to Morris. The claim was examined and decided against her in favor of Ogden, Trumbull, Rogers and others, who were the creditors of Robert Morris. Allen yet believed that his daughter had an indisputable right to the land in question, and got me to go with mother Farly, a half Indian woman, to assist him by interceding with Morris for it, and to urge the propriety of her claim. We went to Thomas Morris, and having stated to him our business, he told us plainly that he had no land to give away, and that as the title was good, he never would allow Allen, nor his heirs, one foot, or words to that effect. We returned to Allen the answer we had received, and he, conceiving all further attempts to be useless, went home.

He died at the Delaware town, on the river De Trench, in the year 1814 or 15, and left two white widows and one squaw, with a number of children, to lament his loss.

By his last will he gave all his property to his last wife, (Morilla,) and her children, without providing in the least for the support of Lucy, or any of the other members of his family. Lucy, soon after his death, went with her children down the Ohio river, to receive assistance from her friends.

In the revolutionary war, Allen was a tory, and by that means became acquainted with our Indians, when they were in the neighborhood of his native place, desolating the settlements on the Susquehannah. In those predatory battles, he joined them, and (as I have often heard the Indians say,) for cruelty was not exceeded by any of his Indian comrades!

At one time, when he was scouting with the Indians in the Susquehannah country, he entered a house very early in the morning, where he found a man, his wife, and one child, in bed. The man, as he entered the door, instantly sprang on the floor, for the purpose of defending himself and little family; but Allen dispatched him at one blow. He then cut off his head and threw it bleeding into the bed with the terrified woman; took the little infant from its mother's breast, and holding it by its legs, dashed its head against the jamb, and left the unhappy widow and mother to mourn alone over her murdered family. It has been said by some, that after he had killed the child, he opened the fire and buried it under the coals and embers: But of that I am not certain. I have often heard him speak of that transaction with a great degree of sorrow, and as the foulest crime he had ever committed—one for which I have no doubt he repented.

## CHAPTER IX

*Mrs. Jemison has liberty to go to her Friends.—Chooses to stay.—Her Reasons, &c.—Her Indian Brother makes provision for her Settlement.—He goes to Grand River and dies.— Her Love for him, &c.—She is presented with the Gardow Reservation.—Is troubled by Speculators.—Description of the Soil, &c. of her Flats.—Indian notions of the ancient Inhabitants of this Country.*

SOON after the close of the revolutionary war, my Indian brother,[23] Kau-jises-tau-ge-au (which being interpreted signifies Black Coals,) offered me my liberty, and told me that if it was my choice I might go to my friends.

My son, Thomas, was anxious that I should go; and offered to go with me and assist me on the journey, by taking care of the younger children, and providing food as we travelled, through the wilderness. But the Chiefs of our tribe, suspecting from his appearance, actions, and a few warlike exploits, that Thomas would be a great warrior, or a good counsellor, refused to let him leave them on any account whatever.

To go myself, and leave him, was more than I felt able to do; for he had been kind to me, and was one on whom I placed great dependence. The Chiefs refusing to let him go, was one reason for my resolving to stay; but another, more powerful, if possible, was, that I had got a large family of Indian children, that I must take with me; and that if I should be so fortunate as to find my relatives, they would despise them, if not myself; and treat us as enemies; or, at least with a degree of cold indifference, which I thought I could not endure.

Accordingly, after I had duly considered the matter, I told my brother that it was my choice to stay and spend the remainder of my days with my Indian friends, and live with my family as I had heretofore done. He appeared well pleased with my resolution, and informed me, that as that was my choice, I should have a piece of land that I could call my own, where I could live unmolested, and have something at my decease to leave for the benefit of my children.

In a short time he made himself ready to go to Upper Canada; but before he left us, he told me that he would speak to some of the Chiefs at Buffalo, to attend the great Council, which he expected would convene in a few years at farthest, and convey to me such a tract of land as I should select. My brother left us, as he had proposed, and soon after died at Grand River.

Kaujisestaugeau, was an excellent man, and ever treated me with kindness. Perhaps no one of his tribe at any time exceeded him in natural mildness of temper, and warmth and tenderness of affection. If he had taken my life at the time when the avarice of the old King inclined him to procure my emancipation, it would have been done with a pure heart and from good motives. He loved his friends; and was generally beloved. During the time that I lived in the family with him, he never offered the most trifling abuse; on the contrary, his whole conduct towards me was strictly honorable. I mourned his loss as that of a tender brother, and shall recollect him through life with emotions of friendship and gratitude.

I lived undisturbed, without hearing a word on the subject of my land, till the great Council was held at Big Tree, in 1797, when Farmer's Brother, whose Indian name is Ho-na-ye-wus, sent for me to attend the council. When I got there, he told me that my brother had spoken to him to see that I had a piece of land reserved for my use; and that then was the time for me to receive it.—He requested that I would choose for myself and describe the bounds of a piece that would suit me. I accordingly told him the place of beginning, and then went round a tract that I judged would be sufficient for my purpose, (knowing that it would include the Gardow Flats,) by stating certain bounds with which I was acquainted.

When the Council was opened, and the business afforded a proper opportunity, Farmer's Brother presented my claim, and rehearsed the request of my brother. Red Jacket, whose Indian name is Sagu-yu-what-hah, which interpreted, is Keeper-awake, opposed me or my claim with all his influence and eloquence. Farmer's Brother insisted upon the necessity, propriety and expediency of his proposition, and got the land granted. The deed was made and signed, securing to me the title to all the land I had described; under the same restrictions and regulations that other Indian lands are subject to.

That land has ever since been known by the name of the Gardow Tract.

Red Jacket not only opposed my claim at the Council, but he withheld my money two or three years, on the account of my lands having been granted without his consent. Parrish and Jones at length convinced him that it was the white people, and not the Indians who had given me the land, and compelled him to pay over all the money which he had retained on my account.

My land derived its name, Gardow, from a hill that is within its limits, which is called in the Seneca language Kau-tam. Kautam when interpreted signifies up and down, or down and up, and is applied to a hill that you will ascend and descend in passing it; or to a valley. It has been said that Gardow was the name of my husband Hiokatoo, and that my land derived its name from him; that however was a mistake, for the old man always considered Gardow a nickname, and was uniformly, offended when called by it.

About three hundred acres of my land, when I first saw it, was open flats, lying on the Genesee River, which it is supposed was cleared by a race of inhabitants who preceded the first Indian settlements in this part of the country. The Indians are confident that many parts of this country were settled and for a number of years occupied by people of whom their fathers never had any tradition, as they never had seen them. Whence those people originated, and whither they went, I have never heard one of our oldest and wisest Indians pretend to guess. When I first came to Genishau, the bank of Fall Brook had just slid off and exposed a large number of human bones, which the Indians said were buried there long before their fathers ever saw the place; and that they did not know what kind of people they were. It however was and is believed by our people, that they were not Indians.

My flats were extremely fertile; but needed more labor than my daughters and myself were able to perform, to produce a sufficient quantity of grain and other necessary productions of the earth, for the consumption of our family. The land had lain uncultivated so long that it was thickly covered with weeds of almost every description. In order that we might live more easy, Mr. Parrish, with the consent of the chiefs, gave me liberty to lease or let my land to white people to till on shares. I accordingly let it out, and have continued to do so, which makes my task less burthensome, while at the same time I am more comfortably supplied with the means of support.

## CHAPTER X

*Happy situation of her Family.—Disagreement between her sons Thomas and John.—Her Advice to them, &c.—John kills Thomas.—Her Affliction.—Council. Decision of the Chiefs, &c.—Life of Thomas.—His Wives, Children, &c.—Cause of his Death, &c.*

I HAVE frequently heard it asserted by white people, and can truly say from my own experience, that the time at which parents take the most satisfaction and comfort with their families is when their children are young, incapable of providing for their own wants, and are about the fireside, where they can be daily observed and instructed.

Few mothers, perhaps, have had less trouble with their children during their minority than myself. In general, my children were friendly to each other, and it was very seldom that I knew them to have the least difference or quarrel: so far, indeed, were they from rendering themselves or me uncomfortable, that I considered myself happy—more so than commonly falls to the lot of parents, especially to women.

My happiness in this respect, however, was not without alloy; for my son Thomas, from some cause unknown to me, from the time he was a small lad, always called his brother John, a witch, which was the cause, as they grew towards manhood, of frequent and severe quarrels between them, and gave me much trouble and anxiety for their safety. After Thomas and John arrived to manhood, in addition to the former charge, John got two wives, with whom he lived till the time of his death. Although polygamy was tolerated in our tribe, Thomas considered it a violation of good and wholesome rules in society, and tending directly to destroy that friendly social intercourse and love, that ought to be the happy result of matrimony and chastity. Consequently, he frequently reprimanded John, by telling him that his conduct was beneath the dignity, and inconsistent with the principles of good Indians; indecent and unbecoming a gentleman; and, as he never could reconcile himself to it, he was frequently, almost constantly, when they were together, talking to him on the same subject. John always resented such reprimand, and reproof, with a great degree of passion, though they never quarrelled, unless Thomas was intoxicated.

In his fits of drunkenness, Thomas seemed to lose all his natural reason, and to conduct like a wild or crazy man, without regard to relatives, decency or propriety. At such times he often threatened to take my life for having raised a witch, (as he called John,) and has gone so far as to raise his tomahawk to split my head. He, however, never struck me; but on John's account he struck Hiokatoo, and thereby excited in John a high degree of indignation, which was extinguished only by blood.

For a number of years their difficulties, and consequent unhappiness, continued and rather increased, continually exciting in my breast the most fearful apprehensions, and greatest anxiety for their safety. With tears in my eyes, I advised them to become reconciled to each other, and to be friendly; told them the consequences of their continuing to cherish so much malignity and malice, that it would end in their destruction, the disgrace of their families, and bring me down to the grave. No one can conceive of the constant trouble that I daily endured on their account—on the account of my two oldest sons, whom I loved equally, and with all the feelings and affection of a tender mother, stimulated by an anxious concern for their fate. Parents, mothers especially, will love their children, though ever so unkind and disobedient. Their eyes of compassion, of real sentimental affection, will be involuntarily extended after them, in their greatest excesses of iniquity; and those fine filaments of consanguinity, which gently entwine themselves around the heart where filial love and parental care is equal, will be lengthened, and enlarged to cords seemingly of sufficient strength to reach and reclaim the wanderer. I know that such exercises are frequently unavailing; but, not-withstanding their ultimate failure, it still remains true, and ever will, that the love of a parent for a disobedient child, will increase, and grow more and more ardent, so long as a hope of its reformation is capable of stimulating a disappointed breast.

My advice and expostulations with my sons were abortive; and year after year their disaffection for each other increased. At length, Thomas came to my house on the 1st day of July, 1811, in my ab-sence, somewhat intoxicated, where he found John, with whom he immediately commenced a quarrel on their old subjects of differ-ence.—John's anger became desperate. He caught Thomas by the hair of his head, dragged him out at the door and there killed him, by a blow which he gave him on the head with his tomahawk!

I returned soon after, and found my son lifeless at the door, on the spot where he was killed! No one can judge of my feelings on seeing this mournful spectacle; and what greatly added to my distress, was the fact that he had fallen by the murderous hand of his brother! I felt my situation unsupportable. Having passed through various scenes of trouble of the most cruel and trying kind, I had hoped to spend my few remaining days in quietude, and to die in peace, sur-rounded by my family. This fatal event, however, seemed to be a stream of woe poured into my cup of afflictions, filling it even to overflowing, and blasting all my prospects.

As soon as I had recovered a little from the shock which I felt at the sight of my departed son, and some of my neighbors had come in to assist in taking care of the corpse, I hired Shanks, an Indian, to go to Buffalo, and carry the sorrowful news of Thomas' death, to our friends at that place, and request the Chiefs to hold a Council, and dispose of John as they should think proper. Shanks set out on his errand immediately, and John, fearing that he should be appre-hended and punished for the crime he had committed, at the same time went off towards Caneadea.

Thomas was decently interred in a style corresponding with his rank.

The Chiefs soon assembled in council on the trial of John, and after having seriously examined the matter according to their laws, justified his conduct, and acquitted him. They considered Thomas to have been the first transgressor, and that for the abuses which he had offered, he had merited from John the treatment that he had received.

John, on learning the decision of the council, returned to his family.

Thomas (except when intoxicated, which was not frequent,) was a kind and tender child, willing to assist me in my labor, and to remove every obstacle to my comfort. His natural abilities were said to be of a superior cast, and he soared above the trifling subjects of revenge, which are common amongst Indians, as being far beneath his attention. In his childish and boyish days, his natural turn was to practise in the art of war, though he despised the cruelties that the warriors inflicted upon their subjugated enemies. He was manly in his deportment, courageous and active; and commanded respect. Though he appeared well pleased with peace, he was cunning in Indian warfare, and succeeded to admiration in the execution of his plans.

At the age of fourteen or fifteen years, he went into the war with manly fortitude, armed with a tomahawk and scalping knife; and when he returned, brought one white man a prisoner, whom he had taken with his own hands, on the west branch of the Susquehannah river. It so happened, that as he was looking out for his enemies, he discovered two men boiling sap in the woods. He watched them unperceived, till dark when he advanced with a noiseless step to where they were standing, caught one of them before they were apprized of danger, and conducted him to the camp. He was well treated while a prisoner, and redeemed at the close of the war.

At the time Kaujisestaugeau gave me my liberty to go to my friends, Thomas was anxious to go with me; but as I have before observed, the Chiefs would not suffer him to leave them on the account of his courage and skill in war: expecting that they should need his assistance. He was a great Counsellor and a Chief when quite young; and in the last capacity, went two or three times to Philadelphia to assist in making treaties with the people of the states.

Thomas had four wives, by whom he had eight children. Jacob Jemison, his second son by his last wife, who is at this time twenty-seven or twenty-eight years of age, went to Dartmouth college, in the spring of 1816, for the purpose of receiving a good education, where it was said that he was an industrious scholar, and made great proficiency in the study of the different branches to which he attended. Having spent two years at that Institution, he returned in the winter of 1818, and is now at Buffalo; where I have understood that he contemplates commencing the study of medicine, as a profession.

Thomas, at the time he was killed, was a few moons over fifty-two years old, and John was forty-eight. As he was naturally good natured, and possessed a friendly disposition, he would not have come to so untimely an end, had it not been for his intemperance. He fell a victim to the use of ardent spirits—a poison that will soon exterminate the Indian tribes in this part of the country, and leave their names without a root or branch. The thought is melancholy; but no arguments, no examples, however persuasive or impressive, are sufficient to deter an Indian for an hour from taking the potent draught, which he knows at the time will derange his faculties, reduce him to a level with the beasts, or deprive him of life!

## CHAPTER XI

*Death of Hiokatoo.—Biography.—His Birth—Education.— Goes against the Cherokees, &c.—Bloody Battle, &c.—His success and cruelties in the French War.—Battle at Fort Freeland.—Capts. Dougherty and Boon killed.—His Cruelties in the neighborhood of Cherry Valley, &c.—Indians remove their general Encampment.—In 1782, Col. Crawford is sent to destroy them, &c.—Is met by a Traitor,—Battle.—Crawford's Men surprized.—Irregular Retreat.—Crawford and Doct. Night taken.—Council.—Crawford Condemned and Burnt.—Aggravating Circumstances.—Night is sentenced to be Burnt.—Is Painted by Hiokatoo.—Is conducted off, &c.— His fortunate Escape.—Hiokatoo in the French War takes Col. Canton.—His Sentence.—Is bound on a wild Colt that runs loose three days.—Returns Alive.—Is made to run the Gauntlet.—Gets knocked down, &c.—Is Redeemed and sent Home.—Hiokatoo's Enmity to the Cherokees, &c.—His Height.—Strength—Speed, &c.*

IN the month of November 1811, my husband Hiokatoo, who had been sick four years of the consumption, died at the advanced age of one hundred and three years, as nearly as the time could be estimated. He was the last that remained to me of our family connection, or rather of my old friends with whom I was adopted, except a part of one family, which now lives at Tonewanta.

Hiokatoo was buried decently, and had all the insignia of a veteran warrior buried with him; consisting of a war club, tomahawk and scalping knife, a powder-flask, flint, a piece of spunk, a small cake and a cup; and in his best clothing.

Hiokatoo was an old man when I first saw him; but he was by

no means enervated. During the term of nearly fifty years that I lived with him, I received, according to Indian customs, all the kindness and attention that was my due as his wife.—Although war was his trade from his youth till old age and decrepitude stopt his career, he uniformly treated me with tenderness, and never offered an insult.

I have frequently heard him repeat the history of his life from his childhood; and when he came to that part which related to his actions, his bravery and his valor in war; when he spoke of the ambush, the combat, the spoiling of his enemies and the sacrifice of the victims, his nerves seemed strung with youthful ardor, the warmth of the able warrior seemed to animate his frame, and to produce the heated gestures which he had practised in middle age. He was a man of tender feelings to his friends, ready and willing to assist them in distress, yet, as a warrior, his cruelties to his enemies perhaps were unparalleled, and will not admit a word of palliation.

Hiokatoo, was born in one of the tribes of the Six Nations that inhabited the banks of the Susquehannah; or, rather he belonged to a tribe of the Senecas that made, at the time of the great Indian treaty, a part of those nations. He was own cousin to Farmer's Brother, a Chief who has been justly celebrated for his worth. Their mothers were sisters, and it was through the influence of Farmer's Brother, that I became Hiokatoo's wife.

In early life, Hiokatoo showed signs of thirst for blood, by attending only to the art of war, in the use of the tomahawk and scalping knife; and in practising cruelties upon every thing that chanced to fall into his hands, which was susceptible of pain. In that way he learned to use his implements of war effectually, and at the same time blunted all those fine feelings and tender sympathies that are naturally excited, by hearing or seeing, a fellow being in distress. He could inflict the most excruciating tortures upon his enemies, and prided himself upon his fortitude, in having performed the most barbarous ceremonies and tortures, without the least degree of pity or remorse. Thus qualified, when very young he was initiated into scenes of carnage, by being engaged in the wars that prevailed amongst the Indian tribes.

In the year 1731, he was appointed a runner, to assist in collecting an army to go against the Cotawpes, Cherokees and other southern Indians. A large army was collected, and after a long and fatiguing march, met its enemies in what was then called the "low, dark and bloody lands," near the mouth of Red River, in what is now called the state of Kentucky.* The Cotawpes† and their associates, had, by some means, been apprized of their approach, and lay in ambush to take them at once, when they should come within their reach, and destroy the whole army. The northern Indians, with their usual sagacity, discovered the situation of their enemies, rushed upon the ambuscade and massacred 1200 on the spot. The battle continued for two days and two nights, with the utmost severity, in which the northern Indians were victorious, and so far succeeded in destroying the Cotawpes that they at that time ceased to be a nation. The victors suffered an immense loss in killed; but gained the hunting ground, which was their grand object, though the Cherokees would not give it up in a treaty, or consent to make peace. Bows and arrows, at that time, were in general use, though a few guns were employed.

From that time he was engaged in a number of battles in which Indians only were engaged, and made fighting his business, till the commencement of the French war. In those battles he took a number of Indians prisoners, whom he killed by tying them to trees and then setting small Indian boys to shooting at them with arrows, till death finished the misery of the sufferers; a process that frequently took two days for its completion!

During the French war he was in every battle that was fought on the Susquehannah and Ohio rivers; and was so fortunate as never to have been taken prisoner.

At Braddock's defeat he took two white prisoners, and burnt them alive in a fire of his own kindling.

In 1777, he was in the battle at Fort Freeland, in Northumberland county, Penn. The fort contained a great number of women and children, and was defended only by a small garrison. The force that went against it consisted of 100 British regulars, commanded by a Col. McDonald, and 300 Indians under Hiokatoo. After a short but bloody engagement, the fort was surrendered; the women and children were sent under an escort to the next fort below, and the men and boys taken off by a party of British to the general Indian en-

---

**Those powerful armies met near the place that is now called Clarksville, which is situated at the fork where Red River joins the Cumberland, a few miles above the line between Kentucky and Tennessee.*

†*The Author acknowledges himself unacquainted, from Indian history, with a nation of this name; but as [illegible] years have elapsed since the date of this occurrence, it is highly probable that such a nation did exist, and that it was absolutely exterminated at that eventful period.*

campment. As soon as the fort had capitulated and the firing had ceased, Hiokatoo with the help of a few Indians tomahawked every wounded American while earnestly begging with uplifted hands for quarters.

The massacre was but just finished when Capts. Dougherty and Boon arrived with a reinforcement to assist the garrison. On their arriving in sight of the fort they saw that it had surrendered, and that an Indian was holding the flag. This so much inflamed Capt. Dougherty that he left his command, stept forward and shot the Indian at the first fire. Another took the flag, and had no sooner got it erected than Dougherty dropt him as he had the first. A third presumed to hold it, who was also shot down by Dougherty. Hiokatoo, exasperated at the sight of such bravery, sullied out with a party of his Indians, and killed Capts. Dougherty, Boon, and fourteen men, at the first fire. The remainder of the two companies escaped by taking to flight, and soon arrived at the fort which they had left but a few hours before.

In an expedition that went out against Cherry Valley and the neighboring settlements, Captain David, a Mohawk Indian, was first, and Hiokatoo the second in command. The force consisted of several hundred Indians, who were determined on mischief, and the destruction of the whites. A continued series of wantonness and barbarity characterized their career, for they plundered and burnt every thing that came in their way, and killed a number of persons, among whom were several infants, whom Hiokatoo butchered or dashed upon the stones with his own hands. Besides the instances which have been mentioned, he was in a number of parties during the revolutionary war, where he ever acted a conspicuous part.

The Indians having removed the seat of their depredations and war to the frontiers of Pennsylvania, Ohio, Kentucky and the neighboring territories, assembled a large force at Upper Sandusky, their place of general rendezvous, from whence they went out to the various places which they designed to sacrifice.

Tired of the desolating scenes that were so often witnessed, and feeling a confidence that the savages might be subdued, and an end put to their crimes, the American government raised a regiment, consisting of 300 volunteers, for the purpose of dislodging them from their cantonment and preventing further barbarities. Col. William Crawford[24] and Lieut. Col. David Williamson,[25] men who had been thoroughly tried and approved, were commissioned by Gen. Washington to take the command of a service that seemed all-important to the welfare of the country. In the month of July, 1782, well armed and provided with a sufficient quantity of provision, this regiment made an expeditious march through the wilderness to Upper San-dusky, where, as had been anticipated, they found the Indians assem-bled in full force at their encampment, prepared to receive an attack.

As Col. Crawford and his brave band advanced, and when they had got within a short distance from the town, they were met by a white man, with a flag of truce from the Indians, who proposed to Col. Crawford that if he would surrender himself and his men to the Indians, their lives should be spared; but, that if they persisted in their undertaking, and attacked the town, they should all be massa-cred to a man.

Crawford, while hearing the proposition, attentively surveyed its bearer, and recognized in his features one of his former schoolmates and companions, with whom he was perfectly acquainted, by the name of Simon Gurty.[26] Gurty, but a short time before this, had been a soldier in the American army, in the same regiment with Crawford; but on the account of his not having received the promotion that he expected, he became disaffected—swore an eternal war with his countrymen, fled to the Indians, and joined them, as a leader well qualified to conduct them to where they could annoint their thirst for blood, upon the innocent, unoffending and defenceless settlers.

Crawford sternly inquired of the traitor if his name was not Simon Gurty; and being answered in the affirmative, he informed him that he despised the offer which he had made; and that he should not surrender his army unless he should be compelled to do so, by a superior force.

Gurty returned, and Crawford immediately commenced an en-gagement that lasted till night, without the appearance of victory on either side, when the firing ceased, and the combatants on both sides retired to take refreshment, and to rest through the night. Crawford encamped in the woods near half a mile from the town, where, after the centinels were placed, and each had taken his ration, they slept on their arms, that they might be instantly ready in case they should be attacked. The stillness of death hovered over the little army, and sleep relieved the whole, except the wakeful centinels who vigilantly attended to their duty.—But what was their surprise, when they found late in the night, that they were surrounded by the Indians on every side, except a narrow space between them and the town? Every man was under arms, and the officers instantly consulted each other on the best method of escaping; for they saw that to fight, would be useless, and that to surrender, would be death.

Crawford proposed to retreat through the ranks of the enemy in an opposite direction from the town, as being the most sure course to take. Lt. Col. Williamson advised to march directly through the town, where there appeared to be no Indians, and the fires were yet burning.

There was no time or place for debates: Col. Crawford, with sixty followers retreated on the route that he had proposed by attempting to rush through the enemy; but they had no sooner got amongst the Indians, than every man was killed or taken prisoner! Amongst the prisoners, were Col. Crawford, and Doct. Night,[27] surgeon of the regiment.

Lt. Col. Williamson, with the remainder of the regiment, together with the wounded, set out at the same time that Crawford did, went through the town without losing a man, and by the help of good guides arrived at their homes in safety.

The next day after the engagement the Indians disposed of all their prisoners to the different tribes, except Col. Crawford and Doct. Night; but those unfortunate men were reserved for a more cruel destiny. A council was immediately held on Sandusky plains, consisting of all the Chiefs and warriors, ranged in their customary order, in a circular form; and Crawford and Night were brought forward and seated in the centre of the circle.

The council being opened, the Chiefs began to examine Crawford on various subjects relative to the war. At length they enquired who conducted the military operations of the American army on the Ohio and Susquehannah rivers, during the year before; and who had led that army against them with so much skill, and so uniform success? Crawford very honestly and without suspecting any harm from his reply, promptly answered that he was the man who had led his countrymen to victory, who had driven the enemy from the settlements, and by that means had procured a great degree of happiness to many of his fellow-citizens. Upon hearing this, a Chief, who had lost a son in the year before, in a battle where Colonel Crawford commanded, left his station in the council, stepped to Crawford, blacked his face, and at the same time told him that the next day he should be burnt.

The council was immediately dissolved on its hearing the sentence from the Chief, and the prisoners were taken off the ground, and kept in custody through the night. Crawford now viewed his fate as sealed; and despairing of ever returning to his home or his country, only dreaded the tediousness of death, as commonly inflicted by the savages, and earnestly hoped that he might be despatched at a single blow.

Early the next morning, the Indians assembled at the place of execution, and Crawford was led to the post—the goal of savage torture, to which he was fastened. The post was a stick of timber placed firmly in the ground, having an arm framed in at the top, and extending some six or eight feet from it, like the arm of a sign post. A pile of wood containing about two cords, lay a few feet from the place where he stood, which he was informed was to be kindled into a fire that would burn him alive, as many had been burnt on the same spot, who had been much less deserving than himself.

Gurty stood and composedly looked on the preparations that were making for the funeral of one his former playmates; a hero by whose side he had fought; of a man whose valor had won laurels which, if he could have returned, would have been strewed upon his grave, by his grateful countrymen. Dreading the agony that he saw he was about to feel, Crawford used every argument which his perilous situation could suggest to prevail upon Gurty to ransom him at any price, and deliver him (as it was in his power,) from the savages, and their torments. Gurty heard his prayers, and expostulations, and saw his tears with indifference, and finally told the forsaken victim that he would not procure him a moment's respite, nor afford him the most trifling assistance.

The Col. was then bound, stripped naked and tied by his wrists to the arm, which extended horizontally from the post, in such a manner that his arms were extended over his head, with his feet just standing upon the ground. This being done, the savages placed the wood in a circle around him at the distance of a few feet, in order that his misery might be protracted to the greatest length, and then kindled it in a number of places at the same time. The flames arose and the scorching heat became almost insupportable. Again he prayed to Gurty in all the anguish of his torment, to rescue him from the fire, or shoot him dead upon the spot. A demoniac smile suffused the countenance of Gurty, while he calmly replied to the dying suppliant, that he had no pity for his sufferings; but that he was then satisfying that spirit of revenge, which for a long time he had hoped to have an opportunity to wreak upon him. Nature now almost exhausted from the intensity of the heat, he settled down a little, when a squaw threw coals of fire and embers upon him, which made him groan most piteously, while the whole camp rung with exultation. During the execution they manifested all the ecstasy of a complete triumph. Poor Crawford soon died and was entirely consumed.

Thus ended the life of a patriot and hero, who had been an intimate with Gen. Washington, and who shared in an eminent degree the confidence of that great, good man, to whom, in the time of revolutionary perils, the sons of legitimate freedom looked with a degree of faith in his mental resources, unequalled in the history of the world.

That tragedy being ended, Doct. Night was informed that on the next day he should be burnt in the same manner that his comrade Crawford had been, at Lower Sandusky. Hiokatoo, who had been a leading chief in the battle with, and in the execution of Crawford, painted Doct. Night's face black, and then bound and gave him up to two able bodied Indians to conduct to the place of execution.

They set off with him immediately, and travelled till towards evening, when they halted to encamp till morning. The afternoon had been very rainy, and the storm still continued, which rendered it very difficult for the Indians to kindle a fire. Night observing the difficulty under which they labored, made them to understand by signs, that if they would unbind him, he would assist them.—They accordingly unloosed him, and he soon succeeded in making a fire by the application of small dry stuff which he was at considerable trouble to procure. While the Indians were warming themselves, the Doct. continued to gather wood to last through the night, and in doing this, he found a club which he placed in a situation from whence he could take it conveniently whenever an opportunity should present itself, in which he could use it effectually. The Indians continued warming, till at length the Doct. saw that they had placed themselves in a favorable position for the execution of his design, when, stimulated by the love of life, he cautiously took his club and at two blows knocked them both down. Determined to finish the work of death which he had so well begun, he drew one of their scalping knives, with which he beheaded and scalped them both! He then took a rifle, tomahawk, and some ammunition, and directed his course for home, where he arrived without having experienced any difficulty on his journey.

The next morning, the Indians took the track of their victim and his attendants, to go to Lower Sandusky, and there execute the sentence which they had pronounced upon him. But what was their surprise and disappointment, when they arrived at the place of encampment, where they found their trusty friends scalped and decapitated, and that their prisoner had made his escape?—Chagrined beyond measure, they immediately separated, and went in every direction in pursuit of their prey; but after having spent a number of days unsuccessfully, they gave up the chase, and returned to their encampment.*

In the time of the French war, in an engagement that took place on the Ohio river, Hiokatoo took a British Col. by the name of Simon Canton, whom he carried to the Indian encampment. A council was held, and the Col. was sentenced to suffer death, by being tied on a wild colt, with his face towards its tail, and then having the colt turned loose to run where it pleased. He was accordingly tied on, and the colt let loose, agreeable to the sentence. The colt run two days and then returned with its rider yet alive. The Indians, thinking that he would never die in that way, took him off, and made him run the gauntlet three times; but in the last race a squaw knocked him down, and he was supposed to have been dead. He, however, recovered, and was sold for fifty dollars to a Frenchman, who sent him as a prisoner to Detroit. On the return of the Frenchman to Detroit, the Col. besought him to ransom him, and give, or set him at liberty, with so much warmth, and promised with so much solemnity, to reward him as one of the best of benefactors, if he would let him go, that the Frenchman took his word, and sent him home to his family. The Col. remembered his promise, and in a short time

---

*I have understood, (from unauthenticated sources however,) that soon after the revolutionary war, Doct. Night published a pamphlet, containing an account of the battle at Sandusky, and of his own sufferings. My information on this subject, was derived from a different quarter.

The subject of this narrative in giving the account of her last husband, Hiokatoo, referred us to Mr. George Jemison, who, (as it will be noticed) lived on her land a number of years, and who had frequently heard the old Chief relate the story of his life; particularly that part which related to his military career. Mr. Jemison, on being enquired of, gave the foregoing account, partly from his own personal knowledge, and the remainder, from the account given by Hiokatoo.

Mr. Jemison was in the battle, was personally acquainted with Col. Crawford, and one that escaped with Lt. Col. Williamson. We have no doubt of the truth of the statement, and have therefore inserted the whole account, as an addition to the historical facts which are daily coming into a state of preservation, in relation to the American Revolution.

AUTHOR.

sent his deliverer one hundred and fifty dollars, as a reward for his generosity.

Since the commencement of the revolutionary war, Hiokatoo has been in seventeen campaigns, four of which were in the Cherokee war. He was so great an enemy to the Cherokees, and so fully determined upon their subjugation, that on his march to their country, he raised his own army for those four campaigns, and commanded it; and also superintended its subsistence. In one of those campaigns, which continued two whole years without intermission, he attacked his enemies on the Mobile, drove them to the country of the Creek Nation, where he continued to harrass them, till being tired of war, he returned to his family. He brought home a great number of scalps, which he had taken from the enemy, and ever seemed to possess an unconquerable will that the Cherokees might be utterly destroyed. Towards the close of his last fighting in that country, he took two squaws, whom he sold on his way home for money to defray the expense of his journey.

Hiokatoo was about six feet four or five inches high, large boned, and rather inclined to leanness. He was very stout and active, for a man of his size, for it was said by himself and others, that he had never found an Indian who could keep up with him on a race, or throw him at wrestling. His eye was quick and penetrating; and his voice was of that harsh and powerful kind, which, amongst Indians, always commands attention. His health had been uniformly good. He never was confined by sickness, till he was attacked with the consumption, four years before his death. And, although he had, from his earliest days, been inured to almost constant fatigue, and exposure to the inclemency of the weather, in the open air, he seemed to lose the vigor of the prime of life only by the natural decay occasioned by old age.

## CHAPTER XII

*Her Troubles Renewed.—John's Jealousy towards his brother Jesse.—Circumstances attending the Murder of Jesse Jemison.—Her Grief.—His Funeral—Age—Filial Kindness, &c.*

BEING now left a widow in my old age, to mourn the loss of a husband, who had treated me well, and with whom I had raised five children, and having suffered the loss of an affectionate son, I fondly fostered the hope that my melancholy vicissitudes had ended, and that the remainder of my time would be characterized by nothing unpropitious. My children, dutiful and kind, lived near me, and apparently nothing obstructed our happiness.

But a short time, however, elapsed after my husband's death, before my troubles were renewed with redoubled severity.

John's hands having been once stained in the blood of a brother, it was not strange that after his acquittal, every person of his acquaintance should shun him, from a fear of his repeating upon them the same ceremony that he had practised upon Thomas. My son Jesse, went to Mt. Morris, a few miles from home, on business, in the winter after the death of his father; and it so happened that his brother John was there, who requested Jesse to come home with him. Jesse, fearing that John would commence a quarrel with him on the way, declined the invitation, and tarried over night.

From that time John conceived himself despised by Jesse, and was highly enraged at the treatment which he had received. Very little was said, however, and it all passed off, apparently, till sometime in the month of May, 1812, at which time Mr. Robert Whaley, who lived in the town of Castile, within four miles of me, came to my house early on Monday morning, to hire George Chongo, my son-in-law, and John and Jesse, to go that day and help him slide a quantity of boards from the top of the hill to the river, where he calculated to build a raft of them for market.

They all concluded to go with Mr. Whaley, and made ready as soon as possible. But before they set out I charged them not to drink any whiskey: for I was confident that if they did, they would surely have a quarrel in consequence of it. They went and worked till almost night, when a quarrel ensued between Chongo and Jesse, in consequence of the whiskey that they had drank through the day, which terminated in a battle, and Chongo got whipped.

When Jesse had got through with Chongo, he told Mr. Whaley that he would go home, and directly went off. He, however, went but a few rods before he stopped and lay down by the side of a log to wait, (as was supposed,) for company. John, as soon as Jesse was gone, went to Mr. Whaley, with his knife in his hand, and bade him jogo: (i.e. be gone,) at the same time telling him that Jesse was a bad man. Mr. Whaley, seeing that his countenance was changed, and that he was determined upon something desperate, was alarmed for his own safety, and turned towards home, leaving Chongo on the ground drunk, near to where Jesse had lain, who by this time had got up, and was advancing towards John. Mr. Whaley was soon out of hearing of them; but some of his workmen staid till it was dark. Jesse came up to John, and said to him, you want more whiskey, and more fighting, and after a few words went at him, to try in the first place to get away his knife. In this he did not succeed, and they parted. By this time the night had come on, and it was dark. Again they clenched and at length in their struggle they both fell. John, having his knife in his hand, came under, and in that situation gave Jesse a fatal stab with his knife, and repeated the blows till Jesse cried out, brother, you have killed me, quit his hold and settled back upon the ground.—Upon hearing this, John left him and came to Thomas' widow's house, told them that he had been fighting with their uncle, whom he had killed, and showed them his knife.

Next morning as soon as it was light, Thomas' and John's children came and told me that Jesse was dead in the woods, and also informed me how he came by his death. John soon followed them and informed me himself of all that had taken place between him and his brother, and seemed to be somewhat sorrowful for his conduct. You can better imagine what my feelings were than I can describe them. My darling son, my youngest child, him on whom I depended, was dead; and I in my old age left destitute of a helping hand!

As soon as it was consistent for me, I got Mr. George Jemison, (of whom I shall have occasion to speak,) to go with his sleigh to where Jesse was, and bring him home, a distance of 3 or 4 miles. My daughter Polly arrived at the fatal spot first: we got there soon after her; though I went the whole distance on foot. By this time, Chongo, (who was left on the ground drunk the night before,) had become sober and sensible of the great misfortune which had happened to our family.

I was overcome with grief at the sight of my murdered son, and so far lost the command of myself as to be almost frantic; and those who were present were obliged to hold me from going near him.

On examining the body it was found that it had received eighteen wounds so deep and large that it was believed that either of them would have proved mortal. The corpse was carried to my house, and kept till the Thursday following, when it was buried after the manner of burying white people.

Jesse was twenty-seven or eight years old when he was killed. His temper had been uniformly very mild and friendly; and he was inclined to copy after the white people; both in his manners and dress. Although he was naturally temperate, he occasionally became intoxicated; but never was quarrelsome or mischievous. With the white people he was intimate, and learned from them their habits of industry, which he was fond of practising, especially when my comfort demanded his labor. As I have observed, it is the custom amongst the Indians, for the women to perform all the labor in, and out of doors, and I had the whole to do, with the help of my daughters, till Jesse arrived to a sufficient age to assist us. He was disposed to labor in the cornfield, to chop my wood, milk my cows, and attend to any kind of business that would make my task the lighter. On the account of his having been my youngest child, and so willing to help me, I am sensible that I loved him better than I did either of my other children. After he began to understand my situation, and the means of rendering it more easy, I never wanted for any thing that was in his power to bestow; but since his death, as I have had all my labor to perform alone, I have constantly seen hard times.

Jesse shunned the company of his brothers, and the Indians generally, and never attended their frolics; and it was supposed that this, together with my partiality for him, were the causes which excited in John so great a degree of envy, that nothing short of death would satisfy it.

## CHAPTER XIII

*Mrs. Jemison is informed that she has a Cousin in the Neighborhood, by the name of George Jemison.—His Poverty.—Her Kindness.—His Ingratitude.—Her Trouble from Land Speculation.—Her Cousin moves off.*

A year or two before the death of my husband, Capt. H. Jones sent me word, that a cousin of mine was then living in Leicester, (a few miles from Gardow,) by the name of George Jemison, and as he was very poor, thought it advisable for me to go and see him, and take him home to live with me on my land. My Indian friends were pleased to hear that one of my relatives was so near, and also advised me to send for him and his family immediately. I accordingly had him and his family moved into one of my houses, in the month of March, 1810.

He said that he was my father's brother's son—that his father did not leave Europe, till after the French war in America, and that when he did come over, he settled in Pennsylvania, where he died. George had no personal knowledge of my father; but from information, was confident that the relationship which he claimed between himself and me, actually existed. Although I had never before heard of my father having had but one brother, (him who was killed at Fort Necessity,) yet I knew that he might have had others, and, as the story of George carried with it a probability that it was true, I received him as a kinsman, and treated him with every degree of friendship which his situation demanded.*

I found that he was destitute of the means of subsistence, and in debt to the amount of seventy dollars, without the ability to pay one cent. He had no cow, and finally, was completely poor. I paid his debts to the amount of seventy-two dollars, and bought him a cow, for which I paid twenty dollars, and a sow and pigs, that I paid eight dollars for. I also paid sixteen dollars for pork that I gave him, and furnished him with other provisions and furniture; so that his family was comfortable. As he was destitute of a team, I furnished him with one, and also supplied him with tools for farming. In addition to all this, I let him have one of Thomas' cows, for two seasons.

My only object in mentioning his poverty, and the articles with which I supplied him, is to show how ungrateful a person can be for favors, and how soon a kind benefactor will, to all appearance, be forgotten.

Thus furnished with the necessary implements of husbandry, a good team, and as much land as he could till, he commenced farming on my flats, and for some time labored well. At length, however, he got an idea that if he could become the owner of a part of my reservation, he could live more easy, and certainly be more rich, and accordingly set himself about laying a plan to obtain it, in the easiest manner possible.

I supported Jemison and his family eight years, and probably should have continued to have done so to this day, had it not been for the occurrence of the following circumstance.

When he had lived with me some six or seven years, a friend of mine told me that as Jemison was my cousin, and very poor, I ought to give him a piece of land that he might have something whereon to live, that he would call his own. My friend and Jemison were then

*Mrs. Jemison is now confident that George Jemison is not her cousin, and thinks that he claimed the relationship, only to gain assistance: But the old gentleman, who is now living, is certain that his and her father were brothers, as before stated.

together at my house, prepared to complete a bargain. I asked how much land he wanted? Jemison said that he should be glad to receive his old field (as he called it) containing about fourteen acres, and a new one that contained twenty-six.

I observed to them that as I was incapable of transacting business of that nature, I would wait till Mr. Thomas Clute, (a neighbor on whom I depended,) should return from Albany, before I should do any thing about it. To this Jemison replied that if I waited till Mr. Clute returned, he should not get the land at all, and appeared very anxious to have the business closed without delay. On my part, I felt disposed to give him some land, but knowing my ignorance of writing, feared to do it alone, lest they might include as much land as they pleased, without my knowledge.

They then read the deed which my friend had prepared before he came from home, describing a piece of land by certain bounds that were a specified number of chains and links from each other. Not understanding the length of a chain or link, I described the bounds of a piece of land that I intended Jemison should have, which they said was just the same that the deed contained and no more. I told them that the deed must not include a lot that was called the Steele place, and they assured me that it did not. Upon this, putting confidence in them both, I signed the deed to George Jemison, containing, and conveying to him as I supposed, forty acres of land. The deed being completed they charged me never to mention the bargain which I had then made to any person; because if I did, they said it would spoil the contract. The whole matter was afterwards disclosed; when it was found that that deed instead of containing only forty acres, contained four hundred, and that one half of it actually belonged to my friend, as it had been given to him by Jemison as a reward for his trouble in procuring the deed, in the fraudulent manner above mentioned.

My friend, however, by the advice of some well disposed people, awhile afterwards gave up his claim; but Jemison held his till he sold it for a trifle to a gentleman in the south part of Genesee county.

Sometime after the death of my son Thomas, one of his sons went to Jemison to get the cow that I had let him have two years; but Jemison refused to let her go, and struck the boy so violent a blow as to almost kill him. Jemison then run to Jellis Clute, Esq. to procure a warrant to take the boy; but Young King, an Indian Chief, went down to Squawky hill to Esq. Clute's, and settled the affair by

MARY JEMISON                    199

Jemison's agreeing never to use that club again. Having satisfactorily found out the friendly disposition of my cousin towards me, I got him off my premises as soon as possible.

## CHAPTER XIV

*Another Family Affliction.—Her son John's Occupation.—He goes to Buffalo—Returns.—Great Slide by him considered Ominous—Trouble, &c.—He goes to Squawky Hill—Quarrels—Is murdered by two Indians.—His Funeral—Mourners, &c.—His Disposition.—Ominous Dream.—Black Chief's Advice, &c.—His Widows and Family.—His Age.—His Murderers flee.—Her Advice to them.—They set out to leave their Country.—Their Uncle's Speech to them on parting.—They return.—Jack proposes to Doctor to kill each other.—Doctor's Speech in Reply.—Jack's Suicide.—Doctor's Death.*

TROUBLE seldom comes single. While George Jemison was busily engaged in his pursuit of wealth at my expence, another event of a much more serious nature occurred, which added greatly to my afflictions, and consequently destroyed, at least a part of the happiness that I had anticipated was laid up in the archives of Providence, to be dispensed on my old age.

My son John, was a doctor, considerably celebrated amongst the Indians of various tribes, for his skill in curing their diseases, by the administration of roots and herbs, which he gathered in the forests, and other places where they had been planted by the hand of nature.

In the month of April, or first of May, 1817, he was called upon to go to Buffalo, Cattaraugus and Allegany, to cure some who were sick. He went, and was absent about two months. When he returned, he observed the Great Slide of the bank of Genesee river, a short distance above my house, which had taken place during his absence; and conceiving that circumstance to be ominous of his own death, called at his sister Nancy's, told her that he should live but a few days, and wept bitterly at the near approach of his dissolution. Nancy endeavored to persuade him that his trouble was imaginary, and that he ought not to be affected by a fancy which was visionary. Her arguments were ineffectual, and afforded no alleviation to his mental sufferings. From his sister's, he went to his own house, where he stayed only two nights, and then went to Squawky Hill to procure money, with which to purchase flour for the use of his family.

While at Squawky Hill he got into the company of two Squawky Hill Indians, whose names were Doctor and Jack, with whom he drank freely, and in the afternoon had a desperate quarrel, in which his opponents, (as it was afterwards understood,) agreed to kill him. The quarrel ended, and each appeared to be friendly. John bought some spirits, of which they all drank, and then set out for home. John and an Allegany Indian were on horseback, and Doctor and Jack were on foot. It was dark when they set out. They had not proceeded far, when Doctor and Jack commenced another quarrel with John, clenched and dragged him off his horse, and then with a stone gave him so severe a blow on his head, that some of his brains were discharged from the wound. The Allegany Indian, fearing that his turn would come next, fled for safety as fast as possible.

John recovered a little from the shock he had received, and endeavored to get to an old hut that stood near; but they caught him, and with an axe cut his throat, and beat out his brains, so that when he was found the contents of his skull were lying on his arms.

Some squaws, who heard the uproar, ran to find out the cause of it; but before they had time to offer their assistance, the murderers drove them into a house, and threatened to take their lives if they did not stay there, or if they made any noise.

Next morning, Esq. Clute sent me word that John was dead, and also informed me of the means by which his life was taken. A number of people went from Gardow to where the body lay, and Doct. Levi Brundridge brought it up home, where the funeral was attended after the manner of the white people. Mr. Benjamin Luther, and Mr. William Wiles, preached a sermon, and performed the funeral services; and myself and family followed the corpse to the grave as mourners. I had now buried my three sons, who had been snatched from me by the hands of violence, when I least expected it.

Although John had taken the life of his two brothers, and caused me unspeakable trouble and grief, his death made a solemn impression upon my mind, and seemed, in addition to my former misfortunes, enough to bring down my grey hairs with sorrow to the grave. Yet, on a second thought, I could not mourn for him as I had for my other sons, because I knew that his death was just, and what he had deserved for a long time, from the hand of justice.

John's vices were so great and so aggravated, that I have nothing to say in his favor: yet, as a mother, I pitied him while he lived, and have ever felt a great degree of sorrow for him, because of his bad conduct.

From his childhood, he carried something in his features indicative of an evil disposition, that would result in the perpetration of enormities of some kind; and it was the opinion and saying of Ebenezer Allen, that he would be a bad man, and be guilty of some crime deserving of death. There is no doubt but what the thoughts of murder rankled in his breast, and disturbed his mind even in his sleep; for he dreamed that he had killed Thomas for a trifling offence, and thereby forfeited his own life. Alarmed at the revelation, and fearing that he might in some unguarded moment destroy his brother, he went to the Black Chief, to whom he told the dream, and expressed his fears that the vision would be verified. Having related the dream, together with his feelings on the subject, he asked for the best advice that his old friend was capable of giving, to prevent so sad an event. The Black Chief, with his usual promptitude, told him, that from the nature of the dream, he was fearful that something serious would take place between him and Thomas; and advised him by all means to govern his temper, and avoid any quarrel which in future he might see arising, especially if Thomas was a party. John, however, did not keep the good counsel of the Chief; for soon after he killed Thomas, as I have related.

John left two wives with whom he had lived at the same time, and raised nine children. His widows are now living at Caneadea with their father, and keep their children with, and near them. His children are tolerably white, and have got light colored hair. John died about the last day of June, 1817, aged 54 years.

Doctor and Jack, having finished their murderous design, fled before they could be apprehended, and lay six weeks in the woods back of Canisteo. They then returned and sent me some wampum by Chongo, (my son-in-law,) and Sun-ge-waw (that is Big Kettle) expecting that I would pardon them, and suffer them to live as they had done with their tribe. I however, would not accept their wampum, but returned it with a request, that, rather than have them killed, they would run away and keep out of danger.

On their receiving back the wampum, they took my advice, and prepared to leave their country and people immediately. Their relatives accompanied them a short distance on their journey, and when about to part, their old uncle, the Tall Chief, addressed them in the following pathetic and sentimental speech:

"Friends, hear my voice!—When the Great Spirit made Indians, he made them all good, and gave them good corn-fields; good rivers, well stored with fish; good forests, filled with game and good bows and arrows. But very soon each wanted more than his share, and Indians quarrelled with Indians, and some were killed, and others were wounded. Then the Great Spirit made a very good word, and put it in every Indians breast, to tell us when we have done good, or when we have done bad; and that word has never told a lie.

"Friends! whenever you have stole, or got drunk, or lied, that good word has told you that you were bad Indians, and made you afraid of good Indians; and made you ashamed and look down.

"Friends! your crime is greater than all those:—you have killed an Indian in a time of peace; and made the wind hear his groans, and the earth drink his blood. You are bad Indians! Yes, you are very bad Indians; and what can you do? If you go into the woods to live alone, the ghost of John Jemison will follow you, crying, blood! blood! and will give you no peace! If you go to the land of your nation, there that ghost will attend you, and say to your relatives, see my murderers! If you plant, it will blast your corn; if you hunt, it will scare your game; and when you are asleep, its groans, and the sight of an avenging tomahawk, will awake you! What can you do? Deserving of death, you cannot live here; and to fly from your country, to leave all your relatives, and to abandon all that you have known to be pleasant and dear, must be keener than an arrow, more bitter than gall, more terrible than death! And how must we feel?—Your path will be muddy; the woods will be dark; the lightnings will glance down the trees by your side, and you will start at every sound! peace has left you, and you must be wretched.

"Friends, hear me, and take my advice. Return with us to your homes. Offer to the Great Spirit your best wampum, and try to be good Indians! And, if those whom you have bereaved shall claim your lives as their only satisfaction, surrender them cheerfully, and die like good Indians. And—" Here Jack, highly incensed, interrupted the old man, and bade him stop speaking or he would take his life. Affrighted at the appearance of so much desperation, the company hastened towards home, and left Doctor and Jack to consult their own feelings.

As soon as they were alone, Jack said to Doctor, "I had rather die here, than leave my country and friends! Put the muzzle of your rifle into my mouth, and I will put the muzzle of mine into yours, and at a given signal we will discharge them, and rid ourselves at once of all the troubles under which we now labor, and satisfy the claims which justice holds against us."

Doctor heard the proposition, and after a moment's pause, made the following reply:—"I am as sensible as you can be of the unhappy situation in which we have placed ourselves. We are bad Indians. We have forfeited our lives, and must expect in some way to atone for our crime: but, because we are bad and miserable, shall we make ourselves worse? If we were now innocent, and in a calm reflecting moment should kill ourselves, that act would make us bad, and deprive us of our share of the good hunting in the land where our fathers have gone! What would Little Beard* say to us on our arrival at his cabin? He would say, 'Bad Indians! Cowards! You were afraid to wait till we wanted your help! Go (Jogo) to where snakes will lie in your path; where the panthers will starve you, by devouring the venison; and where you will be naked and suffer with the cold! Jogo, (go,) none but the brave and good Indians live here!' I cannot think of performing an act that will add to my wretchedness. It is hard enough for me to suffer here, and have good hunting hereafter— worse to lose the whole."

Upon this, Jack withdrew his proposal. They went on about two miles, and then turned about and came home. Guilty and uneasy, they lurked about Squawky Hill near a fortnight, and then went to Cattaraugus, and were gone six weeks. When they came back, Jack's wife earnestly requested him to remove his family to Tonnewonta; but he remonstrated against her project, and utterly declined going. His wife and family, however, tired of the tumult by which they were surrounded, packed up their effects in spite of what he could say, and went off.

Jack deliberated a short time upon the proper course for himself to pursue, and finally, rather than leave his old home, he ate a large quantity of muskrat root, and died in 10 or 12 hours. His family being immediately notified of his death, returned to attend the burial, and is yet living at Squawky Hill.

Nothing was ever done with Doctor, who continued to live quietly at Squawky Hill till sometime in the year 1819, when he died of Consumption.

---

*Little Beard was a Chief who died in 1806.

CHAPTER XV

*Micah Brooks, Esq. volunteers to get the Title to her Land
confirmed to herself.—She is Naturalized.—Great Council of
Chiefs, &c. in Sept. 1828.—She Disposes of her Reservation.—Reserves a Tract 2 miles long, and 1 mile wide, &c.—
The Consideration how Paid, &c.*

In 1816, Micah Brooks, Esq. of Bloomfield, Ontario county, was
recommended to me (as it was said) by a Mr. Ingles, to be a man of
candor, honesty and integrity, who would by no means cheat me out
of a cent. Mr. Brooks soon after, came to my house and informed
me that he was disposed to assist me in regard to my land, by procuring a legislative act that would invest me with full power to dispose of it for my own benefit, and give as simple a title as could be
given by any citizen of the state. He observed that as it was then
situated, it was of but little value, because it was not in my power
to dispose of it, let my necessities be ever so great. He then proposed
to take the agency of the business upon himself, and to get the title
of one half of my reservation vested in me personally, upon the condition that, as a reward for his services, I would give him the other
half.

I sent for my son John, who on being consulted, objected to my
going into any bargain with Mr. Brooks, without the advice and
consent of Mr. Thomas Clute, who then lived on my land and near
me. Mr. Clute was accordingly called on, to whom Mr. Brooks repeated his former statement, and added, that he would get an act
passed in the Congress of the United States, that would invest me
with all the rights and immunities of a citizen, so far as it respected
my property. Mr. Clute, suspecting that some plan was in operation
that would deprive me of my possessions, advised me to have nothing
to say on the subject to Mr. Brooks, till I had seen Esquire Clute, of
Squawky Hill. Soon after this Thomas Clute saw Esq. Clute, who
informed him that the petition for my naturalization would be presented to the Legislature of this State, instead of being sent to Congress; and that the object would succeed to his and my satisfaction.
Mr. Clute then observed to his brother, Esq. Clute, that as the sale
of Indian lands, which had been reserved, belonged exclusively to the
United States, an act of the Legislature of New York could have no
effect in securing to me a title to my reservation, or in depriving me

of my property. They finally agreed that I should sign a petition to Congress, praying for my naturalization, and for the confirmation of the title of my land to me, my heirs, &c.

Mr. Brooks came with the petition: I signed it, and it was witnessed by Thomas Clute, and two others, and then returned to Mr. Brooks, who presented it to the Legislature of this state at its session in the winter of 1816–17. On the 19th of April, 1817, an act was passed for my naturalization, and ratifying and confirming the title of my land, agreeable to the tenor of the petition, which act Mr. Brooks presented to me on the first day of May following.

Thomas Clute having examined the law, told me that it would probably answer, though it was not according to the agreement made by Mr. Brooks, and Esq. Clute and himself, for me. I then executed to Micah Brooks and Jellis Clute, a deed of all my land lying east of the picket line on the Gardow reservation, containing about 7000 acres.

It is proper in this place to observe, in relation to Mr. Thomas Clute, that my son John, a few months before his death, advised me to take him for my guardian, (as I had become old and incapable of managing my property,) and to compensate him for his trouble by giving him a lot of land on the west side of my reservation where he should choose it. I accordingly took my son's advice, and Mr. Clute has ever since been faithful and honest in all his advice and dealings with, and for, myself and family.

In the month of August, 1817, Mr. Brooks and Esq. Clute again came to me with a request that I would give them a lease of the land which I had already deeded to them, together with the other part of my reservation, excepting and reserving to myself only about 4000 acres.

At this time I informed Thomas Clute of what John had advised, and recommended me to do, and that I had consulted my daughters on the subject, who had approved of the measure. He readily agreed to assist me; whereupon I told him he was entitled to a lot of land, and might select as John had mentioned. He accordingly at that time took such a piece as he chose, and the same has ever since been reserved for him in all the land contracts which I have made.

On the 24th of August, 1817, I leased to Micah Brooks and Jellis Clute, the whole of my original reservation, except 4000 acres, and Thomas Clute's lot. Finding their title still incomplete, on account of the United States government and Seneca Chiefs not having sanctioned my acts, they solicited me to renew the contract, and have the conveyance made to them in such a manner as that they should thereby be constituted sole proprietors of the soil.

In the winter of 1822–3, I agreed with them, that if they would get the chiefs of our nation, and a United States Commissioner of Indian Lands, to meet in council at Moscow, Livingston county, N. Y. and there concur in my agreement, that I would sell to them all my right and title to the Gardow reservation, with the exception of a tract for my own benefit, two miles long, and one mile wide, lying on the river where I should choose it; and also reserving Thomas Clute's lot. This arrangement was agreed upon, and the council assembled at the place appointed, on the 3d or 4th day of September, 1823.

That council consisted of Major Carrol, who had been appointed by the President to dispose of my lands, Judge Howell and N. Gorham, of Canandaigua, (who acted in concert with Maj. Carrol,) Jasper Parrish, Indian Agent, Horatio Jones, Interpreter, and a great number of Chiefs.

The bargain was assented to unanimously, and a deed given to H. B. Gibson, Micah Brooks and Jellis Clute, of the whole Gardow tract, excepting the last mentioned reservations, which was signed by myself and upwards of twenty Chiefs.

The land which I now own, is bounded as follows:—Beginning at the center of the Great Slide* and running west one mile, thence north two miles, thence east about one mile to Genesee river, thence south on the west bank of Genesee river to the place of beginning.

In consideration of the above sale, the purchasers have bound themselves, their heirs, assigns, &c. to pay to me, my heirs or successors, three hundred dollars a year forever.

Whenever the land which I have reserved, shall be sold, the income of it is to be equally divided amongst the members of the Seneca nation, without any reference to tribes or families.

———

*The Great Slide of the bank of Genesee river is a curiosity worthy of the attention of the traveller. In the month of May, 1817, a portion of land thickly covered with timber, situated at the upper end of the Gardow flats, on the west side of the river, all of a sudden gave way, and with a tremendous crash, slid into the bed of the river, which it so completely filled, that the stream formed a new passage on the east side of it, where it continues to run, without overflowing the slide. This slide, as it now lies, contains 22 acres, and has a considerable share of the timber that formerly covered it, still standing erect upon it, and growing.

## CHAPTER XVI

*Conclusion.—Review of her Life.—Reflections on the loss of Liberty.—Care she took to preserve her Health.—Indians' abstemiousness in Drinking, after the French War.—Care of their Lives, &c.—General use of Spirits.—Her natural Strength.— Purchase of her first Cow.—Means by which she has been supplied with Food.—Suspicions of her having been a Witch.—Her Constancy.—Number of Children.—Number Living.—Their Residence.—Closing Reflection.*

WHEN I review my life, the privations that I have suffered, the hardships I have endured, the vicissitudes I have passed, and the complete revolution that I have experienced in my manner of living; when I consider my reduction from a civilized to a savage state, and the various steps by which that process has been effected, and that my life has been prolonged, and my health and reason spared, it seems a miracle that I am unable to account for, and is a tragical medley that I hope will never be repeated.

The bare loss of liberty is but a mere trifle when compared with the circumstances that necessarily attend, and are inseparably connected with it. It is the recollection of what we once were, of the friends, the home, and the pleasures that we have left or lost; the anticipation of misery, the appearance of wretchedness, the anxiety for freedom, the hope of release, the devising of means of escaping, and the vigilance with which we watch our keepers, that constitute the nauseous dregs of the bitter cup of slavery. I am sensible, however, that no one can pass from a state of freedom to that of slavery, and in the last situation rest perfectly contented; but as every one knows that great exertions of the mind tend directly to debilitate the body, it will appear obvious that we ought, when confined, to exert all our faculties to promote our present comfort, and let future days provide their own sacrifices. In regard to ourselves, just as we feel, we are.

For the preservation of my life to the present time I am indebted to an excellent constitution, with which I have been blessed in as great a degree as any other person. After I arrived to years of understanding, the care of my own health was one of my principal studies; and by avoiding exposures to wet and cold, by temperance

in eating, abstaining from the use of spirits, and shunning the excesses to which I was frequently exposed, I effected my object beyond
what I expected. I have never once been sick till within a year or
two, only as I have related.

Spirits and tobacco I have never used, and I have never once
attended an Indian frolic. When I was taken prisoner, and for sometime after that, spirits was not known; and when it was first introduced, it was in small quantities, and used only by the Indians;
so that it was a long time before the Indian women begun to even
taste it.

After the French war, for a number of years, it was the practice
of the Indians of our tribe to send to Niagara and get two or three
kegs of rum, (in all six or eight gallons,) and hold a frolic as long as
it lasted. When the rum was brought to the town, all the Indians
collected, and before a drop was drank, gave all their knives, tomahawks, guns, and other instruments of war, to one Indian, whose
business it was to bury them in a private place, keep them concealed,
and remain perfectly sober till the frolic was ended. Having thus
divested themselves, they commenced drinking, and continued their
frolic till every drop was consumed. If any of them became quarrelsome, or got to fighting, those who were sober enough bound them
upon the ground, where they were obliged to lie till they got sober,
and then were unbound. When the fumes of the spirits had left the
company, the sober Indian returned to each the instruments with
which they had entrusted him, and all went home satisfied. A frolic
of that kind was held but once a year, and that at the time the Indians
quit their hunting, and come in with their deer-skins.

In those frolics the women never participated. Soon after the revolutionary war, however, spirits became common in our tribe, and
has been used indiscriminately by both sexes; though there are not
so frequent instances of intoxication amongst the squaws as amongst
the Indians.

To the introduction and use of that baneful article, which has
made such devastation in our tribes, and threatens the extinction of
our people, (the Indians,) I can with the greatest propriety impute
the whole of my misfortune in losing my three sons. But as I have
before observed, not even the love of life will restrain an Indian from
sipping the poison that he knows will destroy him. The voice of
nature, the rebukes of reason, the advice of parents, the expostulations of friends, and the numerous instances of sudden death, are all
insufficient to reclaim an Indian, who has once experienced the ex-

hilarating and inebriating effects of spirits, from seeking his grave in the bottom of his bottle!

My strength has been great for a woman of my size, otherwise I must long ago have died under the burdens which I was obliged to carry. I learned to carry loads on my back, in a strap placed across my forehead, soon after my captivity; and continue to carry in the same way. Upwards of thirty years ago, with the help of my young children, I backed all the boards that were used about my house from Allen's mill at the outlet of Silver Lake, a distance of five miles. I have planted, hoed, and harvested corn every season but one since I was taken prisoner. Even this present fall (1823) I have husked my corn and backed it into the house.

The first cow that I ever owned, I bought of a squaw sometime after the revolution. It had been stolen from the enemy. I had owned it but a few days when it fell into a hole, and almost died before we could get it out. After this, the squaw wanted to be recanted, but as I would not give up the cow, I gave her money enough to make, when added to the sum which I paid her at first, thirty-five dollars. Cows were plenty on the Ohio, when I lived there, and of good quality.

For provisions I have never suffered since I came upon the flats; nor have I ever been in debt to any other hands than my own for the plenty that I have shared.

My vices, that have been suspected, have been but few. It was believed for a long time, by some of our people, that I was a great witch; but they were unable to prove my guilt, and consequently I escaped the certain doom of those who are convicted of that crime, which, by Indians, is considered as heinous as murder. Some of my children had light brown hair, and tolerable fair skin, which used to make some say that I stole them; yet as I was ever conscious of my own constancy, I never thought that any one really believed that I was guilty of adultery.

I have been the mother of eight children; three of whom are now living, and I have at this time thirty-nine grand children, and fourteen great-grand children, all living in the neighborhood of Genesee River, and at Buffalo.

I live in my own house, and on my own land, with my youngest daughter, Polly, who is married to George Chongo, and has three children.

My daughter Nancy, who is married to Billy Green, lives about 80 rods south of my house, and has seven children.

My other daughter, Betsey, is married to John Green, has seven children, and resides 80 rods north of my house.

Thus situated in the midst of my children, I expect I shall soon leave the world, and make room for the rising generation. I feel the weight of years with which I am loaded, and am sensible of my daily failure in seeing, hearing and strength; but my only anxiety is for my family. If my family will live happily, and I can be exempted from trouble while I have to stay, I feel as though I could lay down in peace a life that has been checked in almost every hour, with troubles of a deeper dye, than are commonly experienced by mortals.

# MARY GODFREY

Understanding the *Authentic Narrative* requires a brief survey of the First (1817–18) and Second Seminole (1835–42) Wars, and of the interaction between Seminoles and Africans. These were the costliest U.S.-Indian wars in both money and manpower because of sustained Seminole resistance to removal from Florida. In the eighteenth century, the Seminoles separated from the Creeks and fled to Spanish Florida where refugees from other tribes as well as escaped slaves and free blacks joined them. During the Revolution, the Seminoles supported the British. Although some Seminoles held slaves, they allowed their slaves considerable latitude.

In the lead-up to the First Seminole War, the U.S. Congress wanted to annex Florida to bring the Seminoles under control and to destroy a community of free blacks that shielded runaway slaves from Southern plantations. During 1817 and 1818, General Andrew Jackson illegally entered Spanish Florida with white and Creek allied troops, killing many Seminoles and free blacks and returning some runaways to their owners. The First Seminole War was a prelude to the formal U.S. annexation of Florida in 1821 and to another round of hostilities culminating in the Second Seminole War.

Jackson formed a territorial government, and immediately Indians and blacks became vulnerable because white citizens wanted to buy Indian land, and slaveholders wanted more slaves returned. In 1823, the Seminoles agreed to give up their claim to northern Florida, but the U.S. government pressured them to leave Florida altogether and move to Indian Territory. In 1832, after years of friction, some Seminoles signed the treaty of Payne's Landing, in which a delegation of seven chiefs accompanied Seminole Agent John Phagan to Indian Territory to select a suitable site for removal. In the treaty of Fort Gibson, signed on March 28, 1833, the delegation of chiefs resolved that the Seminoles would actually move onto Creek lands in Indian Territory. But owing to internal disagreements, distrust of whites, and fear of the Creeks fanned by black Seminoles, the treaty did not hold. Indeed, the delegation claimed that the agreement was not meant to be binding and that they had been tricked. The Seminole people stated that the chiefs could not decide on their behalf anyway.

The *Authentic Narrative* deals with these incidents as well as key events at the beginning of the Second Seminole War such as Dade's Massacre, Thompson's death, Charley Emathla's murder, and the Battle of the Withlacoochee. The account ends in March 1836 with the Seminole forces under Osceola still intact and powerful; in fact, the war would continue for another six years. Three quarters of the text details verifiable information about the war, and the remaining quarter contains a third-person account of Mary Godfrey's story followed by a supposed verbatim first-person account.

The *Authentic Narrative* appeared as a twenty-four-page pamphlet published by Daniel F. Blanchard (who cannot be traced) and distributed in New York and Providence, Rhode Island. Inside the front cover is a crude but graphic foldout engraving headed "Massacre of the Whites by the Indians and Blacks in Florida." A fascinating handbill prospectus advertising the book provides further insight into its publication, promotion, and readership. Titled "Female Fortitude," the handbill describes the "Authentic Narrative" and "Miraculous Escape" of Godfrey, gives the price of fifteen cents, and only toward the bottom indicates that the booklet also contains information on the "Cause, Rise and Progress" of the war, which in fact comprises the bulk of the pamphlet.

The handbill contains four more pieces of rhetorical or promotional information. At the bottom, a statement establishes that the unnamed author is essentially a war correspondent, a man who has spent three months near the war zone specifically to collect on-site data. With this information, we can appreciate Godfrey's story as a case study of the Seminole War in much the same way that the single individual in Hemingway's "Old Man at the Bridge" crystallizes the Spanish Civil War into a human tragedy. Furthermore, an engraving of Godfrey and her four daughters at the mercy of the escaped slave who brandishes an axe reinforces the individualized verbal case study.

Along the right side of the bill, a printed appeal to prospective purchasers claims that the seller of the pamphlet has lost an arm (not in the Seminole Wars, though!) and is forced to make a living by handing around the suggestive poster and then taking orders for the book described therein. Buyers not only receive an interesting book—the appeal continues—but a sense of having performed a charitable act. Many captivity narratives were similarly hawked in cheap editions, with many a sentimental supplication, to reach a large popular readership.

Finally, and perhaps most interestingly, at the top of the poster a potential buyer's handwritten note describes the hawker's method: he handed the bill and a sample book around in the morning of June 25, 1836 (the date indicates how current the pamphlet was and how quickly it had been printed); the buyer was expected to pay the retail price of fifteen cents, keep the book, but return the graphic handbill so it could be used over and over to hook other purchasers. This particular purchaser, however, decided to break the system. Calling the *Authentic Narrative* "a real catch-penny," he refused to return the handbill but kept it as "a commentary on gulls" (i.e., gullible people).

Whether or not Mary Godfrey existed in the historical record is irrelevant and currently unknown. What was it about the image of a white mother, her four daughters, merciless Indians, and a militant then sympathetic escaped slave that appealed to prospective readers? The image of five vulnerable females in the wilderness swampland is familiar enough, as is the role of divine providence in sustaining the Godfreys and in bringing the ex-slave to their aid. But it is the black figure called variously "the relenting African," "the friendly negro," and "the humane African (our deliverer)" that is particularly interesting and that may make this narrative an unusual example of abolitionist literature. Hearing the cries of Godfrey's starving baby, the runaway at first threatened them with an axe, but when Godfrey begged for mercy, he dropped the axe, overcome by emotion, and offered this rationale for helping them: "that he had two children who were held in bondage by the whites, that to enjoy his own liberty he had left them to their fate, and something now seemed to whisper him, that if he should destroy the lives of her innocent children, God would be angry, and might doom his little ones to a similar fate by the hands of the white men in whose power they were!"

The slave exercises his free will to keep the Godfrey family together, unlike the slaveholders who systematically brutalized and dispersed black families and who sexually abused black women. In other words, presented with the choice of militance or mercy, the runaway chooses mercy. In this way, he conforms to a powerful abolitionist trope: the domestic, "feminized" African who wants to be part of a system of marriage and family, rather than the individual male warrior who resorts to violence when there is no other way to stop slavery's evils.

One last thought: in 1836, Congress passed the gag rule, forbidding discussion of petitions concerning slavery on the House floor.

In time, Northern Representatives began to test the gag rule not by overt violation but by connecting it with other topics. The Second Seminole War proved to be a particularly effective instrument. Indeed, "the war and slavery were seen in Congress to be more and more intimitely related," according to a major study of the subject (Mahon, p. 291). It may well be that the *Authentic Narrative* formed an early part of that ongoing debate.

The text is *An Authentic Narrative of the Seminole War*. Providence, R.I.: D. F. Blanchard, 1836.


## SUGGESTIONS FOR FURTHER READING

*Secondary Sources*

Derounian-Stodola and Levernier; Littlefield; Mahon.

# An Authentic Narrative of the Seminole War; and of the Miraculous Escape of Mrs. Mary Godfrey, and Her Four Female Children

At the termination of the Indian War,[1] in 1833, when, after much bloodshed, a treaty of peace was happily effected, and as was believed, firmly established between the American Government and Black Hawk and his followers, it was then the opinion of many, that in consequence of the severe chastisement received by the latter, that neither they or any of their red brethren would be found so soon manifesting (by offensive operations) a disposition to disturb the repose of the white inhabitants of any of our frontier settlements—but, in this opinion, we have recently found ourselves mistaken, as, at an early period of the present year, tidings of an unpleasant nature were received by the inhabitants of the north, from their brethren at the south, that the *war-whoop* had been sounded by a tribe of Indians denominated *Seminoles;* and in addition to the immense property destroyed by them, many of the defenceless inhabitants (male and female) of the Floridas, had fallen victims to the tomahawk and scalping knife! Since the commencement of offensive operations, by the savages, (which may be viewed as a war of extermination, as they appear disposed neither to give or take quarter) pains have been taken to collect every fact of an important and interesting nature, relative to the cause and progress of the alarming and bloody conflict, with which to present the public.

The name *"Seminole"*[2] *(i. e. wild)* is applied by the Creeks, to all vagabonds of that nation, and as a tribe, their history justifies the application. It was the towns belonging to this tribe that were burnt by General JACKSON,[3] in 1817, when *Francis,*[4] and some others of their principal chiefs were slain; there are, however, numbers of the tribe still remaining, and it is represented that they are not now what they were at that period; they were then, indeed, *Savages,* with but little or no knowledge of civilized warfare—they are now a different race, being a mixture of Creeks, Chickasaws, Chocktaws, Cherokees, Mickasookees, and Blacks. Their intercourse with the whites has not only rendered them more sagacious and adroit in eluding their enemies, more capable of defending themselves, and more provident as to the contingencies against which they ought to guard, and are amply supplied with munitions of war, and with provisions; having, as they have represented, driven nearly 3000 head of cattle into the swamps in the interior, for their subsistence while contending with the whites; and boasting of a force of 2000 warriors fit to take the field, and of an additional force of about 800 captured or runaway negroes from the South, who have united with them in the present contest; and are all well acquainted with every fastness, pass or morass in the territory. The Mickasooky tribe[5] is considered the leading band of the Seminoles; they have always been noted as the most determined and ruthless of the savage race; their head chief is *Micanopy*,[6] a man far advanced in years, and who has never performed much to distinguish himself as a very great warrior; the next in command, is *Jumper*,[7] who bears a truly savage countenance, and possesses a disposition corresponding therewith—his influence is great with Micanopy, and by whom he is altogether dictated. The third in rank, is *Oscala*, alias *Powell*,[8] a chief as cunning as he is brave; he is about 35 years of age, is a half breed, and of slender form, but active and muscular; he possesses unbounded influence over the Indians, which he has acquired by no unbecoming artifices, but by the great superiority of his intellectual powers, his daring courage, and admirable military turn of character. The skill with which he has for a long time managed to frustrate the measures of our government, for the removal of the Indians beyond the Mississippi, agreeable to treaty, entitle him to be superior to Black Hawk.

In so destitute a situation were the Seminoles left after the destruction of their villages by Gen. Jackson, that Congress soon after voted them a very considerable sum of money ($40,000) to keep them from the starvation with which they were threatened—and in consideration therefor, they, agreeable to a treaty concluded with them in May, 1832,[9] agreed to relinquish their present territory (which has been the scene of their present depredations) and at the end of three years, to retire to the prairies of Arkansas; and it appears that the hostility of a very considerable proportion of them, originated in a reluctance to adhere to said treaty, so far as it required of them to quit the land of their forefathers. The three years expired in May last, but as the Indians manifested an unwillingness to move, it was judged expedient by the officers entrusted with their removal, to give them six months longer to prepare for their journey. By the treaty, their cattle and horses were to be surrendered and paid for, and accordingly the Indian Agent advertised the Indians to bring them in

to be sold on the first and fifteenth of December last; to this *Charles*[10]
(who was then their head chief) assented, but others strongly objected, and expressed their determination to die, arms in hand, on
the soil of their forefathers; and in manifestation of this determination, at one of their councils held in December last, nine warriors
entered and discharged nine bullets in the heart of Charles for his
too great subserviency to the whites!—the Agent (General Thom-
mber of Congress) soon after shared
by the hands of Powell, who, it af-
him inveterate hatred, but until this
athies so skillfully, that the general
y! These murders, together with that
iefs, was the signal for a general rise
aration to commence offensive op-
t sending their women and children
Sable and Ten Keys, for the purpose
(so called) of which flour is made,
ity, they live. They next commenced
he whites in the interior, and upon
and Cape Florida, and plundered,
ing of value that came in their way.
ing-houses, barns and cribs of grain
orses, hogs and poultry were shot
tter were cut off, and their mangled
bodies stuck full of light wood splinters!—Families widely separated
from one another, had no other means of safety than flight afforded
them, and that in a way which prevented their providing themselves
with the most necessary articles of clothing, bedding, &c.—their furniture, cattle, grain, agricultural implements, &c. &c. were all left to
the mercy of the savage foe, and years of toil may not enable them
to recover the pecuniary comforts of which they have been deprived.
Several families had got but recently settled, and had just got themselves comfortably situated, when they were obliged to fly for their
lives!—It was estimated that in the month of January, 500 families
were thus driven from their homes, and in almost a state of starvation, sought protection under the walls of St. Augustine and other
fortified places, from the ravages of the enemy!—nor were all so
fortunate as to escape with their lives; many were barbarously butchered by the merciless wretches, regardless of age or sex! among these
was the unfortunate family of Mr. William Cooley, an old and respected inhabitant of New River; Mr. C. was from home—they mur-

dered his wife, three children, and Mr. Joseph Flinton, a teacher in the family, in the most barbarous manner! shot several hogs, plundered his house, and carried away with them all his horses and two negro slaves. The cold blooded massacre of this unfortunate family was attended with many aggravations, as Cooley had always been on the most intimate terms with the Indians; his wife was taken captive by them several years since, and was as such retained by them a sufficient length of time to become acquainted with their language, customs, &c. and has ever since been considered a favorite with them; his son was a particular pet of theirs, whose language he also spoke, and whose skill in shooting, &c. he emulated with a spirit remarkable for a boy of his years.

There were two other children besides this boy, one an infant at the mother's breast. If any family could rely on past friendship for present forbearance from the savage foe, it was this—but all calculations of this sort were horribly disappointed by the awful result.— While the father was absent in a vessel along the coast, his premises were assailed with a brutality unsurpassed even in savage war! His wife and three children were mercilessly butchered! When the disconsolate parent returned to his desolate home, to bury the remains of his murdered household, he found the body of Flinton, (a native of Cecil county, Maryland,) who acted as instructor to his children, shockingly mangled, evidently with an axe—his two eldest children were found near by shot through the heart; one holding yet the book in her hand from which she had been learning, and the book of the other lay by his side; about a hundred yards from thence he found the bodies of his wife and infant—his wife had been shot through the heart, and to appearance, the same shot had broken the infant's arm.

About ten days after the massacre of Cooley's family, the Indians paid a second visit to his house, and took away every thing which they had in the late attack left behind, and ransacked a house but a short distance therefrom, destroyed the furniture, ripped open the beds, &c. One of the negroes belonging to Cooley, who was supposed to have been carried off, afterwards returned, and reported that at the time of the massacre, he succeeded in making his escape by means of a boat; that the outrage was committed by Indians well known to him and the other inhabitants of that part of the peninsula, and who had oftentimes had intercourse with his master's family; they were about fifteen in number.

A family who dwelt but a short distance from the house of Cooley, and were witnesses of the awful butchery of his wife and children, had a very narrow escape from sharing a similar fate—such were their fears and precipitate flight, that a daughter (an interesting girl of 17) fled in dishabille,[13] having sprung with terror from the bed to which she had been confined many weeks by severe sickness! Not far distant dwelt another family—the widow Rigley, her two daughters and an only son—they were closely pursued by the savages, and were compelled to run twelve miles thro' the wood, and when they reached Cape Florida, they had scarcely a garment remaining to their backs, they having been torn off by the bushes; and almost the whole distance they ran without shoes, having lost them at the commencement of their flight, and so completely were they exhausted, that they were unable to walk for several days! All of those who were thus compelled to fly, and were not overtaken by the pursuing savages, took refuge at Cape Florida light, Key Biscayne, being about sixty in number, men, women and children, where, with the keeper of the light, Mr. Deblois, they, for their better safety, resorted to and took up their abode in the Light-House; not having a sufficient supply of provisions and water for so many persons, they were compelled to hoist a signal of distress, which was fortunately discovered by a vessel passing in sight, and which received them on board and conveyed them to St. Augustine.

Among the many unfortunate families who were compelled to leave their late peaceful homes, in quest of aid, or for some place where they would be less exposed, and in less danger of falling victims to the fatal tomahawk and scalping knife of the savages, there was no one instance in which a providential interposition was so remarkable, as that of the miraculous preservation and deliverance of Mrs. Mary Godfrey,[14] the wife of Mr. Thomas Godfrey, and her four female children, one an infant at the breast. The husband of this unfortunate woman had been, with others, drafted and compelled to leave his family unprotected, for the purpose of endeavoring to check the enemy in their murderous career; it was not until she heard the frightful yells of the approaching savages, and saw the dwellings of her nearest neighbors in flames, and the inmates flying in every direction to escape from the awful death with which they were threatened, that she was induced to follow their example; but being impeded in her flight by the burden of her infant, but six months old, she (as the only alternative left her by which she could escape from her pursuers) was obliged to penetrate into a thick and miry swamp! In this dreary and uncomfortable retreat, the unfortunate mother found means to conceal herself and helpless children for the space of four days, with nothing to subsist on but a few wild roots and berries! As she concluded by the almost constant whooping of the Indians, that they had full possession of all the adjacent country, and that it would be impossible to escape discovery should she attempt to seek a more comfortable situation, she came to the conclusion that it would be preferable there to remain, and with her poor children to fall victims to hunger and thirst, than to subject themselves to the tortures, which in all probability, would be inflicted on them were they to fall into the hands of the enemy. As the savages appeared by their yells to approach very near, to prevent a discovery she was obliged to use every exertion to induce her suffering little ones to stifle their cries and lamentations, though driven to it by pinching hunger and burning thirst! On the fourth day, finding that in consequence of her extreme suffering and deprivations, that she could no longer afford the nourishment to her babe that it required, she, with becoming fortitude, endeavored to prepare her mind to part with her precious charge, and to submit, without a murmur, to whatever might be the will of Him to whom alone she could now look for protection. Toward the close of the day, the pitiful moans of her tender babe (produced by its sufferings) were such as to be heard by and to attract the attention of a straggling black, who had enlisted in the cause of the enemy; guided by its cries, and the bitter lamentations of its poor mother and sisters, he was brought full in view of them, and at whose sudden and unexpected appearance, the poor sufferers manifested their terrors by a united shriek of horror and despair! the little girls in the mean time clinging to their parent, and imploring that protection, which she, poor woman, was unable to afford them. The negro, grinning a ghastly smile, as if elated with the discovery, approached them with an uplifted axe, apparently intent on their destruction! The distracted mother at the moment, begged for the lives of her children; and on her pointing to her almost expiring infant, the negro dropped his axe, and after contemplating the sad spectacle for a few moments, appeared much affected, and broke silence by assuring Mrs. G. that she had nothing to fear, that neither herself or her children should be hurt—that he had two children who were held in bondage by the whites, that to enjoy his own liberty he had left them to their fate, and something now seemed to whisper him, that if he should destroy the lives of her innocent children, God would be angry, and might doom his little ones to a similar fate by the hands of the white men in whose power they were! Such, in substance, were the remarks of the relenting African, and who further manifested his pity, by requesting Mrs. G. and her children to remain concealed where they were, and at night he would bring them food and water, and as soon as a favorable opportunity should present, would conduct them to a path which would lead them to the plantation of some of their friends. He then left them, and in proof of his fidelity, he early in the evening returned, bringing with him two blankets and a quantity of wholesome provision; which as he represented, he had succeeded in saving from the house of a planter which had been that afternoon set on fire; having thus provided for their immediate want, he again retired, but early the next morning, once more made his appearance, and apparently much agitated, informing Mrs. G. that a company of mounted volunteers (whites) had just made their appearance in the neighborhood, and had dispersed the Indians, who had been there embodied, and as some of them in their flight might seek shelter in the swamp in which she was concealed, he thought it unsafe for her to remain there any longer, and proposed to her that she now improve the favorable opportunity which presented, to escape to her friends, and that he would accompany her to within view of them, which the friendly negro did, although at the risk of his own life!

The following particulars were received from the lips of Mrs. Godfrey, of the manner in which she passed the four days in her dreary abode:—"The first day,[15] my apprehensions that we should be traced by our tracks, discovered and butchered by the savages, were too great to think for a moment to what extremities we might be driven by hunger, and other privations. Their frightful yells were heard without a moment's cessation during the whole day, at the close of which, I selected as dry a place as could be found, which I overspread with a few pine twigs, on which with my poor helpless children to repose the night, which to me proved a sleepless one; and from the sobs and sighs and bitter moans of my affrighted little ones, I had reason to believe it proved equally so to them. Miserable, however, as was our situation, it might have been still more so. Had an equal quantity of rain fallen that night as the night previous, it is not probable that my tender babe would have survived until morning.

The sun arose bright and cheering on the morning of the second day, but the frightful whoopings of the Indians had not ceased; nor were our prospects of escaping with our lives any better, should we attempt leaving our hiding place. Before the close of the day my youngest children began to complain of hunger and thirst; a few wild berries and a little stagnant water was all that could be procured with which to appease either. My oldest daughter bore her sufferings and privations with remarkable fortitude; when not engaged in conversing (in a low tone of voice) with her two younger sisters, to pacify and to avert their dreadful forebodings of being seized and murdered by the cruel Indians, her time was employed in relieving me of the burden of my helpless babe. We passed the night of this day much as the first, with but little if any sleep; indeed, exposed as we were to the heavy dew and unwholesome night air, and compelled either to sit or lie upon the damp ground, it was not possible for either my children or myself to obtain that repose which nature required; and if more comfortably situated, our fearful apprehensions of being discovered and put to death by the merciless savages, would have prevented it.

The morning of the third day, although clear and pleasant, found us, if possible, in a still more wretched condition, having all contracted bad colds by reason of our thin apparel and exposure; and for the want of proper exercise, our limbs were so benumbed and cramped as to be hardly able to stand erect! and what added still more to my afflictions, I found that in consequence of my long fasting, in addition to other sufferings, I could but a little while longer afford that nourishment to my babe so necessary to support life; and in addition to which, the lamentations of my other children (with the exception of the oldest) it is impossible to describe correctly what were my feelings at this melancholy moment! mothers can best judge, and they can have but a faint conception of them unless similarly situated! But, in this hour of severe affliction, I did not fail to look to and call on One who had power to save and to deliver us, and as He "tempers the storm to the shorn lamb," to revive and protract the life of my tender infant! By the assistance of kind Providence, we were enabled to pass another night, and our lives were spared to witness the rising of another sun, although with a great depression of spirits and relaxation of bodily strength, in consequence of being so long deprived of wholesome nourishment; and, indeed, so visible was it as regarded my infant, as to render it almost certain, that before the close of the day, I should be compelled to part with my precious charge! Although, apparently with insufficient strength to raise its little hands, yet its constant cries were still more shrill and distressing, nor could they be hushed; and fortunate it proved for us that they could not be, for thereby the attention of the humane

African (our deliverer) was attracted, and by them brought to our relief."

There were other instances in which parents were less fortunate—who were not only doomed to witness the total destruction of their property, the fruits of many years labor, but, if not so fortunate as to escape, were treated with most savage barbarity; and in some instances, where, in consequence of the absence of the husband, it was suspected that he had been either draughted or had volunteered his services to assist in repelling the assaults of the savages, but little mercy was shown their wives and children if left behind. In one instance, as was represented to the writer, a house (the only inmates of which were a mother and her two young children) was visited by an Indian and his squaw, and after demanding liquor, and refreshing themselves with whatever they pleased that the house contained, and about to depart, the Indian seized and bound one of the children, a lad about seven years of age, while the other, an infant, was seized by the squaw, and notwithstanding the entreaties and lamentations of the poor distracted mother, would no doubt have carried both off had it not been for two armed white men, who fortunately were discovered, although at some distance, approaching, as the two savages were about leaving the house with their captives.

In addition to the foregoing, many horrid murders have been perpetrated; a great number of the most valuable plantations have been totally destroyed, and whole families missing; and as the Indians have been frequently discovered dancing to and fro around their burning dwellings, there can be but little doubt but some of the missing were consumed in them—and as places have been noticed where fires have been enkindled, with burned stakes erected in the centre; they are doubtless those to which a portion of those who have fallen into their hands, have been inhumanly sacrificed, agreeably to their savage mode of torture.

Upon the first notice of the disturbances, a force of about 500 mounted men were raised, who volunteered for one month, furnishing their own provisions, arms, &c. and supposing that in this short time all would be completed. Between the volunteers and the Indians, there were two slight engagements—in the first the whites lost their baggage and several men, and evidently were worsted; in the second, every Indian was killed who was engaged; the number was 7 or 8— but this proved but a momentary check to the fearless ferocity of the savages; they were dispersed in small parties, and when pursued took refuge in the thickets, and fought with desperation, apparently with the determination, either to kill or be killed without paying any regard to the numbers by whom they were assailed.

The first severe engagement[16] with the savages was on the 28th of December last, when Major Dade having started with a detachment of the fifth regiment of Infantry of United States troops, from Tampa Bay to Camp King, to join Gen. Clinch; at about 8 o'clock in the morning, they were surrounded by a large body of Indians, supposed to number from 800 to 1000, and were cut to pieces!—only three men of the one hundred and twelve of which the detachment was composed, escaped, badly wounded, to recount the lamentable history of the butchery of their fellow-soldiers. Major Dade was shot off his horse on the commencement of the attack; Captains Gardner and Frazer soon after fell, mortally wounded, and their scalps were taken by the savages. Lieutenant Bassinger was wounded on the onset, and was discovered by a negro in the party of savages, crawling off to a place of concealment, and tomahawked! History does not furnish us with an instance, since the defeat of Gen. St. Clair, of a butchery more horrid, and, with the above exception, it stands without an example in the annals of Indian warfare! For a more particular account of the severe engagement we are indebted to Major Belton, being an extract from his official report to the Adjutant General—which is as follows:

"It becomes my melancholy duty to proceed to the catastrophe of this fated band, an elite of energy, patriotism, military skill and constant courage. On the 29th, in the afternoon, a man of my company, John Thomas, and temporarily transferred to C. company, 2d artillery, came in, and yesterday Pr. Ransom Clark, of the same company, with four wounds, very severe, and stated that an action took place on the 28th, commencing about ten o'clock; in which every officer fell, and nearly every man. The command entrenched every night, and about four miles from the halt were attacked, and received at least fifteen rounds before an Indian was seen.—Major Dade and his horse were both killed on the first onset, and the interpreter "Louis." Lt. Mudge, 3d Artillery, received his mortal wounds. Lt. Bassenger, 3d Artillery was not wounded till after the second attack; and at the latter part of that, he was wounded several times before he was tomahawked. Capt. Gardner, 2d Artillery, was not wounded until the second attack, and at the last part of it. Mr. Bassenger, after Capt. Gardner was killed, remarked, "I am the only officer left, and, boys, we will do the best we can." Lt. Keays, 3d Artillery, had both arms broken the first shot, was unable to act, and was tomahawked, the latter part of the second attack, by a negro. Lieut. Henderson had his left arm broken the first fire, and after that with a musket fired at least thirty or forty shots. Dr. Catlin was not killed until after the second attack, nor was he wounded; he placed himself behind the breast work, and with two double barrelled guns, said, "he had four barrels for them." Captain Fraser fell early in the action with the advanced guard; as a man of his company, (B 3d Artillery,) who came in this morning, reports.

On the attack they were in column of route; and after receiving a heavy fire from the unseen enemy, they then rose up in such a swarm, that the ground, covered, as was thought, by Light Infantry extension, showed the Indians between the files. Muskets were clubbed, knives and bayonets used, and parties clinched. In the second attack, our own men's muskets, from the dead and wounded, were used against them; a cross fire cut down a succession of artillerists at the fence, from which 49 rounds were fired—the gun carriages were burnt, and the guns sunk in a pond. A war dance was held on the ground; many negroes were in the field, but no scalps were taken by the Indians, but the negroes, with hellish cruelty, pierced the throats of all, whose loud cries and groans showed the power of life to be yet strong. The survivors were preserved by imitating death, except Thomas, who was partly stifled, and bought his life for six dollars, and in his enemy recognised an Indian whose axe he had helved a few days before at his post. About 100 Indians were well mounted, naked, and painted. The last man who came in brought a note from Capt. Frazer, addressed to Major Mountford, which was fastened in a cleft stick, and stuck in a creek, dated, as is supposed, on the 27th, stating that they were beset every night and pushing on."

By the dreadful massacre, as described in Col. Belton's report, many widows and orphans were made. A few days after the battle, they were to the number of forty or fifty, put on board a vessel bound to New-Orleans, where they arrived in the most forlorn and pitiful condition; but, we are happy since to learn, that, much to the honor of the humane and hospitable inhabitants of that city, seventeen hundred and forty-one dollars have been there subscribed to their relief.

The next important engagement with the Savages, was three days after the fatal defeat of Major Dade's detachment, by a party of regulars and volunteers, under the command of Gen. Clinch—he having assumed the command—and relying on the courage and intrepidity of his men, formed the determination to penetrate into the heart of the enemy's country. His force consisted of two hundred regulars and three hundred and fifty volunteers—they had three or four Indian guides, the relations of the Chief Charles, who was, as before mentioned, killed by the war party of the nation; and under their guidance, it was determined not to take the usual route to Tampa Bay, but to follow a more westerly track, in hopes of taking the enemy by surprise. The Withlacooshe, or, as it is called on most maps, the Amaxura, is a considerable river which runs westerly along the northern border of the Seminole territories, and empties into the Gulf. The usual road to Tampa, crosses the river by a bridge, but the guides promised to take the troops across by a ford lower down. On the morning of the 31st of December, they began to approach the Withlacooshee, and as it was apprehended that the Seminoles, if they had received information of the route which the General had chosen, might dispute the passage of the river, the baggage was left at a point some five miles from the river bank, under a guard, and the spies were ordered to keep a good look out. No signs of the enemy were discovered, except a single track, in the loose sand, which here composed the surface of the country, apparently of a man on a full run, which one of the guides undertook to identify—(such is the nicety of Indian science on matters of this sort)—as the footstep of a certain negro, who had belonged to the Chief Charles. The river on the north side, the direction in which the troops approached it, was lined by a thick hammock, a quarter of a mile in width.—The scouts beat through this without discovering any signs of the enemy. On approaching the river bank, it was found to be a bold and rapid stream, some twenty yards across, and too deep to be forded. An old canoe was found, and after stopping the seams with moss, it served to ferry over the regulars in parties of four and five. After crossing, the trail led obliquely some two hundred yards through a narrow hammock which lined the south side of the river, and then ascended a steep sandy bluff or barren, on the top of which was a clear, open space. Having stationed their sentinels, the regulars stacked their arms on this open space, and laid down to rest and refresh themselves, while the volunteers were crossing. Some were asleep, and others, with true soldier-like nonchalance, were improving this moment of leisure in the enjoyment of a game of cards. A small party of the volunteers had swam their horses across, and were engaged in constructing a bridge for the passage of the others, when the sentinels came running in with the news that the Indians were coming. At first it was believed to be a false alarm, but in a moment after they came rushing down the hammock, along the river bank; they even ventured out of their cover into the open space occupied by the regulars, all the time pouring in a heavy fire. It seemed to be their object, by pushing down the hammock along the river bank, to get possession of the landing place, and cut off the communication between the regulars and the volunteers; but a party of the volunters plunged into the river, some on horseback and some on foot, and others extending themselves along the river bank and firing across, beat back the Indians, and kept open the communication. The enemy were very shy of the rifles of the volunteers, but seemed to have no great fear of the regulars, for whose markship they entertain a good deal of contempt.

The regulars were taken entirely by surprise, but they behaved with great gallantry, forming into platoons and returning the enemy's fire with as much regularity and exactness as if they had been on parade. The Indians, however, had greatly the advantage, as they were posted among the trees at the bottom of the bluff, while the regulars were exposed in the open space at the top of it. The Indians seemed to be coming in during the whole time of the engagement, and those who came in last were observed to have packs on their backs as though they were just off a journey—it was conjectured that they were waiting the approach of the whites at the bridge above, and were obliged to make a rapid movement in order to intercept them at the ford. Osciola, otherwise called Powell, the leader in the war, was observed the foremost of the assailants—he wore a red belt, and three long feathers, and would step boldly out from behind his tree, take a deliberate aim, and bring down his man at every fire!—whole platoons levelled their muskets at him, and the tree behind which he stood was completely riddled by the balls, while he repeatedly called on his followers to stand by him and not to run from "the pale faces." At the beginning of the disturbances, he gave out that there were three men whose lives he would have, viz. Charles, the Chief, who was in favor of a removal, General Thompson, the Indian Agent, and General Clinch—the deaths of the two former he has already effected.

The heat of the engagement lasted about an hour; but the Indians kept up a continual whooping and occasional firing until near dark; the troops had upwards of sixty killed and wounded, principally wounded—the loss fell almost entirely on the regulars, not more than six or seven volunteers having been hurt. It was impossible to ascertain how great was the loss of the Indians; it was conjectured that there were upwards of 400 in the engagement; as soon as they retired the troops fell back beyond the hammock on the north side, carrying with them their wounded, and slept upon their arms through fear of being again surprised.

Throughout the engagement it is represented that Gen. Clinch[17] was in the hottest of the fight—his horse was shot under him in two places, neck and hip—a ball passed through his cap, entering the front and passing out of the back part of the top, and another ball passed through the sleeve of the bridle arm of his coat! At one moment a little confusion occurred among the troops, in consequence of some soldiers giving the word "Retire!" whereupon the General immediately threw himself in front of the men, and his horse staggering under him, he dismounted, advanced to the front, and amidst a shower of bullets from the Indians, exclaimed, that "before he would show his back to the enemy he would die upon the field!"—a gallant charge followed, which routed and drove the enemy from the field!

During the action, the yelling of the savages was incessant, and somewhat appalling; ten times their number of civilized enemies in an open field would not have been so formidable—the regulars were compelled to watch their opportunity, and fire by vollies, as did the volunteers whenever they saw a flash from the thicket; the killed of the whites were interred and fires built over their graves, so that the Indians obtained no scalps.

The following remarkable incident occurred at the battle just mentioned; one of the Jacksonville volunteers who was among the number that remained on the east side of the river, during the fight that remained on the other, on seeing an Indian aim his rifle at one of our men, levelled his own at him from across the stream, about one hundred yards, felled him on the spot, swam over, got his scalp, and with the trophy in his hand, returned to the place he had left! The savage was left on the ground by his comrades, as it is a custom with them never to bury, or even to touch or approach a scalped Indian, for the loss of his scalp renders him in their eyes an unclean thing!

After the engagement on the Withlacoochee,[18] the main body of the enemy moved South, destroying almost every thing of value in their course, burning every house and destroying every plantation between St. Augustine and Cape Florida, a distance of two hundred and fifty miles. The amount of property destroyed is immense. Whenever they set fire to a dwelling house they would dance around it until it was reduced to ashes! In most instances they found the dwellings deserted by the whites, who, on receiving information of the approach of the enemy, had fled for their lives, leaving their most valuable effects behind. In one instance, an aged grand parent, who was too infirm to attempt an escape by flight, and an affectionate little grand-daughter, who was much attached to her grandfather, were left behind. The savages entered and secured both, and having conveyed them to a little distance from the house, set it on fire, after which they returned, and while consulting together in what manner they should dispose of their captives, the poor old man (who entreated only for the life of his grand-child) was fortunately recognised by one of the savages, as one from whom his family had received relief when driven to the greatest extremities by the war of 1818— in consequence, by his kind interposition, they were left uninjured and with sufficient food for their subsistence for several days—an instance in proof of what has been frequently said to be one of the most noble characteristics of a savage, that whether at peace or war, "he never forgets an injury or a favor done him!"

Early in March, Gen. Gaines,[19] with a very considerable body of Carolina and Georgia troops under his command, penetrated as far as the Withlacoochie, where he met with the main body of the Indians encamped on the opposite bank of the river, and by whom during the night he was attacked, (he having by stratagem in concealing a part of his force decoyed them over;) after a short but severe contest, he succeeded in driving them back with loss; but early the succeeding day the attack was renewed by the savages, and continued for three days successively, when finding their number of slain and wounded very considerable, they retired and sought a covert in a neighboring swamp. Gen. Gaines' loss was but four killed and twenty wounded; among the former was Gen. Izard, and among the latter Gen. G. Gen. Gaines having been disappointed in receiving a supply of ammunition and stores, as well as a reinforcement, which, under the command of Generals Clinch and Scott, were to be sent him, was now placed in a very critical situation—entrenched and surrounded by the enemy, his communications cut off, and almost destitute of provisions as well as ammunition. Supplies had been sent him by Gen. Clinch, but the detachment after proceeding within six miles of Gen. Gaines' encampment, found the signs of the Indians so frequent, that they thought it unsafe to proceed further, and therefore returned to Fort Drane.[20] In this alarming condition Gen. Gaines held a council with his officers, by whom it was determined that it would be preferable to kill and eat their horses than to trust to the mercy of the savages; and not only on their horses were they compelled to depend for subsistence, but to such extremities were they finally driven, that even their dogs (with one exception) were butchered, cooked, and distributed sparingly among the men! and the solitary one reserved (although contrary to the positive orders of Gen. Gaines) soon shared a similar fate. This animal for his remarkable attachment to the commanding officer being a favorite, was highly valued; but notwithstanding, the temptation was too great to be resisted by a soldier nearly famished with hunger. Watching a favorable opportunity, he seized the dog, conveyed him a short distance from the camp, and strangled him; and was soon after detected by disposing of one of the quarters to one of his comrades for five dollars! and was severely punished for the act. But at this melancholy period the powers of hunger were too great to be resisted, whatever the consequences might be. One soldier gave six dollars for a piece of horse's entrails of about a foot in length!—five dollars were given for a biscuit, and the same amount for a quart of corn! a soldier was offered one dollar by another for an ounce of tobacco, and refused it. Many other similar instances could be mentioned relative to the woful condition of these unfortunate men, surrounded and suffering beyond the power of conception, in a savage wilderness. In this deplorable condition were they found, when Gen. Clinch happily succeeded in reaching them with supplies and a reinforcement of Alachua militia. They met, as might be supposed, with a joyful reception. The Alachua volunteers cheerfully distributed their biscuits and corn, reserving none for themselves. It was affecting to witness the greediness and thankfulness with which they received a whole or a half biscuit from their deliverers.

The day previous to the arrival of General Clinch, Oseola sent a negro to the camp of General Gaines, requesting an interview, and promising to stop killing white men if he would stop killing Indians.—This proposition was agreed to, and Oseola was told to come next day with a white flag, when they would have a talk with him. The next day, in company with another chief, he came to within about one hundred yards of the fort, waved his white flag around three times, and sat down upon a log. Three officers from the camp went to meet him.

Oseola informed them that Gen. Clinch was on his way to join them with a large number of horsemen.—He expressed his willingness that hostilities cease, and to give up his arms. The officers required him to sign articles of agreement by which he bound himself to proceed immediately to Tampa Bay, and thence embark for the

Mississippi. Some say that Oseola objected to this way of removing, and wished to go by land. Others that he would not promise to go at all, but wished to live on the other side of the Withlachooche, and to have that river for the boundary line between them and the whites. Their discussion was interrupted by the arrival of Gen. Clinch. During the course of it, Oseola inquired how they were off for provisions. They told him they had a plenty. He said, he knew they had not, and if they would come over the river, he would give them two beeves and a bottle of brandy.

The evening of the day on which their interview was interrupted by the arrival of Gen. Clinch, Oseola sent word to Gen. Gaines, that if he would send away the horsemen (Alachua militia,) they would come and surrender their arms. We know not whether from suspicion or otherwise, the horsemen were not sent away. After waiting three days to hear more of Oseola, and not having provisions to remain longer, Gen. Gaines returned to Fort Drane, at which place Oseola was to have met him.

Orseola's request for an interview with Gen. Gaines was no doubt an artifice of that cunning chief, on learning the approach of a reinforcement, either to give time to make a safe retreat, or a stratagem by which, after introducing five hundred Indians within the breastwork under the pretence of surrendering their arms, to make an attack with his main force, and taking advantage of the confusion, to massacre the whole before Gen. Clinch could render them any assistance. Every recent engagement with his followers affords additional evidence of the daring character of this chieftain. He seems to be unacquainted with fear, and no reliance can be placed on his declaration that he was "tired killing white men." Deep-rooted hatred to the "pale faces," and despair of pardon for his unparalleled atrocities, have possession of his heart, and he will no doubt continue to manifest his hatred to the whites, until he is placed where he can no longer raise his murderous arm against the innocent! and yet, he may be supposed almost bulletproof, as forty balls were taken from the trunk of the tree which sheltered him during the battle of Withlicooche!—in that battle the Indians have acknowledged that they lost 138 men. Micanopy, the head chief, they say, had fired but one gun during the war. He had his choice, either to fight or die; he chose the former, raised his rifle and shot Major Dade, and immediately thereafter retired to his town, where he has remained ever since.

After the arrival of Gen. Clinch, the Indians separated into straggling parties, and so far from having been beaten and compelled to sue for peace, the small parties which have been since met with, have fiercely resisted, until put in danger of the bayonet. The face of the country, interspersed with hammocks, cyprus swamps and marshes, almost impenetrable to the white man, presents serious obstacles to the prosecution of a campaign in Florida; and while these fastnesses constitute the natural defence of the Indians, they present difficulties almost insurmountable to their pursuers. As the approaching warm and unhealthy weather, will prevent further operations on the part of the whites, the regular forces have retired into summer quarters at St. Augustine; and thus has ended this unfortunate campaign. The savages, unsubdued, continue fearlessly to stalk over the graves of Major Dade and his brave companions.

# SARAH F.
# WAKEFIELD

In June of 1861, Sarah Wakefield traveled with her family from Shakopee, Minnesota, to the Sioux reservation's Upper Agency at Yellow Medicine, to which her husband had been appointed physician. In her narrative, Wakefield described her initial response upon arrival as ethnocentric and culturally disoriented, but she soon came to appreciate the land's grandeur and to "love and respect" the Dakotas "as well as if they were whites." Her open-mindedness was unusual, since most European Americans on the reservation were traders, soldiers, or farmers who at best ignored the Dakotas and at worst exploited or brutalized them. The exceptions were several missionaries, and from them Wakefield took her cue in developing a radical Christianity. Yet she seems to have gone even further than these male missionaries in adopting what we now call "liberation theology," meaning a type of Christianity whose practitioners' spirituality is defined by their action-based political and social conscience, not just their inner faith.

A year after Wakefield's arrival, a minor incident between several white settlers and starving Dakota youths escalated into the conflict known synonymously as the Dakota War, the Dakota Conflict, and the Sioux Uprising. On August 18, 1862, the great Dakota chief Little Crow led more than a hundred warriors in an attack on the reservation's Lower Agency. During the six-week war, which ended on September 26, they killed close to five hundred white soldiers and settlers and took more than two hundred white and mixed-blood captives. Among the many hostage women and children were Sarah Wakefield and her young son and daughter. Wakefield credits her survival to her faith and adaptability, but, more importantly, to two manifestations of Christianity: her own belief in doing unto others as she would be done by, which in the past meant that she had shown many kindnesses to the Indians which they reciprocated later; and a protector, a Dakota named Chaska who also applied the same commandment and saved Wakefield and her children from harm on many occasions.

Because Wakefield had a protector, and because she cooperated with her captors rather that resisted them (which, she believed, would have further endangered her and her children), other captives viewed her as an "Indian lover." This impression was only reinforced when Chaska said that he had taken Wakefield as his wife; however, the narrative indicates that this was merely a ploy to stop another Indian, Hapa, from sexually harassing and even attempting to rape Wakefield. Of Chaska, Wakefield says, "Very few Indians, or *even white men*, would have treated me in the manner he did. I was in his power, and why did he not abuse me? Because he knew that it was a sin."

As the war continued and Sibley's forces gained the upper hand, Chaska and other less militant Dakotas decided to stay with the captives and hope for American justice. As Chaska had protected Wakefield, she assured him that she would protect him and his family by identifying them as having saved her and by intervening and testifying on their behalf. But she had misjudged white notions of both Christianity and justice, for almost four hundred Dakotas were rounded up—including Chaska—and given hasty military trials. Three hundred and three were found guilty and condemned to death, but only thirty-nine were actually hanged, because President Lincoln, in a move that was extremely unpopular in Minnesota, commuted the others' sentences. But by one of those ironies that signified the extent of cultural misunderstanding and racism, Chaska was hanged instead of a Dakota named Chaskadon, who really was guilty of atrocities. Wakefield was outraged and insisted that Chaska's death was intentional; indeed, she accused the authorities in Mankato of murdering him and claimed that God would punish them at the Last Judgment.

Wakefield's reputation for consorting with the enemy while a captive followed her upon release as she continued to speak out on Chaska's behalf. White patriarchy refused to accept her testimony, which directly contradicted the prevailing view that all Dakotas had murder and destruction in their hearts. At one of the hearings, Colonel Marshall prompted Wakefield to reveal "anything more of a private nature" and simply did not believe her when she refused to implicate the Dakotas in sexual crimes or torture. As Christopher Castiglia points out, Wakefield was useful to the army "only as a 'victim'" (p. 54). Whereas, as the narrative states, many ex-captives "told entirely different stories respecting their treatment, after Sibley came, than they did before," Wakefield herself did not waver in her claims that most Dakotas treated her well while she was a captive and that

SARAH F. WAKEFIELD                239

they had ample reason to rebel in the first place. For this unpopular, if not culturally treasonous, response, "the soldiers lost all respect for me, and abused me shamefully," she says.

Wakefield no longer trusted a patriarchal view of the world: she trusted her own conscience, guilt, and sense of justice, which empowered her to write, publish, and circulate her narrative to vindicate herself and to counteract the other accounts. Most important, composing her own narrative allowed Wakefield to record and then interpret her experiences for herself and her readers without the intervention of a male editor or minister. Thus *Six Weeks in the Sioux Tepees* shows its author as a decoder of signs. She understands, for example, that if the Dakotas had received their annuity and food on time, there would have been no war, so she blames the U.S. government for the hostilities and deaths: ". . . if all these Indians had been properly fed and otherwise treated like human beings, how many, very many innocent lives might have been spared."

Two recent commentators on the narrative focus on Wakefield as an empowered woman (Castiglia) and as an example of woman's response to war (Wakefield, ed. Namias). Yet Wakefield is also writing in the tradition of the Indian captivity narrative as spiritual autobiography. To be sure, the spiritual testament of *Six Weeks in the Sioux Tepees* differs markedly from Rowlandson's *A True History* or Hanson's *God's Mercy Surmounting Man's Cruelty*, but the prevailing theme is that the events of this world offer committed Christians like Wakefield and Chaska an opportunity to put their principles into action, even if they have to wait until the next world to receive true justice.

The narrative also documents the responses of a person who refused to stand passively by during wartime when she could see atrocities and injustices being committed by her own people. As a woman, she could not physically intervene, but she could speak out and later place her narrative alongside other acts of heroism and resistance. She may not quite be an Oskar Schindler, who saved more Jews from the gas ovens than any other single person during the Second World War, or a Hugh C. Thompson, the only American soldier at the My Lai massacre in Vietnam to confront William Calley and his men and helicopter out a dozen terrified survivors, but she is in their mold. Like them, Wakefield reached a point where she had to respond, and even though she was not able to save Chaska's life, she told the story of his sacrifice for posterity. Like them, too, after her heroic act, she slipped back into relative personal obscurity. She died in 1899, thirty-seven years after the events that galvanized her into authorship.

The text is that of the second edition: Sarah F. Wakefield, *Six Weeks in the Sioux Tepees: A Narrative of Indian Captivity*. Shakopee, Minn.: Argus, 1864.


## SUGGESTIONS FOR FURTHER READING

*PRIMARY SOURCE*

Wakefield, ed. Namias.

*SECONDARY SOURCES*

G. C. Anderson; Castiglia; Namias; Schultz.

# Six Weeks in the Sioux Tepees:
# A Narrative of Indian Captivity

### PREFACE

I WISH to say a few words in preface to my Narrative; First, that when I wrote it, it was not intended for perusal by the public eye. I wrote it for the especial benefit of my children, as they were so young at the time they were in captivity, that, in case of my death, they would, by recourse to this, be enabled to recall to memory the particulars; and I trust all who may read it will bear in mind that I do not pretend to be a book-writer, and hence they will not expect to find much to please the mind's fancy. Secondly I have written a *true* statement of my captivity: what I suffered, and what I was spared from suffering, by a Friendly or Christian Indian, (whether such from policy or other motives, time will determine.) Thirdly, I do not publish a little work like this in the expectation of making money by it, but to vindicate myself, as I have been grievously abused by many, who are ignorant of the particulars of my captivity and release by the Indians.

I trust all errors will be overlooked, and that the world will not censure me for speaking kindly of those who saved me from death and dishonor, while my own people were so long—Oh, so long!— in coming to my rescue.

SARAH F. WAKEFIELD

# Six Weeks in the Sioux Tepees

IN JUNE, 1861, my husband was appointed physician for the Upper Sioux Indians[1] at Pajutazee, or Yellow Medicine.

The first day I arrived in the Indian country, I well remember. It was on Sunday, and as I landed from the steamboat, I could not help exclaiming, "Is it here where I am to live?" for all I saw was one log hut and about six hundred filthy, nasty, greasy Indians, and I wondered if I was really at what was called Redwood. But I soon heard that the buildings were upon the hill, some 500 or 700 feet above the river. When I arrived at the Agency I was disheartened, low-spirited and frightened, for the buildings were situated on a high prairie, and as far the eye could reach, was a vacant space. I then felt as if I had really got out of civilization; but when on the following morning, I learned that we were going 30 miles further west, I was alarmed. We at last got ready, and a train of seven wagons, with many women and children, started. We had in our wagons $160,000 all in gold,[2] and we rode in great fear, for the the Indians were grumbling all along the road because of the change in the administration.

Although I was nervous, I enjoyed that ride, for a more beautiful sight than that prairie, I never have seen. It was literally covered with flowers of all descriptions; the tall grass was waving in the breeze, and it reminded me of a beautiful panorama. It seemed really too beautiful for Nature's picture. After riding a few miles we began to meet with annoyances, in the way of sloughs. After leaving the Lower Agency, we traveled ten miles, passing through Little Crow's village,[3] and I little thought then what I should have to suffer in that vicinity. When we arrived at the Redwood River, we all exclaimed, "What a romantic spot!" Very high hills enclose the stream, while huge rocks are thrown around in the valley, giving grandeur to the scene. After crossing the river, we came in sight of a house, used by Government as a school-house for the Indian children. The house consisted of two rooms below and one above. In this Mr. Reynolds and family[4] were already established as teachers, and here also, was kept the only hotel, after passing Fort Ridgely, going west. We only rested long enough to give our horses breath after ascending the high hills, and we were objects of much curiosity to the Indians while we remained, for they all gathered around to catch a glimpse of their new "Father" that had just been sent them.

Our ride over the remaining twenty miles was very unpleasant, for the sun was very powerful, beating down upon us in our open wagons. We got along very well until we would come to a slough, and stick fast in the mud, when all would have to get out, and then putting two or three extra horses to the wagon, we would be able to extricate it. It was all novelty to us, and we enjoyed it, however the poor beasts suffered. After riding a few miles we could not see anything but the road that looked like civilization. It seemed like a vast lake—not a tree or a shrub to be seen. Soon, however, we came to what the driver said was an Indian mound. I do not know whether it was such or not, but it was a very high elevation of land; and there, in the distance we could see our future home, which much resembled a fort, as flags were flying from many of the buildings in honor of our arrival.

We arrived at the termination of the road about three o'clock in the afternoon, and found we must go down and around very steep hills in order to get across the Yellow Medicine River. What a splendid sight was that, as we, after winding and turning in and round great bluffs, came out into the valley of the river. Here we found quite a large Indian village. The houses were all made of bark, and the squaws were cooking outside. It was really a pretty and a novel sight. The waters were rushing and tumbling over the many rocks, and the Indians, playing their flutes, made music quite pleasant to our ears. We found that we were to cross this river, and to ascend a hill 600 feet high, made it seem as if we were going up to some great castle, for we could see the tops of the buildings in the distance, and we all remarked that we enjoyed this as much as pleasure-seekers did their visits to the old castles and scenery on the Rhine. We reached the top of the hill without further inconvenience than having to walk nearly all the way. Very glad was I when we got to our home, for I was exhausted. I found that there were only five buildings there—four large brick, and one frame—and a small brick jail, in which to confine unruly Indians. The situation of the Upper Agency was beautiful, being at the junction of the Minnesota and Yellow Medicine Rivers. On the north side of our house was the Minnesota, and on the south side the Yellow Medicine River, being not more than eighty feet apart.

The first night passed there was one of horror to all, as we were ignorant of Indian customs any further than what we had learned from those who were camped around our town, and this night they were having councils and were talking, shouting and screaming all night, and we, poor, ignorant mortals, thought they were singing our death-song, preparatory to destroying us. Towards morning the noise lulled away, and we dropped to sleep, but not to sleep long, for soon came the tramp and noise of a hundred horsemen close to the house. The men all arose, prepared their arms, waited and watched, but no attack was made. What could be the trouble? why did they not make some manifestation? why were they silent—only that terrible tramp-ing? At last one man, braver than the rest, went down, and, be-hold,——it was our own horses, which had been turned out. They had come up on the platform to get away from the mosquitoes. This gives, in the beginning, an idea of many Indian scares. Many times we were needlessly frightened, but at last came one that was real, as our friends and our country know to their sorrow.

We found that there were employed at the Agency, for the benefit of the Indians, a blacksmith, farmer, and doctor; also, that there was a school taught by a half-breed named Renville who had been edu-cated in Wisconsin, and had returned to his home, his teacher fol-lowing him back and marrying him. They had many pupils, all Indian children. They professed to teach them all kinds of manual labor. The scholars were fed and clothed by Government, the teachers feed-ing their own pockets more than they did the children's mouths. The hotel was kept by the farmer, and during our stay was a good house. We soon knew we could be very happy, although so far away from civilization. After being there a few days, we learned that three miles above us there was a missionary station, conducted by Dr. William-son,[5] a good christian and an excellent man. How I learned to love his family; while there they were so very kind to us all. The old man had been among these Indians 27 years, and had educated and con-verted many of them. Girls and boys brought up by them were equal in learning to white children of the same age. I have employed women educated by the missionaries who could sew or cook much better than girls of the present generation can do. Many persons say the Indian can not be civilized. I think they can, but did not know it until I lived among them. I usually, on the Sabbath, attended the Dakota Church, and was much interested in their services. Sometimes I would go to Mr. Riggs' Mission,[6] which was situated about two miles beyond Dr. Williamson's, at a place called Hazelwood. It was a delightful spot, and the rides to the place I enjoyed exceedingly. The scenery around Rush Brook was grand. Enormous hills—almost mountains—were on every side of this stream, and when a person was at the top and commenced descending, they would tremble with fear for awhile, but at last they would entirely forget all danger, while looking at the beauties of the scene. Away down between the hills, among the brush, could be seen these wild men roaming in pursuit of game, while their wives and children bathed in the stream, and from the top of the bluff they looked like babes, the distance was so great. I often wondered what an Eastern person would think, to ride through those woods, as we did, unprotected. I usually, after the first few weeks, went with my little boy, alone, to Hazelwood, often returning long after the sun was down, and very often passing through the Indian camp, which near the time of payment consisted of about five thousand Indians. I never knew one to be cross, but on the contrary were very kind and pleasant. I often was stopped and asked to take a puff from their pipes, or canduhupa, as Indian women smoke all the time, only when they are at rest. When they cook they smoke. They have a long stem to their pipes, about two feet in length, and they will sit on the ground, mix their bread, and bake it, the pipe resting on the ground, the end in their mouths.

The first Independence Day I passed in the Indian country I passed in great fear. A messenger came from the Indian camp in the morning, saying that the Indians were coming down to make mischief; they were angry because some of their old employees remained whom they thought had defrauded them. We did not know what to do. There were only 15 men there at that time, and it would be useless to try to defend ourselves against thousands. Major Galbraith was absent, and Major Brown[7] (the former agent) was very much alarmed. He proposed that we all should go to the jail and try to keep them off. In the mean time he sent his son on horseback to Fort Ridgely, a distance of 45 miles, for troops. I think all stayed in the jail for many hours, except Mrs. G——h. She said her cooking must be done, as we had invited all the mission people down for a Fourth of July party in the evening, and if she was to die it might as well be at home as any place else; and if we did escape we would all be rushing back for food. During the afternoon a friendly Indian arrived and said they had postponed their attack until Major G—— arrived, as they wished to ask some questions before doing anything; so we were contented and had our dance. The Indians, however, sent down quite a number to guard our buildings, and would not allow any person to go out or in without questioning them. We danced that night, every moment expecting a shot from some of our Indian guards; but when we had eaten our supper, and we had invited some of the Chiefs in, and they eat, for the first time, ice cream, it seemed to calm them down, and they came in and witnessed our dance with great pleasure. I think the Indians all took a fancy to me at that time, for I gave them something of all we had, took them around, showed them our rooms all ornamented for the occasion, they all said that the "Tonka-Winohinca waste," meaning the large woman, was very good. The next day Major G. came home, and they all came down, dressed up finely, for a council. They surrounded the Warehouse, which was a large, fortified building, on the West end of the Agent's house. The Agent took his interpreter, and went up to one of the upper windows and talked with them. They wished for food immediately, and wanted to come in and help themselves. He told them they could not come in. They then began to complain of the Farmer, or Christian Indians.[8] Said they were allowed in, and they every week got food, when they only got it once a year, and if the Farmers would be fed by the white men, and try to be like the whites, they should not have any money at time of payment, for it all belonged to them. They got very saucy, kept firing their guns up in the air, and beating against the doors. At last the Agent told them how much flour he would give them. They refused the quantity, saying it would not make a taste for each. He did not tell them that was all, but such was the case. The provisions had not arrived. Just as they were threatening him, some teams came up the hill, loaded with flour, and he told them they might have all they had; this was accepted, but they soon demanded what was first promised them; then they were satisfied, and after dividing it they went away, contented. That is the only way the wild Indian can be kept quiet, by just filling them with food; for if before eating they feel like fighting, they eat so ravenously that they have to sleep, and then they forget all during their slumbers.

This was all of any consequence that transpired during the first year of our stay. The payment went off quietly, with the exception of a drunken Indian occasionally.

There were at Yellow Medicine, I believe, four trading houses, where were kept groceries and dry goods for the Indians, cheating the creatures very much. Indians would buy on credit, promising to pay at the time of payment. They have no way of keeping accounts, so the traders have their own way at the time of payment. All the Indians are counted, every person giving his name, each Band by themselves. At the time of payment they are called by name from the window to receive their money (which at the Upper Agency was only nine dollars to each person.) As soon as they receive it the Traders surround them, saying, you owe me so much for flour. Another says you owe me so much for sugar, &c., and the Indian gives it all up, never knowing whether it is right or not. Many Indians pay before the payment with furs, still they are caught up by these Traders, and very seldom a man passes away with his money. I saw a poor fellow one day swallow his money. I wondered he did not choke to death, but he said "They will not have mine, for I do not owe them." I was surprised that they would allow such cheating without retaliation; but it came all in God's own time, for at the Trader's was the first death-blow given in the awful massacres of August, 1862. All the evil habits that the Indian has acquired may be laid to the traders. They first carried the minne-wakan[9] among them. The Traders took their squaws for wives, and would raise several children by them, and then after living with them a number of years would turn them off. It was the Traders who first taught them to swear, for in the Indian language there are no oaths against our God or theirs.

The first year of our stay was comparatively quiet, the Indians, after they were paid leaving us for their homes far away, with the exception of those who were farmers, and were living near us as neighbors. And I will state in the beginning that I found them very kind, good people. The women have sewed for me, and I have employed them in various ways around my house, and began to love and respect them as well as if they were whites. I became so much accustomed to them and their ways, that when I was thrown into their hands as a prisoner, I felt more easy and contented than any other white person among them, for I knew that not one of the Yellow Medicine Indians would see me and my children suffer as long as they could protect us.

In the spring of 1862, the Agent, accompanied by my husband and others, visited the Indians living near Big Stone Lake, "Lac Traverse," and that vicinity. They found the Indians quiet, and well contented with what was being done for them, and they seemed much pleased with their visitors.

Before leaving, Maj. Galbraith told them not to come down until he sent for them, as he had doubts respecting the time of payment. He had not been home many weeks when they began coming in, a few at first frightened by some murders committed among them by Chippewas. Not long was it before the whole tribe arrived and camped about a mile from the Agency buildings.

Here they remained many weeks, suffering from hunger—every day expecting their pay so as to return to their homes.

After repeatedly asking for food, and receiving none of consequence, they were told by the interpreter, who belonged at Fort Ridgley, and who accompanied the soldiers to Yellow Medicine a few weeks before the arrival of the Indians, to break into the warehouse and help themselves, promising them that he would prevent the soldiers from firing upon them.

I think it was the fourth day of August, that the Indians commenced hostilities at Yellow Medicine. We were much surprised early Monday morning, to hear them singing and shouting so early in the day. Soon they came driving down the hill toward the Agency, dressed out very finely, and as we thought, for a dance; but we were soon convinced they meant mischief, as they surrounded the soldiers, while part of them rushed up to the warehouse and began cutting and beating the doors in pieces, all the while shouting, singing, and throwing their blankets around them like wild men as they were— driven more wild by hunger.

I was with my children[10] up stairs in my own house, my husband's office being in the building connected with the warehouse. I was very much frightened, and called to my girl to fasten the gate and come in and secure the lower part of the house. Soon the Indians commenced filling our garden and all adjoining. In a short time they surrounded our house and soon came to the door and rapped violently. I caught up a pistol and went down stairs, opened the door, and inquired as calmly as I could what they wanted. They wished axes, and filled the room and followed me around until I gave them all we had. I expected they would kill me, but I knew I could raise an alarm with my pistol before they could get my children. But they offered no violence, and departed quietly; all they cared for was food—it was not our lives; and if all these Indians had been properly fed and otherwise treated like human beings, how many, very many innocent lives might have been spared.

In ten minutes time, after surrounding the warehouse, the door was opened and they were carrying out flour. Soon, however, the soldiers came to the building, and the Indians were obliged to evacuate the premises, but not without many ugly threats and savage looks. The Agent went out and counciled with them, and asked them to give up their flour; but they refused, and he was compelled to give them all they had taken and much more before they would leave.

That night there was little sleep at the Agency; all were expecting an attack before morning.

Just at sunrise the next morning, a friendly or Christian Indian came and told us that the Indians were preparing to make an attack; as they had succeeded so well the day before they would try again. We all knew that matters would be different a second time, as the soldiers intended firing upon them if they came again.

Several families concluded to go down to the Lower Agency, which was thirty miles below us—myself and children being among the number. We remained a week, and while I was there I attended Mr. Hindman's church,[11] and was much pleased with the behavior of the Indians during service. Little did I think while I sat there that my life and my children's would so soon be in danger, and that our deliverer would be one of those wild men that were listening with eager attention to God's word. Surely the missionaries have done good; for where would the white captives now be if the Christian Indians had not taken an interest in their welfare? Monday, August 11th, I returned to my home, my husband coming for me, and saying that the upper Indians had left very quietly, Major Galbraith giving them goods and provisions, and promising to send for them as soon as their money came. I went home with the determination of preparing my clothing for a journey East in a few days, as we were fearful some of the Indians might return and would be troublesome, stealing and begging all summer.

Many who read these pages may not understand about the Indian payment. I will say a few words respecting it: In June these people usually come in for the lands which they have sold to the United States, some coming many hundreds of miles; and if the money is not ready, they expect to find food for themselves, procured at the expense of the Government, as that is part of their treaty. As soon as they are paid they leave, and very few are ever seen until another year has passed away. Last year they came in at the usual time, although many knew they should not come until they were sent for, as before mentioned. But they were all in, and it was no use trying to send them back again, and of course they must live; and the prairie is a very poor place to find any kind of game, and five thousand persons could not long stay where they were without something to support nature. What dried meat they brought was soon eaten, and in a few weeks they were actually starving; the children gathering and eating all kinds of green fruit, until the bushes were left bare.

They had several councils, asking for food which they did not get. Many days these poor creatures subsisted on a tall grass which they find in the marshes, chewing the roots, and eating the wild turnip. They would occasionally shoot a musk rat, and with what begging they would do, contrive to steal enough so they could live; but I know that many died from starvation or disease caused by eating improper food. It made my heart ache to see these creatures, and many times gave them food when I knew I was injuring ourselves pecuniarily; but I always felt as if they were God's creatures, and knew it was duty to do all I could for them. I remember distinctly of the agent giving them dry corn, and these poor creatures were so near starvation that they ate it raw like cattle. They could not wait to cook it, and it affected them in such a manner that they were obliged to remove their camp to a clean spot of earth. This I witnessed. It was no idle story, and it is one of many I witnessed during my short stay among them. I often wonder how these poor deceived creatures bore so much and so long without retaliation. People blame me for having sympathy for these creatures, but I take this view of the case: Suppose the same number of whites were living in sight of food, purchased with their own money, and their children dying of starvation, how long, think ye, would they remain quiet? I know, of course, they would have done differently, but we must remember that the Indian is a wild man and has not the discrimination of a civilized person. When the Indian *wars,* it is blood for blood. They felt as if all whites were equally to blame, I do not wish any one to think I uphold the Indians in their murderous work. I should think I was insane, as many persons have said I was. I wish every murderer hanged, but those poor men who were dragged into this through fear I pity, and think ought to be spared.

When on my way home from the Lower Agency, the soldiers passed us on their return to Fort Ridgley. I was much surprised, and expressed my regret that they should leave so soon, and felt that was a very unwise proceeding; but the Captain assured us there was no longer any need of them, as the Indians had all departed.

That night the Agent had a war meeting, and a company of volunteers were raised, taking about forty men away, the Agent putting his name down first. They left in a few days, passed through the lower Agency, causing the Indians assembled at that place to think their "Great Father" had not many men left or he would not have taken them away from the Agency. They were very angry because the Agent did not stop and have a council with them, and give them goods and provisions, like the upper Indians. There has always been a jealousy among them, as they thought the upper Indians were better treated than they, and this feeling, with what the traders told them, exasperated these men, for they were suffering nearly as much as the upper Indians. The traders said to them they would get no more money; that the Agent was going away to fight, and they would have to eat grass like cattle, etc.

The Indians always blamed the agent for not giving them their goods, and repeatedly said if he had done so they would have scattered back to their homes satisfied, and this awful massacre would not have occurred; but he was deceived respecting these men. He thought they were just like white men, and would not dare to rise, living as near as they did to the Fort; but he must now see his mistake in not explaining matters to these Indians; for only two or three days passed before they commenced their murderous work. I don't think he did this wilfully; it was through ignorance. He did not understand the nature of the people he had in his charge.

· Sunday, the 17th of August, the Indians killed some people in Acton,[12] and on returning to Little Crow's village, said to him, what shall we do? He said they should go to the traders, kill them and all other whites; that they must clear the country of all the whites so they might live. Monday, the 18th, they began their work of destruction at an early hour, killing the traders in their stores; when this was done they began their work of destruction in general. The wine and spirits found in the stores added drunken madness to the madness of despairing vengeance, and soon the Indians were dancing wildly about the dying embers of what had lately been the stores and homes of the traders; then they passed on, killing everything they met. Their savage natures were aroused, and blood-thirsty as wild beasts they raced and tore around, beating crushing, and burning everything they had no use for.

Soon the news came that the soldiers were approaching, when they started for the ferry; but that bloody battle has been many times described, where so many of our kindred were murdered by these savage fiends, made so by liquor and revenge. This affair at the ferry seemed to cheer these people on, and they soon spread over the country, murdering all that were within their reach. How these savage creatures abused the traders after death is not generally known. They broke open the safe at one store, and commenced pelting the dead bodies with gold, filling their mouths and ears, saying to them, you have stolen our money, now take all you will. Some of the Indians acted quite decently, and buried many things belonging to the missionaries, to save them from destruction. Monday, soon after dinner, my husband came in and said I had better get ready and go down to Fort Ridgley that afternoon, instead of waiting for the stage. Mr. Gleason[13] had come up on Saturday and wished to return and had no conveyance, and had offered to drive me and the children to the Fort if my husband would let him take our horses and wagon. (Mr. Gleason was clerk in the warehouse at the lower Agency.) At two o'clock we started. I felt unusually sad, I remember going from room to room, taking a final look. My husband grew impatient and asked me what I was doing, and I made some excuse. I knew he would ridicule me if I told him how I felt. As we were starting he said, "Gleason, drive fast, so as to get to the Fort early." I asked what was the hurry, but he made me some answer that satisfied me then, but many times while I was in captivity I thought of our conversation. I inquired of Mr. Gleason if he had a pistol; he said he had, but it was not so; for after his death no weapons of any kind were found upon him. We drove to the traders, and Mr. Garvie[14] came to the wagon and said he had heard bad news; that the Indians had been killing some persons over in the "Big Woods," and that the Indians were all getting ugly, and at the Lower Agency they were having councils to determine whether they should kill the whites, or if they should give up this country and leave for Red River. He also said that our Indians were only five miles away and were having councils to decide upon the same subject.

I was anxious to go back, as we were only under the hill from the Agency, but Mr. Gleason made great sport of me. He said he had doubt that the upper Indians would make trouble, and he was in a hurry to get home, for he would send four or five hundred lower Indians up to fight for the whites. He then told me that my husband had heard these reports and that this was his object in sending me away in such a hurry; that as soon as we got away from Yellow Medicine all would be right. Poor misguided man! All this day these lower Indians had been committing these awful murders, and, we, not knowing it, were going down into their country for safety. I rode in great fear that afternoon. I was very sad and sorrowful. Death seemed hovering near me. Not a person or a living object did we meet as we rode, and I remarked to Mr. Gleason many times that there was something wrong below, as usually we were constantly meeting teams on that road.

Mr. Gleason was very lively, more so than I ever knew him. He would laugh, sing, shout, and when I would chide him and tell him how I felt, he would say I was nervous, and told me he would never take me anywhere again. I endeavored to have him return with me but he said I would live to see the time I would thank him for taking me away. He tried every possible way to make me feel contented; but it was of no use. I had strong feelings of evil, and it was a presentiment of what was to happen. As we got to the mound which is half way between the two Agencies, we could distinctly see the smoke of the burning buildings. I said to him that the Indians were destroying the Agency. "O, no;" he said, "it is the saw mill or the prairie on fire." I became frightened, and tried again to persuade him to return. I was so excited I could not sit still, and endeavored to jump out of the wagon. Then he really scolded me, saying it was very unpleasant for him to have me act in that way. Very well, said I, go on; they will not kill me; they will shoot you, and take me prisoner. "Why," said he, "who are you talking about? The lower Indians are just like white men; you must not act so hysterical;" for I was now crying. Very soon we came in sight of Mr. Reynold's house, which was near the Red Wood river, twenty-two miles from Yellow Medicine. He said to me, "You now see you have been acting very foolishly, for 'Old Joe's' house is standing." But for all, I could not look or around only at that great body of smoke. As we drove toward the house he looked at his watch, and said: "It is now a quarter past six; we will eat supper here at 'Old Joe's,' and at eight o'clock we we will be at Fort Ridgely." The words had barely passed his lips, when, as we were descending a little hill, I saw two Indians coming toward us. I said, "Mr. Gleason, take out your pistol;" but he said "be quiet! they are only boys going hunting." I then said, "hurry up your horses." Instead of doing so he drew in the lines, and spoke to them, asking them where they were going.

I will here describe the wagon we were in and the way we were sitting: It was an open wagon, with two seats. Mr. Gleason was sitting on the front seat, directly before me, my boy sitting at my right hand, and my baby on my lap. As the Indians passed the wagon, I turned my head, being suspicious, and just then one of them fired, the charge striking Mr. Gleason in his right shoulder, whereupon he fell backwards into my lap, crushing my baby against me. He did not speak, and immediately the savage fired again, striking him in the bowels as he laid across my lap. He now fell backwards out of the wagon as he turned at the fire, bringing his back toward the side of the wagon. O, what a sight was that for a mother! and what were my thoughts, for I supposed I should be shot very soon. As he fell, the horses ran furiously, and the Indian who did not fire ran and caught the horses. As he came up, he asked me if I was the Doctor's Wife. I said I was. He then said, "Don't talk much; that man, (pointing to the one that shot Mr. Gleason,) is a bad man. He has too much whiskey." As soon as he had quieted the horses, he came to the wagon and shook hands with us, and one ray of hope entered my heart; but it was soon dispelled, for when we turned around where poor Gleason lay groaning and writhing in his death agonies, I saw the other Indian loading his gun, and I expected every instant to be launched into eternity. When we rode up near I begged him to spare me for my children's sake, and promised to sew, wash, cook, cut wood, or anything rather than die and leave my children. But he would not speak, only scowl hideously—Chaska,[15] the good man, urging me by his looks to be quiet. Just then, Mr. Gleason spoke for the first time, saying, "O, my God, Mrs. Wakefield!" when Hapa,[16] the savage one, fired again, killing him instantly. He stretched out and became calm without a groan. Now, as I write it, all appears plain before me, and I can scarcely hold my pen. I never can feel worse than I did that night. I passed through death many times in imagination during my stay on that prairie. It now seems so plain before me I cannot keep from trembling; but it must be told. In a moment after poor Gleason breathed his last, Hapa stepped up to the wagon and taking aim at my head, would have killed me but for Chaska, who leaped toward him and struck the gun out of his hands. I begged Hapa to spare me, put out my hands towards him, but he struck them down. I thought then my doom was sealed, and if it had not been for Chaska, my bones would now be bleaching on that prairie, and my children with Little Crow. Three or four times did this demon try to destroy me, when Chaska would draw him away by his arm, and I could hear him tell him of some little act of kindness my husband or myself had shown them in years gone by. But all Hapa would say, was, "She must die; all whites are bad, better be dead." Who can imagine my feelings, exposed as I was to the danger of being shot every moment, and not knowing what might be my fate if I was spared.

I think those men disputed about me nearly an hour, Chaska trying every inducement to influence him in my favor. How many and varied were my thoughts! I felt as if death was nothing if my children were dead; but to die and leave my petted ones to the fate that might be in store for them was agony. I could see them left to starve to death, or partly murdered, lying in agony, calling for their dead mother. Father in heaven, I pray thee impress this upon the minds of an ungenerous world, who blame me for trying to save the man who rescued me from death when it was very near! After a long time, Hapa consented that I should live, after inquiring very particularly if I was the agent's wife. He thought I was; but Chaska knew to the contrary, for he had been at my house in Shakopee[17] many times. He often said that if Hapa could have got the Agent's wife, he would have cut her in pieces on her husband's account.

Chaska and Hapa got into the wagon, leaving poor Gleason on that prairie alone with his God. Unfortunate man! If he only had listened to my entreaties, his life might have been saved, and I been spared six weeks of painful captivity. I rode in much agony; I knew not where I was to be taken, or what might eventually be my fate. I turned and took a last look at Mr. Gleason's remains; his hat was slouched over his face, his dog looking pitifully at him, and just as the sun went down, I bid farewell to him forever, Chaska telling me not to look any more, for Hapa was very cross, and said if I turned around he would kill me now.

Hapa sat facing me all the way, pointing his gun at my breast; and he kept saying, "Those children I will kill: they will be a trouble when we go to Red River." But Chaska said, "No! I am going to take care of them; you must kill me before you can any of them." Chaska was a farmer Indian, had worn a white man's dress for several years; had been to school and could speak some English, and read and spell very little.

Hapa was a wild "Rice Creek Indian," a horrid, blood-thirsty wretch; and here can be seen the good work of the Missionaries. The two men were vastly different, although they both belonged to one band and one family; but the difference was this: the teaching that Chaska had received; although he was not a Christian, he knew there was a God, and he had learned right from wrong.

After riding a few miles, we reached the Indian encampment, consisting of about two hundred persons. As they perceived who I was, their laments were really touching to my feelings. They proved to be old friends of mine. Six years previous to my living at the Agency, I had lived in the town of Shakopee. In the winter there were camped around the town this same band that I was now among. Not a day passed but some of the Indians were at my house, and I had always pitied them, and given them food. But at the time of the battle between the Chippewas and Sioux, near Shakopee, many Sioux were wounded, and my husband attended them, extracting bullets, etc., and they often said he saved many of their lives; and now I was with them they said they would protect me and mine. When they assisted me in alighting, many of the old squaws cried like children. They spread down carpets for me to sit on, gave me a pillow and wished me to lie down and rest. They prepared my supper, and tried every way possible to make me comfortable; but that was an impossibility. They promised me life, but I dared not hope, and felt as if death was staring me in the face.

I had not been there long, when a half-breed approached, saying he felt very sorry to see me, that I would probably be spared a few days, but would at last be killed, as they had sworn to kill everyone that had white blood in their veins. He did very wrong, for he knew better than to try to increase my fears. He was a great rogue.

After the old squaws had given the children supper, Chaska said I had better go with him to a house where there was another white woman, for my children would take cold sleeping on the prairie, as they would not put up their tepees that night. I was afraid to go, and asked the half-breed what I had better do. He advised me to go; he said; "Chaska is a good man, and you must trust him, and you will be better treated" He then gave me some very good advice; he said as long as I was with them I must try to be pleased, and not mistrust them; make them think I had confidence in them, and they would soon learn to love and respect me, and that would be my only way of prolonging my life, which advice I followed, for I never gave them a cross look. If they were telling any of their plans or of their exploits, I would laugh, and say, "That is good; I wish I was a man, I would help you." When they were making preparation for a march or for going to battle, I was as busy as any. I prepared the meat for the warriors, pounding it in leather, and then putting it into skins I would press it, and make it ready to be carried around their waists. I helped paint blankets, braided ribbons to ornament the horses, and in short tried by every way to make myself useful, hoping by such conduct to gain their friendship. I knew I could in that way conciliate them, and a different course would have caused different treatment.

I started with Chaska, leaving my trunk of clothing in the wagon, carrying my baby and leading my boy, Chaska carrying my satchel. We walked about a mile, part of the way through the woods. I was suspicious, but I kept up with him, and tried to talk of the heavy dew which was falling, not letting him know I was frightened. He stopped at a tepee, I suppose to show his prisoner. While I was there the Indians brought in Mr. Gleason's clothes, and his watch, which was still running. I looked at it and saw it was just eight o'clock, the very hour he said he would be at Fort Ridgely. The crystal was broken in the center, with a bullet, I suppose. The Indians were having great sport over his empty pockets. He had no pistol: he had deceived me. It was not safe at any time to go without firearms, and I many times wonder why he did such an unwise thing. There was a white woman at this tepee but I did not learn her name. She was a German, and her greatest trouble seemed to be the loss of her feather beds. She had seen her husband killed, but that was very little compared with her other losses. This woman, through the night, would moan and sob, and at last she would break forth into a wail, saying, "All my five feather beds gone I picked the feathers myself in Old Germany, and now they will not give me one to sleep on." She said that after the Indians killed her husband, father, sister and brother, they were about to kill her, when she said, "Don't! I will give you my house, everything I have, and I have much money." So they spared her. She also said, that, in their hurry to get away with her and her goods, they forgot the money, and after crossing the river, she was compelled to return alone and get the money, which was secreted. I think it very strange they did not murder her, for they had all she possessed, any way. She was a sickly woman, having a babe only two weeks old. She declared she had not been abused by the Indians. She said they were very kind. She only mourned the loss of her feather beds.

They asked me to take off my hoops,[18] which I did. I think I should have cut off my right hand if I could have saved my life by so doing.

We only stayed here a short time, and then went to a bark house where I found another woman. They had a good fire, plenty of candles, and made me as good a bed as could be expected. I was told to lie down and go to sleep, as we would start for Red River in the morning; but sleep was far away from our eyelids that night and many others. After Chaska had made us comfortable, he left us in charge of some old squaws and boys, telling me to go to his mother's tepee in the morning, and tell her to give me a squaw dress, saying I would be more safe in such an attire. The German woman and I managed to get through the night, but she spoke very poor English; still she was white.

No one can imagine the confusion of an Indian camp when the braves come home victorious; it is like Bedlam broken loose. Hour after hour we sat listening to every footstep, expecting death every minute. Guns were firing in every direction; women were mourning over their dead, and the conjurers were at work over the sick or wounded, all tending to increase the confusion.

Morning came at last, and as the sun arose, the Indians began to leave us. They were going to attack Fort Ridgely. Now as it was quiet, I went to Chaska's mother, and soon I was changed from a white woman to a squaw. How humiliating it was to adopt such a dress, even forced by such circumstances! This day, Tuesday the 19th, was an extremely hot day, and I began to suffer. My bonnet was gone, as well as everything I possessed. I thought I would be sun-struck, for we were kept on a constant move. The squaws would get frightened, pack up, and off we would go; when soon they would hear different stories and we would rest awhile. Many, many times that day, was that repeated. Once they heard that the Sissetons, or Upper Indians, were coming, when the old women rubbed dirt into my skin to make me look more like a squaw.—Surely I did not look like a white woman. I had the pleasure of viewing myself, for they had a large glass belonging to Mrs. Reynolds resting against the fence, and the squaws were having a fine time admiring themselves.

I sat down by the roadside, and while we were waiting for news from the Fort, I tried to disguise my children. I rubbed dirt all over my boy, but his white hair would betray him. I tore off the skirt of my baby's dress, took off her shoes and stockings, but did not rub dirt into her flesh, for she is naturally of a very dark skin, and the squaws said she looked like a pappoose after I had her made rugged.

During the morning, an old squaw called Lightfoot came and sat down by me, and said they were going to kill me in a few days, but were going to keep my children, and when they were large, their Great Father would give them much money for them. I became nearly frantic. I had thought of this all night, and I determined I would kill them rather than leave them with those savages. I ran to a squaw, begged her knife, caught up my little girl, and in a moment would have cut her throat, when a squaw said it was false. What I suffered, let every mother imagine, when you think of my trying to cut my child's throat myself. But my thoughts were like this: if my children were only dead and out of trouble, I could die willingly; for I supposed my husband was dead, and I cared not to live, only for my children.

About four o'clock in the afternoon, Chaska's mother came into her lodge, saying that a man was coming to kill me; and she caught up Nellie, my baby, on her back, and told me and my boy to hurry. She stopped at the bark house where I had stayed the night before. She told an old man her story, and he said "Flee to the woods." She gave me a bag of crackers and a cup, and we ran to a ravine. It was very steep, and the banks were like the roof of a house. When we got to the bottom she hid me in the tall grass and underbrush, and bidding me sit still, left me, saying she would come in the morning.

I have passed through many trials and different scenes, but never suffered as I did then. God so willed it that a storm arose as the sun went down, and a furious storm it was. No one, unless a Minnesotian, can judge of our thundershowers, But I did not fear the storm, for I felt that God had sent it for my benefit; still we suffered from the effects of it. The rain and mud washed down upon us from the side of the hill, wetting us completely through in a few minutes. I had one blanket and tried to keep my children warm with that. I had in my satchel a small bottle of brandy, and I put it into my bosom, and during that night, as my children would awaken, I would give them some in their drink; it kept them from taking cold. When I recall that night my heart beats with fear.

Surely God gave me strength, or I would have died through fear, for I am by nature a very cowardly woman;—every leaf that fell during that night was a footstep, and every bough that cracked was the report of a gun. My nerves were so weakened that my heartbeats would sound like some one running, and I would frequently hold my breath to listen. Muskrats looked like wolves, and as they crawled around me in the darkness, I thought they were wolves, and they were going to devour me. I sat all night, my foot in a running brook and I dared not stir for fear I might make some noise that would lead to my discovery, for I could hear the Indians racing around, firing guns, singing, hooting and screaming.

Many persons who may read this may think I was foolish in giving away to my fears, but you cannot tell what you would do or how you would feel; for I many times now, when I think of it, think I was foolish; still I have no doubt I should feel the same under like circumstances. My children would awaken often, and I would hush them, telling them the Indians were near, when the little darlings would lay close to me and tremble with fear. I cannot tell how I lived through that night, but I know God was with me. I passed the time in prayer. I thought of my husband lying murdered in his blood, and my friends in a like manner; then I would beg of God if they were alive to spare them. I know He heard me, for we all know how narrowly they escaped. Can anyone imagine how I suffered? No! they can not. I now do not realize my agony. Just for a moment, my readers, think of a woman at any time, lying in the woods alone, all night. We would all pity a person who was so exposed. Then again think of me, being down in those deep, dark woods, I knew not where I was, or how long I might stay. I felt that my bones might at some future day be found; but O, what thoughts were mine that awful night! when the elements of Heaven were all at work, and devils incarnate were rushing around, seeking whom they might devour! My little boy would awaken at times and say, "Mamma, take me home; put me into my own little bed: what do you sit here for? O, mamma, do go home; my father will not like his boy to stay out of doors all night." I would then in whispers tell him what the trouble was, and he would say, "I forgot about the Indians; I will be still; I have been asleep and dreaming."

After a flash of lightning I would pray for the next to strike me, or else save me to meet my husband. I never knew how to pray before; but I had no one to call upon but God, and I knew He could save me, and I begged and plead with Him all that night, as a child would with a father. Never can I forget His goodness; never can I cease praying to One who brought me out of such dangers.

Morning came at last. Sorry was I to see the light. I felt sure we would now be discovered and our fate sealed. Hour after hour passed, still the old woman came not, and it was all quiet where noise had prevailed during the night; nothing could be heard but the singing of the birds and the running of the brook.

I now began to think she had forgotten me and removed, and that my children and myself would be left to perish in the ravine. I knew I could not climb those banks alone, and our bag of crackers would not last long. I now saw starvation, as well as other evils, staring us in the face. Our situation was truly horrible. We were completely covered with mud, and now the sun was shining, the mosquitos were very numerous. My children's faces were running with blood from their bites, but the darlings were as quiet as if they had been at ease, for their fears were so great they did not notice their stings.

After waiting several hours I saw the old woman coming, and I was overjoyed to see her. We laughed, cried, and I really think I kissed her, for I felt as if our deliverer had now come. She took Nellie on her back, and I tried to get up, but found I could not stand, from the effects of sitting so long in one position, and my limbs in the water had chilled my blood and stopped circulation. But the old woman rubbed me and while doing so said the men had gone who were going to kill me, and I must try to walk to her tepee, and she would give me some dry clothes and some coffee. She said they had removed across the Redwood river, and this accounted for the stillness in the morning.

When I was able to walk we started, she carrying both children up the bank, and then helped me up, for I had not strength to get up alone. I was completely prostrated. I had not eaten a morsel since I left home on Monday; now it was Wednesday. The exposure and fright, combined with nursing a child twenty months old, had reduced my strength exceedingly. When we got up to the bark house, the old woman got me a cup of coffee and some painkiller, which revived me greatly. We walked about three miles, stopping at every tepee for some coffee or tea, and she would make me sit down and warm myself, for I was shivering with fear and disease.

At last we came to the Redwood river, and we commenced fording it, the water in some places being up to my shoulders—the old woman still carrying my baby, and I my boy where he could not walk. But the child was as brave as a man, and ran along through the woods that morning with scarce a murmur, the bushes tearing his little bare feet until the blood ran. Occasionally he would exclaim "Oh! Oh!" I would shake my head and speak in Dakota, that the Indians would hear him, when he would remain quiet, when I knew the little fellow was suffering extremely, for I could not bear my own sufferings without a groan occasionally.

We did not go in paths or roads, but through the tallest and thickest brush, and among all kinds of berry bushes entwined together, with grape vines and ivy. We did not stop to part them, but tore through like wild beasts when driven by fear, and of course we tore our flesh badly. I am completely covered with scars which I will carry to my grave.

Those persons who think I prefer Indian to civilized life, ought to travel as I did last summer. It was because I was carried through so much by that family to save me from death; and what is more, that I was anxious to do all I possibly could for them when they needed assistance.

After crossing the river we arrived safely at their encampment. They had no tepees up, but were getting dinner, each family by their wagon.

When I came to where my home was to be, I felt comparatively happy. I had endured so much the past night, that even squaws seemed like friends, and they proved to be good, true friends. Poor women! how I pity many of them! driven from their good homes, their families broken up and divided. Many of them are as much to be pitied as the whites, and many of them no more to blame.

When I had rested awhile, they gave me my dinner, dry clothes, water to wash my children, and prepared me a bed to lie down.

I learned that Chaska were still absent; that he and his mother were living with Hapa and his wife, she being a half-sister of Chaska. Her name was Winona, and I feared her, for she was like her husband, the murderer of poor Gleason. She tried every way to make me unhappy when Chaska was absent, but was very good in his presence. I will here say that my trunk of clothing, which was very valuable, she appropriated to her own use, and would not give us anything to wear, and the old woman would go around and beg when my children needed a change of clothing. She would not give me a pin to fasten my sacque,[19] and I was compelled to sew it together. She took my embroidered under-garments, dressed herself in them, and then laughed at me because I was so dirty and filthy. One day her boy had a collar (which I prized very highly,) in the dirt, playing with it. I asked him to give it to me. He did so, but she took it from me and tore it in pieces, and then threw it into my face. One day I told Chaska I must have a sacque, for mine was so dirty, when she gave me some cloth to make one. A shower coming up soon it got wet, the colors all faded out, and he saw it was not good, and he was angry. He caught her by the hair, slapped her in the face, and abused her shamefully. At last I coaxed him to desist, but he said she was a "Sica-Winohinca," meaning a bad woman. She took my ear-rings from my ears and put tin ones in their place, and dressed herself in mine; cut up my silk dresses and made her boys coats to tumble around in the dirt with. All little articles, such as miniatures, etc., she would destroy before me, and would laugh when she saw I felt sad. I would like to be her judge, if she is ever brought within my reach. She and her husband are now with Little Crow.

After lying quiet about an hour, I was surrounded by squaws, who commenced talking about some evil that threatened me. The old woman said there was a bad man who would kill me, and I had better go to the woods again. I told her I could not, and I must die, for I was completely exhausted. I arose and looked north where the excitement was, and saw a hut made of green boughs, and women led into it by an Indian wearing a white band on his head; presently I would hear a shriek and see female clothing spread out, and what we all thought were bodies put into an ox wagon, and then driven off. A German (the only man who was spared, except George Spencer,) came where I was hidden under the wagon, and said we were all to be killed in a short time. He said the squaws were much excited, and wished him to hide in the woods, but he thought it useless. The old woman soon came back, and said: "You must not talk, and I will cover you and your boy up with buffalo robes and the tepee cloth," and then taking my baby again on her back, kept marching backwards and forwards, as if she was guarding me.

I made up my mind to die. I knew if Chaska was only near he would save me. I conversed with my boy in a whisper, charging him to try and remember his name and his sister's, and tried to impress upon him the necessity of always staying with her and taking care of her, so that if his father or uncle should be alive, he might some day be able to find them.

Several times I raised the tent cloth and inquired what the news was, but the woman was crying, and would only say, "Chaska dead, and you will die soon; that man is a very bad man." I cannot describe my feelings. I know I prayed; that I begged God to save me from the savages; sometimes I cried, then I would be calm, and once I began to sing. I thought I would not die despairingly; I would try and go to my death cheerfully. At last I felt perfectly happy, and I believe if I had died then, I would have died a Christian. I had bidden the world farewell. My husband I thought dead, and all I had to live for was my children, and I was in hopes they might go with me. I said to my little boy, who was not quite five years of age, "James, you will soon die and go to Heaven." "O, Mamma! I am glad, ain't you? for my father is there, and I will take him this piece of bread," (which he was eating.) Poor child! he was not old enough to know how he was to reach that happy land.

I asked Winona how we were to be killed, and she said, "Stabbed," pointing near the heart. I dreaded death in that way, for I was fearful we might suffer some time. While I sat there thinking of my sad fate and of my friends in the East, and how they would feel when they heard of my death, I thought I heard a neigh from our mare that Chaska had gone away on. Soon I heard her mate, who was tied near, respond, and I felt a sudden thrill, as if my preserver had come. In a moment the tepee cloth was raised, and Winona said, "Come out! Chaska has come; it is all right now." I did not need a second invitation. I went out and surely there he stood. He shook hands, and said: "Don't be afraid; he will not dare to hurt you while I am near; if he comes near I will shoot him." O, how happy was I! My life was again saved, and by him. Had not God raised me up a protector among the heathen? Have I not reason to bless His name, and thank the man and his family for all their goodness towards me and mine? for my little children would now be motherless if he had not taken care of me.

The remainder of this day I passed quietly. That night a violent hurricane arose, upsetting our tepee, which had been put up soon after Chaska had arrived, and we were compelled to go under the wagon and lie down on the wet grass the remainder of the night, while the rain poured down upon us. What a scene was that, as we arose from the wet ground. In every direction could be seen the fires, as the hurricane had upset nearly all the tepees, and it looked like some picture I had seen where witches were holding their revels; for, crooning over the fires, were the old women of the families, who seldom ever sleep in the night, but sit smoking their Kinnikinnick[20] until day begins to dawn; then, with a prayer to the sun, they retire. I have often in the night sat and watched these old creatures, as they smoked, talked and cooked, until I really thought their magic spells were really at work upon me; for they would take the form of very devils, in the midnight hour, over their fires, singing and moaning in their half-stupid state. I don't know as this is always so. It might be they were fearful of losing their prisoners. Such nights as these I have described helped my already diseased imagination, until at times I was nearly frantic, for with all this was the continual firing of guns, and I really thought every one sent some poor creature into eternity, and expected every minute my turn would come.

Thursday, the 21st of August, the Indians were up very early, getting ready for an attack upon the Fort. Chaska was going, and he said he was afraid to leave us where we were, for fear Hapa might return and kill us. He told me I had better go with him to his grandfather's, who lived in a brick house about a mile from where we were. Soon the wagon was ready, and myself and children and the old woman were riding away. Before leaving, Winona painted my cheeks and a part of my hair. She tied my hair (which was braided like a squaw's down my back) with several colored ribbons and ornamented me with fancy colored leggins, moccasins, etc. My children were painted in a like manner; then she gave me my blanket, and told me to start. Who would have known me to be a white woman? I sometimes forgot I was, when I would look around me and see how I was living. If I had been without children I should not have stayed

there and submitted to being painted and dressed out in such a manner. I should have tried to escape, and if I had died in the attempt,
well and good: I should have had no children to leave. As it was I
dared not try, for I knew I would be discovered and then death would
have been certain. I know that after the first few days a person might
have escaped, and I often tried to urge young girls to do so. I know
I could have got away if my children had been large enough to walk;
but as it was I could not, for mine were too large to carry, and not
able to walk but a very little ways. We were at liberty to go where
we pleased, could go to the river, go after plums, or from tepee to
tepee, if we wished, and often as I went down to the Minnesota River
for water, I would stand and form plans respecting my escape. The
water was so low that we could ford the river, and once across I
know a person alone could have secreted themselves, and got back
to the settlements without detection.

The prairie that morning was alive with Indians, all in high spirits,
and confident of taking Fort Ridgely. They were either over dressed
*or else not dressed at all;* their horses were covered with ribbons,
bells, or feathers, all jingling, tinkling, as we rode along, the Indians
singing their war songs. It was a grand but savage sight to see so
many great powerful men mounted on their bedecked animals, going
to war. Many of the men were entirely naked with the exception of
their breech cloth, their bodies painted and ridiculously ornamented.
I little thought one week before when passing over that road, that I
should be in such a train, and the train on its way to kill my kindred.
We arrived at the house of his grandfather just at sunrise. It was a
very cool morning, and a fire which they had in the stove cooking
breakfast, was really comfortable. There were several tepees around
his house. I found, after alighting from the wagon, that I was with
some of my best friends in the Shakopee Band. An old squaw called
by the whites "Mother Friend," was there, and glad was I to see her.
Chaska went soon after I got my breakfast, saying he would stop for
us at night. I passed this day in great anxiety. We could hear the
cannon at the Fort, and see the smoke from the burning buildings.
We were camped just at the head of a small ravine opposite the Fort,
only a few miles above, and we could see the Indians as they fired
run down into the woods and reload, then rush backwards and forward. I expected every minute some one would return and in their
rage destroy us, for they were nearly all drunk at this time, and nearly
every day some one would look at us saying they are going to "Pa
Baksa," meaning you will have your head cut off. We heard many

different stories relative to the fight; sometimes we would hear that the Indians were all killed and that the whites were coming; then the confusion that would ensue was such, that many times we fled to the ravines and hid ourselves in the bushes. The squaws were very cowardly, and I was needlessly frightened many times by them. My children feasted this day, one family having enough nuts, candy, maple sugar, &c., to open a confectionary store.

I never shall forget the kindness of old Mother Friend that day; she would not let me stay in the old man's house, but must pass the day with her. She made my boy new moccasins, brought water and washed my sacque, carried my baby around on her back, and did all in her power to lighten my sufferings. She said when the old grandmother called me to dinner, "No, she is my child, she has given me cooked food in her tepee in Shakopee; now she must stay and eat bread with me." Her daughters tried every way to amuse me, and would tell me that when their father came home he should take me down the river in a boat, but although the father was kind, he never offered to take me down as they promised.

Just at sunset a messenger arrived, saying the Indians were going to stay all night, and that a chief was coming to kill us white women, there being two besides myself in that camp. I was told to flee to the woods again, and Eagle Head, Chaska's grandfather, said he would go with me. He was an old man, nearly eighty years old. Mother Friend said I should leave James, as he was asleep, and she would take care of him. The old man took his gun and I my baby on my back; we started in great haste for the woods, which we roamed all night from dark until daylight, never stopping only long enough to nurse my baby; when we would hear them shouting, we would dive deeper into the gloom. The old man could not keep up with me, but I would wait for him, and he would say, "Stop, I am tired; I will die." As day began to dawn, it became quiet, and we came out of the woods on to the bottom lands of the Minnesota river. He said he would go back to camp, but he must hide me first, for he dared not take me back until he knew how matters were. He proposed hiding me in a hay stack, saying he could pull out the centre and put me into the middle and then cover me up. He did so and left me to sit, as I thought, for a short time; but hour after hour passed. It was noon, and I thought I should suffocate or die with thirst. My baby kept worrying for we started without supper, and the child was hungry; while she was nursing it would pacify her, but made me very weak, for, not having eaten anything, I had very little nurse for her.

I sat hours that day nursing her, when I thought I should faint with the constant drain upon me. I could hear water running but dared not come out of my hiding place, for I had seen Indians very near me twice that day. I nearly choked my child when I heard Indians coming, and she was fretting; I clasped my hands around her throat until she was black in the face, for I knew her cries would lead to our discovery and death. Poor baby, she tho't her mamma very unkind, for she would look so pitifully when I would do so, but it saved our lives.

I sat that way all day until sunset. I thought night never would come. I was miserable on account of my boy. I knew he would cry himself sick, for he never was away from me a night in his life. How I blamed myself for leaving him, but I expected when I left to return in a few hours. Where; oh! where, was my child, I would ask myself. I was fearful he would scream and cry and some ugly Indian would kill him. Soon after sunset I heard a voice and a footstep near, but I dared not speak. Presently the old white head of Chaska's grandfather appeared, and he said, "Come out," at the same time throwing the hay off of me. I was rejoiced to see the old man. He said I must not talk loud for some of the Indians were ugly. I asked for drink or food—he said I must wait until I got to the tepee. It was some time before I was able to stand, as I had sat in one position eighteen hours with my feet drawn up under me. As soon as I could stand, we started and I found I had got to walk several miles. I did not think I could live to walk but strength was given me.

I inquired for my boy but he knew nothing about him. All the gloomy thoughts I had indulged in during the day again arose in my mind, and I was almost sure he must be dead, or he would know where he was; still I knew Mother Friend would save him if possible.

As we walked along we passed through a muddy piece of ground and I dipped up the filthy water in my hands and drank and gave my child. It was refreshing, but I think a dog would refuse to drink such water at ordinary times: but my mouth was parched with thirst. Many times during the day I reached my hand into the middle of the hay stack and would find some moist hay, and would draw it through my lips to try to moisten that awful dryness of my mouth and throat.

We walked I think four miles; every one I met I inquired about my child, but could hear nothing of him. I at last arrived at the tepee. He was not there, but Winona soon came in, saying that he was very near. Presently he came in; what a joyful moment for a mother's heart. He rushed into my arms and cried, as if his little heart would break, "O mamma, I thought you was dead, and I was left alone with the Indians. I have cried until I am sick. O, dear mamma, have you got back? Do kiss me, and keep your arms around me. I thought you and Nellie had gone to Heaven and left your boy all alone." He said he did not awake until morning, and Mother Friend told him I would be back soon. After he had his breakfast Winona came and carried him up to her tepee on her back, He said he had cried so much that Roy, a half-breed, had taken him to see an ox killed, "But, mamma, I thought you might be somewhere shot like the ox, and it made me cry more."

I could not get him out of my arms that night. He clung to me in his sleep, and trembled with fear if I made an attempt to lay him down. I sat all night and held him, and watched the stars through the opening in our tepee, and wondered if his father could see us in our captivity.

I learned after a while, that the Indian who threatened us came and as we were all secreted, they told him we were at the large encampment, They searched around and went to the woods, but it being dark, and they lazy and tired, concluded to wait till morning to put their threats into execution, which it appears was not death, but what would have been worse. Now, my readers, what say you? Am I not indebted to those friendly Indians for my life and honor? What would have been my lot that night if they had not interested themselves to save me, you can imagine. I can never express my gratitude to those who befriended me when in such danger; let people blame me if they will, God, who knoweth all things, will judge me, and I will wait and bear all the reproaches the world may cast upon me, knowing that with Him all will be well.

The next day being Saturday, we arose early, as it was reported we would leave for Yellow Medicine in course of the day. The morning passed quietly, the Indians deciding to remain till Tuesday. Soon after dinner, an Indian called Chaska out. He returned very soon, saying, "I wish I could kill all the Indians." I inquired, what was the trouble. He said an Indian was drunk in the next tepee, and was going to shoot all the white women in our camp. He told his mother to close the teopa, or door, and watch. Just then I heard the report of a gun, and a woman shrieked, "I am shot! I am shot!" The old woman said he had shot her through the legs, as she sat outside the tepee.

Chaska appeared much alarmed. He sat down on the ground, told me to sit back of him, taking my children in my lap; and if the Indian came he must shoot through him before reaching me. We sat in this way a long time, until his mother said he had passed away from our tepee, when she tore up the back part of our tepee, and taking Nellie on her back we again fled to the woods. She found a good place, covered us up with boughs of trees, and left in a hurry, not saying when she would return. I sat awhile, and hearing running water I thought I would follow it, and perhaps I might reach the Minnesota river. I took Nellie on my back (as I had learned to carry her in that fashion) and we followed the brook some ways, until a large tree which had fallen across it completely impeded our progress. I was obliged to stop or retrace my steps, and I decided to remain, as it was a very good hiding place. We sat in the water until sunset, when I heard the old woman calling, "White woman! where are you?" She had been where she had left us and was much frightened when she found us gone. She followed our tracks along the stream, and appeared delighted to see us again. I am sure I was delighted to see her honest old face, and as she took my baby again on her back and arranged my blanket around my shoulders, and scattered my hair over my face to conceal my countenance, I could not refrain from giving her a good kiss. I learned to look upon that woman as I would upon a mother, and I hope some day to be able to do something for her. She said that a large number of Indians had just come in from the Fort, bringing many mules, and that now was a favorable opportunity for me to go back home, as they were so excited over their plunder. We were near our tepee, when she discovered the Indian we were in fear of, and she hurried me into a tepee and covered me up with robes, telling me to lie as quiet and as flat as I could; then the squaws threw their packages on to me, and I looked like a great bundle of goods. The old woman left, telling the squaws to give the children food. Soon some Indians came in and asked whose children they were. They said their father and mother were dead. I expected my little boy would speak and say who he was, for he could speak Dakota very well; but the child showed the good sense and reason of a man all the time we were in captivity. In a few minutes the very Indian who had threatened me, came and inquired if a white woman was there. They said no. I can assure all who read this that my heart beat with fear and trembling, for I did not know these squaws, and I did not know but they might betray me. While I lay there an Indian lad came and sat down on me, thinking I was a bundle of goods piled up against the tepee. Fortunately he sat there only a short time, or I should have been smothered. I could not take a long breath for fear he would notice the motion of my body. Soon Winona came in and told me to hurry back. We went home and had a good supper, and glad was I to lie down and rest, for my feet had become so sore that I could hardly walk, and they were very painful. My left foot was entirely covered with sores, poisoned by weeds, and constantly irritated by running through the prairie grass.

I always felt safe when I was in Chaska's tepee, for he always cautioned me when he went away not to go out unless I was obliged to saying that no man dared enter the tepee of another person and commit any violence, unless it was a drunken person. There was no need of cautioning me, for I had no disposition to run around, as I had travelling enough that was necessary. Many of the white prisoners were roving from morning until night, and would often wish me to accompany them, but I always refused. I could not be happy in any place, and if I could sit with the old woman and have her wash my feet and attend to the sores it was all I cared for. I felt as if this was my home, and I stayed there all the time I was in captivity, and was much better treated than any other female on that account.

I thought I was better off staying there attending to my children than I was roving around gossiping, all the time in danger of being shot down by the Indian soldiers; for of all the places for gossip I ever was in, that Indian camp was the worst. There were several half-breeds that spoke good English, that reported every word spoken by us white women, to the Indians, and so things were exaggerated and misconstrued, going through so many lips and different languages. I always took particular pains to speak in favor of the Indians, many times upholding them in their undertakings, because I knew it would all be repeated again to the Indians; and my sole object was while there to gain their friendship so as to save my life. I hoping that God would pardon me for any deceit used in such a way. I little thought every word would be remembered and told to my injury. I trust God may forgive those that have done this grievous wrong, as fully as I do; for the worst is for themselves.

Saturday night I slept very well until near midnight, when Hapa came home, the first time since my captivity. He was drunk, as usual. He awakened all by his drunken actions, but I little thought of his daring to molest me in the tepee in the presence of all the family. I pretended to be asleep, but soon he asked where the white woman was, He said, "Come here! I wish to talk with you." I dared not speak or move; I thought now he will kill me, as a drunken Indian knows not what he is doing. I asked the old woman in a whisper what I should do; she said, "Lie still! Chaska will not let him hurt you; he will go to sleep soon." But not he, for he soon arose, and, with knife drawn, came towards my place, saying, "You must be my wife or die!" I said, "Chaska, come here; he will kill me!" He said, "Be still! I will take care of you;" whereupon he arose and came toward me, asking Hapa what he wanted. He said, "She must be my wife or die!" Chaska said, "You are a bad man; there is your wife, my sister. I have no wife, and I don't talk bad to the white women." I told Chaska to let him kill me, only kill my children first. He said, "Stop talking, then." He turned to Hapa, who had his knife drawn and was still flourishing it, and said, "You go lie down; I will take her for my wife, for I have none." Hapa said, "That is right; you take her, and I will not kill her." Chaska said, "Yes, as soon as I know her husband is dead. I will marry her;" but Hapa said I must be his (Chaska's) wife immediately. I did not know what to do. I caught hold of the old woman's hand, but she said, "Don't be afraid; Chaska is a good man; he will not injure you." Then Chaska said, "You must let me lie down beside you or he will kill you, he is so drunk. I am a good man, and my wife is in the 'spirit world,' and can see me, and I will not harm you." He came and laid down between his mother and me, and Hapa went back contented, and was soon in a deep, drunken slumber. When Chaska thought he was asleep he very quietly crawled back to his own place, and left me as he found me. My father could not have done differently, or acted more respectful or honorable; and if there was ever an honest, upright man, Chaska was one. He has suffered death, but God will reward him in Heaven for his acts of kindness towards me. This was not the only time he saved me in a like manner. Very few Indians, or *even white men*, would have treated me in the manner he did. I was in his power, and why did he not abuse me? Because he knew that it was a sin; he knew that I was a wife, and he always intended to restore me to my husband, and often said he would give me up as he took me.

It was constantly reported and many believed that I was his wife, and I dared not contradict it, but rather encouraged everyone to believe so, for I was in fear all the while that Hapa would find out we had deceived him. I did not consider the consequences outside of the Indian camp, for I had my doubts all the while of my getting away. I supposed if I was ever so fortunate as to get back I could explain all, never once thinking people would consider me a liar, as many call me. Mine is a sad case, after all I have passed through, to receive now so many reproaches from those that I thought would pity me.

Sunday morning our tepee blew down again, and we were obliged to sit under the wagon and wait for the old woman to go to the woods and cook our breakfast, for the wind was so high they could not cook on the prairie. I was visited this day by a number of white women. They said they had heard I was married, and asked me if that was my husband. I replied that I supposed my husband was dead, and turned the conversation; for there were many near who could understand all we were talking about. These women went away and said I acknowledged it. Now this is the truth, and I am very sorry that women would do such a thing towards one of their own sex.

Sunday afternoon, I think, they decided to kill the prisoners, for Chaska came home soon after the Indian soldiers came in from the war path, and said something in a whisper to his mother, when she turned to me, saying, "Sica! sica! bad! bad!" Presently she got me some stockings and a new pair of moccasins, washed my feet, and put them on. Then she started for the woods, telling me to let James go with her. He started to go, when I caught a look from Chaska, that seemed as if he blamed me, whereupon I started after him, caught him in my arms, and carried him back to the tepee. The old woman was very angry. I don't know what was the matter, but I always thought she was going to take him away that he might not see me murdered. This was very near night! She talked with Chaska, and told me to go inside the tepee. He soon left on horseback. It was with strange and conflicting thoughts that I laid my children down to rest that night, for I was sure my end was near, for they always dress the feet clean when a person is about to die.

I had been in bed, (or what was called my bed, consisting of two strips of carpeting, two blankets and two pillows,) when Chaska came in with two Indians I never saw before, and said I must take my children and go with him. I asked where, and what was the matter. He said he would sometime tell me. I got ready awakened my children, and we started. I knew not what was in store for me, still I trusted him and went along. Chaska carried James and I Nellie, and the two strange Indians walked on each side as a guard. It was very dark; a drizzling rain was falling, and here was I, at the mercy of these men, going I knew not whither; but as I had always found Chaska truthful and honest, I could not feel as I might otherwise. We walked a long way; left our encampment far behind us, and still we went on, and not a ray of light was visible. I began now to be suspicious, but he would only say, "Keep still!" We at last came to a small encampment, and he took me to his aunt's tepee, and told her I should stay there. They whispered together some time, and she looked at me very sadly. He left, saying he would come again in the morning. I never learned why I was carried there, I presume some danger threatened. Surely I was well watched and cared for by these people. Could white people do more? About this time I heard that my husband was dead. The Indians returning from Yellow Medicine said he was shot; then his head was cut off; also that all the rest of them were massacred in some horrible manner. O, what thoughts were mine! I felt that all worth living for was gone. I had just as soon died as not then, for I had always had some hope that he was spared, and would eventually have me rescued. Now I had nothing but my children. Would they be long spared? I could not tell; but God saved us all. Great thanks I return to Him for His goodness.

The Indians were as respectful towards me as any white man would be towards a lady; and now, when I hear all the Indians abused, it aggravates me, for I know some are as manly, honest, and noble, as our own race. I remained at Chaska's aunt's, who was a widow, all the next day. Towards night he came, and soon after his mother, and she said I must go; that the Indians were coming, and the next morning we would certainly start for Yellow Medicine, on our way to Big Stone Lake.

When we were going home, I saw an Indian who exclaimed, "There is the Doctor's wife." I smiled, and the old woman said, "Hurry on; he is a Sisseton, and will kill you." I was not afraid, as I knew the Sissetons would take care of me, and longed to go to Yellow Medicine. I knew the Sisseton chiefs would never allow Little Crow to kill me. He was constantly threatening us all, and myself in particular. He was determined at times to destroy me, I being the only one of the Yellow Medicine people that fell into his hands, and he very often said I should die because they escaped. This caused me more trouble than any other woman there.

I remember one day, while I was still at Redwood, that a half-breed said there had been a council, and that all the whites would be killed very soon. I sent for Shakopee, the chief of the Band I was with, and when he came, I asked him if I was to be killed. I told him if he would only spare me that I would help kill the other prisoners. I also promised never to leave his Band, and that I would sew, chop wood, chop wood, and be like a squaw. I was so frightened that I really did not know what I was saying, nor did I care; for all I thought of was, if I can only live a little while longer, and get away, my husband, if living, will not care what promises are made, if his wife and children were saved.

It was awful the promises I made to kill my own people, but I was nearly crazy, and was expecting the soldiers to come very soon, and wished to live to see them. Many unthinking captives, hearing me make such remarks, have since published it to the world, causing people to believe I really meant all I said. Being naturally timid, and afraid of death under any circumstances, I looked upon such a death with horror. One day the old woman seemed much worried about something, I could not understand what. Chaska was away. Soon I heard guns firing, and I imagined they were shooting the white women. Now this I am about to write, was all imagination, to show people how my mind was a great part of the time.

I sat under the wagon this day, and near us was an ox-wagon and I sat and watched that wagon all day, imagining that it was full of dead bodies, and there being buffalo robes over the bodies. I could not see them, but could see their long hair hanging from under the robes. In course of the day Winona came in with a piece of skin, and I thought as she laid it up to dry, it was to put around my throat, after it was cut. Now this was a piece of the ox (the sinew) they were to sew with; and the hair that I thought was human, was from the buffalo robes. Such a day as I passed! I suffered as much as if it had been real. I often wonder that I was not entirely deranged.

The night before we started for Yellow Medicine there was but little rest. The women were packing and the men preparing for battle, as the report came that the soldiers were coming. Just as it got light they started. My boy was sick with bowel complaint. I was forced to take off his pants, and not having any others, he traveled without anything on except a shirt and a little waist[21] that held his pants up.

I had no moccasins allowed me that day, for squaws go barefoot when travelling, and I had to do likewise. Although they were in a great hurry, they did not neglect to paint my cheeks and ornament my hair. They were anxious to look fine, as they were going up into the Sisseton country. When the train started, in every direction, as far as the eye could reach, were Indians, all hurrying for the Redwood crossing. The old woman became much excited, and said I must hurry, as the Sissetons were coming and would kill me. That day I had my baby to carry, as the old woman had about eighty pounds to carry on her back. Such noises and confusion I never heard. My boy was crying, "I cannot walk so fast." Nellie would slip down nearly to my feet, and she would cry, and the old woman would fret because I could not keep her on my back, squaw style. If I stopped she would scold, and say I must go on. When we got to the river we found it full of teams, some fast in the mud, here a horse floundering in the water, there a boy trying to regain his footing; then you might see a horse with poles attached and an old woman up to her knees striving to urge the beast through; but the noise and confusion excited beasts as well as men, and I was fearful we would be crushed to death, for the Indian soldiers were galloping in every direction, firing their guns, not minding and not caring on what or where they tramped. Fortunately the river is not deep in summer. If it had been, many of us poor females would have drowned. We were all more or less wet. I had my baby on my back, my boy by my hand, and it was very difficult endeavoring to keep myself from being drawn down by the current, for the water in many places was up to my shoulders, when I would have to take my boy in my arms, making quite a burden for a person not accustomed to such labor. When I was striving to get through, an Indian rode up to me and asked, "Where are you going?" I replied, "To Yellow Medicine." He said, "You are the Doctor's wife?" I said, "No, I am an Indian woman," for the old woman just whispered, "He is a Sissiton." He laughed and said, "I know you! you must not tell lies! you are not an Indian woman, your eyes are too light." When we got up the bank after crossing the river, where Mr. Reynolds' house once stood, this Indian, with two others, stopped near the ruins and called me to him. He leaned forward and whispered, "I am Paul; don't you know me? You must go with me to my tepee." This reminds me of how frightened the Indians were just before leaving this neighborhood. They said that an old woman every night came to that (Mr. Reynolds') house, made a bright light, and they dared not go near there. They thought it the spirit of some one they had murdered, for after a little some of them said they would burn the building, which they did; but they continued to see her every night, sitting on the walls of the cellar. At last they said it was Miss Jane Williamson, for they knew her by her singing, and they were going to catch her. I afterwards learned they had her secreted, but it was false, for she escaped with her brother's family. The light they saw was the moon's rays on the glass; but the poor superstitious beings thought they had offended some of their Gods, and this was a mark of their anger.

I knew Paul very well at Yellow Medicine, as he was a farmer but he was disguised in his Indian costume, so I did not recognize him again. He was very anxious I should ride, but I dared not attempt to ride thirty miles on a mule barebacked, when I never rode a horse with a saddle. My little boy knew him very well and was anxious to go with him. I said to the child, "You will cry when night comes, for me, because I shall walk, and not get to Yellow Medicine in two days." "No, no, mamma, I will not cry. It will kill me to walk so far; do let me go with Paul." I asked Chaska, who had just come up, if I had better try to go with Paul. He talked with Paul a few minutes, and then said I could go if I wished to, but that Paul wanted me as a wife, and had been for several days trying to get a white woman. He also said that Paul had told him that my husband was alive; they had all made their escape from the Agency the morning after I left. What glorious news was that for a wife who had mourned for her husband as dead. I laughed, cried, and acted like a wild person. I could have danced for joy; my body as well as mind felt lightened. I felt now as if I must live and try to save my children. A new impulse was given me from that hour.

I told James he might go with Paul, for Chaska had advised me to let him go, as our load was so large he could not ride. He said as he started, "I wish you would go too, mamma," and seemed a little sorry I had consented to let him go. I now can see his little bare legs hanging down against the black ones of the Indian, and his white face looking so pitiful as he rode away. How many times that day I regretted that I let him leave me; sometimes I would think it might not be Paul and that I had been deceived, and probably I would never see him again. I saw him in all kinds of danger. I thought he might be sun-struck, riding that extremely hot day without a shade for his little head. I was looking in all directions for his body. I suffered so much in my mind that I did not realize my bodily sufferings. The more I thought, the less hope I had of ever seeing him again; but then I thought that God could shield him from danger as well away from me as with me, and uttering a prayer in his behalf, I felt more calm and quiet, knowing he was in Gods care.

I wish it was within my power to describe that procession as it moved over that prairie. I think it was five miles in length and one mile wide; the teams were very close together, and of every kind of vehicle that was ever manufactured. Nice coaches filled with young Indians, dressed up in all kinds of finery, the more ridiculous the better they were pleased. White women's bonnets were considered great ornaments, but were worn by men altogether. White crape shawls were wound around their black heads; gold watches tied around their ankles, the watches clattering as they rode. The squaws were dressed in silk short gowns, with earrings and breastpins taken from the whites. It made my heart ache to see all this; still I could not keep from smiling at times to see how ridiculously they were used by these poor savage creatures; they looked indeed more like a troop of monkeys than anything human. Ox carts, chaises, bakers' carts, peddlers' wagons, all well filled with these creatures. Occasionally you would see the faces of the white children intermixed with the Indian children. Sometimes you would see a cow with poles tied to her back Indian style, and such a rearing, tearing and plunging was never seen before. It was ludicrous in the extreme, and many times I laughed until I could scarcely stand; for very often in their plunging they would upset some squaw who had all her possessions on her back, and out would roll a baby, a dog, bread, sugar, and sometimes flour, all mixed together, with a great part of her wardrobe. I saw a very nice buggy, with an Indian pony attached, that never felt a harness before, and such antics never were witnessed. Everything was ornamented with green boughs, horses, men, women, and children. United States flags were numerous, and many times it looked like "Uncle Sam's" camp. The noise of that train was deafening; mules braying, cows (poor animals) lowing, horses neighing, dogs barking and yelping as they were run over or trodden upon, children crying, kittens mewing, for a squaw always takes her pets with her; and then to increase the confusion, were musical instruments played by not very scientific performers, accompanied with the Indians singing the everlasting "Hi! Hi!" All these noises, together with the racket made by Little Crow's soldiers, who tried, but in vain, to keep things in order, was like the confusion of Babel.

I traveled in great distress barefoot, trotting along in the tall, dry prairie grass. In some places it was five feet high. My feet and legs were cut by the grass switching and twirling around them as we drove through, regardless of the many prairie snakes we tred upon. I was obliged to keep up with the other *squaws*, and they will trot as fast as a horse.

At noon we stopped for dinner, which consisted of crackers, maple sugar, and good cool water. Chaska, when seeing my feet, said I must ride, for the skin was all off from one foot, and both were running with blood. His mother washed them and cleaned roots and wrapped them up; and when we started I was provided with a seat on the lead and drove the horses the rest of the day. With what feelings I passed poor Gleason's body no one knows. He was stripped of his clothing, except his shirt and drawers; his head had been crushed in by a stone. Now I was on this road going toward my once happy home, now desolate and destroyed; and he whom I was last with on that road was lying there dead, to be gazed at and stoned by these savages. I could not help rejoicing that my bones were not there also. How I wished for power to punish Hapa on that spot, although I must say he never looked towards the remains of his victim; perhaps his conscience smote him for what he had done.

We did not travel many miles after dinner, as the report reached us that we were pursued by white soldiers. What a scattering there was! all order was gone. All made for a little thicket, for nearly every one knows that this is the Indian's battle ground. Here were made preparations for a fight. Guns were discharged and re-loaded, bullets were run, powder flasks filled, and every man that night was ready for action. We camped two miles away from water, and I thought I would perish with thirst, but soon Chaska came in bringing a large bag of plums which refreshed me. What thoughts passed through my mind as I sat there under the trees with these people. My husband I knew not where he was. My boy gone I knew not whither, as I still had doubts of Paul. I felt sometimes as if I would be carried to Yellow Medicine and be murdered in sight of my home. I felt sure Chaska's family would protect me as long as they could, but every day we heard reports further respecting the disposal of us prisoners.

They had during my stay among the Indians a Soldiers' Lodge, where all business was transacted. The Indians soldiers always go there on returning from battle and report. As soon as they can they send out a man who cries the news, whatever it may be. Every few days, as the Indians would come in, we would hear the cry, "White women to be killed now very soon; they eat too much; we are going away and they cannot travel; they had better die at once." This, of course, kept our minds in a perfect state of phrenzy. I do not know how I lived with my nervous, excitable disposition; but there was One above who was strengthening me, or I should have fallen by the wayside.

The Indians did not put up many tepees the night we camped here; nearly all slept in or under their wagons, to guard their horses or goods, for they were in constant fear of some evil—sometimes Chippewas, Sissetons, or white men. They did not enjoy their plunder very much nor very long. We started very early for Yellow Medicine. Soon we came in sight of Major Brown's house. Where now was all this family with their elegance and comforts? in an Indian's tepee, their home destroyed, and their goods scattered! As we went further, I could see our houses at the Agency. They looked just as they did when we left, as the buildings were not burned until Little Crow's soldiers came up; they were in fear the soldiers would come up and occupy them as forts—they being all of brick. What a loss there was to the country by Sibley not hurrying on his forces, for all our furniture remained good for three weeks after the people fled. When the people fled they left every thing; the Indians soon burst open the houses, robbed them of all kinds of food and such things as they could use in a tepee, leaving all large furniture as they found it. Major Brown's family, who were taken near Red Wood by Little Crow's soldiers, were taken back by their relative Akepa, and when I got up to Yellow Medicine were occupying my house. His son's wife was confined in my bed-chamber, and was quite comfortable there. The next day, however, she had to travel, for as soon as the lower bands went up they drove everything before them. When we got to the top of the hill I had to get out and walk, as the hill was very steep. We crossed the Yellow Medicine river. How different everything looked from what it did only one week before. All the wooden buildings belonging to the traders, which were in the valley of the Yellow Medicine.

Soon we were obliged to rise the hill on the opposite side, as the Agency is situated on a hill six hundred feet above the river; it was just at noon, the sun pouring down on my head until I was nearly mad with headache and excitement, for I lost the old woman, and Winona would not wait for me, and I had to run to keep up with her, as she would say, "If you stop the Indian soldiers will kill you." After rising the hill we waited two miles before we stopped. We then camped for the day. We stopped very near Other Day's house about two o'clock; not a shade of any kind for my head; I thought I must die before I got rest or water. While sitting on the grass with my sick child, I heard Good Thunder, or Hoton Waste's wife say she had water. I went to her and begged for a drop for my child, who was endeavoring to obtain nurse from me; "No," said she, "white woman, get it yourself." She had some little boughs put up to screen herself. I sat down in the shade, but she soon drove me away. I was surprised, for they were *Christian Indians*. But I afterwards learned that Hapa and Good Thunder were great friends, and were, of course, cross to me because he was. They eventually occupied our tepee, and divided my clothing between them, Mrs. Good Thunder cutting up seven of my dresses in one day, all the while laughing because they were so large. My sufferings on that prairie, without shade or drink, cannot be described. I had not yet seen or heard anything from my boy; if I could have had him with me I could have borne all other trouble patiently.

About this time the old woman came, and some trouble arose between her and Winona about some shot that was lost, Winona accusing the old woman of stealing them; they were very abusive, and at last Winona threw a tin kettle at the old woman, and she left, saying she would not stay any longer with her. When Chaska came I told him, and he said he would leave; that Hapa was all the time threatening me and my children because they ate so much. He said, "You go to my grandfathers; my mother is there, and I will soon come." I went to their piece of ground, for they were not going to put up their tepees that night, so I was doomed to pass another night under a wagon. As for sleep, all I got was in the day time, for I was too nervous to sleep in the night.

Next morning after our arrival at Yellow Medicine, the Indian soldiers were determined the encampment should be in a circle, and the old woman got scared and hid me again for several hours. I could not find any one who knew where Paul was. I did not know his Indian name, and they did not know him by the name of Paul. Chaska said if my boy was not brought that night he would go to Hazelwood the next morning for him, as that was where Paul formerly lived. My feet at this time were very bad; proud flesh as large as a silver dollar was eating into my foot, and the old woman said I must not walk any more for several days. Soon after she brought me out of my hiding place; she carried me to the camp. Everything was now still. She took me to her sister's tepee, who was a widow, the same person that I stayed one night with at Redwood. She prepared me a good breakfast of coffee, fried meat and potatoes and fried bread, but I could not eat, my mind was so troubled about my child. While I was sitting on the ground, drinking my coffee, a lady appeared before me whom I had known at Redwood and also at Shakopee, but had not seen her since I was in captivity before. She was feeling very badly, and complained much of her treatment, saying she had no place decent to sleep, or anything fit for a pig to eat, and begged what I had for herself and children. I pitied her very much, for many nights she said she and her children were driven out of the tepee while the medicine men were at work over a wounded man who was with them.

That afternoon, just as I had got my feet done up nicely, and Chaska had started after my boy, some one said the Indians were becoming drunk. I did not feel alarmed until Chaska drove up to the tepee very much excited; his horse was just dripping with perspiration, as if he had been out in the rain, and said a white woman had just been killed by a drunken man, and I must hide somewhere. An old squaw I had known at Yellow Medicine, called "Opa," was just in to see me, and she said she would take me up to the friendly camp of Yellow Medicine Indians, who were always encamped about one mile from us. She took Nellie on her back and we ran for some cornfields, stooping down so we could not be seen, around through potato fields, until we got out of sight of the lower camp, and at last arrived at the tepee, torn, worn, and nearly exhausted. No one knows, unless they have run for their life, how a person feels, expecting every moment to be overtaken; and when they reach a place of safety how relieved they feel. When I got to Bit-Nose's tepee, the name of Opa's husband, I felt so happy that I dropped on my knees and thanked God that he had once more brought me away from death.

I felt that night very happy. Julia Laframbois[22] told me she had seen James that day, and he was well and happy, and old Bit-Nose prepared something for my feet that eased the pain very much. Bit Nose was Chaska's cousin, and he was a very good man. He was a farmer at Yellow Medicine, and was one of my nearest neighbors. I dont wish any one to think he was Cut Nose, for that wretch was hanged, while Bit-nose was taken care of and protected all winter by the government, and now has gone to Missouri.

The morning following my arrival at Bit-Nose's tepee, Chaska drove up in a buggy and had my child with him. I did not at first recognize him, his dress was so different from when I saw him last. As I went towards him saying, "My child, my son," he was busy showing some plaything to the Indian children collected around; the little rogue manifested no joy at seeing me. I said, "James, ain't you glad to see your mother." "Oh! yes, but then I had such a nice time at Paul's, I want to go back again." I tried to take him from the buggy and he said, "Do you think I am a baby, I can get out alone now." I thought he was getting very old, for he was not five until October. This night I was happy. I had my children both in my arms, and I thought I never would murmur again if I only could keep them with me. I knew my husband was alive, and I was out of reach of that villain, Hapa's clutches. I sang for the children that night; we ran around on the prairie, picked flowers, and my spirits were as light as air, although I was a prisoner. Do you who may read this think I did wrong? Many persons say I was happy with the Indians, that I did not mourn over my lot as many. Why should I mourn all the time? could I effect any good by so doing? No; instead of good I should have made trouble for myself. I tried to make myself as pleasant as I could while with my Indian friends, and in that way they learned to respect me more every day. I felt the change from civilized to savage life as much as any one, but it would do no good to keep drawing comparisons; I was there, and it was no use to borrow trouble, but try to be as contented as I could under the circumstances, but every word and action has been remembered, and turned against me to my disadvantage.

While I was at this camp Paul troubled me very much; was continually hanging around me, wanting me to go with him as his wife. One day I got a note from Mrs. Renville[23] saying I should come with Paul and they would protect me. I sent for Miss Laframbois, and in Paul's presence and Chaska's, inquired in what way I could stay with Paul. He said as his wife, but I need not work. His Dakota wife would do the work. I asked Chaska if I should go; he said if I wished to; he did not care; he intended keeping me so as to give me up to my husband. I told Paul I would stay, for I was well treated by Chaska, for he had never asked me to be his wife, and it was wrong in him to ask such a thing, being a Christian.

After remaining at this camp two days, Opa said I had better return, as Paul was determined to have me for his wife, and if I went back to Chaska's tepee I would be more safe than with them. She sent for him to come, but as it drew near night, and he came not, she took Nellie and we started back. We met him, and we all got in and rode back to his aunt's. James was much disturbed to think he should be out that day, as it was raining, for he was very well dressed in his new Indian costume, made for him by Paul's wife, and he was afraid of his soiling it. I went to Chaska's aunt's and he said I must stay there until his mother made her a tepee, and I must help her. Chaska had lived in a house previous to the outbreak, was a good farmer, and worked hard. When forced to leave his house he was obliged to go with his sister and her husband, as they had no tepee. His wife had been dead but a few months and he was still wearing mourning for her. I remained with his aunt, assisting his mother to make our tepee, sitting out in the hot sun sewing, the white cloth drawing more heat towards us. I was afraid my eyes would be in-

jured, but I see no change in my person only the color. I do not think
I will ever recover from the sunburn.

Just before the battle of Birch Coolie,[24] Chaska said he was going
to the Big Woods to drive up cattle, and I had better go back to Bit-
Nose's again, and said his mother would go with me.

I saw Mrs. Decamp[25] again this day; her tepee was near ours. She
was very unhappy, and begged me to ask her people to give her a
squaw dress, as I could speak Dakota. She was very filthy, and so
were her children. She came in one morning and said she was nearly
starved, and I gave her all I had left from my breakfast. She sat a
long time talking about our situation. She remarked several times
during our conversation, that she would be thankful if she was as
comfortable as I was. I told her she took a wrong course with the
Indians; that she cried and fretted all the while, making them feel
cross towards her; that they gave her the best they had, and she must
try and be patient; that her life would be in danger if she kept on
complaining and threatening them; it done no good, only enraged
them towards her. One day after a battle she heard all the Indians
were killed. She felt very glad, as we all did; but I, for one, tried to
restrain my feelings. Not her; she exclaimed, "Oh! that is good; I
wish every one dead; I would like to cut their throats," taking up a
knife and flourishing it. This was very unwise, for many Indians understand every word that is said in our language; and one stood near
her, and made this remark in Dakota. "You die for that talk." Soon
after she went up to a half-breed's about one mile away. He had sent
a girl for her, knowing what the Indians had threatened. Soon she
disappeared entirely, and we all thought she had been secretly murdered, for the Indians disliked her very much. Chaska often told me
to tell her not to come into our tepee, saying that the Indians would
learn to dislike me too. But she made her escape and reached Fort
Ridgely soon after the death of her husband. Poor woman, I feel very
much for her, although she misrepresented many things. But I know
she was about crazy while in camp; and then, the death of her husband must have affected her very much. I well remember her saying
to me, "Mrs. Wakefield, your husband is really dead. I heard an
Indian say he had seen his body." At that time I was in hopes he
was alive, and her words seemed to paralyze me. When I could speak,
I made this remark, "If that is so, I might as well pass the remainder
of my days here as any place. He was my all. I care not to live; life
will be a burden to me." This has been told in a very different way.
Another time she was speaking of our situation, and she said she

could not imagine anything worse than our being in that camp. I said, "Don't say so, Mrs. DeCamp there are many worse things than this." She said no; she thought it worse than "Torment." I told her that I had, in my life, passed through trials that were worse to bear, for I could see no hope, no bright place in the future; that now I could, for I knew that sometime we would be rescued; that we were well treated, and we might be abused; that we were comfortably fed and lodged when we might be left on the plains to starve. I tried every way to encourage the lady, but she was determined to look at the worst, and would not be comforted. But her *situation* at the time had much to do with her feelings, so I will not blame her. My disposition is always to feel that God sends our trials, and I must bear them as well as I can, trusting him to "deliver us from all evils."

I went to Bit-Nose's again, but cannot remember how long I remained there, but it was after the battle of Birch Coolie, for the next morning after that fight I removed with their family farther up the country with sad feelings. I gazed on my home, as it was enveloped in flames the morning we started. I had very little hopes of ever seeing that place again, for the Indians said they were going to the Red River now without stopping again, and I thought I should surely die before reaching there. Chaska had always said the soldiers will soon come and you will be rescued; and he promised me if they came not before the river began to freeze, he would try to take me down in a canoe; but said I had better wait for the soldiers, for if we were discovered by the Indians we would all be killed. I tried to keep up good courage, but it was with a sad heart I drove myself and children over the prairie that day. I have driven many horses, but none ever compared with the one I drove that day. He was an Indian pony, and I should judge, had a good deal of the mule about him, for he would go just contrary to the lines. I was amused but at the same time I was vexed, and I often think of the picture we made. I was kept constantly busy trying to keep all things straight; the back part of our wagon was piled high above our heads with goods, and under our feet; and the seat of our wagon was what had been our pantry. My feet were astride a jar of lard, melted like oil; a crock with molasses, a pan of flour, with bread, vegetables, dishes, all mixed up together. Now it was quite an undertaking to keep all things in order—pony, two children and pantry.

We got along very well, considering all things, until I got to a creek, when the pony, not having had water that morning, became much excited for a drink, and plunged forward regardless of his precious freight; but he did not go far, for he was soon fast in the mud. I unloaded my passengers with help, and gave a jump, thinking I should reach a nice piece of grass; but when I struck I was fast to my knees in a patch of boggy ground. How I was to extricate myself I knew not; but I laughed at the thought of my predicament. At last the children began calling, "Mamma, what are you doing down in the mud?" I found that I could not get out without help, and called to Bit-Nose's girl to come to my assistance. She brought a board and I got out; but what a sight was I! completely covered with mud in my struggles to free myself.

Pony, as soon as released of his load, rushed into the water, got a drink, hurried himself up the bank, regardless of our provisions. My blanket was considerably soiled, but everything was otherwise safe. We rode the rest of the way quietly, but my boy would occasionally say, "Mamma, why don't you turn round and drive to Shakopee?" I said, "Why, you know the Indians will not let us." "Oh, dear me! mamma, what do you suppose God made Indians for? I wish they were all dead, don't you mamma?"

We camped about three miles west of Hazelwood, but it was a long time, as usual, before they could decide upon the best place. This day I was treated to bread and molasses; the children thinking it a treat. As we sat eating it under the wagon, on a piece of carpet which they always provided me with, I heard a voice in my own language, and Miss E. B——[26] came towards me. Glad was I to see her. I knew she was a prisoner, but had not caught a glimpse of her since I had been in captivity. She looked finely in her squaw dress, but did not compliment me very highly on my looks. She said she would not have known me if she had met me on the prairie, for I was so much changed. My hair turned as white as an old woman's with fright the night I was taken prisoner.

After being at Bit-Nose's some days, I got nervous, and wished to go to the old woman's, for the Yellow Medicine Indians were expecting to be attacked by the Lower Indians, because they wo'd not come and join them in their camp.

Opa said she would like me to stay, but told me I would be more safe if I was back with Chaska, so they sent for him. He disliked to have me leave Bit-Nose's, because if we traveled I could ride, if I was with them, and if with him I must walk, as they had but one horse now, he and Hapa had separated, but all I thought of was life. I preferred to go back even if I had to walk, rather than stay, expecting death every minute as I did. Chaska and his cousin Dowonca, came for me; one took Nellie, the other James, on their horses, and I followed by their side.

Little Crow's camp had not crossed the creek, therefore it was three miles from the Yellow Medicine camp. When we were going along I could see Mr. Rigg's church and house all in flames.

I think I suffered in my mind more at Yellow Medicine and that neighborhood, than at any other spot, as it recalled so many pleasant scenes past and gone; it spoke so forcibly of home, husband, children, all united; now where were we, and what would be our fate? Would we ever be together again?

I got back to Chaska's tepee, and it seemed good to get back, for everything was so clean, new and sweet. I was nearly devoured with fleas at Bit-Nose's, for they had thirteen dogs. About this time my baby became quite sick, and I thought for many days she would die. I was told that in Dr. Williamson's house, which was as yet unburnt, I would find medicine. I asked Chaska to take me there, as it was several miles, and I dared not go alone. One day he took James, his cousin and myself, and we visited the house, where I often went while at home. What a change! Their once happy home was all destroyed. It looked as if an earthquake had done its worst work, for everything was broken up and mixed together. Bedsteads, stoves, books and medicines. I could not keep from shrieking as I thought of the old people that had passed all their lives among these same people, and now how they were repaid! They had been compelled to flee, forsaking all, after passing nearly all their lives among these Indians. They had a delightful home with many of the comforts of eastern farmers around them. Oh! how my heart ached as I passed through the rooms where I had so often seen their friendly faces. Now where were they? Turned out into the world to seek a home in their old age; and why, I asked myself, have these Indians lived quietly so long, and never, until this late day, done any wrong towards the whites? I could not think of any other cause than this—it may be right, it may be wrong; but such is my belief—: That our own people, not the Indians, were to blame. Had they not, for years, been sutlering?[27] had they not been cheated unmercifully, and now their money had been delayed; no troops were left to protect the frontier and their Agent, their "father," had left them without money, food or clothing, and gone off to the war. I often said to the Indians that if they had let innocent people alone, and robbed us all they would never have been blamed. But they knew no justice but in dealing out death for their wrongs.

I sat down on the door-step and cried while taking a view of my situation now and what it was only two weeks before. At last my boy said, "Don't cry, mamma, you know we shall get away soon," and for his sake I dried my tears and endeavored to put on a cheerful face.

The bell from the top of the building was being rung furiously by some boys; the Indians were tearing, crushing everything within their reach. I went into the garden and gathered a few tomatoes, and came away feeling sad, very sad.

While at this camp I suffered very much bringing water, as the bank was almost perpendicular; all the way I could get up would be by catching a twig with one hand, and pull myself up, and then catch another. Many times a twig would break, and down I would go, feet foremost, to the bottom, deluged by the water I was carrying. One day I went for water, and as my feet were dirty, I tho't I would wash them; as the pail was an old one I thought I would wash my feet in it, for I could reach the water only by lying down on my face; so I thought I would dip it up and wash, and then wash the pail. When I got back to the tepee the family were all in great commotion. Chaska brought in an interpreter, who said I had committed a great sin by putting my feet in the pail, for all vessels belonging to a tepee are sacred, and no women are allowed to put their feet in them or step over them. I told him I could scrub the pail, but he said it would not do, for they would never use it again, and they did not. It was turned upside down, and when we removed they left it on the prairie.

Speaking of their superstitions, reminds me of many things that were interesting to me, and I will relate them here. Their war spears and medicine bags are sacred things; a female is never allowed to touch them. By day they are tied to a pole in front of the tepee; at night they are brought in and tied high above the head of the chief man in the tepee. One morning I noticed they were about to fall down and was going towards them to fasten them up, when the old woman said, "Stop, stop, white woman, stop, I will call some man." She appeared much frightened, and run in a great hurry and brought in a boy. When the men go to battle they always take their spears with them, thinking a few painted sticks will assist them in their undertaking.

I offended many an Indian God by stepping over axes, pipes, or persons' feet, or some such silly thing. They never wash their hands in any dish; they fill their mouths and then spit it out on to their hands. I could not do this way, so they begged me a wash dish from some half-breeds.

I don't remember what time in the month we started for Red Iron's village,[28] but I have not forgotten what I suffered that day, for I had to walk all the distance, which was sixteen miles. My mare that Chaska had, was this day, for the first time, hitched to the poles, Indian fashion. Poor animal, I felt bad for her, as she had been made a great pet of by myself and husband. When the poles were first fastened on and she took a few steps, she began prancing, which threw everything in all directions. As soon as she got quiet they put James on her back, and I with Nellie on mine, the old woman leading the horse, we commenced our march towards Lac Que Parle; we walked without resting even for a drink of water, for sixteen miles. They seemed to feel very bad because they could not give me a ride, but it was no use to mourn; every one had a load without taking me, and so I plodded on. Sometimes as Nellie would fall asleep the old woman would tie her on to the bundle which was fastened to the poles, and she would ride until a sudden jolt would awaken her, then I would have to quiet her and would be forced to walk as fast as the horse to keep her quiet. The sun is very powerful on these prairies, and the dust was stifling, and the perspiration and dust did not add to my looks. I would hear the Indians say, "White woman got a dirty face," but had no idea how I looked until I went to the river (my looking glass) to arrange my dress. The last few miles we traveled that day I experienced more pain than I ever did in my life before. I might have been tracked by the blood that ran from my feet and legs, cut by the tall, dry grass; We could not go in the road, but right on the prairie, the carriages filling the road. Glad was I when we made a stop, and I told Chaska that I would certainly die if I had to walk any further. He said he was sorry, but he wanted me to stay at Bit-Nose's so I could ride, but I would not, and all he could do he had done, and he said I had better go back now, but I preferred to remain with his family to going back and being killed by Little Crow.

We remained at Red Iron's village some little time. While there letters were carried to Fort Ridgely, from Little Crow to H. H. Sibley.[29] One morning Tom Robertson and another man, a half-breed, went with letters; soon after the Indian soldiers left, crossed the river, and all in our neighborhood believed they had gone to intercept and murder them. There was great alarm, for the Indians said if they killed them they would return and kill all the rest of the half-breeds and prisoners. When I heard this I dropped as one struck with apoplexy; I could not speak for awhile, my teeth chattered and I shivered with fear. I then thought of what Chaska had many times told me, that if I was in danger, to tell the Indians I was his wife, and I would be saved. So I said to an Indian, "I am Chaska's wife, will they kill me." He said, "No," but he believed I was telling an untruth. I went back to the old woman's and told Chaska. He said I done very wrong in saying so, for there was no truth in the story. But I did not consider how it would sound. I would have called myself the evil spirit's wife if I thought by so doing I could save my life. I suppose many Indians really thought I was his wife, for there was such an excitement all the time I forgot all about contradicting it. One day before this a half-breed woman came in and Mrs. Decamp with her. They said Little Crow was going to destroy all the whites, but would spare all who had Indian blood in them. I made up this story, which I will relate here. I said I was safe, as I was part Indian. I knew the lady had known me in Shakopee many years, and she did not believe me. I said I was about an eighth-breed; that my grandfather married a squaw many years ago in the west, and took her east, and I was one of her descendants; that I had some pride about acknowledging it, but now perhaps it would save my life. I then asked her if she did remember how very dark my mother was, when she became convinced. I was sure this half-breed woman would tell it all around, and I would be spared. I know it was wrong to tell such falsehoods, but I felt as if my God knew my thoughts and he would pardon me for doing as I did. Now to this day that woman believes me part Indian, because I never had an opportunity to contradict it.

While we were camped at Ma a ha's, or Red Iron's, the camp was quiet; soldiers would go off in scouting parties, but the majority of the Indians were around playing cards, shooting at ducks, &c. The old women were busy drying corn and potatoes, cutting and drying beef, laying in a stock for winter. I assisted at all these operations willingly, for I thought I might save my childred from starvation on those plains, where we were bound, for I had given up all hopes of being rescued by Sibley.

I had not many idle moments. I made short gowns for squaws, made bread, fried meat and potatoes, brought water, and went to the river three or four times a day to wash my baby's clothing, for her diarrhœa was growing worse daily.

It was quite amusing to see us white women at the river washing. The banks for several miles usually were lined with Indians with their horses and cattle, boys and squaws swimming, causing it to be very muddy, so we would go out up to our waists to get a clear drink or a place to wash. When we finished we would come out and shake ourselves like dogs and go back to our tepee with our wet bundles on our backs, I have slept many a night in my wet clothes, and never took cold while I was there.

The Indians were all very kind to me; they brought me books and papers to read, and I would make them shirts, so as to return their favors. Many times when I have been coming up the steep bank of the river, all out of breath, bringing water, some Indian would take my pails out of my hands and carry them for me. Now this for a white man would not be considered much, but for an Indian it is a great thing, for they never bring wood or water. Every little act like that I remember, and let who blame me that may, I shall say there are many, very many good, kind hearted Indians. One day I was down by the river waiting to get a chance to fill my pails, when I saw an Indian approaching. I was standing near a tree resting my head against it. He came very near and spoke to me in English, "Mrs. Wakefield, this makes me feel very bad." I then recognized him: it was a Christian Indian called "Cosonka," who had been at my house. His wife worked for me all one winter and he knew I was suffering very much carrying water. He got off his horse, shook hands, and burst forth crying. I sat down on the ground and cried for near an hour, while this man, Indian as he was, gave me such advice as would have astonished persons. He said I must put my trust in God; never forget that he had power to save, and feel as if his eye was upon me, his arms around me, and all would would be well. He said he would do all he could for me, and he had often prayed for me. Now this was an evidence of God's love, for he stood firm in His truth although surrounded by savage and heathen Indians, trying to have him forsake the white man's God and return to the worship of sticks and stones.

In the nights, while at Red Iron's we had a good chance to sleep, for the young men had great dances and councils, so it left the old women and myself time to rest. Before that time hardly a night passed without our cooking all night, as they would have a tepee full of company playing cards and singing. The old women would fill the kettles with beef and potatoes as soon as it was dark, pound their coffee and commence frying their bread. The company would soon assemble; they would generally commence eating as soon as they came in, each one bringing his own dish or "wooden trencher." Then they would smoke, (I must take a whiff with them, or they would be offended) then they would play cards, for they are inveterate gamblers, often losing all they had in the world, taking off shirt, blanket and mocasins, and going home entirely naked except their "breech-clout." After playing many would lie down and commence pounding their breasts as a drum, all the while singing, "Hi! Hi!" with some thing about the "Isau Tonkas," or white men, (meaning Big Knives, as they called the whites from their wearing swords when they first came among them.) They would sing, shout and pound their breasts, when up would jump one, then another, and then the "Wacipa," or dance, would commence; keeping constantly on the move, one foot shuffling before the other, until they were completely exhausted, when, one by one, they would fall back and go to sleep, after which it would be quiet. Soon, however, one would awaken and then another; the kettles would be re-filled and the programme would be repeated, and this would be kept up until day began to dawn.

After leaving Red Iron village there was no rest, either night or day, for they knew when the soldiers left the Fort, and they expected they would come right on. Many a time I have run for the woods with the squaws, thinking the soldiers were very near, and they said Sibley was going to shell the camp.

Every night now, the old women kept watch, keeping the door open so as to watch their horses, for we were drawing near the Sisseton country, and Standing Buffalo[30] had threatened to take all their horses and cattle, if they came up where he was.

I should have suffered with the cold at this time if Chaska and his mother had not been so kind as to lend me their blankets to cover me, and they would draw around the fire to keep warm. Where could you find white people that would do like that? Go without to cover others. Was this kindness or not, let me ask you?

The Indians made much sport of the slow movements of Sibley; said the white people did not care much about their wives and children or they would have hurried on faster.

Many nights the old crier would go around, saying the soldiers are coming, make ready for battle. Sometimes he would say the white women are to be killed in the morning; and our feelings were dreadful living in that way. Then when morning came they would tell a different story. Little Crow had a plan like this: when the soldiers came he was going to send us out in our squaw dresses, thereby causing the white men to kill those they came to rescue. I had no fears of anything of this kind. When Standing Buffalo came, Chaska was very nervous. The lower Indians are very much afraid of the Sissetons, and they thought he would kill the white women, but he came and shook hands with some of us, and said that, if the Indians brought us up into his country, he would take us and bring us back to our friends.

When the news came that Sibley was near Yellow Medicine, and that the Indians were going down to fight him, I felt very uneasy, for Chaska said he and his cousins were going, and I would be left without any protection. He and many others went, and I passed a wretched day. We heard all kinds of reports about the friendly Indian camp, that Little Crow had threatened before leaving.—About nine o'clock in the evening, Chaska returned, saying that Little Crow was a bad man, and he would not go again unless he was forced to. He remained at home two days, when it seemed as if the squaws were crazy; they would move their tepees every few hours, sometimes on the prairie, then into the timber.

One morning a messenger came, saying that every man that could carry a gun should come down immediately, or he would shoot all that refused. I tried to urge Chaska not to go, but he said Little Crow would say I had prevented him, and that he would destroy us both. The morning he left he seemed very anxious to impress upon my mind the necessity of remaining with his mother. Several times he came in and said, "You stay where you are; don't go up to the friendly camp; don't you talk to any half-breed or white women, if you do you will be killed." I knew these friendly Indians were trying to get the prisoners, now they knew Sibley was coming, and I thought he was fearful I would go off, as some had done. After he had been gone sometime, his cousin, a half-breed, told me that Little Crow intended to destroy the friendly camp as soon as he returned; therefore Chaska's anxiety to have me stay where I was.

I stayed with his mother as I promised, although all left but two other Americans besides myself. If Little Crow had been victorious, all would have been killed; but God ordered otherwise, and they were all saved.

Chaska was gone two days and one night. When he returned, I inquired how the battle had gone; he said they had killed one hundred and fifty white men, and only lost two Indians. I felt as if all hope was now gone, and could not help saying that I believed the Lord was on their side. But night told different stories, and I should have known it from the mourning and crying from the many tepees, if they had not told me. Any one that has heard one squaw lament can judge of the noise of four or five hundred all crying at once. As soon as it was dark Chaska advised me to lie down so my shadow would not show on the tepee cloth, as he was afraid they would shoot through and kill me, they were so excited. They held a council that night, and decided to give us up, and I was told that a letter would be sent to Sibley the next morning, requesting him to come for us in the morning. They had many plans. They did not get breakfast—only roasted potatoes in the ashes, and commenced packing up preparing for a start. I asked if they were not going to give us up; they said five half-breeds would take us down to Sibley's camp. I then said I would not go, for I knew we would all be killed by Little Crow's soldiers. I told them I had rather remain with them and wait until Sibley came. Soon the camp began to break up, and the old woman gave me some potatoes, saying that I must eat them, as upon the plains where we were going, we could get no more. I threw myself down, crying, on the ground. Chaska said, "What are you crying about?" I said, "I do not want to go away with the Indians." He said, "You did not wish to go with the half-breeds; what will you do? The Indians are all going very soon." I told him I thought the Indians were going to wait for Sibley, and try to make peace. He said they were afraid to stay for fear they would all be killed, and were going on, leaving us with the half-breeds. Soon after this conversation, two chiefs came in, saying that Joe Campbell was going for Other Day, the Indian who rescued the people from death at Yellow Medicine. In the meantime they wished me to write an account of my treatment by Chaska, and the other Indians I had been acquainted with. I told them it was very foolish for me to write, for I could tell the people just as well as to write, and I began to be suspicious of some evil. I was afraid they would murder us and hide our bodies, and carry our notes to the Fort. I wrote the note, however, but was determined I would not go without more protection than five men over that prairie.

Soon after writing the note, I was told to hurry and change my dress for one of my own, as the soldiers were coming, and it would be wrong for them to see me in a squaw dress. I dressed in a great hurry. I could not tell what was to be done, there were so many stories. At last we were ready, and we left our tepee and my Indian friends, who had given me a home and protected me for six weeks. The old woman shook hands and kissed me, and said, "You are going back where you will have good, warm houses and plenty to eat, and we will starve on the plains this winter. O, that 'bad man,' who has caused so much trouble," meaning Little Crow. They cried over James, and begged me to leave him with them. He was a great favorite with the Indians all the time I was with them. Chaska led Mr. Gleason's dog. Dowanca carried James, and I with Nellie, we started for the Indian soldiers' camp. A large American flag was flying, and we sat ourselves down on the grass beneath its folds, awaiting the decision of our captors relative to our going or staying. All seemed anxious to have us go, still none wished to go below, but a few half-breeds. At last they said they would carry us down; then I began to act like one crazy. I declared I would not go; whereupon Mr. Campbell said I could go and stay with his wife, who was a white woman, until his return, as the friendly Indians were going to stay where they were. We stayed on this hill until Little Crow's camp had gone, then we went over to the friendly camp, Chaska and his mother bidding me good-bye, and leaving.

I went to Mrs. Renville's tepee. Her husband is a half-breed. She was like a wild woman. She was afraid to speak, fearing she might be heard by Indian spies. There were about sixty tepees left in the morning after the others had gone. Instead of taking us below, the Indians left us and went on horseback carrying letters to Sibley, hurrying him on—telling him how we were situated—that we were liable to be attacked at any moment by Little Crow's soldiers. I had not been in Mrs. Renville's tepee more than an hour, when her husband came in saying many Indians were returning and were anxious to camp with us. Among them was Chaska and all his family. Soon Eagle Head appeared, and said I had better come back to Chaska's tepee; that they had decided to remain, and would feel more safe if I was with them when Sibley came. He also said if Little Crow returned, as they expected he would at night, I would be more safe with them than with the half-breeds; so I decided to go, as his tepee was not more than three rods[31] from Mrs. Renville's. She was quite angry because I left, and said I must be crazy for he would kill me. I told her they had protected me for six weeks, and I was not afraid of their injuring me now. But I knew her object in having me stay, for she said that Mazcoota-Meni had no prisoner to give up to Sibley, and she wished me to go to his tepee, so he could have the credit of releasing me. I felt if I could be of service to any one, I would rather benefit those who had taken care of me when I was in danger, than to favor strange Indians. I many times sent for this lady, when I was a prisoner, but she dared not come, so she knew not of their kindness to me.

Among those that decided to remain were Wabasha, Wacota, and parts of several bands.

The half-breeds returned from Sibley's camp early in the afternoon. We looked for the soldiers all night, but they came not. There was no sleep. Every man was on guard. Intrenchments were dug around our tepees, and pits within, for we expected we would be attacked before morning, as Little Crow's brother had remained around as a spy, and surely would notify Little Crow of the non-appearance of our soldiers.

We passed a very anxious night. Morning came, but no soldiers were visible. "What can be the matter?" was the cry. Some Indians came in, saying they had returned because their force was not large enough. Chaska became frightened, and said he thought I had better go to some half-breeds, and take his mother with me, and he would go off. Miss E. B—— and I persuaded him to remain, promising him our protection. He said he felt as if they would kill all the Indians; but we told him if Sibley had promised to shake hands with all that remained and gave up their prisoners, he would do as he said. At last he decided to stay, saying, "If I am killed, I will blame you for it." Now I will always feel that I am responsible for that man's murder, and will reproach myself for urging him to remain.

How we looked for Sibley all the next day, but he did not come; all that night we watched also, but no signs of him yet. Where can he be? he was only twenty-five miles away. We at last concluded he was afraid. The Indians began to get uneasy, and said, "Little Crow will be back and kill us, if Sibley does not soon come." How we blamed him for making us suffer as we did, for we expected death every instant. The second night we waited for him, an Indian came in saying they had only traveled eight miles, and it was now thirty-six hours since he got our message, and they had camped for the night, spending hours to intrench themselves. An army of over two thousand leaving us, a little handful of persons, with only about one hundred men to protect us! The time taken to intrench themselves, passed in marching, would have brought them to our relief; but God watched over us, and kept those savages back. To him I give all the honor and glory; Sibley I do not even thank, for he deserved it not.

The second night of our stay, Dowonca had a religious performance in our tepee. The females were excluded. They were trying to ascertain by their conjuring if the soldiers would hurt them.

That night every Indian was on guard, the report reaching us that Little Crow was advancing towards us for battle. There were no more midnight councils and dances; all was still and quiet except the medicine men at their performances over the sick. The Indians believe when a person is sick they are possessed with evil spirits, and these conjurers stand over them and rattle gourds, thinking by so doing they will drive out the evil spirits; and when some are about leaving, the squaws rush at the imaginary beings and pretend to shoot them, or stab them with their knives, all the time singing, talking, imploring their gods to help them. It is enough to make a well person sick. I was one day in a tepee where an Indian woman was in labour; she had been suffering many hours, and these conjurers were at work rattling and singing. Her husband soon came in, and began cutting out little images of stained hide. I was told that he would stand at the door of the tepee, and, as occasion required, throw one at her, expecting this would assist nature in bringing forth the child.

Poor superstitious beings, how much they are to be pitied! Very few of them believe in any God besides a painted stone or stick; ought we to expect these creatures to act with reason and judgment like ourselves?

Just for one moment, think of all they have borne for years, and you will wonder, as I do, that they saved as many lives as they did, for their religion teaches them that evil for evil, good for good, is right. Many ask me why they killed so many that had befriended them. I myself asked that question many times while I was with them, and I will give one answer that was given me.

An Indian, having plenty of ducks, went one day to Beaver Creek and wished to exchange them for potatoes. He said, when telling me of it, that his ducks were fresh and good; that they took them and gave him potatoes that a hog could not eat, they were so soft. Now, this is the way many befriended the Indians; gave them what they could not eat themselves. This is the way the Indians have been treated for years. I know the Indians have butchered the whites, and I wish every guilty one punished: but I cannot blame them as many do, for I am sure they had cause, and very strong reasons for being revenged on some persons who have been living off their lands and money, while they were starving. If these Indians had commenced this outbreak out of pure wickedness, I would feel as many do—that they ought to be exterminated; but it is not so; they took the only way they knew of getting restitution and we all want that when we are wronged.

I have many very firm friends in the Indian camp, and I feel for them as much pity and sorrow as if they were white; for I have sat and listened to their tales of suffering and distress until my heart bled for them. I pray God they may for the future be more mercifully dealt with by those that are in authority over them.

To return to my narrative: the night passed without an attack, as anticipated; but we could hear no tidings of the soldiers, and we really thought they had returned. Sibley had requested us to remain where we were, or we should have gone down. That was the message brought back by the half-breeds. Now it was the third day, and we were getting very impatient, but not as much so as our Indian friends, who often said, "We will go on; there is no use waiting longer." About noon of the third day we saw them coming, and then, instead of joy, I felt feelings of anger enter my breast, as I saw such an army, for I felt that part at least might have come to our rescue before that late hour. While they were coming up we saw a party of Indians near us, and several half-breeds and Indians started for them, and found them to be a party of Sissetons who had come up just in advance of the soldiers, bringing with them three prisoners—one girl and two boys. Joe Campbell demanded the children, but they refused to give them up, and said they were going to kill them; but Joe made a sudden spring and secured the girl, while the Indians saved the boys, when the Sissetons fled. I conversed with the girl; she said they were near the soldiers for a long time, so she could hear their voices; that they crawled on their knees much of the time, to avoid being seen. Her feet were all blisters, but the boys the Indians carried part of the way. It seems very strange they should spare so many helpless children and murdur their parents, when they are such a trouble to them. I have seen squaws carry white children nine and ten years old on their backs, and let their own walk. Now this was out of real good feeling, for they certainly had no selfish motives in so doing, and the world does the Indian great injustice when they say they saved *persons only for selfish purposes.*

As Sibley's forces drew near, the Indians became much alarmed, and drew within their tepees. We were all eager to get to them immediately, but we were told we should remain where we were until Sibley came over. The soldiers encamped about a quarter of a mile from our camp. Sibley sent a messenger, saying he would come over after dinner and talk with the Indians.

About this time some squaws brought me a dress belonging to Mrs. Dr. Humphrey.[32] How strange are God's ways! How little did I think, when I assisted her in making this dress, of my ever wearing it, and at such a place and under such circumstances. Now she was dead, and I, where was I? In a camp of Indians, not knowing but I should be, at last, murdered by them, for I had many miles to travel before reaching civilization.

It may be well to speak of this family here. It was with them, you will remember, that I passed one week previous to my captivity. On the first day of the outbreak, Dr. Humphrey and wife, with three children, fled, crossed the Minnesota River, ascended the high hills and entered a house for a drink of water. The family had all left. Johnny, aged twelve went to the spring for water, and on returning, heard a shot and saw his father fall dead before the door. He said his mother closed the door and fastened it. The Indians tried to get in, but finding it secured, fired the building, and she and her two beautiful children perished in the flames. The boy secreted himself and made his escape. When near Fort Ridgely he met the soldiers, returned with them, and was in that fatal fight at the Ferry. Still he was unhurt, and with the remnant of that brave band reached Fort Ridgely an orphan, homeless, but not friendless, for God was with him and raised up kind friends for him.

My dinner was eaten for the last time with my Indian friends; they were very sad; seeming to be dreading some evil. About three o'clock Sibley and staff arrived, and after conversing a few minutes with the Indians, ordered those having prisoners to bring them forward and give them up. Old Eagle Head and Chaska came for me: before leaving the old woman tore her shawl and gave me half, as I had none.

Chaska trembled with fear. He said, "You are a good woman, you must talk good to your white people, or they will kill me; you know I am a good man, and did not shoot Mr. Gleason, and I saved your life. If I had been a bad man I would have gone with those bad chiefs." I assured him he need not fear, they would not injure him; but how vain were all my promises; poor man, he found the whites deceitful, even unto his death.

After I was introduced to Sibley, Mr. Riggs, and others, they requested me to point out the Indian who had saved me. He came forward as I called his name; and when I told them how kind he had been they shook hands with him, and made quite a hero of him for a short time. I was compelled to leave the circle about this time, on account of my baby, and went to a tepee near, and while there the company broke up, taking the white women with them; two or three officers remained to escort me over. When I got to the camp I found the soldiers in a state of great excitement, and all were eager to catch a glimpse of us. I was conducted to a large tent and soon it was surrounded with soldiers. We nearly suffocated for want of air. The tent I was in contained twenty-four persons. We suffered much for want of bedding, for there was no provision made for us, although they were so many weeks preparing for a start to rescue us. My children took very bad colds, and I wished many times I had a tepee to sleep in. Now I wish to be distinctly understood in this remark: I did not wish myself back in a tepee, I only wanted the comforts of one, for I was a vast deal more comfortable with the Indians in every respect, than I was during my stay in that soldier's camp, and was treated more respectfully by those savages, than I was by those in that camp, when we were given some straw to lie on, and a blanket for each. We had to cook our own food, exposed to the gaze of several hundred ignorant men, that would surround our fires as soon as we commenced cooking, so we could not breathe for want of air. I have many times been forced to go to some officer and request a guard around us, so we could cook without molestation. With the Indians my life was very different; the old squaws doing all the cooking, unless I took a fancy to assist.

The nights had got to be very cold now, and our tent was constructed for a stove, but we had none. Sometimes we would make a fire on the ground, and we would be forced to lie down on our faces, the smoke was so dense.

My clothing consisted of a thin gingham dress, one cotton skirt, no under garments of any kind. I had a pair of moccasins, but no stockings of any kind, and half of a shawl. I am a large woman, and the squaws could not find any that would be large enough. I weighed, three days before the outbreak, two hundred and three pounds. When I got to Shakopee, eight weeks after, I weighed one hundred and sixty-three pounds. My travels and anxiety had worn upon me so much.

The first evening I passed at Camp Release was a very pleasant one. We were serenaded, and all the dainties of the camp were brought to us. I think the soldiers must have thought we had fasted for many weeks, to judge by the quantity brought to us. My children never knew what it was to be hungry in the Indian camp, for food was plenty, and that which was good. Nearly every day some little dainty was brought to "Pajute Wicaste Tawicu"—English doctor's wife. I really thought my children would be made sick by the Indians, for they were continually feeding them.

I will here say, that the family I was with were not the greasy, lousy, filthy Indians, we used to see around begging. There is a great difference in them, and a person visiting the Agencies would have been astonished to see the hard working men and women, but clean and neat as our own farmers. I have employed squaws in my family that were educated by the missionaries, that could read and write in their own language, and could make coats, pants, or shirts, far better than many a white girl of the present generation. Such are some of the good works of the missionaries.

I always had in our tepee, a towel, soap, and wash dish, and I never knew any of the family to neglect washing and combing before eating. I had my own corner of the tepee, and was not allowed to go over to the other part, and they never came near mine.

They are foolishly particular about some things. The fire is in the centre of the tepee, and I never was allowed to pass around the fire. I must go out on my own side, for I would be going into my neighbor's domains, if I went across. I used to get very tired sitting in one place with my baby. My little boy, however, enjoyed his life while there, for I could raise the tepee cloth and watch him; and he would play for hours on the grass, with the Indian boys.

I often asked him if he would not like to see his father, and he would answer, very indifferently, "Yes, but I wish he would come here, I would like to stay if he would."

The morning after my arrival at Camp Release I went over to the Indian's camp for some articles I left, in company with a woman who was taken near Hutchinson. She was taken captive by an Indian who had a wife, and this woman caused great trouble in their tepee. She declared to me she was not his wife, but said she slept on the same pillow and was covered with his blanket. But his wife got very jealous, and one day threw a knife at her husband, inflicting a severe wound. He was very angry, and Mrs. A——s was obliged to go over to the friendly camp for protection.

We attended, while there, a Dakota prayer meeting. Chaska was much frightened. He called me to the door, and said they had arrested two Indians, and if he was arrested he would know I had told falsehoods about him, and then he would lie too.

I told him I had a long conversation with one of the officers, and he said that he should be pardoned on account of his kindness to me and my children. He appeared much pleased, and I went back to Camp Release. In the afternoon they had a sort of court of inquiry, and we were all questioned by Col. Crooks and Marshall, J. V. D. Hurd, S. R. Riggs, and others. I was the first one questioned. I related to them briefly what I have here written, after which, Col. Marshall said, "If you have anything more of a private nature to relate, you can communicate it to Mr. Riggs." I did not understand until he explained himself more fully. I told them it was just as I related, it was all. They thought it very strange I had no complaints to make, but did not appear to believe me. I was then told I might go, and not wishing to walk a quarter of a mile alone, I went to a tepee near by occupied by Miss La Flambois. While there I sent for Chaska. He was looking very pale and frightened. He said the white men were not doing as they promised, and he knew they would kill him. I endeavored to persuade him to leave, promising to take care of his mother. He said, "No; I am not a coward, I am not afraid to die. All I care about is my poor old mother, she will be left alone." He said he was sorry I persuaded him to remain; that his mother was very angry with me for not letting him go. I still held out strong hopes to him, insisting that he should be spared. Soon after I left he was arrested. I was not much concerned at first, for I supposed he would soon be liberated, unless they could find something more against him than I knew of. That evening many of the officers were in, laughing and talking. We were all acting like little children let loose from school, not really sensible of what we were saying, when some one remarked, "We have seven of those Indians fast." When Capt. Grant said, "Yes; we have seven of the black devils, and before to-morrow night they will hang as high as Haman." I asked if they had him who had protected me. He said, "Yes; and he will swing with the rest." Then I made this remark, "Capt. Grant, if you hang that man, I will shoot you, if it is not in twenty years." Then thinking how it sounded, I said, "But you must first teach me to shoot, for I am afraid of a gun, unloaded even." Now this remark has been reported throughout the State. Any one well acquainted with me knows my violent impulsive disposition, and would not heed what I say when I am excited, for I very often say to my children, when I am out of patience, "Do be quiet, or I will whip you to death." Now I never meant to do one any more than I did the other; it is a rude way I have of expressing myself.

The first man tried was the negro, and several days were passed in bringing in testimony, when every one knew he was guilty. But it gave Little Crow a good chance to escape, thereby prolonging this war; for Little Crow was only six miles away when Sibley arrived. Now arises a thought—an inquiry: If Sibley had not found us waiting on that prairie for him, would he have returned or would he have gone farther? If he intended to go farther, why did he stop where he did? for he was sure of the Indians who had been waiting two days and nights for him. Why did he not push on and capture those murderers? Instead of so doing, the whole command stopped, and spent days and weeks trying men who had willingly given themselves up, leaving their chiefs and bands. I, as a woman, know very little about war; but I know Little Crow and his soldiers might have been captured last fall, but now it is very doubtful if he is ever overtaken. But I suppose the troops were fatigued, if they marched all the way from St. Paul as fast as they did from Yellow Medicine—taking over fifty hours to travel twenty-five miles.

I don't wish to censure those that were compelled to do as they were bidden, but their leaders. If those officers had known their wives and daughters were in danger, they would have found ways and means to travel more than five miles a day.

From the way the affair was conducted, I suppose if Sibley had not found us on that prairie, he would have returned, and we would have passed the winter on the plains; for he went no farther, as he said he could not pursue them without cavalry. He did, after a few weeks had passed, send out scouting parties, when he knew the Indians were returning to surrender. But he nor his troops never captured an Indian, (and I don't believe ever will, until there is a change made in our officers,) only those that wished to be taken, they preferring captivity to death by starvation. I never can give Sibley any credit in releasing the prisoners, or capturing Indians, for do you, my readers, consider it a capture when men willingly wait two days and nights for their captors to march twenty-five miles? It was a wonderful affair! Glory, honor, and renown, ought to be written on their brows! God influenced those Indians to remain with us, and to God and the Indians I give my thanks.

After I heard Chaska was in prison, I was unhappy. I felt as if the Indians, as well as myself, had been deceived. All the solemn promises I had made to Chaska were as naught. What would he think of me? I could not eat or sleep, I was so excited about him. I felt as bad as if my brother had been in the same position.

The women knowing I felt sad, tried every way to aggravate me, some saying, "I know he is a murderer. I know he killed my brother, sister, or some other relative." I would reply, "If he has done such things, how could you be so friendly with him?" for these same women would come in and laugh, sing, and play cards with him very often, and Mrs. A——, from the neighborhood of Forest City, used to comb his hair, arrange his neck-tie, and, after he was arrested, abused him shamefully.

When Chaska was to be tried, I was called upon to testify. I told them all I could say would be in his favor. They thought it very strange I could speak in favor of an Indian. I went into court, and was put under oath. Chaska was present, and I shook hands with him. I am particular in relating every interview I had with him, as many false and slanderous stories are in circulation about me.

He was convicted of being an accomplice in the murder of Geo. Gleason, without any evidence against him. I was angry, for it seemed to me as if they considered my testimony of no account; for if they had believed what I said, he would have been acquitted. All the evidence was his own statement, wherein he said that he snapped his gun at Mr. Gleason; but through misrepresentation, it was made to appear as if he intended to try to kill him.

I know he had no more idea of killing the man than I had, or did no more towards it than I did. He was present, so was I; and they might as well hang me as him, for he was as innocent as myself.

After Mr. Gleason was dead, as we rode away from his body, I heard Chaska say to Hapa, "Get out and shoot him again; don't leave him with any life to suffer." Hapa said, "You have not shot to-day; you go with me, and I will go." Then they both got out, giving me the lines to hold, and went to the body, but it was still and motionless. Hapa fired at him; Chaska raised his gun, but it snapped fire. I don't believe his gun was loaded at all. That was what convicted him. Afterwards, in speaking to me of the affair, he said he had done as he would wish any one to do by him. He was afraid there was a little life, and he wished him put out of suffering.

I know that after he was convicted I said many things I need not have said, and would not at ordinary times; but every one ought to know that my mind was in a dreadful state, living as I had for six weeks in continual fear and anxiety, and I was not capable of acting rationally. The Indian who saved George Spencer's life was lauded to the skies, and I could not refrain from saying that I considered my life and that of my two children as valuable as his; but the Indian that saved me must be imprisoned, while that Indian was carried around and shown as a great hero, and at the same time was known to be the murderer of Mr. Divoll, and at the time George Spencer was wounded, was murdering the whites.

But I soon discovered that the Commission was not acting

according to justice, but by favor; and I was terribly enraged against them. The more angry I got, the more I talked, making matters worse for Chaska as well as myself. I can now see wherein I failed to accomplish my object. They soon at the camp began to say that I was in love; that I was his wife; that I preferred living with him to my husband, and all such horrid, abominable reports. I know I am innocent; that I acted from right motives; and sure am I if I am condemned here on earth, God will see me righted—if not here, I hope in Heaven.

I never could love a savage, although I could respect any or all that might befriend me, and I would willingly do everything in my power to benefit those that were so kind to me in my great hour of need. I have strong feelings of gratitude towards many of them. I can not feel as many persons do, for I lost no friends, and I was kindly treated by all but Hapa. I feel very sorry for those that have suffered at their hands in any manner. I do not know of but two females that were abused by the Indians. I often asked the prisoners when we met, for we were hearing all kinds of reports, but they all said they were well treated, that I saw. It is true that there were many persons there that I never saw until I was brought into Sibley's camp, for the Indian camp was so large it was like a city, and a person was in danger of losing themselves unless there was something particular that would indicate the locality of the tepee. Many kept small white flags and such things flying, to notify members of the family where their homes were.

I think it was two days before I left Camp Release that I went to the Indian camp. Miss E. B—— accompanied me. I saw Chaska's mother, and such a cry as burst from her at the sight of me. She put her arms around me, saying, "My boy! my boy! they will kill him! Why don't you save him? He saved your life many times. You have forgotten the Indians now your white friends have come," I was much affected at her reproaches, and I told her I was doing everything I could to save him, but the Indians were lying about him. She told me she had been to carry him some bread, but the soldiers would not let her go in where he was, and she begged me to go and see him. I had not been to see the prisoners until that day, although the women were going several times every day. I had always refused, for I knew it would make me feel sad to see those who had been so kind to me tied together like beasts, and felt that they would reproach me for not trying to assist them, now they were in danger.

This day, when I returned to camp, I went to the prisoners' tent, accompanied by Major Cullen and Miss E. B——. When I entered I went towards Chaska to shake hands, but he refused to take my hand. I inquired what was the cause of his acting so unfriendly. He said I had told falsehoods to the soldiers, or I would not now see him tied hand and foot. He then repeated all he had done for me and my children, and reproached me for so soon forgetting his kindness. It affected me to tears, for he spoke of many things he had done, such as selling his coat for flour, sleeping without his blanket so my children might be warm, &c. I said to him that I had lost all my friends now by trying to save him, and it was very wrong for him to blame me. I am not ashamed to acknowledge that I cried. I am naturally very sensitive, and cannot see tears or hear reproaches without shedding tears.

I at last convinced him that I was not to blame for his imprisonment, and I said I would like to shake hands and bid him goodbye in friendship. He shook hands with me, and that is all that passed between us. I never saw him again, for I left very soon for my home.

There were at that time twenty-one Indians all fastened together by their feet. I did not go any nearer to him than four feet, but there have been outrageous reports put in circulation of that visit I made that poor forsaken creature. Any one doubting my story may inquire of the persons who were with me—not of the soldiers. I was not aware of the excitement that existed throughout the country. I knew there had been awful murders committed, but I knew not the particulars, or how people were enraged against the Indians. I was so happy, and rejoiced so greatly, over my safe deliverance from death and dishonor, through the kindness of the Indians, that I wished to sound their praises far and near.

That night before leaving, I heard from Capt. Grant that Chaska would not be executed, but would be imprisoned for five years. I was very well contented, and troubled myself no farther, for he gave me his word as a gentleman that that was the truth. He cautioned me not to speak of it, as it was a secret. I never told any one until he was dead.

I came from Camp Release with four ladies who had been prisoners. We were sent without any escort over seventy miles, through the scene of those awful murders. The day before we left, Sibley sent down a train of forty wagons, and a number of prisoners, mostly French and Germans, with eighty soldiers as an escort. When we got to Yellow Medicine I found them there, on their way to Wood Lake to camp for the night, and we ladies proposed camping with them, as the man who drove our team said he was going to Redwood to camp, saying there was no danger, for there were no Indians within one hundred miles of us, except those at Camp Release. I got frightened, as usual, and said I was afraid to go on to Redwood to camp; for I had suffered so much in that neighborhood I cared not to stay there over night; so I concluded to leave the horse team, and stay with the ox train, as I saw a lady in the train that I knew very well. Mrs. H—— and I remained at the soldiers' camp until after supper, when we proposed to go back to Yellow Medicine—three miles distant—and stay in the tepees, for my baby was very low, and I did not dare to stay out all night without some covering, for our blankets we had left at Camp Release, as they were borrowed from the soldiers, and the tents the soldiers had up were just large enough for four persons sitting, no fire in them, and the wind was blowing a hurricane, for it was now October. My children were both without shirts, Nellie had a dress, no shoes or stockings, nor anything else. My boy had an Indian jacket and leggings. I knew we would be comfortable at the tepees, and there were several half-breeds there who could speak English as well as myself.

The farmer Indians were at Yellow Medicine under Major Galbraith's directions, digging potatoes. We went to John Moore's tepee, and stayed with his family all night. Capt. McClarthy promised to wait for us; but when we arrived at the camp they had all gone. Not a vestige of the camp was discernible.

I afterwards learned that the wagon master, hearing of our going to the tepees, said he would hurry on; and if we liked the tepees so well, we might stay there, for he was going to hurry off.

Capt. Kennedy[33] and one of his soldiers were detailed to come for us in the morning from the camp of soldiers that were guarding the Indians, and they were only ordered to take us to Wood Lake. Now we were in great trouble; they dared not go any farther without orders, and we did not wish to stay at the tepees. The soldiers at length decided to go on with us to Fort Ridgely without orders, thinking we could overtake the other teams when they stopped for dinner at Redwood. Mrs H—— and myself traveled in great fear all day. I was now going toward the spot where poor Gleason was killed, and she where her husband laid, still unburied. We imagined Indians in every bush. We had but one gun, and now I think how reckless we were to start on such a journey in such an unprotected way.

The men laughed at our fears, but I told them Mr. Gleason also laughed, going over the same road; and I felt sure there were Indians now near us, for Little Crow sent out one hundred men the night before the battle of Wood Lake, and they had never returned to camp. No one can imagine my feelings as I passed poor Gleason's grave, for he was now covered from sight; the whole scene was again before my eyes. I got so nervous that my teeth chattered, and I shook like one with the palsy. As we got to the river, my fears increased, for it was a dreary place. Now we had to go down through the woods for some ways, and we all expected to be fired upon by Indians hiding in the bushes; but God in his mercy delivered us from death by them, for it afterwards proved that Indians were secreted in those woods. We at last arrived at Little Crow's village; the buildings were all standing, and everything was looking well, only so desolate; not a sound to break the stillness, not a living thing visible. The soldiers proposed leaving the road and going to a farm house to get some corn for their horses, for we had all come without breakfast. We sat in the wagon, Mrs. H., myself and children, while they gave their horses feed; and while they were eating, the men roamed through the gardens, gathering tomatoes, &c. In a few minutes after they left we heard a dog bark, and I told Mrs. H. there were Indians in the neighborhood. In a moment we heard a gun, and then another; Mrs H—— being much alarmed, jumped and ran into a corn field. As she did so I saw two Indians just going down into the woods not ten rods from where we sat, I beckoned to the men, and they very hurriedly hitched up the horses, and they drove them on a run for the other teams which we had seen some three miles beyond us, on a hill. The soldiers' object in going that way was to save five miles, but we came near losing our lives by so doing. As we drove over the prairie, regardless of road or track, we turned, and five Indians were coming toward us on foot running very fast. About that time, the teams on the hill seeing us, and thinking we were Indians, started some men to capture us. The Indians, seeing the horsemen, turned around and made for the woods, where we could see their tepees. We were very glad to meet with the train, and we arrived at the Fort at 5 o'clock that evening, very tired, but O, how happy to be within its walls, How refreshing that bath, and the clean clothes, given us by the kind lady of the Surgeon, and with what feelings of joy I laid myself and little ones down to rest, undressed—it being the first time I had taken my clothes off to sleep, in nearly eight weeks.

The next morning, as Mrs. H—— and I were preparing for break-fast, my little boy exclaimed, "There is my father!"—and so it was.

There was my husband I had mourned as dead, now living—coming toward me. I was happy then, and felt that I would have died then willingly, and said, "Thy will not mine be done," for I knew my children had a protector now.

I left the Fort about noon that day, and arrived at Shakopee in a few days. I did not hear any more respecting Chaska, but felt it was all right with him. I was in Red Wing when the President sent on the list of those who were to be executed. I noticed the name of Chaskadon, but knew it was not Chaska's number, and that he was not guilty of the crime that Chaskadon was to be punished for.

Sunday after the execution, when the papers were brought in, I noticed my name immediately, and I then saw that a mistake had been made. The Indian named Chaskadon, that the President ordered to be hanged, killed a pregnant woman and cut out her child, and they hung Chaska who was only convicted of being present when Mr. Gleason was killed.

After passing eight weeks in Red Wing, I returned to St. Paul. I then saw Rev. S. R. Riggs, formerly missionary among the Sioux, and who was present at the time Chaska was hung, and he said he was really hanged by mistake, as his name was on the list that were recommended to mercy. In a letter I received from him, he explained the matter in this way:

"MRS. WAKEFIELD—*Dear Madam:*—In regard to the mistake by which Chaska was hung instead of another, I doubt whether I can satisfactorily explain it. We all felt a solemn responsibility, and a fear that some mistake should occur. We had forgotten that he was condemned under the name of We-chan-hpe-wash-tay-do-pe. We knew he was called Chaska in the prison, and had forgotten that any other except Robert Hopkins, who lived by Dr. Williamson, was so called. We never thought of the third one; so when the name Chaska was called in the prison on that fatal morning, your protector answered to it and walked out. I do not think any one was really to blame. We all regretted the mistake very much, &c.

"With kind respects, yours truly,
"S. R. RIGGS."

Now I will never believe that all in authority at Mankato had forgotten what Chaska was condemned for, and I am sure, in my own mind, it was done intentionally. I dare not say by whom, but there is One who knoweth every secret, either good or bad, and the time will come when he will meet that murdered man, and then he will find the poor Indian's place is far better than his own.

If the President had not plainly stated what the man was convicted for, then, probably, there might have been a mistake made, but as it was, it was either carelessness, or, as I said before, intentional; for every man was numbered as he was arrested, and the President sent the number, as well as the cause of his punishment. It has caused me to feel very unkindly towards my own people, particularly those in command at Mankato. There have been all kinds of reports in circulation respecting Chaska and myself, but I care not for them. I know that I did what was right, that my feelings were only those of gratitude toward my preserver. I should have done the same for the blackest negro that Africa ever produced; I loved not the man, but his kindly acts.

I *know* that many Indians now paid by Government are murderers, but being connected with the officers by blood are saved, while the true-hearted full blood savage has been hung for these men's crimes. I know of one who came into a tepee one night. He had not seen me in a squaw dress, and did not know but what I was a squaw. He then and there related scenes that made my very blood curdle in my veins. He told of meeting a mother and three children, and after violating the oldest daughter, who was about fourteen years old, he beat them all to death with a club. When the Indians asked why he did it, he said they were only Dutch, and it was just like killing hogs. He now calls himself a friendly Indian, or a white man, as he is three-fourths white. Most of the half-breeds are treacherous like him. I would sooner trust a full blood than any of them. When they heard that Sibley's forces were coming, they began to show great feeling for the *poor captives*. Previous to that if a prisoner went to them for protection they were driven away, fearing they might be blamed by the Indians. A Mrs. Earle,[34] who lived near Beaver Creek, with a little girl nine years of age, was held by Little Crow himself. She always stayed in his tepee with his wives. At the time of the battle of Wood Lake, he turned them away, telling them they might find friends elsewhere. They went to John Renville's a half-breed, of whom I have spoken in this work. He said he could not protect them; that they must leave immediately. Mrs. Earle was in great fear. She told them she would not eat much. He said, "No matter! go somewheres! go hide yourself on the prairie!" She started to go, she knew not whither, when she met an Indian who told her to come with him. He took her in, gave her food, and cared for her like a brother, when this part-white man would not do anything for her. Such is the way with the part breeds, or many of them. I would not trust myself with

one of them. There is too much art and duplicity in them. All of
them helped rob the whites. Now at this time they are bringing large
bills against Government for what they have lost, when they have at
the same time hundreds of dollars worth of goods stolen from the
whites.

There are many things I would like to speak about in this narrative, but I would be obliged to mention particular names, and I will
forbear; but I will say this, that many persons told entirely different
stories respecting their treatment, after Sibley came, than they did
before. One lady very often visited me, and she often complained of
being uncomfortable from eating so heartily, but said the squaws
forced her to eat, as that is their way of showing their kindness towards a person. Now many times I have listened to her telling the
soldiers that she was nearly starved by the squaws, going days without food of any kind. It shocked me, and I reprimanded her severely
for telling such untruths; but she was only one of a class of females
that were endeavoring to excite the sympathies of the soldiers. My
object was to excite sympathy for the Indians and in so doing, the
soldiers lost all respect for me, and abused me shamefully; but I had
rather have my own conscience than that of those persons who
turned against their protectors, those that were so kind to them in
that great time of peril.

All the time I was with the Indians the women seemed to be en-
vious of me, saying that the Indians thought more of me than any
other female. They did of course think more of me than they did of
strangers, for they had known me many years. I could talk with them
of things that had transpired in Shakopee that they knew about, and
they considered me an old friend. No Indian ever came to my house
hungry without being fed, or if in need of clothes, I gave if I possibly
could do so. They all came to me for medicine as much as they did
to my husband, both in Shakopee and Yellow Medicine, and their
actions have proved the bible true to me, for it says. "Cast your bread
upon the waters, and after many days it shall return to you."

I will draw my work to conclusion by giving an account of my
husband's escape from Yellow Medicine on Tuesday, August 19th,
He says that soon after I left, Mr. Garvie came to the Agency, informing them that the Indians were returning from above, and he
was afraid they intended mischief. Soon after he left, Akepa and
Other Day came in, and said the Indians were going to make an
attack that night. The inhabitants were all soon assembled together
in the ware house, every one ready to protect him or herself, the

friendly Indians remaining with them. Soon after dark they heard reports of guns, and they knew they had attacked the trading post, under the hill. One by one the friendly Indians left, except Other Day. Having a white wife, I presume, kept him from going. They were in great fear, expecting every moment to be attacked. Very often during the night some three or four Indians would ascend the hill, look towards the buildings, then retire, seeming to be keeping an eye on them. What must those poor creatures have suffered during that long night! Soon they heard some one at the door, and poor Garvie, wounded and covered with dirt, was found and taken in. He was attended to as well as could be under the circumstances. About daylight some one of the party proposed trying to escape. Other Day was very anxious, and said he could get them across the Minnesota river at an old Indian crossing, but to get there they must ascend a high hill, showing themselves to the Indians in the valley of the Yellow Medicine. But they knew it was death to remain, and they had little, if any, hopes of getting away. The hope was so faint that they did not even take their watches or papers with them. They only had seven vehicles, some only large enough to hold two persons, but they started. The Indians were so busy plundering the stores that they did not notice them. They crossed the river,—sixty-one persons, piloted by Other Day,—and when across they were obliged to stop and cut their road through the thick woods that skirts the north bank of that river. Every stroke of the ax, they thought, would lead to their discovery; but no! They went on; on, on in a very slow way, as they had no roads, as I said before. They did not stop until near midnight, when they camped at a deserted house. The women made a few biscuits out of flour and water, but they did not want much, for a person has no appetite when they are fleeing for their lives. They remained there the remainder of the night, and in the morning they again started, not having seen or heard any Indians, Other Day going two or three miles in advance of the train, trying to beat up the enemy if any were hidden. They rode all day in great excitement, and at night arrived at a place called Cedar City. Here they found quite a party of settlers trying to fortify the place. They remained together all night. In the morning when they were about to leave, Mr. Garvie requested to be left, saying he would die if he rode farther, jolting over the rough roads. Bidding him be careful, they again started, going right through the Big Woods, past the scene of many murders; but still an All-wise Providence kept them from all harm. They arrived at Chaska on Saturday morning, after travelling four days and nights, expecting every moment to be struck down by some foe. My husband came into Shakopee, holding in his hands an account of his own death, as it was reported they were all killed. He had on at the time of the outbreak, a thin suit of clothes and a pair of slippers, as the day had been extremely warm, and when he got down to Shakopee he was barefoot; everything gone: wife, children, home, property,—all he then thought destroyed by the Indians. But through God's mercy we were all saved, and are now re-united.

In conclusion, I will say that the Indian Expedition of this year[35] has not accomplished any thing of importance. They met the Indians, had a few skirmishes, driving them across the Missouri river. Dr. Weiser, of Shakopee, was killed, being shot down by some Indians with whom he was conversing in a friendly manner. This brought on a fight. If this *had not occurred* there would not have been any fight; for Sibley would have had a parley and the Indians would have been brought down and been fed and *petted* as those were last winter. They did take Little Crow's son, who from starvation and fatigue had secreted himself in the grass. This is all that has been done by this large force. Another year the scenes of the two last years will be repeated, and this war will be prolonged for many, many years, unless we have a change of officers. The army on the Missouri, under Gen. Sully, has done a good work, killing many Indians and destroying their property, while our army has been only enriching the officers, and shielding murderers from justice. An account I have received from the new agency is not very good. The land is very poor. The Indians cannot raise any thing only on the bottom lands. The water is all alkali, causing the deaths of many after they reached there. The Indians are all dissatisfied, and the Winnebagoes are building canoes and threaten to leave very soon. They have no good hunting grounds unless they cross the Missouri river, and there they are in danger of being killed by the Brules and Tetons, who are at war with them. So this poor down-trodden race is in a dreadful condition. They must starve unless food is sent them by Government. There is at the Agency 3,600 Indians. Three missionaries are with them, and more are still going. But what a place for white people where nothing can be raised! I think they have begun to realize some of the sufferings I often tried to paint out to them during my stay with them.

Their reservation in this State was a portion of the most beautiful country that was ever known, and they had everything they wished to make them comfortable if they could have only stayed there; but a few evil men commenced their murderous work, and all has gone to ruin. I feel very sorry for many of my neighbors who for years have lived like the white man; now they are wanderers, without home, or even a resting place. A few days since a number of families passed through here, and as I saw them I ran with eagerness to see those old faces who were so kind to me while I was in captivity. I went down to the camp (for they stayed all night in Shakopee), and was rejoiced to be able to take them some food, and other little things which I knew would please them, and for this I have been blamed; but I could not help it. They were kind to me, and I will try and repay them, trusting that in God's own time I will be righted and my conduct understood, for with Him all things are plain. And now I will bid this subject farewell forever.

# EMELINE L.
# FULLER

As with so many of the narratives in this collection, the main character and purported author of *Left by the Indians*, Emeline Fuller (1847–?1923/24), did not write her own story. The Methodist minister James Hughes, though deliberately vague about authorship in his introduction, implied that the first-person narrative in the story proper belonged to Fuller. An outside source clarifies the issue. A letter written by Geraldine Hughes, the minister's daughter, states categorically that her father wrote the book. She continues to say that Fuller had attended Rev. Hughes's evangelical meetings and that he had heard her story from others: "My father met her, urged her to let him write an account of her story. She was a frail, sad, timid little woman and consented reluctantly. My father thought perhaps the booklets could be sold to people in his meetings in the various towns and she could be helped financially." Geraldine Hughes mentions that there were many leftover copies of the book in her father's house, so either it did not sell well or it was overprinted.

The woman whom James Hughes met in 1891 was Emeline Fuller, a survivor of the Utter-Myers disaster on the Oregon Trail in which two-thirds of the party died. Denied adequate protection by the army, the wagon train of forty-five people was vulnerable to a series of Indian raids between September 7 and October 18, 1860, in the Snake River country of Idaho and Oregon. Those who were not killed in the initial Shoshone/Snake Indian onslaught died in later attacks, were captured, or starved to death as they roamed around scavenging off the land and waiting for rescue. Contemporary news reports played up the most shocking aspect of the affair: that some survivors, including Fuller, were driven to cannibalism. When help finally arrived, thirteen-year-old Fuller was the only person from her family of twelve still alive.

While the narrative's seeming detachment and detail about the attack make for compelling reading, perhaps the most haunting aspect is Fuller's physical dislocation that parallels her psychological distress. Throughout her life—sometimes by chance, sometimes by choice; sometimes for better, sometimes for worse—Fuller moved around the country. She was born in Wisconsin, lived in other parts of the Midwest, and then with her stepfather and extended family set out for Oregon. After her family's death in Idaho, Fuller lived in Washington Territory and Oregon until, at sixteen, she married John Whitman in 1863.

The Whitmans were together for twenty-three years, and the narrative shows that Emeline obtained some emotional and financial stability during that time. Yet the couple opted to relocate to different parts of the Northwest, and they found that success followed success: "Every turn we made seemed to be in the right direction, for we made money fast, and were happy," the text recalls. After Whitman died in an accident in 1886, his widow returned to Wisconsin, where she remarried, to Melvin Fuller, but separated from him after four years. Between 1892 and 1900, Emiline Fuller went back to Washington where she married a third time, to widower Andrew J. Calhoun, and the couple moved to Tennessee until Calhoun's death in 1909. After that, according to one source, Emeline Calhoun kept moving south, to Mississippi or Florida, and died about 1923 or 1924 (Fuller and Schlicke, p. 9).

Fuller's story can be seen as an emblem of the American nineteenth-century female frontier experience. From the Midwest, to the West and Northwest, then the South, Fuller followed her menfolk (stepfather and husbands) and sometimes her own inclination. But while she was clearly a survivor, she was not a frontierswoman in the Hannah Dustan mold. For Fuller, survival carried permanent psychological and physical scars. The narrative is pervaded by Fuller's sense of loss, depression, and bitterness heightened by residual problems in her legs from her traumatic experiences in the wild. In his introduction, Hughes notes Fuller's "careworn face," and Geraldine Hughes's letter quoted above refers to Fuller's sadness and frailty. By the end of Left by the Indians, Fuller's only lasting consolation (assuming this claim is not merely Hughes's editorializing) was religion.

It is interesting to compare the Rowlandson and Fuller texts, published almost exactly three hundred years apart, which mark both the first full-length, fact-based captivity narrative to appear as a separate book (Rowlandson's) and one of the last to do so (Fuller's). Although Rowlandson was a middle-aged mother of three from an educated and influential family when attacked and Fuller a mere teenager from a humble background, both women's accounts focus on family dispersal, psychological loss, and the role of religion in human suffering (Fuller more obliquely than Rowlandson). Indeed, these three themes characterize many women's narratives in the captivity literature.

The text is Emeline L. Fuller, *Left by the Indians: Story of My Life*. Mt. Vernon, Iowa: Hawk-Eye, 1892.

## SUGGESTIONS FOR FURTHER READING

*PRIMARY SOURCE*

Fuller and Schlicke.

*SECONDARY SOURCES*

Derounian-Stodola and Levernier; Shannon.

## Left by the Indians. Story of My Life

My father[1] was born in Mt. Vernon, O. in 1824 and my mother[2] was born in Gelena, Wis. July 12th 1827. Her maiden name was Abagel Payne. They were married Jan. 1st 1846 at Sugar Creek Walworth co., Wis. To them were born three children of whom I was the oldest. Christopher was born Nov. 28th 1850. He was always vigerous and full of fun. Libbie was born Jan. 9th 1852. She was always a delicate child, and hence a great care to me. I was born Feb. 21st 1847 at Mercellon, Columbia co., Wis. When I was five years old we moved to Keokuk, co., Iowa. We traveled with oxen and wagon. When all was in readiness to start as we supposed, father noticed that he had not fixed a place to carry a pail with which to water the oxen on the way. He took a nail and while driving it in a cross-piece under the wagon, the nail flew and struck my right eye as I was looking on, causing almost total loss of vision ever since. We arrived at uncle Wm. Trimble's after a journey of over two weeks. Father rented a house for us, and went to work at what ever he could get to do. In the fall of 1852 father being away with a threshing machine, was called home on account of mother's sickness. She had the Typhoid-fever. Soon after she recovered father took the same disease and died. After father's death uncle George Trimble came after mother and us children, and took us back to Walworth co., Wis. where we remained for a year. The next spring we went to Winnebago co., to my grandfather Payne's and stayed till the fall. Then we went to my mother's brother, Uriah Payne. He was a widower, with three children. My mother kept house for him till the following spring. Here I wish to mention a little incident that occured, because of what follows. I loved my little brother Christy dearly. One day mother hid the axe from him for fear he might cut himself, but I found it and gave it to him. Soon after I was passing where he was chopping and accidently fell, and my left hand went under the axe as it came down and I lost my large finger for finding the axe, Children do suffer for not minding their parents. But poor Christy felt worse about it than I did. He cried as though his heart would break, and we could not get him to come in the house till late that night. From there we moved to Fondulac co., near Brandon, and

remained about a year and a half. Then we moved back to Columbia co. to my uncle Jason Payne's, and remained till spring. From here my uncle Geo. Trimble's son took us back to Walworth co., where we helped to care for grandfather and grandmother.

In 1858 mother married Elijah Utter,[3] of Walworth co. a blacksmith by occupation, and a large-hearted, honest man, who proved a good husband to mother, and good father to us children. He had three sons and three daughters, making in all eleven in the family. The next year a baby daughter was born to them, making twelve in the family.

My father and mother often talked of going to the far west to make themselves a home, and settle their numerous family in homes adjoining their own in that broad country, where settlers were so much needed to till the lands, and improve the country, and after much deliberation and very much advice from friends and neighbors, they decided to go, and commenced preparations forthwith, selling their home and converting other property into money, buying oxen and wagons, and preparing for our long journey, for we had decided that we would go to Oregon, which was full six months journey in our way of travel. I could but contrast the old ways of travel with the new, as I made the journey a short time ago in six days, comfortably seated in a palice car.[4] The first day of May, 1860, dawned upon us clear and bright, and with all prepared for starting, we yoked our oxen to the wagons, gathered our cows and young stock together, taking sixteen head and four yoke of oxen, our family dog, clothing, provisions, household utensils, &c. Although tears were in our eyes at the thought of parting with our friends and relatives, still we were hopeful, for we dearly loved each other, stepfather, stepbrothers and sisters all being united and happy, and the thought that in that far land to which we were to go, we would be so fortunate as to live an unbroken family in nice homes, near father and mother, and if the Lord so willed it, with not a face missing in our family circle, gave strength to pass through the sorrowful parting. But I shall never forget the tearful faces of my dear old grandparents as they stood at the end of the lane, leading to the road, with tears streaming down their wrinkled faces bid a last adieu to their youngest child and her family.

I was then a girl of 13 years, and with a heart untouched by cares, but bitterly did I cry over leaving home, and lonely, most lonely were the first few nights of camping, and feeling that we were going farther and farther from home each day.

We fell in with three other teams about noon of the first day, that like ourselves were started for Oregon and California.⁵ As these families were with us during our entire journey, I will give their names: John Myers, who left his wife and children and went to find a home for them, Michæl Myers, a brother, and Edward Prine. With this addition to our company we felt a little stronger and better satisfied. We soon became accostomed to camp life, and after a little time really enjoyed it.

Everything had been planned before starting on our journey, and we had prepared all things for convenience on the road. We took ten milch cows, and had kegs made before starting, and we milked our cows and strained the milk into our kegs, put them into our wagons, and every night the milk was churned by the motion of the wagons into nice butter, which we salted and worked into balls for use.

We stopped and rested our teams occasionally, and did our washing and such work as it was possible to do up ahead under the circumstances.

We kept falling in with emigrant teams, and by the time we had reached Ft. Laramie we had quite a train.

There are many incidents of our journey which I should like to narrate if time and space would allow. One young man by the name of John Green, who overtook us at Ft. Laramie, while handling his revolver, had the misfortune to get his hand shot, and so badly hurt that he had to go to Ft. Kearney and have it amputated.

We were much amused by the intelligence and acuteness of the little prairie dogs. Some nights we scarcely slept at all for the barking and yelping of the noisy things, which were alarmed at having strange neighbors and wished to alarm their friends. They had little owls and a kind of dormant rattlesnake in the burrough with them all on friendly terms, it seemed. We stopped at Fort Laramie a few days to rest and shoe our teams, also to wait for teams which we heard were behind us, and like ourselves bound for Oregon. We fell in with a large California train, and traveled with them until the Californian trail separated from the Oregon, and then we were left more lonely than before. We had felt the security of traveling with such a large number. While with the Californian train, when we camped at night we would prepare the ground by cutting down the brush, leveling and sprinkling the ground, and have a good old-fashioned dance.

It was not much work to make our toilets, for the most of us wore for convenience the costume called Bloomers and did not have many changes. We would also sing songs, tell stories, and amuse ourselves with all the sports of our school days, feeling perfectly safe and secure, for in union was our strength, but how soon all changed when we parted with our friends of the California train, and traveled westward, knowing that we were every day nearing the dangerous part of our journey. But still we kept on over hills, through forests, across mountains and rivers, until we came to Ft. Hall, where soldiers were stationed. As we deemed it unsafe to go farther alone, we called for troops to go with us. There had one company already gone with a train but a few days ahead of us, and we had to wait for the soldiers to make preparations.

While waiting, Col. Howe,[6] in command of Ft. Hall, sent in a request to have the women and girls of the train come into their tents and have a dance, which we refused to do, which very much displeased the Col., and at first he refused to send one of his men with us, but upon considering the matter over he dared not refuse, so sent out a small force, with instructions not to go more than half as far with us as those he sent with the train ahead. The soldiers, when they turned back, told us that we were just in the edge of danger, and so we found it, for in a few days we found the Indians meant mischief, as they did not come to our wagons, but would occasionally come in sight at a distance, seemed to be watching us, and acted as though they were not friendly to us. One of the soldiers deserted and went with us. He was a bugler, and took his bugle with him, but we did not enjoy music as well as when we felt safer.

After we had traveled for about one week, perhaps longer. I write from memory, having kept no diary, and all know that twenty-five years will dim the memory of the past in one's mind, we camped late one night. We had not been in camp long when three Indians and two squaws came into camp and all agreed that the leader among them must be a white man,[7] as his dress and appearance was different from the rest. He had a beard, and you could see plainly that he was painted. He wore an old white hat, with the top of the crown gone.

We could tell him as far as we could see him, he was so different from the rest. They stayed around our wagons until late, when our men told them that they must go to their homes, as we wish to go to bed. They waited to be told a number of times, and finally went away.

We started early next morning, and did not go far before we came to good feed and water, and as we had a dry camp the night before, the men decided to stop part of the day and water and feed the teams and stock, and let the women wash. In a short time the same Indians came to us, talked a while, and told us they were going off into the mountains to hunt, said good bye, and left us. We were suspicious of them, and the men consulted together, and thought the safest way would be to kill them, but hardly dared to do so, for fear of its being found out by the Indians. Still we all thought them spies, and, I often wish that we had done as our better judgment told us, and killed them and secreted the bodies, but it seemed it was not to be so. All went well for a week.

We saw no Indians to alarm us, and had almost regained our cheerfulness, and were very hopeful that our fears were unfounded, when on reaching Salmon Falls, on Snake river, who should we meet but our supposed white man and the two Indians who were with him before, and a number of other Indians with them. They came to our wagons and pretended to be glad to see us. We bought some dried salmon of them, and hurried away, thankful to be rid of them, but it worried us as we were followed. We went on for another week with all quiet, and we were another hundred miles nearer our destination, when we reached a small river, I think it was called Bruno. There we found a good place for our stock to graze. We always sent a man out with the cattle and horses, for fear they would be stolen, and when our cattle were brought into camp at night there were one or two yoke of oxen missing. The men searched for them and found their tracks where they had been driven up a canyon by Indians.

We kept a good watch that night and were not molested. In the morning Mr. Vanornam, the man who lost the oxen, threw away everything that he could spare and someone let him have a yoke of oxen to hitch to his wagon, and we all started along feeling glad to leave what seemed to us to be a dangerous place. We traveled only a short distance before we came to a grave where a man belonging to the train ahead of us had been buried, and the Indians had dug him up, taken his clothing, and then partly buried him, leaving one hand and foot out of the grave. You cannot imagine what a terror struck to our hearts as we gazed on the awful sight and reflected that we too might share the same fate, for on looking about us we saw a board on which was written an account of his being killed by the Indians, and warning anyone who came that way to be very cautious. But the warning came too late to do good, for we had not gone more than a mile before we were attacked by them. This was the 9th day of September, 1860. As we came up the hill and turned down towards Snake river again, we came in full sight of the Indians who were singing their war songs, and their shrill war whoop I can never forget. It was too terrible to even attempt to describe, but suffice it to say that although so many years have elapsed since that awful, awful scene, I can never hear a shrill yell without shrinking with much the feelings which I experienced as that terrible noise reached our ears.

We saw at a glance what we must do and corrected our wagons as quickly as possible. There were only nine wagons in the train, but we had sixteen men and boys capable of bearing arms, and were well armed. There were also five women, and twenty-one children between the ages of one and fourteen years.

Perhaps it might be of interest to tell you of the families in the train. Elijah Utter and wife, with their ten children, Mr. and Mrs. Myers, with five children, Mr. and Mrs. Vanornam, and five children.

After a short time the Chief rode up and down the road waving a white cloth and motioning for us to go on at noon. Two or three of the Indians came up close to us and motioned that they wished to talk with us. Some of the men went out and met them, and they said they would not hurt us, that they were only hungry, and that we were to go on after noon, but I can tell you that dinner time did not find us with our accustomed appetites that day.

Shortly after noon we started, but did not go by the road as they expected us to do, but kept up the hill from them, and the last wagon had hardly started before they commenced their terrible war songs and dancing again, and coming toward us all the time. We corrected our wagons as soon as possible, but before we could get the last one in place, the man who was driving was shot dead. His name was Lewis Lawson, from Iowa. Shortly after two more were killed, Mr. Utley and Mr. Kithual. We fought them all that afternoon all of that long, awful night, picking them off as often as we could get a chance. We had no chance to get away under cover of night, as they were watchful, and if they heard the least noise would commence whooping and shooting at us. We talked it over, and made up our minds that we were all to die, but thought we would try leaving all the wagons but one for each family, and take some provisions, leave all our stock and other property, and see if they would not let us go our way. There were with us three discharged soldiers from Fort Hall, and the deserter before mentioned. They were mounted on horses and were to go ahead and clear the way for us to follow with our wagons. But instead of doing so, the discharged soldiers put spurs to the horses, which belonged to Mr. Vanornam, and galloped off for dear life, and left us to our fate. The deserter stayed as long as he could and stand any chance to save himself, and then taking with him the Reath brothers, Joseph and Jacob, they left, taking the one horse with them which belonged to the deserter. In the horrible tumult of the fight we did not see them go, and did not know but they were killed.

The Indians now seemed to redouble their frenzy and showered upon us a continual fire, until it seemed impossible for one to escape. The first one who fell there was John Myers, who it will be remembered left his family at home either at Hebron, Ill., or Geneva, Wis. As Joseph Reath was helping my oldest step-sister, Mary Utter, from his wagon, a ball passed through his clothes and entered her breast. She only lived a few minutes. The next one to go was my step-father, who had his baby, one year old that day, in his arms. As I stepped up and took her from him, so he could the better use his gun, I kissed him and turned to mother, who was bending over my dying step-sister, Mary, when father was shot in the breast and fell. He got up, but hardly got up when he fell close to his daughter Mary, and soon died. We gave up then. It seemed as though our whole dependance had been taken from us, and leaving our wagons, we started, each one for himself. I turned to my poor mother who was standing by the dead bodies of husband and children, and begged her to go with us, but she said no, there was no use in trying that we were all to be killed, and that she could not leave father, and when I found that I could not persuade her to go, I took one last lingering look at her dear face, and taking my poor little baby sister in my arms and telling four of the little brothers and sisters to follow me, I started, I knew not whither, but with the one hope of getting away from the wretches who seemed to thirst for the blood of everyone of us. I turned and motioned to my mother, who still stood by the wagon where I left her, with two of my step-sisters and a little step-brother. She shook her head, but the oldest step-sister started to come to me and they shot her down. I turned and ran a little way, and looked back, and they had all been shot down, and were lying with the rest of the dead. I felt then that all that I held dear on earth was dependant upon my feeble care, and child as I was, I nerved myself for that terrible struggle for life which I could see was before me.

Will the reader of this narrative please to pause a moment and reflect upon my situation. A child of barely thirteen years, and slender in build and constitution, taking a nursing babe of one year, and four other children, all younger than herself, and fleeing for life without provisions and barely clothing enough to cover us, into the pathless wilderness or what is worse yet, across the barren plains of the west. It was now the 10th day of Sept., and getting dark, the second day after the attack. Others also fled, and we got to gether as much as possible and made for the river, for we were very thirsty, as we had had but little water through the fight, for we did not fill our kegs as usual that morning, as we knew we should travel along the river. After we got a drink of water we rested a little, if it could be called resting, with the awful fear in our minds that we should be followed and killed. We decided upon the course that we would keep away from the road and travel in single file, and as near as possible cover our tracks by having a man step in each track.

We traveled by night and hid in the willows that grew along the river, by day. We traveled only a short distance that night and we could see the fire from our burning wagons and such goods as they could not well carry away, and before morning we hid in the willows on the river bank and lay there all day. We saw some of the Indians going past us driving off some of our cattle, for it seemed that they divided up into small bands and dividing their spoil, each one went his way. While they were passing I held my hand over the mouth of my baby sister, who, frightened, perhaps by the scared faces around her commenced crying. Poor little sister, how my heart did ache for her. Words can not describe my agony as I looked on the faces of my little brothers and sisters, poor orphans now, and heard them cry piteously for father and mother, and if possible worse yet, cry for bread when I had none to give them. God grant that none of the readers of this story may ever realize from experience the awful bitterness of the cup which I was forced to drink to the very dregs.

Just about dark of that day three Indians went past us shooting off their guns and whooping and yelling. We laid very quiet until after dark, then got up and traveled as fast as possible. When tired out we would lie down and sleep a short time, then get up and travel along.

The Indians followed us four days, coming onto us about the same hour each night. We supposed they tracked us all day. The fourth night they did not come until later. We had camped under a hill on the creek, and above us were rocks, and they went up above us and rolled rocks down, trying to roll them onto us. They came close, but we were so far under that they did not strike us. We started as soon as it was dark enough for us to travel with safety, and kept on all night, feeling sure that we would be safer elsewhere. One night brother Christopher was missing when we camped. You will remember that we travelled by moonlight and starlight, and we could not guess what had become of him, and one of the men went back and found that he had taken the road and gone on, instead of turning out where we did to camp. He found his tracks, but we did not see him until the next day, when we met him coming back to us.

After the fourth day we did not see nor hear anything to alarm us, and travelled by day and camped by night.

You will perhaps wonder what we could get to eat. Well, we got so hungry during the third night's travel that we killed our faithful family dog, that had shared our hardships through all that long journey. We also killed Mr. Vanorman's, roasted and ate some of the meat, and carried the rest along for future use.

We kept on our journey through the wilderness until we came to the Oyhee river, near where Fort Boisee used to stand, and all being tired out with travel and weak with hunger, we camped there.

We had found a cow the day before, which had strayed away from the train ahead of us, and was trying to go back home. She was very poor, but we shot her, the first shot which had been fired since we left the wagons. We roasted her, and carried the meat over to the Oyhee.

We had traveled more than 100 miles, although it would not have been much over 80 by the road, since leaving the wagons, but so far all were alive, although our sufferings were terrible, both from hunger and exposure. It was getting cold weather, and we were without extra clothing nights, and commenced to suffer from the cold. Our shoes were worn off, and we were barefoot, or nearly so, and nights we would bury our poor bruised feet in the sand to keep them warm. We set to work and built us camps out of the boughs and brush which we could find along the river, for we could see little probability of getting away from there, and tried to make things as comfortable as possible.

Mr. Myers had escaped so far with his whole family, and had it not been for him I think we should have traveled along a little way each day toward the Fort, which was to us the haven of safety, but he begged so piteously for us not to leave him, as he was not able to travel, that we would not go without him.

When we had been in camp some time, my brother Christopher was down by the river fishing one day, when an Indian came to him and seemed much surprised at seeing him, and wanted him to go home to his camp with him, but Christy told him that he had a camp of his own and must go to that. He went away, and Christy came home and told us. In about an hour the same Indian came back and had four more with him, and brought us one fish, but when they saw how many there were of us they went back and brought some more fish for us, and urged us to go to their camp with them, but we would not go. We had a great horror of being taken captive by them. We traded some of our clothes with them for fish, and they wanted Christy to go home with them, and he told us that he would go home with them, as he was afraid that if none of us went they would not like it, and might do us harm. He was a brave little fellow, and although only eleven years of age, had before started with a man by the name of Goodsel to see if they could not reach the fort and bring us help, and after getting quite a long way from us they met the deserted soldier and the Reath boys, who got away, it will be remembered, at the time of the massacre, taking one horse among them, and in trying to reach the fort they had taken the wrong road, and brother and Mr. Goodsel met them coming back to take the right trail. When they heard that we were starving they killed their horse and roasted it, and started my brother back to us with all he could carry, and he, poor boy, knowing how great was our need, loaded himself so heavy that he had to throw pieces away as it became so heavy that he could not carry it. The man Goodsel went on with them, traveling with all speed to reach the fort and send help to us.

But to return to my subject, Christy said that if the Indians did not let him come back that he could run away the next summer and get in with some emigrant train and reach us if we ever got through, which looked very doubtful. The Indians took a dislike to the children of Mr. Vanornam, as they were so hungry that they snatched the fish from them and ate it greedily.

They went back to camp taking Christy with them, and said they would be back in three days and bring him with them. After they went away we talked it over and thought when they came back they would surely kill us, and Mr. Vannornam and wife, with two sons and three daughters, Mr. Gleason and Charles and Henry Utter, my step-brothers started along to try and reach Fort Walla Walla.

At the end of three days the Indians came back as they had agreed to, and brought Christy with them, and they brought fish again. Mr. Chase ate so much of it that he was taken with the hiccough and died. We buried him, but the Indians dug him up, took his clothes, and buried him again. My poor sister Libbie, nine years old, used to help me gather buffalo chips for fuel, and rosebuds, pusley[8] and other things to eat. She and I went to gather fuel as usual one morning, and she was tugging along with all she could carry and fell behind. I carried mine into camp and went back to meet her. I called her by name and she made no answer. Soon I found her, and I said, "Libbie, why did you not answer?" She said, "I could not talk I felt too bad," and before night she was dead. Soon the Indians came again bringing Christy with them I did not see him this time as I was away after fuel. Mr. Myers asked him where they camped. Christy asked why he wished to know, and he said "because when the soldiers come we want to come and get you." The Indians, as soon as they heard the word "soldiers" spoken, said it over to each other and talked among themselves and went away taking Christy with them again. I came back with my fuel, and when on my way out quite a ways from camp I heard a frightful noise. It seemed to me more like dogs fighting than anything else I ever heard. I was scared, and made haste into camp, and they told me Christy had been there and gone back again. We waited with as much anxiety as we could feel about anything until the three days were passed, and the Indians did not come back, and we felt afraid of them, and we began to talk about trying to start along, but I could not go without finding something of the fate of Christy. We waited a few days and then I went over to Snake river, about two miles, and I could see their camps, but could not see any living thing around them. I called Christy loud and long, but the echo of my own voice was all the answer I could hear. I went back to camp feeling sure that something had happened to the boy. The next day Mr. Myers took the trail which went from our camp to theirs, and had not gone far when he found where the wolves had dragged something along, and soon he found some of his hair, and then he knew that my brother had been killed by the Indians and his body torn to pieces by the wolves. He came back to camp and told us, and words cannot describe my feelings as I heard of his horrible fate. I knew then that the noise which I heard that day was my poor brave Christy whom I loved so well. I thought I had passed through all the suffering which I could endure, and God knows how I longed to lie down and die and be at rest, but it was not to be so, nor had I drained the cup to the dregs yet. Starvation was making sad inroads on our little band, and none but those who endured the awful pangs of starvation can have even a faint idea of such horrible sufferings and death. We became almost frantic. Food we must have, but how should we get it? Then an idea took possession of our minds which we could not even mention to each other, so horrid, so revolting to even think of, but the awful madness of hunger was upon us,[9] and we cooked and ate the bodies of each of the poor children, first sister Libbie, then Mr. Chase's little boys, and next my darling little baby sister, whom I had carried in my arms through all that long dreary journey and slept with hugged to my heart, as though if possible I would shield her from all danger. She too had to leave me. In vain had I saved the choicest morsel of everything for her, chewed fish and fed it so her, boiled pusley which we found on Snake river, and fed her the water, and everything which I could plan had been fed to her to keep her alive. Mrs. Myers and Mrs. Chase each had babies about her age, but neither could spare a share of nature's food for our poor little motherless one, for fear of robbing her own. For over forty days I had carried her, but had to give her up at last, and I was left alone. All who had depended upon me had been taken away except the two step-brothers, who had gone on and from whom we had heard nothing. We also dug up the body of Mr. Chase, intending to eat that, but thank God, relief came. The first one to reach Fort Walla Walla was one of discharged soldiers,[10] who it will be remembered, ran away with Mr. Vanornam's horses from the wagons at the time of the massacre. They told so many lies on getting to the fort, that they did not believe that there was any train in trouble. He got in a number of days before the Reath brothers, Mr. Goodsel and the deserted soldier gave out on the way and did not reach Fort Walla Walla. They camped there till the soldiers came after us.

When they reached the fort, which was between eighty and a hundred miles from us, one of the Reath boys came back with two companies of soldiers, one of dragoons and one of infantry. They started back immediately and traveled along without resting night or day.

Upon nearing us, they found a sad sight. The company who had gone on ahead when the Indians took brother Christy away, which you will remember consisted of Mr. and Mrs. Vanornam, three daughters and two sons, Samuel Gleason, and Charles and Henry Utter, the Indians had followed and killed Mr. and Mrs. Vanornam, their son Mark Samuel Gleason, and the last of our family except myself, Charles and Henry Utter. Their bodies lay unburied, showing marks of torture too devilish for any human beings to inflict except Indians. Let those who have neer suffered as I have pity the fate of the noble red man of the forest. My pity all goes out for their poor unfortunate victims, and I can never look even upon one of our poor, degraded, harmless Winnebagoes without such feelings as I do not like to entertain towards any of God's created beings, and I almost doubt if they are a part of our great Maker's work.

Mrs. Vanornam had evidently been tortured too terribly to mention. Her ankles were tied with strong ropes when found, and she had been scalped. Three of the Vanornam girls and one boy had been carried away by the Indians.[11] The next year we heard, by some emigrant trains, something of them. The oldest girl, 13 years old, was killed. In attempting to get away she killed two squaws, and the Indians then killed her. The boy was bought by an emigrant train, and reached his uncle in Oregon. The Indians were seen leading the two little girls with collars around their necks, and chains to them to lead them by. A thousand pities that they had not all been killed with their parents. I have that one consolation, that in all my troubles none of my folks were taken captive by them.

The dragoons commenced to bury the dead, who it was very evident had been dead but a short time but the Reath boy begged of them not to stop there for the night, as it was getting late in the afternoon, but to push on for he told them there were certainly more somewhere, and it was possible they might find them alive. So the infantry traveled all night without resting. I may say here there is no doubt but we owed our lives to that night's work of those brave, tender-hearted men, for we were sure that the Indians were on their way to kill us when scared away by the approach of soldiers.

About ten o'clock in the morning we saw signal fires off a few miles from our camp, and we knew that either they were coming to kill us, or help was close at hand, and strange as it may seem to my readers my heart was so benumbed by my terrible sufferings that I hardly cared which it was. I was alone in the world and had suffered enough in the past few months to change me from a light-hearted child into a broken-hearted women,[12] and my wish was that I might lie down and die, and join my kindred in a world free from cares and troubles like those I had passed through. I was out after fuel as usual, when I saw the soldiers coming, but was too weak to feel much joy at seeing them. They rode up to me and a few dismounted, and coming to me asked if I did not want something to eat. I answered that I did not care. I shall never forget the pitying looks bent on me by those strong men. Tears stood in every eye as one of the officers gave me a part of a biscuit. I ate that, but did not care for more, but in a few days I was hungry enough to eat anything. I could not have lived many days longer if help had not reached us.

The soldiers commenced at once making preparations for return to the fort. They took us about three miles from our camp the next day after their arrival, and went into camp there, and waited for us to get ready. They told us to make us some clothing before starting. We made some skirts out of blankets which they gave us, and we wore some of their underclothes, and their short blue coats, which were comfortable, for it was getting to be cold days and nights, as it was now the 25th or 26th of October. I cannot speak half well enough of the soldiers to express their kind and gentlemanly treatment of us, and I shall carry through life the recollection not only of the kindness but even of the features of those large-hearted soldiers, and I almost think I should recognize any of them, should I ever see them. They made saddle-bags, hung them across their saddles, and put a child in each one; made a litter for those who were too feeble to ride on horseback, or rather on mules, for they were mounted on mules. Mrs. Chase and myself changed, and each rode a part of the time on a litter. I have neglected to say that Mrs. Chase had the misfortune to lose the use of one limb, and the arm on the same side, and was almost entirely helpless, for a part of the time we were in camp, and it was very hard for her to travel in any other way than on a litter. She got thrown off from the mule and hurt, and then I gave up my place on the litter to her. After traveling a few days, the government wagons sent to our relief from Fort Walla Walla met us. Then we had clothes to keep us warm, and an easy wagon to ride in.

Perhaps some of my readers will wonder why we ventured so much danger with so small a train. The reason is we did not intend to cross those dangerous plains alone. We fully expected to overtake a train that was a short distance ahead which got through all right except the one man above mentioned, who left the train to go after some strayed sheep, and was then killed by the Indians. Having failed to overtake them, we were left to our sad fate in spite of all we could do.

There was one family which I cannot forbear to make special mention of, and that is the family of Mr. Myers. The reader will recollect that I spoke of them in the beginning of this narrative. There were seven in the family, father, mother, and five children, and strange as it may seem every one of them were spared, and reached the fort in safety. Mr. Myers, in answer to the question asked him how they all happened to get through, when other families were entirely annihilated, answered, "It was prayer saved my family," but I can say that my idea is that extreme selfishness had more to do with their being saved than prayer. The hardship of gathering fuel and subsistence was not shared by Mr. Myers' family. He said they were not able. Even the task of washing for their baby was allotted to me, and often when we would go out after pusley, rosebuds, and such other vegetation as we could find, which we could eat, and leave Mr. Myers praying, I suppose in a selfish way, for his own family, in camp, instead of helping in our hardships, on our return the other children would cry and beg for something to eat and say the Myers family had been eating fish, or whatever we had stored away for rations, for we had to allow each one just so much at a meal. Perhaps the good Lord, who is the searcher of all hearts, heeded his selfish prayers, but I would quicker believe that shirking duty and stealing from others was what saved the Myers family.

After I arrived at Walla Walla, Washington Territory, I stayed with the family of Lieutenant A. J. Anderson until my cousin came for me from Salem, Oregon. It was the Lieutenant that rescued us at Oyhee river near old Fort Boysee. They were very kind to me. Mrs. Chase and her little girl stayed at the home of Captain Dent. He was a brother-in-law of U. S. Grant, and captain of the infantry. They were there when I left.

It was now about the middle of December, 1860. Cousin took me to his sister's who had married Mr. T. J. Pomeroy. My cousin's father, Edward Trimble, was killed on the plains in 1846 by the Indians. From Salem I went to Linn Co., Oregon, to my only relatives in Oregon that I had ever seen before. Uncle Pierce H. Trimble and his family moved to Oregon in 1853 from Walworth Co., Wisconsin. With them I made my home part of the time, and part of the time with Mr. W. W. Allingham's family, and went to school. They were very kind people; in fact, all I met with in the west were kind to me and often tried to help me to forget my troubles. I shall always hold in grateful remembrance the kindness of the people in Washington Territory and Oregon. They were so liberal in making up money for us. My uncle took what was raised for me and bought sheep with it for me. I had twenty-one head. Uncle gave me a cow, and Mr. John Clark gave me another. So I had plenty of stock. My schooling did not cost me nor my uncle one cent, as the people paid for it. Neither did their kindness stop here. They often came and took me along to entertainments that were going on in the country. The best horse and saddle were always provided for me. They wanted me to learn to ride on horseback, as that was their mode of traveling there. I soon learned to ride, and often went with the young people to church and singing school. Sometimes eight or ten couple of us went together. The country was beautiful to ride over, and the scenery was lovely to look at. When the snow was three or four feet deep in Wisconsin, I picked wild flowers in Oregon. Everything around me, so far as nature was concerned, was charming to behold. If father, mother, brothers, and sisters had only been with me, my joy would have been complete; but they were gone, and with all that beauty spread before me, I could not help but turn my longing heart toward them, and weep in my lonliness. While in the school-room trying hard to learn, the scenes of the past would come up before me, and it seemed that my heart would break. Nobody knew how hard it was. Many times I was happy with my young friends, and tried to be so; but night would come on, and I would pray for dear mother to come and take me, and cry myself to sleep. My feet were so injured from walking after the fight, having no shoes, and from the cold, I could not always walk to school. Then I rode on horse back, and picketed my horse out till I returned home. I still suffer much pain in my feet.

I lived in Linn Co. about two years, and then went forty miles to Manmoth, Polk Co., Oregon, with a lady I had met a few times. She had me go to the Christian College in that place. I went two terms, and then came back to Linn Co. in the spring. The next fall (Nov. 12th, 1863), Mr. John M. Whitman and I were united in marriage.[13] Mr. Whitman was born September 8th, at Monmouth, Ill. When he was eight years old his parents moved to Monmouth, Oregon, taking him along. His parents still live there. Here we began house-keeping, and remained till the following July. During this time I received a letter from my mother's uncle, Rev. Aaron Payne of Yamhill Co., Oregon. His brother was a Quaker preacher, and Blackhawk's first victim. They captured him on the way to his appointment. He carried no arms, according to the Quaker custom. The Indians said he was a brave man to travel there in this way; but even this heroic spirit did not prevent them from taking his defenseless head and carrying it on a pole. Rev. A. Payne had been a widower since 1847. His family had all died with the consumption, except one son. He wanted me to come and live with them. He came twice to see me before I was married, and if possible to get me to go and live with a family near them and go to school. The first time he came he talked to my uncle, but did not mention it to me, lest I should become uneasy. Uncle did not want me to go. After we were married we went and lived on his place two years, and he lived with us. Then we moved to Tillomook Co. on the coast, about fifty miles distant, to another place of his, taking with us some of his stock with our own. We took a pre-emption joining his place for ourselves, and got along well. Every turn we made seemed to be in the right direction, for we made money fast, and were happy. We lived in that part five years. To get there we had to cross the Coast Range of mountains on horse-back, or go around on the water. We usually preferred to cross the mountains. Those mountains are covered with the finest timber that can be found. The timber in Wisconsin looks like shrubbery beside those great trees. The fruit was abundant and delicious. The climate was very mild. They hardly ever had snow to lie long enough to have a sleigh-ride. It is a great place for fishing and boating. We used to have some good times with our neighbors, sailing and rowing. Three or four couples of us often went to the beach, and camped all night. Some would take their bathing-suits along, and go out in the water as the tide came in, and let the waves roll over them. We often walked miles on the beach, dug clams, gathered shells, etc. to pass the time away, and amuse ourselves. When we got tired we would return to our camp-fire and sing songs, and visit to make life as pleasant as possible. It was amusing to see some strangers trying to go out with a boat on the tide. Not being aware that the water was so shallow, they sometimes neglected till the tide left them on a clam-bed or mudflat. There they might play themselves for six hours, until the tide would return and bring them back. As I looked on those majestic mountains, the dark, briny ocean, and the blue, etherial sky; I thought of Him, who made the mountains rise;

> "That spread the flowing seas abroad,
> And built the lofty skies."

In 1870 we sold the property we had there, and went to Eastern Oregon. The damp winter seasons did not agree with my poor health in the west. Here we rented a good farm from a brother-in-law for two seasons and did well. We raised feed, and bought and sold stock. Then we moved about one hundred and thirty miles into Washington Territory. Here we took a homestead timber claim, and bought some railroad land adjoining. We farmed, kept a store and stagestand, or travelers home. Many of the officers and soldiers of the late war stopped with us; Generals Howard and Wheaton I remember well. I shall never forget the thrill that went through my heart when I saw Gen. Howard's empty sleeve. He was the first officer, or soldier, that I had seen who lost a limb in the war. I tho't of my own cousins and friends, who had been killed or wounded fighting for the same cause.

After the death of my husband our property there was sold and passed into the hands of strangers, and now there is a city on our old place. I should like to see it once more. While residing there we adopted a nephew of my husband. He was eleven years old, and lived with us till he was twenty-one. Now he is married and settled in Rosalia, Wash.

Since I returned to Wis. Mr. Melvin Fuller of Pardeeville, Wis., and I were married. He was a widower with seven children at home. We lived together for four years and a few months and then separated on account of trouble with the older children. Now I live beside my uncle Payne, and his family in Marshfield, Wis., and Miss Nettie Reid stays with me most of the time. In 1861 I was converted to God, and joined the Close Communion Baptist church. Since then I have found Jesus to be a "friend that sticketh closer than a brother."

In 1873 we took Frank Riggs to raise. He was only six years old. His mother was from Wisconsin. She went to Idaho to keep house for her brother, Joe Baker. She married Mr. Riggs and in a few years he left her and the children to the mercy of strangers in Western Oregon. If any of her folks should happen to read this, I should like very much to hear from them. But before this when we were in Eastern Oregon we took his baby brother only two weeks old. Their mother having four children. Baby Willie (as we called him) grew to be a sweet and good little fellow but he was permitted to stay with us only six years and seven months. He died, Aug. 22, 1879. It was hard to give him up but God knows best. I shall meet my dear ones some sweet day in that beautiful heaven beyond,

> Far from a world of grief and sin;
> With God eternally shut in.

MRS. EMELINE L. FULLER.

# EXPLANATORY NOTES

## MARY ROWLANDSON

1. *Feb. 1. 1675:* In the Old Style (Julian) calendar, which stayed in effect in Britain and New England until 1752—seventy years after the publication of this narrative—the new year did not begin until March 25. When England adopted the New Style (Gregorian) calendar in 1752, it observed the beginning of the New Year on January 1 and also accommodated a ten-day difference of dates. By the modern calendar, then, the date referred to here was actually February 11, 1676.

2. *United Colonies:* An informal alliance of the New England colonies of Massachusetts Bay, Plymouth, and Connecticut.

3. *devoured those to whom they went:* That is, when the Narragansetts fled to join the Nipmucks, they quickly used up the Nipmucks' provisions.

4. *some time before:* The English were forewarned of an Indian attack on Lancaster by a Nipmuck named James Quanapohit, who supported the English.

5. *Lot . . . beside others:* Genesis 14:12.

6. *three Children too:* Daniel 3.

7. *Were there not . . . the nine:* Luke 17:16–18.

8. *It is better . . . and not pay:* Ecclesiastes 5:5.

9. *what dost thou:* Job 9:12.

10. *Out of the Eater . . . the strong:* This citation ("Samson's Riddle") is from Judges 14:14. The quotation that follows, beginning *"The worst of evils,"* is, as indicated, from Romans 8:28.

11. *PER AMICUM:* By a Friend. Very likely the noted Puritan minister Increase Mather.

12. *Flankers:* Projecting defensive fortifications or anything that flanks a building or adjoins it laterally, such as side wings, according to *The Oxford English Dictionary (OED)*.

13. *my Children:* Joseph, born in 1661; Mary, born in 1665; and Sarah, born in 1669. Apart from Rowlandson and her three children, there were thirty-three others in the Rowlandson garrison house at the time of the attack.

14. *one of my Sisters, hers:* Rowlandson's sister Hannah Divoll. It is not clear which of her sister's children Rowlandson took.

15. *my dear Child in my Arms:* Sarah.

16. *My elder Sister:* Elizabeth Kerley.

17. *Come . . . in the Earth:* Psalms 46:8.

18. *Remove:* Literally, encampment, but also figuratively, "The space or interval by which one person or thing is remote from another in time, place, condition, etc." *(OED).*

19. *the Bay:* Joseph Rowlandson had gone to Massachusetts Bay to request additional defenses for Lancaster.

20. *it:* In seventeenth-century usage, "it" rather than "he" or "she" could be used to refer to small children.

21. *one-ey'd John:* "One-eyed" John Monoco was a Nashoway sachem (chief). The Nashoways were part of the Indian confederacy that attacked Puritan settlements throughout Metacom's (King Philip's) War. Rowlandson refers here to an attack on Lancaster in August 1675 led by Monoco. Although promised amnesty, Monoco was imprisoned and executed in Boston in September 1676.

22. *Marlberough's Praying Indians:* Praying Indians were Christianized Indians, who occupied ambivalent positions in both Native American and English cultures. The Christian Indians of Marlborough were accused of complicity in Monoco's attack on Lancaster in 1675. However, Captain Samuel Moseley's attempt to prove this in court was unsuccessful. Rowlandson scorned "praying Indians" and frequently refers to them in her narrative.

23. *Capt. Mosely:* Samuel Mosely, a captain in the English army, was a well-known Indian-hater who harassed and killed many Indians. Rowlandson seems to approve of his tactics.

24. *Furniture:* Tack (e.g., harness and saddle) for a horse.

25. *Robert Pepper:* One of Captain Richard Beers's company attempting to evacuate Northfield in September 1675. They were ambushed by Nashoways led by Monoco, and although Pepper escaped, half the company died.

26. *miserable comforters . . . he said:* "He" refers to Job; see Job 16:2.

27. *Quannopin:* Narragansett sachem and war chief who led his people in the Lancaster attack in which Rowlandson was taken. He himself was captured, court-martialed, and executed in August 1676.

28. *King Philips wives Sister:* Weetamoo (Wettimore) was the squaw sachem of the Pocasset Wampanoags. Her first husband was Wamsutta, Metacom's brother. Her second husband was also the sachem of a Wampanoag community; she left him when he allied himself with the English. After she and her followers joined the Narragansetts in 1675, she took Quinnapin as her third husband. Apart from her sachem spouses, she

was an extremely powerful figure in her own right. She drowned in August 1676 after escaping an English attack on her camp.

29. *Me . . . against me:* Genesis 42:36.

30. *Goodwife Joslin:* Ann Joslin was twenty-six when she and her child were captured. They were killed in March 1676.

31. *ver. ult.:* The last verse; that is, Psalms 27:14.

32. *like Jehu . . . furiously:* See II Kings 9:20.

33. *Bier:* A frame for a corpse or a litter for a noble person.

34. *my Mistress:* Weetamoo.

35. *Lots Wife's Temptation:* See Genesis 19:26.

36. *crickled down:* Presumably, crunched down.

37. *the hungry Soul . . . sweet:* Proverbs 27:7.

38. *King Philip:* Metacom (or King Philip, as the English called him) was chief sachem of the Wampanoags. He was married to Weetamoo's sister. Two weeks after the English captured and enslaved his wife and son, Metacom was killed in August 1676.

39. *Sannup:* Married Indian man.

40. *Mary Thurston:* Believed to be a housewife captured in the attack on Medfield in February 1676.

41. *Naananto:* Naananto (Canonchet), main war chief of the Narragansetts, led many anti-English raids. Captured in April 1676, he is said to have met his brutal death with great dignity.

42. *Nux:* Yes.

43. *outragious:* Furious or enraged.

44. *Have pity . . . touched me:* Job 19:21.

45. *I will go . . . from him:* Judges 16:20.

46. *Thomas Read:* Apparently an English soldier guarding farmers near Hadley.

47. *Mohawks:* The Mohawks were English allies who fought against the New England Indians.

48. *worse with him . . . remaining with the Indians:* Like most Puritans, Rowlandson was vehemently anti-Catholic. She preferred that her son remain an Indian captive than risk conversion to Catholicism if sold to the French.

49. *John Gilberd:* A teenage boy from Springfield. He escaped in April 1676.

50. *flux:* Dysentery.

51. *Remember now . . . in truth:* Isaiah 38:3.

52. *As David said . . . me a sinner:* Psalm 51:4 and Luke 18:13.

53. *For a . . . gather thee:* Isaiah 54:7.

54. *nice:* Fastidious or particular.

55. *Letter . . . Saggamores:* This letter, dated March 31, 1676, was from Governor John Leverett and the Massachusetts Council.

56. *Samp:* Porridge made from ground corn.

57. *Ruffe or Ridding:* Rough or discarded parts.

58. *Tom and Peter:* Tom Dublet (Nepanet) and Peter Conway (Tatatiqunea), Christian Nipmucks who agreed to mediate between the English and the Narragansett alliance for the captives' ransom.

59. *Twenty pounds:* Close to five hundred dollars in today's money. Evidence suggests that this was a very large ransom.

60. *It was . . . for them:* Thought to be James Printer (Wowaus), a Christian Indian and printer's apprentice who later typeset the second and third editions of Rowlandson's narrative in 1682.

61. *Kab:* A biblical measurement.

62. *Sudbury Fight:* At the battle of Sudbury, the last major victory for the Indian alliance, the English incurred heavy losses.

63. *Powaw:* Ritual war dance.

64. *Powaw:* Here referring to an Indian shaman or holy man.

65. *Hollandlaced Pillowbeer:* Pillowcase made of, or laced with, Holland cloth (a type of linen).

66. *My Sister:* Hannah Divoll.

67. *Goodwife Kettle:* Elizabeth Kettle, another captive from the Lancaster attack.

68. *Mr. John Hoar:* A lawyer from Concord engaged by Joseph Rowlandson. Owing to his contacts with the Nashobas, Hoar persuaded Tom Dublet and Peter Conway to help with ransom negotiations.

69. *Matchit:* Bad.

70. *Kersey Coat:* Coarse wool coat.

71. *Tuesday morning:* The date would have been May 2, 1676.

72. *Philip . . . among them:* Some of the Nipmucks hoped to coordinate ransom negotiations for the captives with more wide-ranging peace agreements. Metacom did not think this strategy would work.

73. *after the Fort-fight:* After the English attacked a Narragansett stronghold in December 1675.

74. *Shall there be . . . in our Eyes:* Amos 3:6 and 6:6–7; Psalms 118:23.

75. *did not see . . . with Hunger:* Rowlandson does, in fact, mention Indians who have starved. This clear inconsistency may indicate that the numbered section of "remarkable passages of Providence" is an editorial interpolation.

76. *Hartychoaks:* Artichokes.

77. *Agag-like . . . past:* I Samuel 16:32.

78. *Help Lord, or we perish:* Matthew 8:25.

79. *not one . . . or action*: Northeastern Indian tribes did not rape captive women, so we can take at face value Rowlandson's claim that she was not sexually abused.

80. *Boston Gentlewomen, and M. Usher*: Some of the other seventeenth-century editions state "Boston Gentlemen" and "Ms. Usher," but scholars cannot agree on a definitive reading. The rhetorical counterpointing here of the "Boston Gentlewomen" and "M. Usher" (i.e., Mr. Usher) seems to make the best sense. If Rowlandson is referring to a Mr. Usher—as seems likely—then it was Hezekiah Usher, a Boston merchant and bookseller.

81. *Thomas Shepherd*: Son of the better known Thomas Shepherd of Cambridge.

82. *the Governour*: John Leverett, governor of Massachusetts.

83. *William Hubbard*: Minister of Ipswich who published a history of Metacom's War, *A Narrative of the Troubles with the Indians* (1677), based partly on information from Rowlandson.

84. *Major Waldrens*: Richard Waldron, who ran an Indian trading post in Dover, New Hampshire, acted as agent in ransom negotiations that led to the release of several captives.

85. *Thus saith . . . of the Enemy*: Jeremiah 31:16.

86. *Governour of Road-Island*: William Coddington.

87. *Mr. Newman*: Noah Newman, minister of Rehoboth.

88. *Hirtleberries*: Whortleberries, bilberries, or huckleberries (related to blueberries).

89. *Money answers all things*: Ecclesiastes 10:19.

90. *Mr. James Whitcomb*: A wealthy Bostonian whose house the Rowlandsons lived in for about nine months in 1676–77. Some of his money came from enslaving Indians and selling them overseas.

91. *But now . . . out of the rock*: Psalm 81:16.

92. *instead of . . . fatted Calf*: Luke 15:16–27.

93. *It is good . . . afflicted*: Psalm 119:71.

94. *Vanity of vanities . . . spirit*: Ecclesiastes 1:2.


## HANNAH DUSTAN

1. *Dux Faemina Facti*: Literally, a woman leader in the deed; in other words, a heroic woman.

2. *Mary Neff*: Mary Corliss Neff was a local midwife and neighbor of the Dustans.

3. *Husband*: Thomas Dustan (c. 1652–?1732). He married Hannah Emerson in 1677 and they had thirteen children. He held various town offices in Haverhill until his death.

4. *Forty Rod:* A rod was equal to five and a half yards; forty rods was about 220 yards away.

5. *sent unto their Long Home:* Killed.

6. *Instructions which . . . given them:* As a Puritan, Mather was strongly anti-Catholic. Here he discusses how Dustan's Indian captors, who had been converted to Catholicism by the French, prayed more regularly than many English families but would not allow the Puritan captives to say their own prayers.

7. *English Youth:* Samuel Leonardson had been captured in September 1695 from his father's farm near Worcester.

8. *Penacook:* Near what is now Concord, New Hampshire.

9. *Run the Gantlet:* Running the gauntlet was an initiation rite common among certain Indian tribes. Many terrified captives described as torture what was apparently intended to test the survival of the fittest and to serve as an introduction—even a welcome—upon arrival at an Indian village.

10. *Jael:* The Book of Judges, chapters four and five, tells how Jael, wife of Heber the Kenite, offered hospitality to the Canaanite general Sisera and then killed him. Following the Israelite militia's miraculous victory over superior Canaanite forces, Sisera had sought refuge with the Kenites, who had long-standing ties to the Israelites. Traditionally, the heroine Jael is seen as an example of how unlikely figures served the Israelite cause. In the same way, Mather suggests that an improbable heroine like Dustan could serve the English cause. Mather's reference a few lines later to the Indians bowing, falling, and lying down paraphrases Judges 5:25–27.

11. *Colonel Nicholson:* Francis Nicholson was governor of Maryland from 1694 to 1698.


## ELIZABETH HANSON

1. *God . . . for ever:* Hebrews 13:8.

2. *6th Month:* The writer is using the Old Style calendar here and elsewhere in the narrative although the dating is a little off here since August should presumably be the fifth, not the sixth, month. See Rowlandson, note 1.

3. *four Children:* Hanson's captured children were Sarah (sixteen), Elizabeth (fourteen), Ebenezer or David (six), and the unnamed baby whom the French christened "Marie Anne Françoise." Two other children died in the initial attack.

4. *As soon as:* Hanson's supposed first-person narrative begins here.

5. *gave me Quarter:* Gave me mercy or spared my life.

6. *screaking:* Shrieking or screeching.

7. *Match Coats:* Capes or loose coverings of fur worn by the Indians.

8. *to the . . . is sweet:* Proverbs 27:7. This was a frequently quoted scriptural reference in the religious captivity literature as captives tried to come to terms literally with an unfamiliar and irregular diet and figuratively with providential affliction.

9. *short Commons:* Scanty provisions or insufficient supplies.

10. *prudent Management . . . a Week:* The European cultural practices of husbandry and harvest caused many colonists, including Hanson, to respond ethnocentrically by criticizing the nomadic agricultural customs of some American Indian groups.

11. *Remove:* See Rowlandson, note 18.

12. *Chapman:* Buyer.

13. *Mary Ann Frossways:* "Frossways" is a phonetic misrendering of the French name "Françoise."

14. *married to the Frenchman:* In 1727, Hanson's daughter Sarah married Jean Baptiste Sabourin, a Canadian officer from a wealthy family.


## PANTHER CAPTIVITY

1. *as follows:* At this point, Panther's frame narrative ends and the lady's story begins.

2. *Albany:* Albany, New York.

3. *a few rods:* A rod was 5½ yards.

4. *tell my tale:* These words end the lady's narrative; Panther's voice resumes in the next sentence.


## JEMIMA HOWE

1. *three women and some children:* At Bridgman's Fort were Jemima Howe, her two daughters from her first marriage, Mary and Submit Phipps, and three of the five boys from her second marriage, Squire (four), Caleb (two), and a six-month-old baby (her elder boys, William [8] and Moses [6], were captured outside the Fort); Submit Grout and her three children; and Eunice Garfield and her daughter.

2. *Mr. William Phipps:* In 1744, at Great Meadow (Putney), Vermont, Howe's first husband died from wounds received in an Indian attack.

3. *Mr. Doolittle's history:* Thomas Doolittle, *A Short Narrative of Mischief Done by the French and Indian Enemy,* was published in Bos-

ton in 1750. It gives a daily account of Indian attacks in western Massachusetts from March 1743/44 to August 1748.

4. *The Indians:* Howe's supposed first-person account begins here.

5. *de Vaudreuil:* Marquis Pierre de Vaudreuil-Cavagnal became governor of Canada in June 1755 as New France was on the verge of war with England. He allowed himself to become part of the corrupt political establishment, and, on his cronies' advice, refused adequate support to General Montcalm, the French military commander. When de Vaudreuil returned to France in 1760, he was held responsible for French defeats ultimately leading to the French loss of Canada in 1760.

6. *St. Francois:* The village of St. Francis, or Odanak, in Quebec. The British and Americans referred to the Western Abenakis as St. Francois Indians.

7. *Messiskow:* The homeland of the Missisquois, on the northern shore of Lake Champlain. The Missisquois were one of the many Algonquian-speaking Indians known collectively as Abenakis.

8. *great earthquake:* In November 1755, a series of severe earthquakes hit parts of Europe and North America, causing great damage and loss of life (the Lisbon earthquake alone on November 1, 1755, caused an estimated 30,000 to 60,000 deaths). The earthquake Howe refers to struck the Northeast on November 18.

9. *sanhop:* See Rowlandson, note 39.

10. *English gentleman:* Colonel Peter Schuyler, a wealthy New Jersey landowner, was stationed at Oswego, New York, when hostilities against the French resumed in 1754. In 1756, General Montcalm captured Schuyler and half his regiment and imprisoned him in Canada until October 1757. While detained, Schuyler used his considerable wealth and influence to help his fellow captives. Howe was one of his beneficiaries.

11. *superstition and bigotry:* Gay and/or Howe reveal(s) anti-Catholic prejudice.

12. *Count de Estaing:* Charles Hector Comte D'Estaing, commander of the French fleet, intended to help America against Great Britain. In 1778, before he was able to attack the British fleet under Lord Howe, many of his ships were damaged in a storm and he had to put into Boston for repairs.

13. *I have spun:* Bunker Gay's voice resumes with these words.

14. *Mrs. Tute:* Jemima Sartwell Phipps Howe Tute was widowed a third time.

15. *agent to go to Europe:* Humphreys's version of Howe's captivity stated that the people of Hinsdale had chosen her as their agent to Europe in a land dispute. Gay says that no one in Hinsdale had ever thought of Howe's being a representative until the statement appeared

in print; in other words, that Humphreys's supposedly factual claim was completely bogus.

## MARY KINNAN

1. *It would be:* Kinnan's first-person narrative begins here.

2. *Tiger's Valley:* Tygarts Valley.

3. *imbecility:* Weakness or frailty.

4. *Wherein the . . . fur dry:* Shakespeare, *King Lear*, Act 3, Scene 1, lines 12–14.

5. *trimmed their scalps:* To carry as many scalps as possible either as trophies or for bounty, scalpers needed to remove a small circle of skin with its hair from the top of the head. If, in haste, scalpers cut too large a piece, they could trim it later to about two inches in diameter. Since scalping involved the removal of only a layer of skin and hair, people who were scalped did not necessarily die, though Kinnan's husband and child did.

6. *recked not:* Did not care about or did not pay attention to, or reckoned not.

7. *from whose . . . returns:* Shakespeare, *Hamlet*, Act 3, Scene 1, lines 79–80.

8. *scalp-whoop . . . five times:* Repeating the scalp-whoop five times indicated to the Shawnee villages the number of enemies killed. This ritual was performed by other Native American groups, too.

9. *each person . . . senseless:* The ritual Kinnan describes is comparable to running the gauntlet.

10. *defeat of St. Clair:* On November 4, 1791, General Arthur St. Clair's forces were severely defeated by Miamis and Wyandots.

11. *Grand Glaize:* Au Glaize, in present-day Ohio.

12. *procuring my escape:* A letter written for Kinnan on July 29, 1793, to be delivered to her brother in Basking Ridge, New Jersey, was mislaid and did not arrive until mid-October.

13. *General Wayne:* General Anthony Wayne succeeded St. Clair and scored a number of decisive victories against the Indians.

14. *Plead like . . . the wind:* Shakespeare, *Macbeth*, Act 1, Scene 7, lines 19–25.

15. *native of the United States:* Jacob Lewis's American citizenship was a problem since the Indians were British sympathizers, and Detroit was then held by the British.

16. *Commodore Grant:* Commodore Alexander Grant, British naval commander of the Upper Lakes until the British relinquished control to the United States.

17. *Simcoe:* John G. Simcoe, British commander at Niagara.

18. *what kind . . . hope deferred:* Proverbs 13:12.


## MARY JEMISON

1. *Peace of 1783:* The Treaty of Paris, which formally recognized American independence and ended the Revolutionary War.

2. *Thomas Clute:* Jemison's neighbor, lawyer, and trusted friend.

3. *one hundred rods:* About 550 yards; see Mather, "Hannah Dustan," note 4.

4. *George Jemison:* A man claiming to be Jemison's cousin to whom she offered financial assistance for eight years. While the narrative says clearly that Mary ultimately considered George to be an impostor, Seaver says she still referred him to George for information, especially on Hiokatoo, Mary's second husband.

5. *descendants of William Penn:* That is, the Quakers, known for their tolerance and civic responsibility.

6. *spring of 1755:* Jemison's dating is systematically incorrect by three years. She was actually captured in 1758.

7. *Dickewamis:* Also spelled variously Dehgewanus and Degiwene's.

8. *Washington's war:* The French and Indian War (1754–63) began in 1754, not 1757. Called "Washington's war" here because George Washington undertook several daring missions for the English. Jemison's dating of the war is another example of the three-year error mentioned in note 6.

9. *Sheninjee:* Jemison married Sheninjee, a Delaware, in the summer of 1760. They had two children: an unnamed daughter who died after only a few days and a son named Thomas Jemison.

10. *Thomas Jemison:* Born in 1762, Thomas Jemison was killed by his stepbrother, John, in 1811.

11. *Genishau:* Variant of Genesee, a large Seneca town with many inhabitants.

12. *When we arrived . . . month preceding:* The British took Fort Niagara from the French on July 25, 1759.

13. *Gardow:* Variant of Gardeau, referring to the Gardeau flats on the Genesee River, Jemison's property from 1797 until she sold it in old age and moved onto the Senecas' Buffalo Creek Reservation.

14. *Sir William Johnson:* Sir William Johnson was appointed Superintendent of North American Indian affairs in 1756 and held this office until his death. He helped lead the expedition to take Fort Niagara in 1759 and in 1760 led the successful Canadian campaign. He concluded the treaty with the Indians at Fort Stanwix in 1768. During Johnson's

latter years until his death in 1774, he lived with Molly Brant, sister of Joseph Brant (Thayendanegea), the famous war chief of the Mohawk Valley Mohawks.

15. *Hiokatoo . . . Gardow:* Jemison married the Seneca warrior Hiokatoo (Big Lance) in 1765 or 1766. They were married for over fifty years until his death in 1811 and had six children: John (1766–1817), Nancy (?1773/1776–1839), Betsey (probably after 1773–1839), Polly (before or early in 1779–1839), Jane (1782–1797), and Jesse (1784/85–1812).

16. *my daughter Nancy:* Nancy married Billy Green and had seven children.

17. *battle at Fort Stanwix:* On August 3, 1777, a combined British force mostly of Loyalists and Indians besieged Fort Stanwix, which was garrisoned by several hundred men under Colonel Peter Gansevoort. American troops coming to aid Gansevoort were ambushed by a force of Loyalists and Native Americans led by Joseph Brant.

18. *Col's Butler and Brandt:* In June/July and November 1778, Sir John Butler and Joseph Brant led Loyalists and Indians in attacks on outlying settlements in Pennsylvania's Wyoming Valley.

19. *General Sullivan:* John Sullivan, Revolutionary general and statesman. In March 1779, he headed an expedition to western Pennsylvania and New York to devastate Iroquois country. On August 29, 1779, he routed combined Indian and Loyalist forces near modern-day Elmira, New York. He moved northwest, destroying Seneca villages and food supplies but turned back on September 15 after reaching Geneseo. He died in 1795.

20. *William Boyd:* Actually Thomas, not William, Boyd, First Lieutenant in the First Pennsylvania Regiment, killed near Geneseo on September 13, 1779.

21. *Corn Planter:* Corn Planter (Kaiiontwa'ko), known by the English as John O'Bail, was a Seneca war chief and statesman. He was a mixed-blood whose mother was a Seneca but whose father was an Anglo trader. In the action referred to here, Corn Planter and others attacked the Mohawk Valley in August 1780, taking approximately fifty prisoners (including, for a while, his own father) and destroying two forts and over fifty farms.

22. *Ebenezer Allen:* Ebenezer Allen, an adventurer and a Tory during the Revolutionary War, came from Pennsylvania to the Gardow flats apparently because of his knowledge of, and alliance with, the Senecas during the war. As Jemison indicates, while Allen lived with the Senecas he caused mayhem by taking several wives, both white and Indian, committing adultery, and exploiting land claims. He moved to Canada and

was granted three thousand acres of land, but in the early 1800s he was arrested for forgery and larceny, and died a poor man in 1814.

23. *my Indian brother:* Kau-jises-tau-ge-au (Black Coals). Through him, at the Treaty of Big Tree on September 15, 1797, Jemison became a significant landowner in the Genesee Valley with property extending to almost 18,000 acres.

24. *William Crawford:* Colonel William Crawford, a close friend of George Washington, resigned his regimental commission in 1777, but in 1778 and 1779 he served on the western frontier in Virginia. Commanding an expedition against Moravian Indians in 1782, he was captured, tortured, and killed in Ohio on June 11, 1782, in revenge for the earlier attack on Moravian Indians led by David Williamson.

25. *David Williamson:* Virginia militiamen under Colonel David Williamson's command massacred many Moravian Indians at Gnadenhutten in March 1782, then decided to attack the remainder in May. In conjunction with Crawford, Williamson attacked the Moravian Indians but was able to escape back to the settlements when the initiative failed, whereas Crawford was killed in retaliation.

26. *Simon Gurty:* Simon Gurty, a Pennsylvania adventurer who was captured by Senecas and held in captivity for several years when young. As an adult, he alternated allegiance between the Americans and the British, aiding the latter during the War of 1812.

27. *Doct. Night:* Doctor John Knight fought with the Seventh Virginia Regiment in 1781 and retired from the military in 1783.


## MARY GODFREY

1. *termination of the Indian War:* The opening paragraph indicates that after Black Hawk's crushing defeat in the North in 1832, whites thought that other Indian tribes would realize the futility of fighting the U.S. troops. It was thus a surprise to Northerners when in 1835 they received word from Florida of sustained Seminole attacks and resistance.

2. *Seminole:* The name is said to derive from the Spanish "cimarron," meaning "wild" or "runaway."

3. *General JACKSON:* A reference to Jackson's role in the First Seminole War and to his burning of the Seminole Mikasuki and Suwannee settlements.

4. *Francis:* Known as Josiah Francis, the Prophet Francis, or Hillis Hadjo, Francis was a Creek chief and British sympathizer in the War of 1812. Following Andrew Jackson's victory over the Creeks in 1814, Hillis Hadjo fled to Florida to join the Seminoles and continue hostilities

against the Americans. Lured into American hands, he was ordered hanged by Jackson in 1817.

5. *Mickasooky tribe:* The Mikasuki Indians were considered one of the most warlike Seminole tribes.

6. *Micanopy:* Micanopy, grandson of the founder of the Seminole nation, became the principal chief shortly before the Second Seminole War. He was passively opposed to tribal removal until moved to resistance by more militant chiefs, including Osceola. It was Micanopy who shot Major Francis Dade and initiated the Second Seminole War. He surrendered to General Thomas S. Jesup, was removed to Indian Territory (Oklahoma), and died there in 1848.

7. *Jumper:* Jumper (Ote Emathla) has been called the intellectual leader of the Second Seminole War. He was married to Micanopy's sister and was one of the seven chiefs who visited Oklahoma after the treaty of Payne's Landing. He fought alongside Micanopy at Dade's Massacre in 1835 and at the Battle of Withlacoochee against General Edmund P. Gaines in 1836. He surrendered in 1837 but died the following year awaiting removal to Indian Territory.

8. *Oscala, alias Powell:* Osceola (Billy Powell) achieved national renown as a Seminole warrior and an outspoken opponent of American expansionism. The mixed-blood child of a Creek mother and a British father, Osceola joined the Seminoles with the flight of some Creeks to Florida. Osceola and the Seminole agent, Wiley Thompson, were bitter enemies, and Osceola's killing of Thompson on December 28, 1835, helped precipitate the Second Seminole War. After initial successes early in 1836, Osceola's forces were driven south into the Florida swampland, where he contracted malaria. He agreed to a parley in 1837 but was detained and sent to Fort Moultrie, South Carolina, where he died on January 30, 1838.

9. *treaty . . . May, 1832:* The treaty of Payne's Landing, discussed in more detail in the introduction.

10. *Charles:* Charley (Chalo) Emathla was one of the few Seminole chiefs who favored removal to the West. In November 1835, he was killed by Osceola.

11. *General Thompson:* Wiley Thompson earned his title as major general of the Georgia militia from 1817 to 1824. In 1833, he replaced Phagan as Seminole agent but was unable to mediate successfully among whites, Indians, and blacks. In 1835, Thompson degraded Osceola by placing him in chains. In revenge, Osceola and his forces killed and scalped Thompson.

12. *County Root:* A cooling jelly called "conte" prepared from the powdered root of the China briar.

13. *in dishabille:* Undressed or scantily dressed.

14. *Mrs. Mary Godfrey:* Neither Mary nor Thomas Godfrey can be traced in the historical record.

15. *The first day:* Told in the first-person supposedly by Mary Godfrey, this two-page passage in quotation marks is embedded within the larger, third-person military account.

16. *The first severe engagement:* On December 28, 1835, Indians and blacks under Micanopy, Alligator (Halpatter Tustenuggee), and Jumper destroyed U.S. troops commanded by Major Francis L. Dade in the battle known as Dade's Massacre. On the same day, Seminoles under Osceola killed Wiley Thompson. These dual hostilities marked the formal beginning of the Second Seminole War. References to the military dead include Captain G. W. Gardiner, Brevet Second Lieutenant R. Henderson, and First Lieutenant W. E. Basinger, from the Second Regiment of Artillery; Captain U. S. Fraser, Brevet Second Lieutenant J. L. Keais, and Second Lieutenant R. R. Mudge, from the Third Regiment of Artillery; and Assistant Surgeon J. S. Gatlin.

17. *Gen. Clinch:* General Duncan L. Clinch was expected to regain control of Seminole country, to protect the Florida plantations, and to oversee the removal of the Seminoles to Indian Territory. He resigned his army commission in April 1836.

18. *engagement on the Withlacoochee:* On December 31, 1835, Osceola and Alligator moved to cut off two military parties converging on the River Withlacoochee: General Clinch with his army regulars and Brigadier General Call's Florida volunteers. The Battle of the Withlacoochee involved considerable casualties and hardships to the army and was the first major confrontation between the official forces of the U.S. government and the anti-removal Seminoles. The River Withlacoochee was the site of several other skirmishes during the war.

19. *Gen. Gaines:* General Edmund P. Gaines, bitter at General Winfield Scott's being named to the overall field command, precipitously marched his troops into Florida and on February 28, 1836, set up an improvised camp on the River Withlacoochee called Camp Izard. Lieutenant (not General, as the narrative says) James F. Izard and others were killed or wounded over the course of a week when Seminoles attacked the besieged troops, and their expected reinforcements and rations were delayed. Gaines and Osceola agreed to talks, but the Seminoles dispersed, fearing a trap, when relief troops suddenly arrived and fired shots. Gaines's men were on the point of starvation, as the narrative indicates, by the time help arrived.

20. *Fort Drane:* Built on General Clinch's plantation, Ft. Drane was about eighty miles southwest of St. Augustine.

## SARAH F. WAKEFIELD

1. *Upper Sioux Indians:* The Sioux are divided into the Dakotas, Nakotas, and Lakotas, culturally and geographically. By 1855, most of the Sioux in Minnesota, who were Dakotas, had moved onto a reservation that had two agencies: the Upper Agency, also called the Upper Sioux Agency or Yellow Medicine, and the Lower Agency, also called the Lower Sioux Agency or Redwood. At the Upper Agency were mainly Sisseton and Wahpeton Dakotas; at the Lower Agency were Mdewakanton and Wahpekute Dakotas. The Wakefields were traveling to the Upper Agency.

2. *$160,000 all in gold:* The Wakefields were carrying the annuity money promised to the Dakotas in recent treaties. The change in the administration refers to the Republican election victory and the appointment in 1861 of Thomas Galbraith as Dakota agent.

3. *Little Crow's village:* Little Crow (Taoyateduta) was a Mdewakanton chief and Dakota leader. Instrumental in supporting the 1851 treaty in which the Dakotas sold land to the Americans in the promise of a permanent reservation on the upper Minnesota River, debt repayment, and cash and food annuities, Little Crow began to lose influence among the Dakotas when the U.S. government did not meet these obligations. In the summer of 1862, when annuity payments and provisions were late, Little Crow was asked to lead the four Minnesota tribes in a war against the whites. Angered by the U.S. government's broken promises, he agreed. The Dakota Conflict proved unsuccessful, and Little Crow fled to Canada, but soon returned to the Minnesota frontier, where he was killed on July 3, 1863. His village was at the Lower Agency.

4. *Mr. Reynolds and family:* Joseph and Valencia Reynolds were teachers at the government school.

5. *Dr. Williamson:* Thomas Williamson was a Presbyterian missionary and doctor.

6. *Mr. Riggs' Mission:* Stephen Riggs and his wife began their missionary work among the Dakotas in 1837. They survived the Dakota War and continued to preach to the Indians afterwards.

7. *Major Galbraith . . . and Major Brown:* Joseph Brown, a Democrat, had been named the Indian agent for Minnesota upon the area's statehood in 1858 and was instrumental in furthering programs to encourage the Dakotas to adopt white ways. With the Republican election victory, Thomas Galbraith replaced Brown.

8. *Farmer, or Christian Indians:* Farmer Indians, or progressives, were those who agreed to adopt white ways, encouraged by government incentives such as a house, land to farm, clothing, and extra provisions.

They dressed European-style, converted to Christianity, and sent their children to the mission schools. Opposed to the farmer Indians were the so-called blanket Indians, or traditionalists, who held onto tribal ways and (correctly) believed that the farmer Indian program was designed to splinter tribal unity.

9. *minne-wakan:* Presumably, liquor.

10. *my children:* At the time of the attack, Wakefield had two children: James, born in 1858, and Lucy Elizabeth or Nellie, born in 1860.

11. *Mr. Hindman's church:* Samuel D. Hinman, an Episcopalian minister, was later beaten up by whites for his missionary work among the Dakotas and for his attempts to convert those Indians condemned to die after the war.

12. *the Indians killed some people in Acton:* On August 17, 1862, in a minor incident that escalated into the Dakota War, four Dakotas from the Lower Agency killed several whites on the property of Robinson Jones, near the small settlement of Acton.

13. *Mr. Gleason:* George Gleason clerked at the Lower Agency warehouse.

14. *Mr. Garvie:* Stewart Garvie was manager of a store at the Upper Agency.

15. *Chaska:* Chaska (We-Chank-Wash-ta-don-pee), a Mdewakanton Dakota, was a Christian farmer Indian.

16. *Hapa:* Chaska's brother-in-law, a traditional blanket Indian.

17. *Shakopee:* Town built on the site of a Dakota village named after a Dakota chief, approximately fifty miles southwest of Minneapolis. In 1851, the Dakotas moved from this village to the Lower Agency, to a place they called Shakopee's village, leaving the original area open to white settlement.

18. *hoops:* The whalebone hoops worn by nineteenth-century women beneath their skirts or dresses to make the garments' circumference larger.

19. *sacque:* Slip, shift, or loose gown (*OED*).

20. *Kinnikinnick:* Tobacco or other substance that the Dakotas smoked.

21. *waist:* Underwear for children to which petticoats or drawers are buttoned (*OED*).

22. *Julia Laframbois:* A mixed-blood woman living near the Upper Agency.

23. *Mrs. Renville:* Mary Renville, another captive.

24. *battle of Birch Coolie:* On September 2, at the battle of Birch Coolie (or Coulee), more than three hundred Dakotas attacked American troops, causing substantial casualties.

25. *Mrs. Decamp:* Jannette De Camp, wife of Joseph De Camp, who had been appointed to supervise the sawmill at the Lower Agency.

26. *Miss E. B——:* Ellen Brown, daughter of the previous Dakota agent for Minnesota, Joseph Brown.

27. *sutlering:* Technically, following an army or living in a garrison town and provisioning soldiers. *OED* also defines the word as performing low or mean duties. In Wakefield's usage, the word clearly implies overinflating prices and cheating.

28. *Red Iron's village:* Red Iron (Mazasha), a Sisseton chief, opposed Little Crow's decision to go to war. His village was near the confluence of the Chippewa and Minnesota Rivers.

29. *H. H. Sibley:* Henry H. Sibley was a fur trader, politician, and soldier. In 1858, running as a Democrat, he became the first governor of Minnesota. He unsuccessfully urged Congress to change Indian policy, and when the Dakota War erupted in 1862, he led the military against the Indians. From 1863 to 1864, he commanded punitive raids against the Dakotas, but in 1865–66, he was one of the commissioners who negotiated peace treaties between the U.S. government and the Dakotas. Until his death in 1891, he continued to be an important figure in Minnesota politics.

30. *Standing Buffalo:* Standing Buffalo was a Sisseton chief who opposed Little Crow in waging war on the whites.

31. *three rods:* About 18 feet; see Mather, "Hannah Dustan," note 4.

32. *Mrs. Dr. Humphrey:* Susan Humphrey, the wife of Doctor Philander Humphrey, physician at the Lower Agency, had been killed while she and her family were trying to escape.

33. *Capt. Kennedy:* John Kennedy was a member of the Seventh Minnesota Regiment.

34. *Mrs. Earle:* Amanda Earle was one of Little Crow's captives.

35. *Indian Expedition of this year:* In the summer of 1863, General Sibley led an expedition against the Sioux in Dakota Territory.

## EMELINE L. FULLER

1. *My father:* Christopher Trimble.

2. *My mother:* Abagel (Abigail) Payne Trimble Utter. In her first marriage, Abagel Trimble had three children: Emeline, Christopher (Christy), and Elizabeth (Libbie). In her second marriage, Abagel Utter had one child, Susan.

3. *Elijah Utter:* Utter's children from his first marriage were Mary, Charles, Henry, Wesley, Emma, and Abby, aged from twenty-three to under five.

4. *palice car:* A palace car was a railroad car or coach fitted out luxuriously.

5. *We fell in . . . California:* Fuller does not always remember or spell names correctly. Following is a list of the Utter-Myers party: Elijah and Abagel Utter and their ten children; Joseph and Mary Myers, their five children, Joseph's brother, John, and Mary's brother, Edwin Prime; Daniel and Elizabeth Chase and their three children; Alexis and Abigail Van Ornum and their five children; six men boarding with the Van Ornums: Judson Cressey, Samuel Gleason, Lewis Lawson, Goodsel Munson, and the brothers Jacob and Joseph Reith. At the Pontneuf encampment on the Snake River, a bugler, Lucius Chaffee, and five discharged soldiers (Charles Schamberg, Theodore Murdock, Henry Snyder, Charles Kishnell, and William Utley) joined the train. Only fifteen of the forty-five emigrants survived.

6. *Col. Howe:* Lieutenant Colonel Marshall Howe, the army commander at the Pontneuf encampment (seven miles from the abandoned Fort Hall to which Fuller refers), aroused the Utter party's distrust when he intervened in an internal dispute between emigrants, capriciously refused them adequate military protection, and tried to force the women to attend a military dance.

7. *white man:* Renegade whites may well have instigated and participated in the attacks.

8. *pusley:* Purslane or pussley is a plant that can be used in salads.

9. *awful . . . upon us:* Military records confirm that the survivors did indeed resort to cannibalism.

10. *one of the discharged soldiers:* Henry Snyder reached help at the end of September but was so exhausted that his garbled story initially was disputed.

11. *Three of . . . by the Indians:* Much of this is probably hearsay. Of the four Van Ornum children captured by Shoshones, Minerva starved, Eliza either starved or was killed, Lucinda died after being rescued, and Reuben was rescued but apparently disappeared and may have returned to the Shoshones.

12. *broken-hearted woman:* Fuller was not the only survivor to suffer severe psychological trauma. Indian agent George Abbott, who met the survivors about a week after they had been found, said that none of them "appeared to have the intelligence or mental strength of a child of three years of age."

13. *united in marriage:* As far as can be determined, Fuller married three times: to John M. Whitman from 1863 to 1886; to Melvin Fuller from about 1887 to about 1891; and to Andrew J. Calhoun from 1901 to 1909.